American Foreign Relations

Relations

VOLUME 1

A History • to 1920

BRIEF EDITION

Thomas G. Paterson

J. Garry Clifford

Shane J. Maddock

Deborah Kisatsky

Kenneth J. Hagan

HOUGHTON MIFFLIN COMPANY

Boston   New York

Publisher: *Charles Hartford*
Senior Sponsoring Editor: *Sally Constable*
Senior Development Editor: *Jeffrey Greene*
Project Editor: *Kerry Doyle*
Senior Marketing Manager: *Sandra McGuire*
Manufacturing Coordinator: *Priscilla Manchester*

Cover art: Albert Fountain Jr., *Celebration of the Gadsden Purchase,* 1854 oil on canvas.
© Mary V. Alexander, The Gadsden Museum, Mesilla, NM.

Printed in the U.S.A.

Library of Congress Control Number: 2005930482

ISBN: 0-618-38221-6

1 2 3 4 5 6 7 8 9-CRS-09 08 07 06 05

for

Colin Graham Paterson

Carol Davidge

Vera Low Hagan

Emily Rose Maddock

About the Authors

Thomas G. Paterson, professor emeritus of history at the University of Connecticut, graduated from the University of New Hampshire (B.A., 1963) and the University of California, Berkeley (Ph.D., 1968). He has written *Soviet-American Confrontation* (1973), *Meeting the Communist Threat* (1988), *On Every Front* (1992), *Contesting Castro* (1994), *America Ascendant* (with J. Garry Clifford, 1995), and *A People and a Nation* (with Mary Beth Norton et al., 2001). Tom has also edited *Cold War Critics* (1971), *Kennedy's Quest for Victory* (1989), *Imperial Surge* (with Stephen G. Rabe, 1992), *The Origins of the Cold War* (with Robert McMahon, 1999), *Explaining the History of American Foreign Relations* (with Michael J. Hogan, 2004), and *Major Problems in American Foreign Relations* (with Dennis Merrill, 2005). With Bruce Jentleson, he served as senior editor for the *Encyclopedia of American Foreign Relations* (1997). A microfilm edition of *The United States and Castro's Cuba, 1950s–1970s: The Paterson Collection* appeared in 1999. He has served on the editorial boards of the *Journal of American History* and *Diplomatic History.* Recipient of a Guggenheim fellowship, he has directed National Endowment for the Humanities Summer Seminars for College Teachers. He is a past president of the Society for Historians of American Foreign Relations. In 2000 the New England History Teachers Association awarded him the Kidger prize for excellence in teaching and mentoring. Besides visits to many American campuses, Tom has lectured in Canada, China, Colombia, Cuba, New Zealand, Puerto Rico, Russia, and Venezuela.

J. Garry Clifford teaches at the University of Connecticut, where he is a professor of political science and director of its graduate program. Born in Massachusetts, he earned his B.A. from Williams College (1964) and his Ph.D. in history from Indiana University. He has also taught at the University of Tennessee and Dartmouth College and has taught in two National Endowment for the Humanities seminars for high school teachers at the Franklin D. Roosevelt Library. For his book *The Citizen Soldiers* (1972), he won the Frederick Jackson Turner Award of the Organization of American Historians. With Norman Cousins, he has edited *Memoirs of a Man: Grenville Clark* (1975), and with Samuel R. Spencer, Jr., he has written *The First Peacetime Draft* (1986). He also co-authored *America Ascendant* (with Thomas G. Paterson) in 1995. Garry's essays have appeared in Gordon Martel, ed., *American Foreign Relations Reconsidered* (1994), Michael J. Hogan and Thomas G. Paterson, eds., *Explaining the History of American Foreign Relations* (1991 and 2004), Arnold A. Offner and Theodore A. Wilson, eds., *Victory in Europe, 1945* (2000), and in the *Journal of American History, Review of Politics, Mid-America, American Neptune,* and *Diplomatic History.* Garry has served on the editorial board of *Diplomatic History* as well as on the editorial board of the Modern War Series of the University Press of Kansas. He frequently participates in American professional conferences and has also lectured in Russia and Northern Ireland.

Shane J. Maddock is associate professor of history at Stonehill College in Easton, Massachusetts, where he also serves on the faculty of the Martin Institute for Law and Society. Born in North Dakota, he earned his B.A. from Michigan State University (1989) and his Ph.D. from the University of Connecticut (1997). He has also taught at the U.S. Coast Guard Academy. Shane has edited *The Nuclear Age* (2001) and has published in the *Journal of American History, International History Review, Pacific Historical Review, Presidential Studies Quarterly, Mid-America, Journal of Military History, American Jewish History, Canadian Journal of Latin American and Caribbean Studies, History in Dispute,* and *The Encyclopedia of U.S. Foreign Relations.* He has received fellowships from the Institute for the Study of World Politics, the U.S. Arms Control and Disarmament Agency, and the Hoover, Truman, Eisenhower, Kennedy, and Johnson presidential libraries. Shane has presented lectures and papers on his main research interests—U.S. nuclear nonproliferation policy and the intersection of popular culture and foreign relations. He is currently working on a book titled *The Nth Country Conundrum: The American and Soviet Quest to Halt the Spread of Nuclear Weapons, 1945–1970.*

Deborah Kisatsky is assistant professor of history at Assumption College in Worcester, Massachusetts. Born in Pennsylvania, she earned both her B.A. (1990) and her Ph.D. (2001) from the University of Connecticut. Deborah is the recipient of numerous awards and fellowships: the 1998–1999 Alexander von Humboldt Foundation Bundeskanzler (Federal Chancellor's) Scholarship for research in Germany, where she also served as a Junior Fellow of the Center for European Integration Studies, University of Bonn; the Myrna F. and Stuart L. Bernath Dissertation Grants of the Society for Historians of American Foreign Relations (1996 and 1999); a Franklin D. Roosevelt Library Lubin-Winant Fellowship (1996); and a Harry S. Truman Institute Research Grant (1996). She has published in *Intelligence and National Security, The Historian, Presidential Studies Quarterly,* and *The Journal of Interdisciplinary History,* as well as in the *Encyclopedia of U.S. Foreign Relations.* Deborah's book *The United States and the European Right, 1954–1955* was published by Ohio State University Press in fall 2005.

Kenneth J. Hagan is an adjunct professor on the faculty of the U.S. Naval War College, Monterey Program, and professor emeritus of history and museum director at the U.S. Naval Academy, Annapolis. He previously taught at Claremont McKenna College, Kansas State University, and the U.S. Army Command and General Staff College. A native of California, he received his B.A. and M.A. from the University of California, Berkeley (1958, 1964) and his Ph.D. from the Claremont Graduate School (1970). Ken is the author of *This People's Navy: The Making of American Sea Power* (1991), a comprehensive history of American naval strategy and policy since the Revolution, and *American Gunboat Diplomacy and the Old Navy, 1877–1889* (1973). His scholarship also includes two edited collections of original essays: *In Peace and War: Interpretations of American Naval History, 1775–1984* (1984) and *Against All Enemies: Interpretations of American Military History from Colonial Times to the Present* (1986). He frequently contributes articles to the journal *Naval History* and lectures annually at the Canadian Forces College in Toronto. Besides regularly participating in panels at conferences in the United States, he has given papers on the history of naval strategy in Sweden, Greece, Turkey, France, and Spain. A retired captain in the naval reserve, he served on active duty with the Pacific Fleet from 1958 to 1963 and currently advises the Naval ROTC college program on its history curriculum.

Contents

3 *Extending and Preserving the Sphere,*
1815–1848   **58**

4 *Expansionism, Sectionalism, and Civil War,*
1848–1865   **90**

5 *Global Rivalry and Regional Power,*
1865–1895   **114**

6 *Imperialist Leap, 1895–1900*   143

7 *Managing, Policing, and Extending the Empire, 1900–1914*   164

8 *War, Peace, and Revolution in the Time of Wilson, 1914–1920* **188**

Index **217**

Maps and Graphs

Preface

Since the first edition of *American Foreign Relations: A History* was published in the 1970s, a generation of teachers and students has used this textbook in college courses through six revised editions, the last of which appeared in 2005. Because the text is too long for many instructors, we have written an abridged version of *American Foreign Relations,* cutting the length by more than one-fourth. As colleagues and students have suggested, a briefer text allows instructors to assign more collateral reading. In preparing this abridgement, we have retained the basic narrative structure, chapter sequence, broad chronological and geographic coverage, and interpretive themes of the longer edition. Because we have deleted all endnotes in this brief edition, readers might wish to consult the 6th edition for the sources of quotations.

Cataclysmic events of the past few years have rekindled interest in the history of America's foreign relations. The triumphal ending of the Cold War fifteen years ago did not, as some have argued, signal the end of history. Nor has the passing of America's "greatest generation" of World War II heroes reduced history to nostalgic memories. Consider some recent headlines—shocking photographs of American military personnel inflicting torture and humiliation on Iraqi prisoners in Abu Ghraib prison near Baghdad, serious debates on the limits of dissent and whether terrorist enemies should be protected by the Geneva Convention, the reelection of President George W. Bush after a heated electoral campaign in which the Vietnam War records of both candidates became the focus of partisan debates, the death of Yasir Arafat and a possible new opportunity for peace between Palestinians and Israelis, the reorganization of America's intelligence agencies under a new director of national intelligence, ongoing concern about weapons of mass destruction, including possible "dirty" bombs from terrorists and putative nuclear threats from Iran and North Korea, continued complaints about America's behavior as a "hyperpower" despite efforts to repair rifts with allies, increased alarm over environmental decline and fast-spreading diseases such as AIDS, and finally a graphic demonstration of American humanitarianism as U.S. naval task forces airlifted food, expertise, and funds to tsunami victims in the Indian Ocean region in early 2005, followed by more extensive relief efforts personally led by former presidents Bill Clinton and George H. W. Bush. Indeed, much of what has happened since September 11, 2001, has riveted attention on America's global travails and how and why they came to be. *American Foreign Relations* seeks to introduce students to this complex history.

In this abridged edition we engage influential approaches and interpretations, especially those articulated by younger scholars. We seek to explain foreign relations in the broadest manner as the many ways that peoples, organizations, states, and systems interact—economic, cultural, strategic, environmental, political, and more. Our text emphasizes the theme of expansionism, explaining its many manifestations. We also show that on almost every issue in the history of American foreign relations, alternative voices unfailingly sounded among and against official policymakers. Americans have always debated their place in the world, their wars, their overseas commitments, and the status of their principles and power, and they have always debated the people of other nations about the spread of U.S. influence. We try to capture with vivid description and quotation the drama of the many debates.

A historical overview such as this one necessarily draws on the copious work of scholars in the United States and abroad. Their expertise informs this book throughout and helps lend it the authority instructors and students expect. Our "Further Reading" sections are one way to thank them for their books, articles, and conference papers. We have also appreciated their recommendations for text revisions and their suggestions for teaching the courses for which this book is intended. We thank them, too, for challenging us to consider the many different approaches and theories that have commanded attention in this field, including world systems, corporatism, dependency, culture, psychology and personality, medical biography, lessons from the past ("thinking in time"), bureaucratic politics, public opinion, executive-legislative competition, gender, national security and power, impact on recipients of foreign aid, the natural environment, and ideology. This book also presents the findings of our own ongoing archival research and writing as we discover and rediscover the past.

The traditional topics of diplomacy, war, economic intercourse, and politics remain central to our presentation of the foreign-relations story. We also discuss the cultural dimensions of foreign relations: race-based and gender-based images of other peoples that condition the decisionmaking environment; how the "reel" world of films reflects cultural myths and captures public perceptions of international events; the proliferation abroad of American mass culture (such as rock and roll and sports); the foreign responses to "Americanization"; travel and tourism that help create a pool of knowledge about foreign places that promotes an expansionist consciousness; and cultural transfer through "public diplomacy"—the presentation of a positive image of the United States abroad through, for example, propaganda, radio and television, and trade fairs. We especially stress the self-conscious expansion of American "empire" from its westward displacement of Native Americans in the eighteenth and nineteenth centuries to its overseas incarnations in the twentieth and twenty-first centuries. Issues that spring from human interaction with the natural environment and the international conferences convened to deal with damage to the environment also receive attention, as does the linkage between the civil rights movement and American foreign relations with the Third World in the 1940s through the 1960s. New scholarship prompted by anniversaries—such as the Louisiana Purchase and Lewis and Clark expedition, the Spanish-American-Cuban-Filipino War, victory in World War II, the Cuban Missile Crisis, and the Vietnam War, among others—have enabled us to bring fresh insights to these important events.

Equally important, with the Cold War International History Project providing scholars with a treasure trove of declassified documents from foreign archives (Russian, East German, Cuban, and Chinese among them), we offer fresh insights into Joseph Stalin's goals and tactics during and after World War II, the origins of the Korean War, Sino-American relations, Cuban policy toward Africa, the Soviet invasion of Afghanistan, the failure of détente in the 1970s, and the end of the Cold War in

1989–1991. Similarly, recently declassified U.S. government documents made available via "electronic briefing books" from the National Security Archive have added nuance to our coverage, for example, of the India-Pakistan War of 1971 and the Indonesian invasion of East Timor in 1976, as well as new evidence regarding Washington's Cold War initiatives toward the Soviet Union, the People's Republic of China, and Fidel Castro's Cuba. The declassification, duplication, and public release of presidential audiotapes from the Kennedy, Johnson, and Nixon years help to recapture their colorful language and reveal how the assumptions, styles, and emotions of these leaders influenced their decisionmaking.

In preparing this edition, we once again immersed ourselves in the memoirs, diaries, letters, speeches, recorded tapes, and oral histories of U.S. and international leaders. We often let them speak for themselves in the frankest terms, guarded and unguarded. We have sought to capture their anger and their humor, their cooperation and their competitiveness, their truths and their lies, their moments of doubt and times of confidence, their triumphs and setbacks. This brief edition, in short, strives to capture the erratic pulse of international relations through peoples' struggles to plan, decide, and administer. We study not only the leaders who made influential decisions, but also the world's peoples who welcomed, resisted, or endured the decisions that profoundly influenced their lives. In this regard, we have drawn on the growing scholarship that studies non-state actors, including peace groups, African Americans, and international bodies such as the World Health Organization.

Each chapter opens with a significant and dramatic event—a "Diplomatic Crossroad"—that helps illustrate the chief characteristics and issues of the era. The introductory and concluding sections of each chapter set the themes. Illustrations from collections around the world are closely tied to the narrative in image and caption description. The maps, graphs, and "Makers of American Foreign Relations" tables in each chapter provide essential information. The up-to-date chapter bibliographies guide further reading and serve as a starting point for term or research papers.

In the late 1970s, the People's Republic of China adopted a new system for rendering Chinese phonetic characters into the Roman alphabet. Called the Pinyin method, it replaced the Wade-Giles technique, which had long been used in English. Use of the Pinyin method is now common, and we use it in *American Foreign Relations.* Many changes are minor—Shantung has become Shandong and Mao Tsetung has become Mao Zedong, for example. But when we have a possibly confusing Pinyin spelling, we have placed the Wade-Giles spelling in parentheses—for example, Beijing (Peking) or Jiang Jieshi (Chiang Kai-shek).

Instructors and students interested in the study of foreign-relations history are invited to join the Society for Historians of American Foreign Relations (SHAFR). This organization publishes a superb journal, *Diplomatic History,* and a newsletter; offers book, article, and lecture prizes and dissertation research grants; and holds an annual conference where scholars present their views and research results. Dues are very reasonable. For information, contact the SHAFR Business Office, Department of History, Ohio State University, 106 Dulles Hall, 230 West 17th Avenue, Columbus, OH 43210, or visit their website, *http://www.shafr.org.*

Another informative website is H-Diplo: Diplomatic History, found at *http://www.h-net.org/~diplo/.* Besides presenting provocative on-line discussions on foreign-relations history, this site also provides research and bibliographic aids and an extensive list of links to other useful resources, including journals, newspapers, archives and presidential libraries, research organizations such as the National Security Archive, and government agencies such as the Central Intelligence Agency and Department of State.

Many colleagues, friends, students, and editors contributed to this brief edition and to earlier editions of *American Foreign Relations* by providing research leads, correction of errors, reviews of the text, library searches, documents and essays, and editorial assistance. At Houghton Mifflin we give our heartiest thanks to Jean L. Woy, senior consulting editor; Frances Gay, senior development editor; Jeff Greene, senior development editor; Kerry Doyle, project editor; and Nancy Benjamin at Books By Design.

We are also eager to thank the many people who helped us in the previous editions of the longer book: Philip J. Avillo, Jr., Richard Baker, Ann Balcolm, Michael A. Barnhart, Derick Becker, Robert Beisner, R. Christian Berg, Kenneth J. Blume, Mark Boyer, Richard Bradford, Kinley J. Brauer, John Burns, Richard Dean Burns, Michael Butler, Robert Buzzanco, Charles Conrad Campbell, Chen Jian, John Coogan, Alejandro Corbacho, Frank Costigliola, Carol Davidge, Mark Del Vecchio, Ralph Di Carpio, Justus Doenecke, Michael Donaghue, Regina Egan, Robert H. Ferrell, David S. Foglesgong, Xavier Franco, Irwin Gellman, Paul Goodwin, James Gormly, Eric Hafter, Peter Hahn, Robert E. Hannigan, Hope M. Harrison, Alan Henrikson, Gregg Herken, George Herring, Ted Hitchcock, Joan Hoff, Kristin Hoganson, Reginald Horsman, Michael Hunt, Edythe Izard, Holly Izard, Richard Izard, Leith Johnson, Burton Kaufman, Melville T. Kennedy, Jr., Thomas Lairson, Lester Langley, Thomas M. Leonard, Li Yan, Terrence J. Lindell, Florencia Luengo, Martha McCoy, David McFadden, Charles McGraw, Elizabeth McKillen, Matt McMahon, Robert McMahon, Elizabeth Mahan, Paul Manning, Herman Mast, Dennis Merrill, Jean-Donald Miller, William Mood, Jay Mullen, Carl Murdock, Brian Murphy, R. Kent Newmyer, Arnold Offner, John Offner, Marc O'Reilly, Chester Pach, Jerry Padula, Carol Petillo, David Pletcher, Salvadore Prisco, Stephen G. Rabe, Carol S. Repass, Wayne Repeta, Barney J. Rickman III, Michael Roskin, John Rourke, Nicholas Evan Sarantakes, Kenneth E. Shewmaker, Kent M. Schofield, David Sheinin, Anna Lou Smethurst, Elbert B. Smith, Kevin Smith, Thomas G. Smith, Larry Spongberg, Jennifer Sterling-Folker, Kenneth R. Stevens, Mark A. Stoler, Stephen M. Streeter, William W. Stueck, Jr., Duane Tananbaum, George Turner, Jonathan G. Utley, Thomas Walker, Wang Li, Kathryn Weathersby, Ralph E. Weber, Edmund S. Wehrle, Immanuel Wexler, Lawrence Wittner, Sol Woolman, Sherry Zane, and Thomas Zoumaras.

We welcome comments and suggestions from students and instructors.

T. G. P.
J. G. C.
S. J. M.
D. K.
K. J. H.

CHAPTER 1

Embryo of Empire: Americans and the World Before 1789

DIPLOMATIC CROSSROAD

✳ *Jay, Franklin, Adams, and Negotiations for Independence, 1782*

TWO DISGRUNTLED AMERICANS rode the same carriage from Versailles in August 1782. John Jay and Benjamin Franklin had just spent two frustrating hours with the French foreign minister, the Comte de Vergennes. These American peace commissioners, seeking to end the Revolutionary War for independence waged since 1775, had asked for advice on two problems in their negotiations with British and Spanish representatives. Because they had instructions to make no decisions without the "knowledge and concurrence" of the French, Jay and Franklin had asked Vergennes whether they should insist on explicit recognition of independence from England *prior* to a final peace treaty and whether the western boundary of the new American nation should be the Mississippi River. On both points Vergennes seemed to deny American interests. Do not worry about technicalities, he advised. If the British granted independence in the final treaty, Americans should not fuss about formal titles during the negotiations. On the western boundary, Vergennes hinted that Americans claimed "more than we had a right to," and that Spain and England had valid territorial claims east of the Mississippi.

Jay and Franklin wondered why their French ally seemed so negative. Jay suspected that Vergennes was plotting to delay negotiations with England so that Spain, having captured West Florida, could acquire the whole Gulf Coast and additional territory to the north. Franklin agreed that Spain wanted to "coop us up within the Allegheny Mountains," but he did not think that the French were conniving with the Spanish at American expense.

Franklin invited Jay inside his apartment to continue their now animated conversation. "Have we any reason to doubt the good faith of the King of France?" asked Franklin. "We can depend on the French," Jay rejoined, "only to see that we

1

French Snuffbox. Benjamin Franklin's reputation as a representative of frontier America is captured in a contemporary French snuffbox. In this complement, the revered gentleman from Pennsylvania joins two other philosophers, Rousseau and Voltaire. (The Metropolitan Museum of Art, Gift of William H. Huntington, 1883 [83.2.228] Photograph, all rights reserved, The Metropolitan Museum of Art)

are separated from England, but it is not in their interest that we should become a great and formidable people, and therefore they will not help us to become so." Franklin asked on whom the United States should rely. Only "on God and ourselves," Jay solemnly answered. The Pennsylvanian shot back: "Would you deliberately break Congress's instructions [on not negotiating separately]?" "Unless we violate these instructions the dignity of Congress will be in the dust," Jay asserted. The septuagenarian Franklin pressed further: "Then you are prepared to break our instructions if you intend to take an independence course now." Jay stood up. "*If* the instructions conflict with America's honor and dignity I would break them—like this!" Jay threw his clay pipe hard into Franklin's fireplace. It shattered.

Nothing that happened in the next several weeks elevated John Jay's opinion of the French and Spaniards. In early September, Vergennes's secretary gave Jay his "personal ideas" to expedite peace negotiations with England as well as a boundary settlement with Spain. Again the Frenchman urged the Americans not to press for the Mississippi. When that same official suddenly left on a secret mission to London, Jay became immediately suspicious. Even the usually unflappable Franklin fretted. Perhaps the French would bring the same arguments to the British that they were making to the Americans; perhaps France supported British claims north of the Ohio River and wanted Spain to have full control over the Mississippi.

Jay had seen enough. On September 11, without first even informing Franklin, Jay boldly sent his own secret emissary to London with the proposal that secret and separate negotiations for peace begin at once. The British jumped at the chance to split the Franco-American alliance. When he learned what his younger colleague had done, Franklin protested, but he went along.

By late October, when the third American peace commissioner arrived in Paris, private talks with the British had gone on for several weeks. John Adams had just successfully negotiated a commercial treaty with the Dutch. As a diplomat in Paris earlier in the war, he had come to distrust both the French and Franklin, an "old conjurer" who seemed too cozy with Vergennes. The disputatious New Englander immediately found a kindred spirit in Jay, who confided that the French were "endeavoring to deprive Us of the Fishery, the Western Lands, and the Navigation of the Mississippi." Like Jay, Adams thought that Vergennes opposed American expansion and kept "his hand under our chin to prevent us from drowning, but not to lift our heads out of the water." On meeting Franklin, Adams immediately launched into a lecture. Everything Jay had done was correct. Jay was right in his suspicions toward Vergennes. Jay was right to insist on prior independence, access to the fisheries, and extensive western boundaries. Adams waxed enthusiastic about the decision to negotiate separately with the British on these issues. To do otherwise would be leaving "the lamb to the custody of the wolf."

Franklin hardly replied to Adams's outburst. Suffering from the gout, the old philosopher listened patiently to the person he later described as "always an honest man, often a wise one, but sometimes, and in some things, absolutely out of his senses." Franklin agreed that the United States should remain firm on both the fisheries and the Mississippi boundary. Access to the Newfoundland fishing grounds was vital to New England's economy, while the Mississippi stood as an indispensable highway for trans-Allegheny commerce—"a Neighbor might as well ask me to sell my Street Door," he said. What bothered Franklin most was the failure to consult Vergennes. French loans had kept America solvent through six years of war, and French ships and troops had contributed mightily to the decisive victory at Yorktown in 1781. "If we were to break our faith with this nation," Franklin warned, "England would again trample on us and every other nation despise us." Franklin did not believe that the French were dealing with Spain and England behind American backs. He nonetheless recognized the importance of a united American front in negotiations. Just prior to meeting with the British commissioners, Franklin startled Jay: "I . . . will go with these gentlemen in the business without consulting this [French] court."

Franklin kept his word, and on November 30, 1782, England and the United States signed a "preliminary treaty" of peace. The terms, enumerated in a comprehensive treaty some ten months later, guaranteed American independence and provided generous boundaries. The historian Samuel Flagg Bemis has called the accord "the greatest victory in the annals of American diplomacy."

The American decision to negotiate separately in 1782 was both symbolic and successful. By going to war with England, the colonies had sought to win their independence, enlarge their commerce, and expand their territorial domain. Patriot leaders hoped to attain these goals without getting entangled in European politics.

"Blessed Are the Peacemakers." In this critical British cartoon of 1783 a Spaniard and a Frenchman lead George III by the neck while Lord Shelburne carries the "Preliminaries of Peace." The procession is commanded by an American wielding a whip and tugging a sulking, boorish Dutchman. (British Museum)

Blessed are the PEACE MAKERS

One motive for independence was to escape the constant wars that embroiled eighteenth-century Europe. But victory required help. France became America's ally in 1778, and in the next two years Spain and the Netherlands also joined the war against England. The war for American independence had evolved into a world war. The entanglements Americans hoped to avoid inevitably followed. At the critical moment in peace negotiations, Jay and Adams rightly suspected that their French ally, although committed to American independence, did not share the expansive American vision of that independence. The two commissioners thereupon persuaded Franklin to pursue an *independent* course, take advantage of European rivalries, and extract a generous treaty from the British. In Adams's eyes especially, they were upholding American honor by breaking instructions that French diplomats had forced on a pliant Congress. It was an ironic moment. Americans said they pursued independence and empire not merely for selfish motives, but also for a more civilized mode of international relations, free from the monarchical double-dealing of European power politics. To gain their ends, however, Franklin, Jay, and Adams employed the same Machiavellian tactics that they so despised in Europeans.

Reaching for Independence: Ideology and Commercial Power

The United States could not have won independence from England without assistance from France. However much the patriots of 1776 wanted to isolate themselves from the wars and diplomatic maneuverings of Europe, European rivalries provided them with the opportunity for national liberation.

The century-old contest between France and England for preeminence in Europe and control of North America provided the immediate backdrop for the American Revolution. Four wars fought between 1689 and 1763 originated in Europe but had profound consequences in the New World. The most recent war, called the French and Indian War in America (1754–1763), had eliminated French power from North America. By the Treaty of Paris (1763) the defeated French ceded Canada and the Ohio Valley to the British and relinquished Louisiana to the Spanish. Spain, in turn, gave up the Floridas to England.

Most colonial leaders cheered the victorious British war for empire. The Reverend Jonathan Mayhew of Boston envisaged the colonies as "*a mighty empire . . . mighty cities rising on every hill, and by the side of every commodious port, mighty fleets . . . laden with the produce of . . . every other country under heaven.*" Benjamin Franklin, then a colonial agent in England, had urged removal of the French from Canada. "The future grandeur and stability of the British empire lay in America," he wrote in 1760. "All the country from the St. Lawrence to the Mississippi will be in another century filled with British people." With the American population doubling every twenty-five years, a British visitor predicted that "this vast country will in time become the greatest and most prosperous empire that perhaps the world has ever seen."

Once the French and Indian War ended, however, London began to tighten the machinery of empire. A standing army of 10,000 men was sent to America for imperial defense. To pay for its upkeep, Parliament levied new taxes on the colonies. London now enforced mercantile regulations banning direct American trade with foreign ports in the West Indies. Hoping to pacify Native Americans beyond the Alleghenies, the British ministry issued the Proclamation of 1763, which delineated the headwaters of rivers flowing into the Atlantic as a line beyond which settlers had "forthwith to remove themselves." The Treaty of Fort Stanwix (1768) moved the line to the Ohio River, but settlers soon swarmed beyond the Ohio with "utter disregard for Indian rights," thus renewing conflict along the frontier from Pennsylvania to Kentucky by 1774.

In response to London's apparent disregard for their interests, the colonials retaliated with petitions, economic boycotts, and sporadic outbreaks of violence. Parliament responded with more taxes. The Tea Act of 1773 led to the Boston Tea Party, which, in turn, triggered the Coercive Acts. When the Quebec Act of 1774 made the Ohio Valley an integral part of Canada, some colonial leaders who had speculated in western lands supported revolution to obtain empire. Armed resistance exploded at Lexington and Concord in the spring of 1775, followed by battles around Boston. Then came an abortive American invasion of Quebec in December 1775. By this time John Adams and Benjamin Franklin were urging ties with the same French they had helped to defeat twenty years before.

As Americans moved cautiously toward independence, the emerging republican ideology, which embraced the "rights of Englishmen" and the principles of representative government, also contained the roots of an independent foreign policy. Americans specifically looked to their immediate colonial past. As British mercantile restrictions tightened in the 1760s, colonial leaders argued that the imperial connection with England was one-sided, and that Americans became constantly embroiled in England's wars against their will. Attacks by the French and Indians along the northern frontier usually had their origins in European quarrels, yet Americans nevertheless had to pay taxes, raise armies, and fight and die. Britain did not always value colonial sacrifices, most notably in 1742 when New Englanders captured the strategic French fortress of Louisbourg on Cape Breton Island, only to have the British hand it back later in exchange for French conquests in India.

Not wanting to be pawns in England's colonial wars, Franklin exaggerated when he told Parliament in 1766 that the Americans had enjoyed "perfect peace with both French and Indians" and that the recent conflict had been "really a British war." He nonetheless expressed what one scholar has called "a deep-seated feeling of escape from Europe and a strong tendency, encouraged by European diplomacy, to avoid becoming entangled in European conflict, whenever it was to their interest to do so."

Americans also cited recent British history. Many of the same English Whig writers quoted in defense of "no taxation without representation" had also taken part in a great debate over British foreign policy during the first half of the eighteenth century. These Whigs had criticized British involvement in continental European wars. Since the European balance of power always seemed unstable, they argued that continental entanglements might improve the German territorial interests of the House of Hanover but certainly not those of England. England's true interests, these Whigs emphasized, lay in expanding its commerce and empire which "will turn deserts into fruitful fields, villages into great cities, cottages into palaces, beggars into princes, convert cowards into heroes, blockheads into philosophers." One pamphleteer posited a general rule: "A Prince or State ought to avoid all Treaties, except such as tend towards Commerce or Manufactures. . . . All other Alliances may be look'd upon as so many Incumbrances." The similarity between these arguments for British isolation from Europe and the later American rationale for independence is striking. American leaders became familiar with the British debate. In their desire to avoid British wars and British taxes, Revolutionary leaders not surprisingly appropriated British precepts.

Another source of American thinking on foreign policy came in the writings of the French *philosophes*. As Enlightenment enthusiasts and advocates for the rising bourgeoisie, the *philosophes* launched an attack on all practices that thwarted the proper rule of reason in international affairs. Traditional diplomacy, they argued, had become "an obscure art which hides itself in the folds of deceit, which fears to let itself be seen and believes it can succeed only in the darkness of mystery." Like English Whigs, the *philosophes* emphasized commercial expansion over power politics. Unlike political barriers, commerce tied the "family of nations" together with "threads of silk." Trade should be as free as possible, unfettered by colonial restrictions. Baron de Montesquieu, who believed that "the natural effect of commerce is to lead to peace," postulated that "everywhere there are gentle mores, there is commerce and that everywhere there is commerce, there are gentle mores." More radical *philosophes* wanted to take diplomacy out of the hands of princes. "Alliances," wrote the Marquis de Condorcet, "are only means by which the rulers of states precipitate the people into wars from which they benefit either by covering up their mistakes or by carrying out their plots against freedom." Diplomacy should consist mainly of commercial interchange between individual persons rather than governments.

Thomas Paine (1737–1809). This working-class Englishman found his way to Philadelphia in 1774, where he took a job as a journalist. The irascible Paine joined the Continental Army and later participated in the French Revolution. John Adams later called Paine "the Satyr of the Age . . . a mongrel between Pig and Puppy, begotten by a wild Boar on a Bitch Wolf." (John Wesley Jarvis, *Thomas Paine.* Image © Board of Trustees, National Gallery of Art, Washington, D.C.)

Along with Whig writings, such continental ideas provided Revolutionary leaders with a missionary credo as they sought to win independence and an empire from the British Crown. Like John Winthrop's Puritans, they would not merely benefit themselves but also erect a model for the rest of the world. John Adams made this point when he told Vergennes in 1781 that "the dignity of North America does not consist in diplomatic ceremonials. . . . [It] consists solely in reason, justice, truth, the rights of mankind, and the interests of the nations of Europe." Indeed, the Revolutionary generation believed itself "providentially assigned . . . to lead the world to new and better things" and to create "an exemplary state *separate* from the corrupt and fallen world." Americans also shared with Europeans the belief that a single dominant power always carried forward civilization, and that historically such empires always moved "from east to west, and this continent is the last western state" wherein God is "erecting a stage on which to exhibit the great things of his kingdom."

The movement for an independent foreign policy reached its climax with the convocation of the Second Continental Congress in summer 1775. Some Americans desiring to remain within the British Empire held out hope that continued commercial pressure would force London to negotiate. More radical delegates wanted to continue the war and declare independence. Benjamin Franklin proposed "articles of confederation" that would give Congress full power to make war and peace. John Adams called for construction of an American navy. Others urged the opening of American ports to foreign trade, arguing that only with protection from foreign navies could American merchant ships reach European ports. Foreign trade required foreign assistance. The argument for independence, made repeatedly behind the closed doors of Congress, became popularized on January 10, 1776, with the appearance of Thomas Paine's pamphlet *Common Sense.*

Tom Paine was an English Quaker who had come to America in 1774. Once in Philadelphia he became friends with those members of Congress who urged independence. Paine's pamphlet summarized their arguments. Opposing further petitions to the king, urging construction of a navy and immediate formation of a confederation, emphasizing the need for foreign assistance, and calling for the opening of American ports, Paine's celebrated call to "begin the world over again" also spelled out the benefits of an independent foreign policy. With reconciliation with England no longer possible, as Paine put it with some exaggeration, there was no "advantage" to "being connected with Great Britain." On the contrary, "France and Spain never were . . . our enemies as Americans, but as Our being subjects of Great Britain." For Paine and his American friends, "Our plan is commerce, and that, well attended to, will secure us the Peace and friendship of all Europe. . . . As Europe is our market for trade, we ought to form no partial connection with any part of it. It is the true interest of America to steer clear of European contentions." Declare independence, he claimed, and Europe would compete for America's commercial favors. Paine assumed that a foreign nation would assist America to protect that trade. America would benefit, and so would the rest of the world.

Of course, part of what Paine wrote was more nonsense than "common sense," particularly his playing down of privileges that Americans enjoyed as part of the British Empire. After independence, Americans would miss British naval protection and easy access to the British West Indies. The pamphlet nonetheless served as effective propaganda. *Common Sense* sold more than 300,000 copies—one copy for every ten persons living in the thirteen colonies in 1776. Indeed, Paine's pamphlet thus embedded "decidedly nontraditional—indeed, revolutionary—ideas in early American foreign relations."

With the abortive invasion of Canada in the winter of 1775–1776 and the arrival of British reinforcements, it became obvious that some foreign help was imperative. Congress opened American ports in April 1776, but Paine's logic seemed irrefutable: No foreign power would openly aid the American rebels until independence was a declared fact. "No State in Europe," Virginia's Richard Henry Lee argued in June, "will either Treat or Trade with us so long as we consider ourselves Subjects of G.B." Thomas Jefferson thereupon wrote the Declaration of Independence, and Congress endorsed it on July 4, 1776.

To solicit foreign support, Congress designated a committee to prepare a "model treaty" to be presented to the French court of Louis XVI. The committee's so-called Plan of 1776, which Congress debated in August, would also serve as the basis for alliances with other countries. A final, amended version then accompanied Benjamin Franklin to France when he became American minister at the close of the year. John Adams drafted the Model Treaty. Like Paine, the lawyer from Braintree eschewed "any political connection, or military assistance, or indeed naval, from France," as he told a friend. "I wish for nothing but commerce, a mere marine treaty with them." Adams's imprint on the Model Treaty became clear, for it was almost purely a treaty of commerce and navigation, which would permit American ships free entry into French ports while French military supplies entered American ports in ever-increasing quantities. Included also were elaborate rules protecting neutral commerce in wartime. The Model Treaty suggested that the United States and France grant the nationals of each country the same "Rights, Liberties, Privileges, Immunities and Exemptions" in trade, or at least agree to a most-favored-nation clause, whereby American merchants would receive the same commercial benefits enjoyed by other nations.

Some in Congress, Adams later recalled, "thought there was not sufficient temptation to France to join us. They moved for cessions and concessions, which implied . . . political alliance that I had studiously avoided." Like most Americans in 1776, he feared that France, if offered inducements, might demand Canada and the Newfoundland fisheries, both of which the new republic sought for itself. Somewhat naively, Adams and his colleagues convinced themselves that breaking England's monopoly over North American commerce, accomplished through American independence, would by itself gain French support. Franco-American trade should be "ample Compensation to France for Acknowledging our Independence," Adams insisted. The only political obligation in the Model Treaty came in Article VIII, which stipulated that America would not aid London in any war between Britain and France.

The neutral-rights provisions of the Model Treaty deserve special attention. Although these articles would not apply to the war against England, they formed the basis of America's historic policy of "freedom of the seas." These commercial clauses guaranteed the principles of "free ships, free goods" (that is, the neutral flag protected noncontraband cargoes from capture), the freedom of neutrals to trade in noncontraband between ports of belligerents, and a restricted and narrowly defined list of contraband (illegal cargo) exempting naval stores and foodstuffs from seizure. Regarding the neutral flag as an extension of territorial sovereignty on the high seas, Americans claimed broad freedom to trade in wartime, except in contraband articles and with places blockaded or besieged. Such principles of neutral rights were becoming increasingly accepted in the late eighteenth century, particularly by countries lacking large navies. Having adopted liberal provisions in a few treaties, London was understandably reluctant to endorse them as international law. If Britain went to war against an inferior naval force, the British enemy might very well encourage neutral shipping to carry its commercial goods to protect its own vulnerable vessels from British warships. If neutrals could also supply an enemy nation freely, especially with naval stores, they could eventually undermine Britain's maritime supremacy. Americans, looking past independence, envisaged future European wars and hoped to expand their commerce at such times. France, in a naval war against the more powerful British, would benefit from American neutrality. Americans could fatten their pocketbooks and at the same time serve humanity by supporting more civilized rules of warfare.

The Model Treaty, then, introduced the main themes of early American foreign policy. It set forth the ideal of commercial expansion and political isolation. By specifically binding France against acquiring Canada, it also projected a continental domain for America beyond the thirteen coastal settlements. As one historian has written, the Model Treaty underscored "the faith of the leaders of the new nation in the power of trade, and a concomitant desire to stay out of European struggles," and a belief "that America, now liberty's home, must be maintained as 'an asylum for mankind.' "

Opportunity and Necessity: Alliance with France

Patriot leaders did not err in thinking that France would aid American independence. Indeed, since 1763, when France had been stripped of its empire, the compelling motive of French foreign policy became *revanche*. "There will come in time a revolution in America," the French foreign minister in the 1760s predicted, "which will put England into a state of weakness where she will no longer be a terror in Europe." Americans knew of intense French interest. "All Europe is attentive to the dispute," Franklin wrote from London in 1770, and "our part is taken everywhere." Aside from strengthening the Bourbon Family Compact with Spain and sending secret observers to North America, France made no overt moves to intervene before 1770.

The decision to succor the Americans fell to Charles Gravier, the Comte de Vergennes. Suave, polished, outwardly unemotional, Vergennes looked every inch the epitome of a successful diplomat of the ancien régime. In actuality, he could act impetuously. When the American colonies began their armed rebellion, he adopted the motto *Aut nunc aut nunquam* ("now or never").

A perfect scheme for aiding the insurrectionaries short of war appeared early in 1776 in the person of Pierre Augustin Caron de Beaumarchais. The adventurous author of *The Barber of Seville* created a dummy trading house, Rodrigue Hortalez and Company, through which he could secretly ship military supplies to the American colonies. The French court could provide secret financing. Vergennes jumped at Beaumarchais's scheme. In a persuasive memorandum, Vergennes argued that American independence would "diminish the power of England and increase in proportion that of France." Assistance to the Americans might also permit France to recover "the possessions which the English have taken from us in America, such as the fisheries of Newfoundland. . . . We do not speak of Canada." By May 1776, before any American agent reached France, Paris took the plunge. The French Treasury quietly transferred 1 million livres (about $200,000) to Beaumarchais's "company." Charles III of Spain made a similar grant, and the first shipments of muskets, cannon, powder, tents, and clothing soon crossed the Atlantic. When Franklin arrived in December 1776, French assistance already existed. Whether this aid could evolve into recognition and a formal treaty remained to be seen.

Franklin took Paris by storm. The seventy-year-old philosopher was already well known in France. *Poor Richard's Almanac,* with its catchy aphorisms, had run through several French editions, and Franklin's electrical experiments and philosophical writings had earned him honored membership in the French Academy. Franklin's kindly features soon adorned medals and snuffbox covers—so much so that "my Face is now almost as well known as that of the Moon." A jealous John Adams complained that the Philadelphian was "so fond of the fair sex that one was not enough for him, but he must have one on each side, and all the ladies both old and young were ready to eat him up." Franklin explained physics to Queen Marie Antoinette, played chess with the Duchesse de Bourbon, and even proposed marriage to the wealthy Madame Helvetius. Withal, Franklin captivated his host country. Thomas Jefferson did not exaggerate when, on becoming minister to France in 1784, he said that he was merely succeeding Franklin, for no one could replace him.

Benjamin Franklin (1706–1790) at the Court of France. The elderly philosopher-journalist-humorist-politician-diplomat fascinated the snobbish court of France. A recent biographer, Edmund S. Morgan, *Benjamin Franklin* (2002), writes that Franklin's "style of dealing with the French was not the suspicious, secretive, aggressive assertion of American demands . . . but an openhanded confession of American needs and American gratitude for French help. And it had worked." (Courtesy of The Old Print Shop, Kenneth M. Newman)

Social popularity did not ensure diplomatic success. Vergennes might have recognized American independence prior to Franklin's arrival had not the successful British military campaign in New York in summer 1776 made the French court cautious. Recognition meant war with England, and the French hesitated without Spanish assistance. Spain was dragging its feet. Although French loans and supplies continued through 1776 and 1777, Vergennes avoided a formal commitment until there was a sure sign of American military success. Then came Saratoga on October 17, 1777, a battle in which 90 percent of American arms and ammunition had come from French merchants. The defeat of "Gentleman Johnny" Burgoyne's troops in the forests of northern New York helped persuade England to send out peace feelers. Franklin used the threat of reconciliation with England as a lever on Vergennes. When asked what could prevent Congress from coming to an agreement with England short of full independence, Franklin replied: The immediate conclusion of a treaty of commerce and alliance.

On February 6, 1778, Vergennes and Franklin inked two pacts. The first, a treaty of amity and commerce, gave Americans most-favored-nation privileges (they would enjoy any commercial favors granted by France to other countries). The two nations also accepted definitions of contraband and neutral rights that followed the Model Treaty.

The second pact, however, a treaty of alliance, contained political commitments that departed from John Adams's original plan. Instead of the meager promise not to aid England if France entered the war for independence, Franklin agreed not to make peace with the British without first obtaining French consent. Vergennes made a similar promise. Although retaining the ban against French territorial gains on the North American continent, the United States agreed to recognize any French conquests in the Caribbean and to guarantee "from the present time and forever" all French possessions in North America and any others obtained at the peace table. France paid an equivalent price. According to Article II, France also guaranteed "from the present time and forever" American "Possessions, and the additions or conquests . . . during the war, from any of the Dominions now or heretofore possessed by Great Britain in North America." In short, Vergennes seemed ready to guarantee whatever territories could be wrested from England.

The French alliance posed the very political dangers that John Adams had warned against. Certainly the stipulation prohibiting any peace without French consent, as well as the guarantee of territories, entangled American interests in the foreign policies of another nation. Congress had already offered political inducements when it had instructed Franklin to seek an alliance with Spain in which the United States would assist Spain in conquering Florida and declare war against Portugal in return for diplomatic recognition and outright military assistance. Such a treaty did not materialize, but the instructions indicated that Congress, after two years without a major victory, could compromise its ideals for military help against Britain. Both Paine and Adams embraced the French alliance, Paine so enthusiastically that he named his next daughter Marie Antoinette after the French queen. Adams was soon calling the treaty "a Rock upon which we may safely build." The treaty did fulfill the most important of Adams's original expectations—that American independence from England would be too great a prize for France to pass up. The French, said Adams, dreaded "the United British Empire" so much that they could not possibly "let slip the opportunity of striking one pistol at least" from "an enemy who constantly threatened them with two." In fact, Vergennes had no wish to replace Britain with a great American empire that might eventually chase the French and the Spanish out of the New World. "[T]hey would not stop here," he said in 1775, "but would in process of time advance to the Southern Continent of America . . . and in the end not leave a foot of that Hemisphere in the possession of any European power." The French made a commitment to American independence, not to American expansion.

The French commitment was tested at the very beginning of the alliance. When the Elector Maximilian of Bavaria died, on December 30, 1777, Joseph II of Austria promptly occupied and annexed that German principality. Frederick the Great of Prussia went to war on behalf of Bavarian independence. Austria urged France, allied to Austria since 1756, to join the War of Bavarian Succession against Prussia. The Austrian Netherlands would be France's reward, but Vergennes resisted temptation. Toward Austria, he slyly assumed the role of benevolent mediator, hoping to keep Europe quiet to concentrate on the maritime war against England. This mediation was successfully accomplished in 1779.

Ironically, Emperor Joseph resented French interference, and when the opportunity presented itself in the summer of 1781, he returned the favor and offered to mediate between Britain and France. Russia also joined in the mediation offer. Since it came at a low point in the military struggle in America, Vergennes might have felt compelled to accept Austro-Russian mediation (the terms would *not* have recognized American independence) in 1781 had not English king George III stubbornly resisted any solution short of complete submission by the colonies. The point is clear: France, whatever the entanglements of the European continent, was bent on defeating England by backing American independence. By 1783 France had expended some 48 million livres ($9.6 million) on behalf of American independence.

Suspicious Suitors in Europe

Franklin had argued that "a virgin state should preserve the virgin character, and not go about suitoring after alliances, but wait with decent dignity for the application of others." Congress, needing money and hoping for military assistance, ruled otherwise. Thus did American diplomats scurry to Berlin, Madrid, Vienna, St. Petersburg, Amsterdam, and other capitals in quest of alliances that never quite materialized. Frederick the Great had intimated that Prussia would recognize American independence if France did, but when envoy William Lee arrived in Berlin, Frederick told his chief minister: "Put him off with compliments." Fear of revolutionary principles, the danger of British retaliation, trading opportunities, and territorial ambitions closer to home—all made the European monarchies reluctant to challenge Britain. Neutrals should recognize America and join the war, John Adams grumbled: "Without it, all may nibble and piddle and dribble and fribble, waste a long time, immense treasures, and much human blood, and they must come to it at last."

The Dutch exemplified the point. With institutions of representative government firmly entrenched in the Dutch Estates General, the Netherlands might have been the first to recognize American independence. Not so. The burghers of Amsterdam preferred making money. The Dutch busied themselves by carrying naval stores from the Baltic to France, as well as using their West Indian island of St. Eustatius as an entrepôt for contraband trade with the Americans. These activities, plus a willingness to join Catherine the Great's League of Armed Neutrality in 1780, led to war with England, but the Dutch steadfastly refused any treaty with the United States until October 1782. Although the Dutch treaty came too late to give military assistance in the war, John Adams secured a loan of 5 million guilders in June 1782 from Amsterdam bankers, the first of a series of Dutch loans, totaling some 9 million guilders ($3,600,000), that sustained American credit through the 1780s.

American efforts to join the Armed Neutrality of 1780 marked another episode in futile diplomacy. Organized by Catherine II of Russia, the Armed Neutrality also included Denmark, Sweden, Austria, Prussia, Portugal, and the Kingdom of the Two Sicilies. Its purpose was ostensibly to enforce liberal provisions of neutral rights ("free ships, free goods," no paper blockades, narrow definition of contraband) in trading with belligerents. Because the Armed Neutrality's principles so closely resembled the Model Treaty, Congress immediately adopted its rules by resolution and sent an envoy, Francis Dana of Massachusetts, to St. Petersburg to gain formal adherence to the league by treaty. It was an impossible mission. Aside from the obvious incongruity of a belligerent nation attempting to join an alliance of neutrals, Catherine would not risk war with England by granting recognition prematurely. Her real purpose was to divert British attention while preparing to seize the Crimea from Ottoman Turkey. Dana returned home "most heartily weary of the old world" after two long years in the Russian capital without ever being received officially. Indeed, formal relations with Russia did not begin until 1809, when Catherine's grandson, Tsar Alexander I, received as American minister John Quincy Adams, who as a fourteen-year-old had been Dana's secretary during the abortive wartime mission.

Once peace negotiations in Paris had established American independence in 1783, however, the Dutch urged the United States to join the Armed Neutrality through a formal treaty with the Netherlands. At this point with the war all but over, Congress reconsidered and rejected any formal treaty. The reason? "The true interest of these [United] states requires that they should be as little as possible entangled in the politics and controversies of European nations." Thus, however much Americans desired freedom of trade for both profit and principle, they shunned political entanglements to achieve such an objective.

The most frustrating diplomacy of all occurred with Spain. Despite previous financial support for the embattled colonials, and notwithstanding the outwardly close alliance with France, the government of King Charles III was in no hurry to take up arms against England—especially if Spain could obtain its principal objective, the return of Gibraltar, by other means. Given its own extensive American empire, moreover, Spain was understandably less eager than France to encourage overseas revolutions. Not only might colonial rebellion grow contagious, but a powerful American republic could threaten Spanish possessions as effectively as an expanding British Empire. Determined to "make our decisions without rushing," Spanish foreign minister Count Floridablanca played a double game by dickering with both France and England in the hope of regaining Gibraltar. Only by the Treaty of Aranjuez, signed on April 12, 1779, did Spain agree on war against England, and even then the alliance was with France, not with the Americans. One article held enormous importance. Because of Madrid's obsession with Gibraltar, France agreed to keep on fighting until they wrested that rocky symbol of Spanish pride from the British. According to the alliance of 1778, the United States and France had pledged not to make a separate peace and to continue the war until England recognized American independence. Now France was promising to fight until Gibraltar fell. In this circuitous, devious fashion, without being a party to the treaty or even being consulted, the Americans found their independence "chained by European diplomacy to the Rock of Gibraltar."

Congress dispatched John Jay to Madrid in September 1779 to obtain a formal alliance. The thirty-four-year-old New Yorker of Huguenot descent did not have an easy time of it. Not once during his two-and-a-half-year stay did the Spanish court officially receive Jay. Rarely did Count Floridablanca deign to communicate with him. Even more frustrating, Jay ran out of money and had to ask the Spanish for funds. The Spanish count did give Jay some $175,000, but only to keep the American dangling while the count secretly negotiated with a British agent in the hope that Britain would accept outside mediation and cede Gibraltar. The Spanish ploy failed because George III remained as stubborn about Gibraltar as he did about American independence.

In summer 1781, Congress instructed Jay to concede navigation on the Mississippi River if Spain would recognize American independence and make an alliance. Such a message reflected the military dangers the colonists faced in autumn 1780, following the successful British invasion of the South. Jay obediently sought an interview with the Spanish foreign minister and made his proposal: a treaty relinquishing navigation rights on the Mississippi south of 31° north latitude, a Spanish guarantee to the United States of "all their respective territories," and an American guarantee to the Spanish king of "all his dominions in America." Floridablanca refused. Had he accepted, the navigation of the "Father of Waters" and the boundary of West Florida would have been settled to Spain's advantage. But Floridablanca preferred to gamble. Already Spanish troops from New Orleans had occupied West Florida, and possibly they could claim more territory between the Mississippi and the Alleghenies.

Rebuffed, Jay withdrew the concession on Mississippi navigation. If Spain refused to make an alliance during the war, the United States should reassert its Mississippi claims in any final peace treaty, he explained. Congress concurred. Jay had also begun to suspect that the French were encouraging Spain in its trans-Appalachian territorial ambitions. Indeed, following his sojourn in Spain, this "almost xenophobic American" and his suspicions of European intentions helped shape the American posture at the 1782 peace negotiations.

A Separate Peace: The Treaty of Paris

The surrender of Lord Cornwallis's army at Yorktown on October 19, 1781, precipitated serious peace talks. George III stubbornly tried to fight on, but the burgeoning public debt and war weariness finally caused the ministry of Lord North to fall early in 1782. The king reluctantly accepted a new ministry under the Marquess of Rockingham, committed to a restoration of peace but undecided as to the terms.

The British sent Richard Oswald to Paris in April 1782 to sound out Benjamin Franklin. Old friends from before the revolution, the two men talked candidly as Franklin "opened his mind" about the "desirability of restoring American goodwill toward England" and how to achieve it. After introducing the British envoy to Vergennes, Franklin privately intimated to Oswald the possibility of a separate peace if England granted complete independence and generous boundaries. The American did not demand Canada, but its voluntary cession would have "an excellent effect . . . [on] the mind of the [American] people in general."

Peace talks stalled as another cabinet crisis distracted the British. Not until Rockingham's death and Lord Shelburne's succession as prime minister on July 1 could the British agree on a negotiating position. During this interval, Franklin summoned his fellow peace commissioners, Jay and Adams, to Paris. Jay arrived by the end of June. Adams continued commercial negotiations in the Netherlands and did not reach the French capital until October 26.

The success of the separate negotiations, which began in October and ended on November 30, owed much to the conciliatory attitude of Shelburne. A believer in natural rights and free trade through his friendship with French *philosophes,* the prime minister wanted to break up the French-American alliance, and by "encouraging the expansion of American territory and population," he now envisaged new markets for "British goods to conquer." The peace terms were thus exceedingly generous; as Vergennes later put it:"The English buy the peace more than they make it." Not only did the United States gain complete independence, but also extensive boundaries (the Great Lakes and St. Lawrence River to the north, Mississippi River to the west, 31° north latitude line across Florida to the south) that far surpassed what Americans had won on the battlefield. Further territorial gains were probably thwarted by eleventh-hour British naval victories in the Caribbean and the failure of a French-Spanish siege of Gibraltar in September 1782. Canada thus remained British. Henceforth, in one scholar's words, "American expansionism had a westward, but not a northward gaze."

With independence and boundaries easily settled, much wrangling focused on the Atlantic fisheries. The British argued that access to the fishing grounds off the Grand Banks of Newfoundland, as well as the right to dry and cure fish on Canadian shores, should be limited to members of the British Empire. The Americans disagreed. New England, where "Tom Cod," not George III, was king, had a stubborn advocate in John Adams, who claimed that the fisheries were "indispensably necessary to the accomplishment and preservation of our independence." The Americans finally won their point, although the treaty ambiguously granted the "liberty" to fish, not the "right," thus perpetuating a controversy over which generations of diplomats battled for more than a century.

Sharpest disagreement arose over Loyalists and pre-Revolutionary debts. The British sought generous treatment for the thousands of colonials who had fled into exile for their loyalty to the Crown, demanding restitution of confiscated property, or at least compensation. The Americans adamantly disagreed. Even the moderate Jay spoke of Loyalists as having "the most dishonourable of human motives" and urged that "every American must set his face and steel his heart" against them. As to the 5 million pounds owed by Americans (mostly southern planters) to British merchants, Americans hesitated to repay obligations contracted prior to 1775. Adams found acceptable compromise language whereby British creditors would "meet with no lawful impediment" in collecting their debts. This particular clause helped gain the support of the British commercial classes for what was an otherwise unpopular treaty. As Adams put it, concession on the debts prevented the British merchants "from making common Cause with the Refugees [Loyalists]." The British accepted an article that "earnestly recommended" to the states that properties seized during the war be restored. Because Congress could not dictate to the states under the Articles of Confederation, both British and American commissioners understood that the "earnest recommendations" might not be followed.

Americans enthusiastically greeted the preliminary peace terms but worried about alienating France. After two weeks of silence, Vergennes wrote plaintively to Franklin: "You perfectly understand what is due to propriety; you have all your life performed your duties. I pray to you to consider how you propose to fulfill those which are due to the [French] King?" Franklin thereupon delivered one of the most beguiling replies in the history of diplomacy. He admitted that the American commissioners had been guilty of a lack of *bienséance* (propriety) in not keeping the French fully informed, but he hoped that it would not harm the alliance. "The English," he told Vergennes, "flatter themselves they have already divided us." The French foreign minister said nothing more. In fact, he even agreed to an additional loan of some 6 million livres, which Franklin had requested earlier.

Why did the French respond so mildly? Vergennes, with Paris honeycombed with spies, knew all along about the secret negotiations. He did not protest, because he understood that England was indeed trying to break up the Franco-American alliance. The separate American peace, moreover, offered Vergennes a way out of a sticky tangle with Spain. He could now tell the stubborn Spaniards that Gibraltar was no longer a viable objective with the Americans effectively out of the war. To Vergennes American independence counted far more than Gibraltar. While preferring a treaty that left the United States more dependent on France, he was not displeased with what Jay, Adams, and Franklin had accomplished.

The final Treaty of Paris was not signed until September 3, 1783. Except for some complications regarding Florida (Britain finally ceded all of Florida to Spain, whose military forces had captured West Florida in 1780–1781), the terms were precisely those of the preliminary treaty between England and the United States. America's diplomats had done well in overcoming political entanglements and exploiting European rivalries. "Undisciplined marines as we were," said John Adams, "we were better tacticians than we imagined." A Spanish diplomat predicted that the United States, "born a pygmy, . . . will grow up, become a giant, forget the benefits" of allies, and "only think in its own aggrandizement." Nonetheless, to obtain both independence and empire ranks as an impressive achievement.

Diplomatic Frustrations Under the Articles of Confederation

Americans were in an exuberant, expansive mood in 1783. Two years earlier all thirteen states had ratified the Articles of Confederation, giving them a new, if cumbersome, government. "This ball of liberty," wrote Jefferson, "is now so well in motion that it will roll around the world." Nearly half the national territory, some 220 million acres of wilderness, lay across the Appalachian chain, and the flood of emigrants westward, fleeing from heavy taxes to lower ones, from poorer to better lands, became inexorable. More than 100,000 Americans settled in Kentucky and Tennessee alone in the years between 1775 and 1790. As Jay put it in 1785, "the seeds of a great people are daily planting beyond the mountains." For George Washington, roads and canals would turn the trans-Allegheny region into a field almost too extensive for imagination. A Spanish official in Louisiana complained that Yankees were "advancing and multiplying . . . with a prodigious rapidity."

The "Thunder-Gust of Peace" also meant that foreign ships could now enter American ports without fear of British retaliation. Americans could regain British markets for their agricultural exports and develop as extensive and free a trade as possible with the rest of the world. As the geographer Thomas Hutchins boasted, Americans "have it in their power to engross the whole commerce," and "to possess, in the utmost security, the dominion of the sea throughout the world."

Impressive trade expansion fueled American optimism. Some 72,000 tons of shipping cleared America's busiest port, Philadelphia, in the year 1789, compared with an average of 45,000 tons in 1770–1772. Boston's tonnage increased from 42,506 in 1772 to 55,000 in 1788. Clearances in Maryland and Virginia doubled in volume over the figures from 1769. Tobacco exports brought a favorable balance of more than $1 million a year in trade with France during the 1780s. By 1788 the Netherlands was importing more than $4 million annually of tobacco, rice, and naval stores from the United States.

Merchants found new markets. The *Empress of China,* the first American ship to trade with Asia, set sail from New York in February 1784 and reached Guangzhou (Canton) six months later. The cargo was ginseng, which the Chinese believed would restore sexual potency to the aged. Another pioneering vessel, the *Columbia,* left Boston in 1787, wintered on the Pacific coast near Vancouver Island, and traded metal trinkets to the Indians for otter furs. The *Columbia* then voyaged to China, exchanged the furs for tea, and returned to Boston—the first American ship to circumnavigate the globe. Other ships soon followed. Thus began a curiously complicated trade, which often included a stop at the Hawaiian Islands to pick up sandalwood for Chinese consumers. The Pacific trade thus became "Boston's high school of commerce for forty years." On its second voyage, in 1792, the *Columbia* entered the mouth of the river named after it and helped establish the American claim to Oregon. In December 1785, Elias Hasket Derby of Salem sent the *Grand Turk* to the French island of Mauritius in the Indian Ocean, beginning a lucrative trade with India and other Asian ports. In their search for cargoes, American captains made the first contacts in the Indian and Pacific Oceans at least a generation prior to official diplomatic attention from the U.S. government.

Spanish America also loomed as a new market in the 1780s. Shipments of wheat, flour, and some reexported manufactures went to Cuba, Venezuela, and Argentina, and in particular to Santo Domingo, which served as an entrepôt for New Orleans, where American smuggling flourished as never before. By 1785 the viceroy of Buenos Aires in Argentina was reporting numerous *bostoneses* vessels plying southern waters "on the pretext of whaling and probably with hidden intentions." By 1788 American whalers and China traders had reached the west coast of South America, where they took on pelts and specie for the Asian market.

Despite the expansion of trade, the instant prosperity that many Americans expected in 1783 did not materialize because the United States had to adjust from a favored position within the British Empire to independent status in a world dominated by mercantilist restrictions. The bulk of American trade continued to be with England. In 1790, nearly half of all American exports went to England, and 90 percent of American imports originated in England. Contrary to Paine's *Common Sense,* however, independence brought an end to privileges that had been part of the imperial connection. New England suffered when London prohibited American ships from trading with the British West Indies. By 1786 the exports of Massachusetts totaled only one-fourth of what they had been in 1774. Because each state had its own customs service and tariff schedules, moreover, American diplomats could not threaten commercial retaliation against England. George Washington complained: "One State passes a prohibitory law respecting some article, another State opens wide the avenue for its admission. One Assembly makes a system; another Assembly unmakes it."

Indeed, as peacetime problems multiplied, structural weaknesses under the Articles of Confederation hamstrung diplomacy. Beyond commercial policy, states' rights thwarted national power in other respects as well. Congress had raised a continental army and constructed a small navy during the war, but in peace these "implied" powers collapsed; all naval vessels were sold or scrapped by the mid-1780s, and the army dwindled to a mere regiment. Congress remained nominally in charge of foreign policy. Yet during the war this large body had proven so faction-ridden and irresponsible that it had given the French foreign minister veto power over American peace commissioners. The legislative body did take a forward step in 1784 by creating a Department of Foreign Affairs and selecting John Jay as secretary. Although retaining the right to make war and peace and to make treaties and alliances, Congress lacked the power to enforce its diplomacy. Individual states violated the 1783 peace treaty with impunity. Instead of a world in which America would be "friends to all, and enemies to none," the reality seemed quite the opposite.

Relations with England quickly deteriorated after 1783. In the first flush of peace, Lord Shelburne's grand scheme of rapprochement might have continued the benefits Americans had enjoyed under the Crown, including free access of American goods and ships to British and West Indian ports. But Shelburne was soon forced from office for having given the Americans too much, and his successors rejected commercial reciprocity with the United States. Mercantilist thinking still held sway in England. Officials argued that the United States, if allowed the privileges of the British Empire, would eventually outstrip Britain in shipping, trade, and the production of manufactured goods. A restrictive policy, however, would allow England to increase its carrying trade, particularly in the West Indies, where colonial shipping

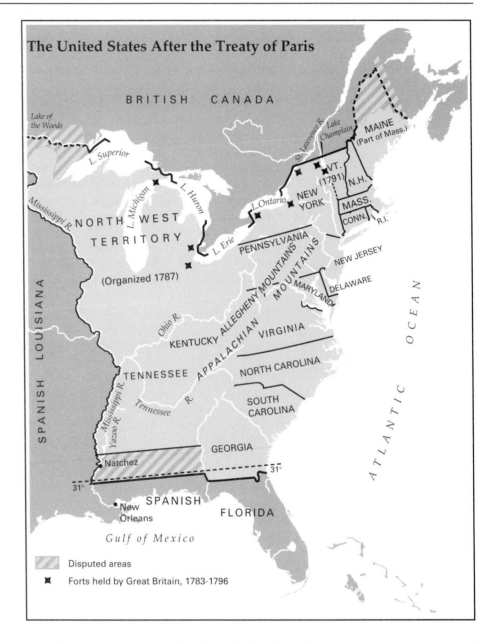

The United States After the Treaty of Paris

BRITISH CANADA

Lake of the Woods

L. Superior

Mississippi R.

NORTH WEST TERRITORY

L. Michigan

L. Huron

(Organized 1787)

L. Erie

St. Lawrence R.

Lake Champlain

MAINE (Part of Mass.)

VT. (1791)

N.H.

L. Ontario

NEW YORK

MASS.

CONN.

R.I.

PENNSYLVANIA

NEW JERSEY

DELAWARE

MARYLAND

Ohio R.

KENTUCKY

ALLEGHENY MOUNTAINS

APPALACHIAN MOUNTAINS

VIRGINIA

SPANISH LOUISIANA

TENNESSEE

Tennessee R.

NORTH CAROLINA

SOUTH CAROLINA

Mississippi R.

Yazoo R.

GEORGIA

Natchez

31°

31°

New Orleans

SPANISH FLORIDA

ATLANTIC OCEAN

Gulf of Mexico

Disputed areas

✖ Forts held by Great Britain, 1783-1796

had long predominated. Canada and Ireland could serve as alternative sources of provisions for the West Indian planters.

Such mercantilist precepts were codified in a series of orders in council, according to which American raw materials and foodstuffs, but not manufactures, could enter the British home islands aboard American vessels, while Canada and the West Indies remained closed to American shipping. Such restrictions, it was believed, would not hurt British exports. As the Earl of Sheffield prophetically observed: "At least four-fifths of the importations from Europe into the American

States were at all times made upon credit; and undoubtedly the States are in greater want of credit at this time than at former periods. It can be had only in Great Britain." As for possible commercial retaliation, the British scoffed at whether "A DISUNITED PEOPLE" could ever agree on uniform tariffs. "Pish! . . . What can Americans do?" boasted one Briton. "They have neither government nor power. Great Britain could shut up all their ports."

The British refusal to evacuate the northwest forts also rankled. These fortified posts, which ranged from Lake Champlain to Lake Michigan, strategically controlled the frontier, including the fur trade. Indian tribes between the Great Lakes and the Ohio River continued to resist white encroachment. Abandoned by the Paris Treaty, "we are determined to pay no attention to the Manner in which the British Negotiators have drawn out the lines," vowed the Creek leader Alexander McGillivray. Indian claims to trans-Allegheny lands remained valid under their previous treaties, Native Americans insisted.

Partly to placate the Indians, the British did not lower the Union Jack from the forts, despite their treaty promise to relinquish them with "all convenient speed." They later justified retention on the grounds that Americans themselves had violated the treaty by their failure to repay debts and by the shabby treatment accorded Loyalists. The British adopted a "wait-and-see" policy in the west, holding the forts, encouraging the Indians, but refusing Indian requests to guarantee their territorial claims. American shipping was thus effectively excluded from the Great Lakes after 1783, and new settlements were confined largely to Kentucky and Tennessee. In 1786, British officials in Canada entered into secret talks with separatist leaders in Vermont, luring them with special trade privileges along the Champlain–St. Lawrence water route. If the confederation were to dissolve, Vermont could easily be attached to Canada, along with the lightly populated territories north of the Ohio.

Other issues troubled Anglo-American relations, including slaves the British had carried off during the war and a controversy over the Maine–New Brunswick boundary. Americans could only watch, helpless. With no army, no navy, no executive, no power to control the national commerce, the United States under the Articles of Confederation could do little to force British respect for the 1783 peace treaty. Indeed, British policies "may well have contributed more to the convoking and to the success of the Federal Convention of 1787 than many who sat in that august body."

The thankless task of enduring humiliation fell to John Adams, the first American minister to the Court of St. James's in 1785. When Adams protested British failure to send a minister to the United States, he was curtly asked whether there should be one envoy or thirteen. Adams could make no dent in British policy toward trade or the forts. "If we cannot obtain reciprocal liberality," he wrote in 1785, "we must adopt reciprocal prohibitions, exclusions, monopolies, and imposts." British arrogance infuriated the New Englander. "If an angel from heaven," he noted sarcastically, "should declare to this nation that our states will unite, retaliate, prohibit, or trade with France, they would not believe it." Adams repeated one message in dispatch after dispatch from England: Congress must have the power to regulate commerce; otherwise the British would not negotiate. Thomas Jefferson also complained that trade talks "have been treated with a derision which shew their [Britain's] firm persuasion that we shall never unite to suppress their commerce or even to impede it."

Thomas Jefferson (1743–1826). Before serving as secretary of state (1790–1793) and president (1801–1809), the eloquent Virginia lawyer and graduate of the College of William and Mary wrote the Declaration of Independence and represented the new nation as minister to France (1784–1789). ("Thomas Jefferson" by John Trumbull. © White House Historical Association/Photo by National Geographic Society)

Diplomacy with Spain after 1783 fared little better. Just as the British refused to evacuate the Ohio Valley after the war, so did the Spanish try to retain control over the Southwest. The peace treaty had created ambiguities. According to Article VII of the Anglo-American treaty, the United States gained free navigation of the Mississippi, and the northern boundary of Florida was set at 31° north latitude. Yet Spain had not agreed to either stipulation. British Florida prior to the war had extended northward to the Yazoo River, and Spain had no intention of yielding territory or guaranteeing free navigation. Spanish troops continued to hold Natchez on the Mississippi. Like the British north of the Ohio, Spain made Indian alliances and attempted to bribe frontier leaders. The most threatening move came in 1784 when Spain closed the mouth of the Mississippi to American commerce. Westerners exploded in violent protest against this stifling of agrarian expansion. George Washington, visiting the frontier territories that summer, reported: "The western settlers . . . stand as it were upon a pivot; the touch of a feather would turn them any way."

Unprepared for a war on the frontier, the Spanish opted to negotiate. Don Diego de Gardoqui arrived in New York in 1785. The crafty, charming envoy had instructions to obtain the Mississippi by dangling trade concessions with respect to Spain and the Canary Islands, including an offer to intercede with the Sultan of Morocco, whose pirates were seizing American merchant ships. Since such a treaty would obviously benefit the commercial Northeast at the expense of southern expansionists and western farmers, the Spanish envoy worked hard at flattering Secretary John Jay and the other easterners. He passed out "Havanna Segars," gave splendid dinners with the finest wines, brought a Spanish jackass for George Washington, and squired Mrs. Jay to numerous festivities. In 1786 Jay asked Congress for permission to negotiate a treaty whereby the United States would relinquish the *use* of the Mississippi River for twenty-five or thirty years while reserving the *right* to navigate until a time when American power would be sufficient to force Spanish concessions. Dividing geographically, seven northern delegations voted to make the necessary concession, while the five southern delegations stood opposed. Concluding that "a treaty disagreeable to one-half of the nation had better not be made," Jay told Congress that it must decide "either to wage war with Spain or settle all differences by treaty on the best terms available." Congress did neither.

Spain temporarily reopened the Mississippi River to American shipping in 1788 after the payment of special duties. Although a definitive treaty did not come until 1795 (see Chapter 2), Spanish officials began to permit American immigrants to settle in Louisiana and Florida provided they take an oath of allegiance. The Americanization of Spanish borderlands thus commenced long before the United States acquired those territories officially, eventually providing, as Jefferson prophesied, "the means of delivering to us peaceably, what may otherwise cost us a war." In the short run, the Jay-Gardoqui talks consolidated a political alliance between the South and West and ensured a clause in the new Constitution that provided for a two-thirds majority for Senate approval of treaties.

Relations with France also proved frustrating. Thomas Jefferson, as minister to France in 1784, hoped that France could replace England as America's principal trading partner, and he worked to convert the French to liberal commercial theories. Except for the opening of some French West Indian ports in 1784 and a consular treaty four years later, he ran into the same mercantilist restrictions John Adams faced in England. Whenever Jefferson pressed for commercial concessions, he was reminded of the outstanding Revolutionary debt of 35 million livres. The inability of Congress to retaliate distressed Jefferson. He momentarily thought of abandoning commerce and diplomacy and having the United States "stand, with respect to Europe, precisely on the footing of China." Jefferson understood that such isolation was impossible, so he advocated constitutional reform instead. "My primary object," he wrote in 1785, "is to take the commerce of the states out of the hands of the states, and to place it under the superintendence of Congress, so far as the imperfect provisions of our constitution will admit, and until the states by new compact make them more perfect."

The Barbary "pirates" also spurred constitutional reform. These rulers of the North African states—Algiers, Tunis, Tripoli, and Morocco—had transformed piracy into a national industry. By capturing merchant ships, holding sailors and cargoes for ransom, and extorting protection money from nations willing to pay, the sultans nearly drove U.S. shipping out of the Mediterranean. With Spanish assistance, the United States obtained a satisfactory treaty with Morocco in 1787, at the bargain price of only $10,000, but other negotiations proved fruitless. The young republic had neither the revenue to pay for protection nor the armed force to coerce the North African pirates. Thomas Jefferson asked for a fleet of 150 guns, but Congress took no steps toward constructing a navy. Yankee sailors continued to languish in North African jails. John Jay saw a blessing in disguise: "The more we are ill-treated abroad the more we shall unite and consolidate at home."

The New Constitution and the Legacy of the Founding Generation

Amid this troubled international setting, fifty-five delegates attended the Federal Convention in Philadelphia from May to September 1787. Although economic woes and Shays's Rebellion provided the immediate impetus for reform, the Founders had foreign relations in mind, too. The federal Constitution, approved by the Philadelphia assembly and ratified by the states over the next two years, eliminated most of the weaknesses that had plagued diplomacy under the Articles of Confederation. A central government consisting of an executive, a bicameral legislature, and a judiciary—all designed to balance one another—replaced the weak confederation of sovereign states.

Responsibility for diplomacy rested with the president, who would make treaties "by and with the advice and consent of the Senate." The impunity with which the individual states had violated the 1783 treaty with England prompted Benjamin Franklin's proposal that treaties shall be "the Supreme Law of the land . . . any thing in the Constitution or laws of any State to the contrary notwithstanding." Southerners, remembering the Jay-Gardoqui negotiations, hesitated to allow Congress too much power over commerce. In return for a constitutional prohibition against taxes on exports and a twenty-year moratorium on interference with the slave trade, however, southern delegates granted Congress the right to regulate imports by a simple majority. The way now seemed clear for commercial retaliation against England. The Constitution also provided for a standing army and navy, thus freeing national defense from dependence on requisitions from the various states. "We are no longer the scoff of our enemies," one delegate bragged.

A heated discussion at Philadelphia erupted over the warmaking power. The early drafts of the Constitution granted Congress the power to "make" war. Delegates soon perceived, however, that both houses might lack sufficient knowledge and unity to act quickly in the event of attack. Congress might not even be in session. Someone suggested that the president be responsible, whereupon delegate Elbridge Gerry of Massachusetts exclaimed that he "never expected to hear in a republic a motion to empower the Executive alone to declare war." Virginia's George Mason advocated "clogging rather than facilitating war; but . . . facilitating peace." Fearful of executive tyranny, but not wanting to leave the country defenseless, Gerry and James Madison of Virginia proposed a compromise whereby Congress retained the power to "declare" war, while the president, as commander in chief, could still "repel sudden attacks." With Congress empowered to raise and support armies and navies, call out the militia, and make rules and regulations for all of the armed forces, it seems evident that the Philadelphia delegates intended to subordinate the executive on this issue.

The size of the federal republic also aroused debate at Philadelphia. According to classic political theory, republics stood the best chance of survival if their territory remained small. What about the obvious disparity between the thirteen coastal states and the vast trans-Allegheny expanse stretching to the Mississippi? It took the thirty-five-year-old Virginia lawyer James Madison to articulate the philosophy of a growing republican empire. According to Madison, the greatest threat to a republic arose when a majority faction tyrannized others. Expansionism could benefit a republic by defusing the influence of factions, especially those that formed over economic issues. As Madison argued in *Federalist 10,* once you "extend the sphere" of government, "you take in a greater variety of parties and interests; you make it less probable that a majority . . . will have a common motive to invade the right of other citizens; or, if such a common motive exists, it will be more difficult . . . to act in unison." Whether or not continual expansion would be necessary to ensure survival, the man who later as secretary of state presided over the huge Louisiana Purchase in 1803 welcomed westward expansion from the outset. So did most delegates at Philadelphia. Still, they had not yet answered a basic question—"whether domestic liberty could flourish alongside an ambitious and strongly assertive foreign policy."

Congress's last official measure under the Articles of Confederation during the same summer of 1787 dealt with this very issue of westward expansion. With a bare quorum of eight states represented, the dying Congress enacted the Northwest Ordinance of 1787, which set up guidelines for governing the territories of the Old Northwest. Its terms called for Congress to appoint a governor, secretary, and three judges, who would govern until the population of a territory reached 5,000, at which time the settlers would elect a legislature. The territorial legislature would then rule in conjunction with a council of five selected by the governor and by Congress. When the population grew to 60,000, inhabitants could write a constitution and apply for statehood. Slavery was forbidden. The Founders at Philadelphia took cognizance of the new law, and stipulated, according to Article IV, Section 3 of the new Constitution, that "Congress shall have Power to dispose of and make all needful Rules and Regulations respecting the territory or other property belonging to the United States." A blueprint for an American colonial system was thus established. The same process that led to statehood for Ohio, Indiana, Michigan, Illinois, and Wisconsin continued into the twentieth century, including the admission of Hawai'i and Alaska as states in 1959.

Concurrent with these plans for a territorial system, American commissioners negotiated with representatives of the Indians who still occupied these territories. At Fort Stanwix, New York, in 1784, and at Hopewell, South Carolina, in 1785–1786, officials signed treaties opening new lands for white settlement with the Iroquois, Choctaw, Chickasaw, and Cherokee nations. The United States regarded these treaties as confirmation of its sovereignty over the trans-Allegheny interior. The Creeks, who did not sign the Hopewell treaties, continued to resist along the Georgia frontier until 1790. Although these treaties later became mechanisms for national expansion (or "licenses for empire"), the military power to defend frontier settlements was conspicuously lacking under the Articles.

When George Washington took the oath of office as president at Federal Hall in New York on April 30, 1789, he could look optimistically at the international prospects of the new republic. Not only could Washington employ the new diplomatic tools fashioned at Philadelphia, but he and his compatriots could also make good use of the foreign-relations experiences of the past thirteen years. The American Revolution and its aftermath had produced a remarkable reservoir of leaders who had become sophisticated in world affairs. Diplomats such as Jefferson, Jay, and Adams soon contributed their expertise to the new administration. Washington himself, as his wartime collaboration with the French attested, understood the intricacies of alliance politics, as did his wartime aide, Alexander Hamilton. Because intellectual and political leaders were often the same people in this era, and because domestic, economic, and foreign policies were inextricably related, the founding generation gave rise to a foreign-policy elite of exceptional skills.

The diplomatic goals of independence and expansion were both practical and idealistic. Adams's Model Treaty of 1776 had projected a vision whereby American commerce would be open to the entire world, thus diminishing one of the major causes of war and increasing American profits. Independence and extensive boundaries would protect a republican experiment that, in turn, could serve as a countervailing model for a world of monarchies. Invoking divine sanction, John Jay told the Spanish in 1780 that "Americans, almost to a man, believed that God Almighty had made that river [the Mississippi] a highway for the people of the upper country to go to the sea by." Even more expansive, the geographer Jedidiah Morse predicted in 1789 that America would soon become the world's largest empire, including "millions of souls, west of the Mississippi." Of course, before Americans could move beyond the Mississippi, the boundaries of 1783 had to be made secure.

The Revolutionary generation that looked westward held the optimistic belief that "they could teach the peoples of the rest of the world to govern themselves in happiness and prosperity; they did not believe that the majority of other peoples were unteachable or expendable." Yet as Americans moved across the Alleghenies, they entered "a cultural contact zone" of blurred boundaries and contested terrain, a frontier in which "no culture, group, or government can claim effective control or

hegemony over others." Agents of rival European empires, overlapping legal jurisdictions, alien customs and religions, and especially heterogeneous Indian populations with established linkages to European metropoles, all blocked the path of
peaceful westward expansion. Over time, the Enlightenment belief in an innate
general human capacity for progress gave way to the racist belief in Anglo-Saxon superiority over those whom Americans destroyed or dominated.

Americans sought independence and empire without resort to European-style
power politics. The attractions of American commerce proved insufficient to bring
automatic aid and recognition; so Franklin in 1778 negotiated the alliance with
France. The American preference for commercial treaties instead of political alliances did not diminish after 1778, however, and the commercial and neutral-rights
provisions of the Model Treaty remained central to American foreign relations.
Commercial treaties in the 1780s with Sweden, Prussia, and the Netherlands followed those principles. Americans believed, however, that the emphasis on commerce did not exalt profits over principles. As James Monroe later wrote, "People in
Europe suppose us to be merchants, occupied exclusively with pepper and ginger.
They are much deceived. . . . The immense majority of our citizens . . . are . . . controlled by principles of honor and dignity."

The United States, of course, had been forced to compromise principle—to
make the alliance with France to win independence. Without Comte de Rocham-
beau's army and Admiral de Grasse's fleet, Washington could not possibly have forced
Cornwallis's surrender in 1781. French loans had kept an impecunious Congress
solvent during the war. To be sure, Vergennes wanted to limit American boundaries;
French agents in Philadelphia used their influence with Congress to hamstring
American diplomats abroad; and as late as 1787 the French chargé d'affaires predicted that America would break up and urged his government to plan the seizure
of New York or Rhode Island before the British could act. Still, the French alliance
had helped secure American independence, and the treaty remained valid in 1789,
including the provision guaranteeing French possessions in the New World.

The French alliance notwithstanding, the eschewing of foreign entanglements
remained a cardinal American tenet in the 1780s. "The less we rely on others," wrote
Connecticut's Roger Sherman, "the more surely shall we provide for our own
honor and success and retrieve that balance between the contending European powers." Americans regarded the European balance of power as a "vortex of death and
destruction, not a sensitive mechanism that could be made to work for neutral
rights, free trade and world peace." American diplomats abroad simply did not trust
European countries. Europe had its own set of interests, America another. Even a
Francophile like Jefferson could write: "Our interest calls for a perfect equality in
our conduct towards [England and France]; but no preferences any where."

Americans, in short, sought fulfillment of their goals without war or foreign allies. The federal Constitution strengthened national power. With abundant federal
revenue came stronger national credit. A flourishing foreign commerce and the
power to regulate that commerce, it was hoped, would provide an important diplomatic lever. American military power hardly existed. The United States with its
3.5 million population seemed a slight threat to the 15 million British or 25 million
French. The traditional Anglo-Saxon fear of standing armies, and the expense of

naval construction, made Americans slow to build a defense establishment. Even Hamilton, the most military-minded Founder, predicted that it would be fifty years before "the embryo of a great empire" could tip the balance between competing European powers or between the Old World and the New. Without military power or a foreign ally, the United States might find it difficult to maintain its independence, claim and extend its boundaries, and expand its commerce.

FURTHER READING FOR THE PERIOD TO 1789

For the colonial period, see Fred Anderson, *Crucible of War* (2001); Frank W. Brecher, *Losing a Continent* (1998); Marc Egnal, *A Mighty Empire* (1988); Peggy K. Liss, *Atlantic Empires* (1983); Michael McConnell, ed., *Army and Empire* (2004); James Pritchard, *In Search of Empire* (2004); and Robert W. Tucker and David C. Henrickson, *The Fall of the First British Empire* (1982).

Revolutionary-era issues are treated in Samuel Flagg Bemis, *The Diplomacy of the American Revolution* (1957); Thomas E. Chavez, *Spain and the Independence of the United States* (2002); Stephen Conway, *The British Isles and the War of American Independence* (2000); John Crowley, *The Privileges of Independence* (1993); Jonathan R. Dull, *A Diplomatic History of the American Revolution* (1985); John Ferling, *Setting the World Ablaze* (2000) and *A Leap in the Dark* (2003); Eliga Gould and Peter Onuf, eds., *Empire and Nation* (2005); Julie Flavell and Stephen Conway, *Britain and America Go to War* (2004); David C. Hendrickson, *Peace Pact* (2003); Ronald Hoffman and Peter J. Albert, eds., *Diplomacy and Revolution* (1981) and *Peace and the Peacemakers* (1986); Lawrence S. Kaplan, ed., *The American Revolution and "A Candid World"* (1977); Robert Middlekauf, *The Glorious Cause* (2005); Richard B. Morris, *The Peacemakers* (1965); J. W. S. Nordholt, *The Dutch Republic and American Independence* (1986); Peter Onuf and Nicholas Onuf, *Federal Union, Modern World* (1993); Andrew Jackson O'Shaughnessy, *An Empire Divided* (2000); Bradford Perkins, *The Creation of a Republican Empire, 1776–1865* (1993); Norman E. Saul, *Distant Friends* (1991) (on Russia); H. M. Scott, *British Foreign Policy in the Age of the American Revolution* (1990); Reginald C. Stuart, *United States Expansionism and British North America, 1775–1871* (1988); William Earl Weeks, *Building the Continental Empire* (1996); Peter Whitely, *Lord North* (1996); and Gordon S. Wood, *The Creation of the American Republic* (1969).

Foreign relations under the Articles of Confederation and foreign-policy questions during the making of the Constitution are discussed in Joyce Appleby, *Inheriting the Revolution* (2000); Richard Beeman et al., eds., *Beyond Confederation* (1987); Daniel G. Lang, *Foreign Policy in the Early Republic* (1985); Frederick W. Marks III, *Independence on Trial* (1986); Richard B. Morris, *The Forging of the Union, 1781–1789* (1987); Peter S. Onuf, *Statehood and Union* (1987); Jack N. Rakove, *The Beginnings of National Politics* (1979); and Charles R. Ritcheson, *Aftermath of Revolution* (1969).

For the frontier and relations with Indians, see Andrew Clayton and Fredrika Teute, eds., *Contact Points* (1998); Gregory Evans Dowd, *A Spirited Resistance* (1992) and *War under Heaven* (2004); Walter S. Dunn, *Opening New Markets* (2002); Eric Hinderaker, *Elusive Empires* (1997); Dorothy Jones, *License for Empire* (1992); Jane T. Merritt, *At the Crossroads* (2003); and David M. Weber, *The Spanish Frontier in North America* (1992).

For individuals, see Joyce Appleby, *Thomas Jefferson* (2003); H. W. Brands, *The First American* (Franklin) (2002); John P. Diggins, *John Adams* (2003); Jonathan R. Dull, *Franklin the Diplomat* (1982); Joseph Ellis, *Founding Brothers* (2000); John Ferling, *John Adams* (1992); Edwin S. Gaustad, *Benjamin Franklin* (2004); Don Higginbottom, *George Washington* (2002); James H. Hutson, *John Adams and the Diplomacy of the American Revolution* (1980); Walter Isaacson, *Benjamin Franklin* (2003); John Keane, *Tom Paine* (1995); Edward Larkin, *Thomas Paine and the Literature of Revolution* (2005); David McCullough, *John Adams* (2001); Robert Middlekauff, *Benjamin Franklin and His Enemies* (1996); Evan Thomas, *John Paul Jones* (2003); and Gordon S. Wood, *The Americanization of Benjamin Franklin* (2004); and books on diplomatic leaders listed in Chapter 2.

See also Robert L. Beisner, ed., *Guide to American Foreign Relations Since 1600* (2003).

For a comprehensive survey of foreign-relations topics, see the articles in the four-volume *Encyclopedia of U.S. Foreign Relations* (1997), edited by Bruce W. Jentleson and Thomas G. Paterson.

CHAPTER ❈ 2

Independence, Expansion, and War, 1789–1815

DIPLOMATIC CROSSROAD

❈ *The* Chesapeake *Affair, 1807*

AT 7:15 A.M. on June 22, 1807, the thirty-six-gun American frigate *Chesapeake* weighed anchor from Hampton Roads, Virginia. Commanded by Commodore James Barron, the *Chesapeake* was bound for the Mediterranean Sea as flagship of the small naval squadron that protected American merchant vessels from the Barbary states. The ship's crew numbered 329, several of whom had deserted the Royal Navy and enlisted on the *Chesapeake* under assumed names. Sick sailors, recovering from a drinking bout of the night before, sought relief in the sunny air on the upper deck. Loose lumber cluttered the gun deck. Four of the guns did not fit perfectly into their carriages. Only five powder horns used in priming the guns were actually filled. In fact, officers had not exercised the crew at the guns during the ship's fitting out in Hampton Roads. Barron set sail anyway. Already four months behind schedule, the ship would have ample opportunity for gunnery practice during the long sea voyage.

At 9:00 the *Chesapeake* passed Lynnhaven Bay, where two seventy-four-gun British ships of the line, *Bellona* and *Melampus,* lay anchored. It was rumored that the captain of the *Melampus* was threatening to seize deserters from the *Chesapeake,* but Barron took no special precautions. Neither British ship stirred. Soon after midday the *Chesapeake* sighted the fifty-six-gun ship H.M.S. *Leopard.* At approximately 3:30 P.M., some ten miles southeast of Cape Henry, the *Leopard's* captain hailed that he wanted to send dispatches to the Mediterranean through the courtesy of the American commodore. The *Chesapeake* then hailed back: "We will heave to and you can send your boat." Barron then made a serious mistake by allowing a foreign warship to approach close alongside without first calling his crew to battle stations. But to Barron the idea of a British naval attack "was so extravagant that he might as well have expected one when at anchor in Hampton Roads."

British lieutenant John Meade came aboard at 3:45 and handed Barron orders instructing him to search the *Chesapeake* for British deserters. Barron replied cor-

28

rectly; he could never allow his crew to be mustered "by any other but their own officers. . . . I hope this answer . . . will prove satisfactory." As Meade returned to the *Leopard,* Barron ordered the gun deck cleared for action.

It was nearly 4:30. To prepare the frigate for battle required a full half hour. The *Leopard* used the windward advantage to move closer. Captain S. F. Humphreys called through the hailing pipe: "Commodore Barron, you must be aware of the necessity I am under of complying with the orders of my commander-in-chief." Barron tried to gain time by shouting: "I do not hear what you say." He ordered the men to stations without drumbeat. The *Leopard* fired a shot across the *Chesapeake*'s bow. Another shot followed a minute later. Then, from a distance of less than 200 feet, the helpless *Chesapeake* was pounded by an entire broadside of solid shot and canister. In ten minutes the *Chesapeake* was hulled twenty-two times. Its three masts badly damaged, the ship suffered three men killed, eighteen wounded, including Commodore Barron, who stood exposed on the quarterdeck throughout the barrage. Finally Barron ordered the flag struck. The Americans salvaged a modicum of honor by firing a lone shot. A lieutenant had managed to discharge the gun by carrying a live coal in his fingers all the way from the galley. The eighteen-pound shot penetrated the *Leopard*'s hull but fell harmlessly into the wardroom.

British officers took only four sailors from the deserters and identifiable Englishmen aboard the *Chesapeake.* Of the four, three were undeniably Americans, deserters from the *Melampus* the previous March. The fourth deserter was a surly Londoner, Jenkin Ratford, who had openly insulted his former British officers on the streets of Norfolk. The British eventually hanged him from a Halifax yardarm; the three Americans received lesser punishment.

Americans exploded in anger when they heard about the *Chesapeake.* Heretofore the Royal Navy's practice of impressing alleged British sailors from U.S. merchant ships had caused much diplomatic wrangling. Just a few months earlier, President Thomas Jefferson and Secretary of State James Madison had rejected a treaty with

England largely because it failed to disavow "this authorized system of kidnapping upon the ocean." British warships constantly stopped and searched merchant vessels in American waters. But the *Chesapeake* affair lacked precedent: The British had deliberately attacked an American *naval* vessel, a virtual act of war.

Federalists and Republicans alike expressed outrage. In the historian Henry Adams's words, "the brand seethed and hissed like the glowing olive-stake of Ulysses in the Cyclops' eye, until the whole American people, like Cyclops, roared with pain and stood frantic on the shore, hurling abuse at their enemy." The citizens of Hampton Roads destroyed some 200 water casks ready for delivery to the thirsty British squadron in Lynnhaven Bay. An angry British admiral proposed a retaliatory attack on New York City. Only "red hot [cannon] balls" can keep the British "from our Rivers & Bays," warned one American veteran of the Revolutionary War.

Jefferson issued a proclamation on July 2 closing coastal waters to British warships. Two weeks later he vowed: "If the English do not give us the satisfaction we demand, we will take Canada." Treasury Secretary Albert Gallatin believed that war with England might salvage "the independence and honor of the nation" and "prevent our degenerating, like the Hollanders, into a nation of mere calculators."

The *Chesapeake* affair did not lead to war—at least not immediately. Jefferson first tried military preparations and diplomatic alternatives. Even before Congress convened late in the year, the president called all naval and merchant vessels home, ordered naval gunboats to be readied, armed seven coastal fortresses, sent field guns to state militia, gave war warnings to all frontier posts, and planned to call 100,000 militia members to federal service. In readying the ramparts, however, Jefferson discovered the inadequacy of U.S. defenses. The navy could not even send a ship to the East Indies to call home American merchant ships because it lacked funds for such a voyage. Even Washington, D.C., seemed vulnerable. Gallatin warned prophetically that the British could "land at Annapolis, march to the city, and re-embark before the militia could be collected to repel [them]." When Congress met in December 1807, Jefferson persuaded reluctant Republicans to triple the size of the regular army—not to fight the British but to enforce embargoes against them; he similarly asked for inexpensive coastal gunboats in preference to oceangoing frigates.

Nor did diplomacy quiet the crisis. The British government might have settled the matter amicably if Jefferson had asked only for an apology and reparations for the *Chesapeake* incident. Foreign Secretary George Canning told the U.S. minister James Monroe exactly that, in July 1807, but Jefferson insisted that England abandon impressment altogether. Canning would disavow the incident but not the practice. The British did not formally apologize for the *Chesapeake* attack until 1811, by which time America's wounded honor and England's stubbornness made war almost unavoidable. The *Chesapeake* affair also advanced American thoughts about invading Canada, and the British, in turn, began to repair their alliances with Native Americans in the Ohio Valley. In this way were maritime grievances linked to frontier friction. By 1812, most Americans could agree with South Carolina politician John C. Calhoun's declaration of a "second struggle for our liberty" that "will prove" that "we have not only inherited the liberty which our Fathers gave us, but also the will and power to maintain it."

The French Revolution and American Debates

The *Chesapeake* affair came during the series of wars that engulfed Europe after 1789. The wars initially proved advantageous to the United States. The economic prosperity of the young republic depended on disposing of agricultural surpluses abroad on favorable terms, and war in Europe created new trading opportunities for neutral carriers. U.S. exports amounted to $20,750,000 in 1792; by 1796 exports had jumped to $67,060,000. War in Europe also gave the United States more diplomatic leverage over territorial disputes in North America. Since England and Spain were embroiled with France, and both sides desired American trade, the administration of George Washington could proceed more forcefully in negotiating with Spain over the Mississippi and Florida, and with Britain over the still occupied northwest forts.

Yet Europe's battles also posed the danger that the United States might get sucked in. France might demand assistance under the terms of the 1778 alliance. England and Spain might fight rather than concede territorial claims in North America. Belligerent nations might still disrupt America's neutral commerce. Americans differed over the proper response to Europe's wars, and the ensuing debate over foreign policy helped give rise to national political parties. The stakes were high indeed.

George Washington always sought the best counsel before making decisions. Accordingly, the making of foreign policy during Washington's first administration often resembled an essay contest between Secretary of State Thomas Jefferson and Treasury Secretary Alexander Hamilton. Hamilton usually won, sometimes by unscrupulous tactics, and around his policies coalesced the first national political party in the United States, the Federalists. Washington tried to remain above partisanship and accepted Hamilton's advice because he thought it in the national interest. As Hamilton admitted, however, the popular Founding Father "was an *Aegis very essential to me.*"

Hamilton dominated diplomacy because early on he formulated and won congressional approval for a fiscal program with foreign-policy implications. By funding the national debt at par, assuming the Revolutionary debts of several states, and paying the arrears on the national debt owed abroad, Hamilton sought to attract

Makers of American Foreign Relations, 1789–1815

Presidents	Secretaries of State
George Washington, 1789–1797	Thomas Jefferson, 1790–1794
	Edmund Randolph, 1794–1795
John Adams, 1797–1801	Timothy Pickering, 1795–1800
	John Marshall, 1800–1801
Thomas Jefferson, 1801–1809	James Madison, 1801–1809
James Madison, 1809–1817	Robert Smith, 1809–1811
	James Monroe, 1811–1817

financial support for the federal experiment from wealthier commercial interests. Such a program required revenue. Hamilton provided the necessary monies through a tariff on imports and a tax on shipping tonnage. The revenue laws, passed in July 1789, levied a tax of fifty cents per ton on foreign vessels in U.S. ports and attached a 10 percent higher tariff on imports in foreign ships. Such navigation laws served to stimulate U.S. shipping by discriminating moderately against foreigners, but not enough to curtail trade. Hamilton particularly opposed a bill sponsored by James Madison in 1791 that would have prohibited imports from countries that forbade American imports in American bottoms (as England did with respect to Canada and the British West Indies). In Hamilton's eyes, any interference with Anglo-American commerce spelled disaster. Fully 90 percent of American imports came from England, more than half in British ships; nearly 50 percent of U.S. exports went to British ports. If trade were curtailed, national credit would be "cut up . . . by the roots," warned Hamilton. This brilliant illegitimate son of a West Indian planter devoted his tenure at the Treasury Department defending the sanctity of Anglo-American trade and hence Anglo-American diplomatic cooperation.

Opposition to Hamilton's definition of the national interest quickly developed, particularly among southern agrarian interests seeking new markets in Europe. Echoing Jefferson, who resented Hamilton's encroachment on his prerogatives, Madison raised questions in Congress. As spokesmen for southern planters whose crops had long been shackled to British markets and British credit, Madison and Jefferson wanted to loosen Anglo-American patterns through favorable commercial treaties with other European states and by legislation favoring non-British shipping. Britain might retaliate, but, as Madison bragged: "The produce of this country is more necessary to the rest of the world than that of other countries is to America. . . . [England's] interests can be wounded almost mortally, while ours are invulnerable." In particular, he calculated that the British West Indies, in the event of a European war, would starve without vital U.S. supplies. Hamilton's supporters blocked Madison's navigation bill in the Senate, but the mere threat of commercial reprisals induced the British to send their first formal minister, George Hammond, to the United States in October 1791.

The French Revolution of 1789 exacerbated the "heats and turmoils of conflicting parties" over trade policy. The initial phase, with familiar figures such as Thomas Paine and the Marquis de Lafayette in positions of leadership, elicited almost universal approbation in America. Then came the spring of 1793 and news that King Louis XVI had been guillotined and France had declared war on England and Spain. While conservative Federalists recoiled at the republican terror in France, an enthusiastic Jefferson wrote: "rather than it [the French Revolution] should have failed I would have seen half the earth desolated; were there but an Adam and Eve left in every country, and left free, it would be better than it now is."

Federalists feared that the "murderous orgies of Paris" would spread to America via the French alliance. Hamilton sneered that Jefferson and his friends harbored "a *womanish attachment to France and a womanish resentment against Great Britain*." The Jeffersonians, in turn, advocated a "manly neutrality" that would tilt toward France and accused Federalists of plotting against "human liberty." In actuality, the rising political passions in 1793 obscured the fact that neither party placed the interests of France or England above those of the United States. If Hamilton sometimes talked indiscreetly to British diplomats, he did so in the belief that the twin American goals of commercial and territorial expansion could be best achieved in close relationship with Great Britain. As for Jefferson's celebrated Francophilism, the French minister Pierre Adet commented in 1796: "Jefferson . . . cannot be sincerely our friend. An American is the born enemy of all the European peoples." Nonetheless, Americans would favor one side or the other in the symbolic struggle between "Jacobin and Angloman," between "revolutionary France and conservative England."

President Washington's proclamation of neutrality on April 22, 1793, received the unanimous backing of his cabinet advisers. How to reconcile neutrality with the French alliance was another matter. In receiving France's new republican minister, Citizen Edmond Charles Genet, Jefferson refuted Hamilton's claim that the 1778 treaties had lapsed with the death of Louis XVI. Jefferson thereby set two important diplomatic precedents: American respect for the sanctity of treaties and quick diplomatic recognition of regimes in de facto control over a country. The thirty-year-old Genet did not ask the United States to become a belligerent and offered new commercial concessions if American merchants would take over France's colonial trade with the West Indies.

Citizen Edmond Charles Genet (1763–1834). From Charleston to New York City, the French representative recruited Americans for anti-British activities, setting off political fireworks and complicating the nation's neutrality. (Albany Institute of History and Art)

Complications soon followed. Genet outfitted some fourteen privateers—privately owned American ships, equipped in American ports for war under French commission. Before long they had captured more than eighty British merchant ships. Such activities openly violated neutrality regulations announced in August. British minister Hammond protested and Jefferson warned Genet, but pro-French juries often acquitted those Americans who were arrested. Genet infuriated Jefferson by promising not to send a captured British prize, *Little Sarah,* to sea as a privateer only a few hours before the vessel slipped down the Delaware River to embark on a career of destroying commerce. "Mr. Jeff" did wink at Genet's scheme to "excite insurrections" in Spanish Louisiana through an expedition comprising mostly American volunteers. Although the plan fizzled, the French envoy dramatically informed Paris: "I am arming the Canadians to throw off the yoke of England; I am arming the Kentuckians, and I am preparing an expedition by sea to support the descent on New Orleans." Genet also encouraged pro-French editorials in the press of the nation's capital and at one point appealed to the American people to disobey the president's neutrality proclamation. Even Madison admitted that Genet's "conduct has been that of a madman."

The furor abated somewhat by late summer 1793. By this time Genet had made himself so obnoxious that the Washington administration agreed unanimously to ask the French government to recall its envoy. Meanwhile, Washington replaced Gouverneur Morris as American minister in Paris. Morris had proven a shrewd judge of the French Revolution but had alienated his hosts by befriending French aristocrats. The nomination of James Monroe, a firm Virginia Republican, to replace Morris patched up quarrels temporarily, as did the arrival of Genet's successor, Joseph Fauchet, in February 1794.

Commerce, Politics, and Diplomacy: Jay's Treaty

No sooner had the crisis with France eased than the country found itself on the edge of war with England in the winter of 1794. Indignation raged in Congress when it learned that British cruisers, under a secret Admiralty decree declaring foodstuffs contraband, had seized more than 250 American merchant ships trading with the French West Indies. These maritime actions, coupled with an inflammatory speech to the western Indians by the governor-general of Canada, posed a direct threat to the young republic. Congress responded, on March 26, 1794, by imposing a thirty-day embargo on all U.S. shipping bound for foreign destinations. Although ostensibly impartial, the legislation targeted England.

Cool heads sought to prevent a rupture. Fearful that permanent embargoes might cause war with England, Federalists suggested a special mission to London. By a vote of 18 to 8, the Senate on April 18 confirmed the appointment of Supreme Court Chief Justice John Jay. Hamilton conceived the special mission and drafted the bulk of Jay's instructions. Only after strenuous argument from Edmund Randolph, who had replaced Jefferson as secretary of state, was a reference inserted to the possibility of sounding out Russia, Sweden, or Denmark about an alliance of neutrals. The Anglophilic Hamilton defused this threat when he leaked to British minister Hammond the information that Washington's cabinet, ever wary of entanglements, had actually decided not to join a neutral alliance. Except for forbidding any agreement that contradicted obligations under the 1778 alliance with France, the special minister's instructions afforded him considerable discretion. Jay's concern for maintaining peace and commerce with Great Britain, moreover, stood almost as high as Hamilton's.

Amid much wine, dining, and expressions of "most sincere esteem and friendship" from the British foreign secretary, Lord Grenville, Jay negotiated the Treaty of Amity, Commerce, and Navigation, signed on November 19, 1794. England, locked in deadly combat with France, found it prudent to conciliate the United States on North American issues but did not yield on the vital questions involving its maritime supremacy. Jay did gain the British surrender of the northwest forts, which London had promised in the 1783 peace treaty. This time the redcoats actually left.

London's abandonment of the West also aborted efforts to unite the Indians north and south of the Ohio River against American encroachment. When General Anthony Wayne defeated the Miami confederacy in the Battle of Fallen Timbers in August 1794, the British commander at nearby Fort Miami closed his gates to the retreating Indians. In the Treaty of Greenville (1795), the Indians ceded much of what soon became the state of Ohio. In return, the U.S. government formally recognized Indian sovereignty over unceded lands. The agreement pacified the Ohio Valley for a decade.

Another British concession, opening the British East Indies to American commerce, held promise for future trade with Asia. Jay also obtained trade with the British Isles on a most-favored-nation basis. As for the British West Indies, however, the treaty limited U.S. shipping to vessels of less than seventy tons and also forbade the American export of cotton and sugar to those islands. Other controversial matters, including pre-Revolutionary debts still owed by Americans and the disputed northeast boundary of Maine, would be decided by arbitration. In regard to neutral rights, Jay made concessions that violated the spirit of treaty obligations to France. Under certain circumstances American foodstuffs bound for France might be seized and compensation offered, while French property on American ships constituted a fair prize. In short, "free ships" no longer meant "free goods." The commercial clauses were to remain in effect for twelve years, thus ensuring a "twelve year moratorium" on Republican efforts to discriminate against British trade.

Despite Republican opposition, Jay's Treaty accelerated the nation's sovereignty. Faced with the loss of American trade, England had compromised on territorial issues in North America. By avoiding war, the treaty also sparked a short-term trading boom with both England and Europe, "a golden shower," as one merchant called it. In the long run, it also linked American security and development to the British fleet, which provided "a protective shield of incalculable value throughout the nineteenth century." In view of the contempt England had shown American diplomacy since 1783, any concession by treaty constituted real proof that the United States could maintain its independence in a hostile world. By inaugurating a critical period of relatively amicable relations with England, Jay's Treaty gave the young republic time in which to grow in territory, population, and national consciousness. When war with Britain did occur in 1812, the United States had fought France and the Barbary states and doubled in territorial size.

George Washington (1732–1799). The esteemed Virginia gentleman farmer and first president always maintained a regal, if not cold, countenance. (National Portrait Gallery, Smithsonian Institution/Art Resource, N.Y.)

The treaty signed in November 1794 arrived in Philadelphia on March 7, 1795. The Senate had just dispersed, so Washington did not actually submit the treaty for approval until early June. The senators debated in executive session, and only by eliminating the West Indian trade restrictions could Federalists secure a bare two-thirds vote of 20 to 10 on June 24. While Washington pondered whether he needed to resubmit the accord to England before formally ratifying it, a Republican senator leaked Jay's Treaty to the press, which spread it "like an electric velocity to every part of the Union." Critics quickly charged that Jay had surrendered American maritime rights for minor British concessions and betrayed the French alliance. "Foes of order," as Washington put it, "working like bees, to distill their poison," staged protests in most cities. In Philadelphia a mob hanged John Jay in effigy and stoned the residence of the British minister. A would-be poet called the treaty "truly a farce, fit only to wipe the national _ _ _."

Always a deliberate man, Washington might have put off ratification indefinitely had not suspicions of treason intervened and thereby removed Edmund Randolph, the chief obstacle to normalizing relations with England. In March 1795, a British man-of-war had captured a French corvette carrying dispatches from Minister Joseph Fauchet to Paris. Dispatch Number Ten recounted conversations in which Randolph had allegedly sought from Fauchet money for Republican leaders in Pennsylvania during the Whiskey Rebellion of 1794. Foreign Minister William Grenville sent Dispatch Number Ten to Minister Hammond suggesting that "the communication of some of [the information] to well disposed persons in America may possibly be helpful to the King's service." Hammond showed the dispatch to Secretary of War Timothy Pickering, a diehard Federalist. Convinced of Randolph's treason, he deliberately but subtly mistranslated certain French passages in Number Ten to make the evidence on Randolph look more incriminating. Then he wrote to Mount Vernon asking for a special meeting with Washington.

Washington arrived in Philadelphia in August, read Pickering's translation of Number Ten, and apparently pronounced his secretary of state guilty. On August 18, 1795, the president put his official signature on Jay's Treaty. The next day he confronted Randolph. Washington handed him Fauchet's dispatch, pronouncing coldly, "Mr. Randolph! here is a letter which I desire you to read, and make such explanations as you choose." The young Virginian defended himself to no avail. Even though most scholars accept Randolph's innocence, he quarreled openly with the revered President Washington, and in the heated political atmosphere of 1795 neither Republicans nor Federalists would take up his cause. Randolph resigned.

The Republicans made one last effort in the House of Representatives to negate Jay's Treaty by trying to block appropriations for its implementation. During the House debates in March 1796, Republican leaders asked to see all official correspondence relating to the treaty. In a precedent-setting decision, Washington refused, citing the need for secrecy. The debate raged on. Federalist Fisher Ames of Massachusetts evoked the fear of Indian warfare in the Northwest if Congress rejected appropriations, and another Federalist tried to blackmail his congressman: "If you do not give us your vote, your son shall not have my Polly." A bare majority (51 to 48) of the House voted the necessary funds on April 30.

Pinckney's Treaty, France, and Washington's Farewell

One reason why the House, despite a Republican majority, voted appropriations for Jay's Treaty was the fear that its negation might jeopardize the more popular Pinckney's Treaty with Spain. This treaty obtained everything that the United States had sought from Spain since the Revolution, which especially delighted the South and West. Signed by Thomas Pinckney in Madrid on October 27, 1795, the agreement secured free navigation of the Mississippi River and the right to deposit goods at New Orleans for transshipment. Spain also set the northern boundary of Florida at 31° north latitude. The Senate approved the accord unanimously on March 3, 1796. With America's southeastern frontier now settled with "quiet neighbours," some Republicans did not want to risk losing a similarly favorable settlement in the Northwest by voting against Jay's Treaty. In the sense that they redeemed America's borderlands from foreign control, Jay's Treaty and Pinckney's Treaty stood together.

The popular treaty with Spain followed logically from Jay's handiwork in England. When Thomas Pinckney arrived in Spain in June 1795, the Spanish knew of Jay's Treaty, but no one had seen the actual text. The Spanish prime minister, Don Manuel de Godoy, feared "the greatest evil" if the United States "should succeed in uniting with England." Already "a new and vigorous people" were "advancing and multiplying in the silence of peace," the Spanish governor of Louisiana warned. Godoy extricated Spain from the war against France in July 1795, and he hoped to renew the old alliance with France. Fearing England's wrath after Madrid switched sides, Godoy sought to appease the grasping Americans before they could align with the British and seize Louisiana. Concessions on the Mississippi and Florida boundary would serve as a temporary stopgap. "You can't put doors on an open country [the United States]," Godoy lamented. With the war in Europe diverting Spain's attention from North America, Pinckney's Treaty stands, in the historian Samuel Flagg Bemis's famous phrase, as a classic case of "America's advantage from Europe's distress." European wars facilitated American expansion.

Nevertheless, the pact with England generated only trouble with France. James Monroe had to bear the brunt of French outrage over Jay's surrender of "free ships, free goods." The only foreign diplomat to remain in Paris during the Reign of Terror, Monroe had ingratiated himself by hailing France's contributions to human liberty in a speech before the National Convention. When news of Jay's Treaty reached Paris, however, Monroe erred in predicting that the treaty would be defeated. In July 1796, the angry French government announced that American ships would no longer be protected under the neutral-rights provisions of the 1778 treaty. A disgruntled Washington ordered Monroe home. French agents in America, meanwhile, stepped up their efforts to wean American policy from its pro-British orientation. Minister Pierre Adet tried to bring about "the right kind of revolution" by lobbying unsuccessfully in the House of Representatives against Jay's Treaty and openly backing Thomas Jefferson for the presidency. Adet's electioneering efforts could not prevent John Adams from winning by an electoral vote of 71 to 68.

The well-timed publication of Washington's Farewell Address on September 19, 1796, contributed to Adams's victory. The first president and Hamilton, who revised Washington's draft of the speech, had French intrigues very much in mind in making the famous warning: "Against the insidious wiles of foreign influence . . . the jealousy of a free people ought to be *constantly* awake." Washington's valedictory also stands as an eloquent statement of American diplomatic principles. It reiterated the "Great Rule" that "in extending our commercial relations" the United States should have "as little *political* connection as possible" with foreign nations. "Europe," said Washington, "has a set of primary interests which to us have none or a very remote relation. . . . Our detached and distant situation invites and enables us to pursue a different course." Then came perhaps his most memorable words: " 'Tis our true policy to steer clear of permanent alliances, with any portion of the foreign world. . . . Taking care always to keep ourselves . . . on a respectable defensive posture, we may safely trust to temporary alliances for extraordinary emergencies." Washington did not preclude westward expansion. Even though he seemed to fear a French connection more than a British linkage in 1796, the evenhandedness of his phraseology gave the Farewell Address an enduring quality. "Our countrymen," Jefferson commented in agreement, "have divided themselves by such strong affections to the French and the English that nothing will secure us internally but a divorce from both nations."

The XYZ Affair and the Quasi-War with France

"My entrance into office," John Adams wrote, "is marked by a misunderstanding with France, which I shall endeavor to reconcile, provided that no violation of faith, no stain upon honor, is exacted." In July 1796, the French decreed that they would

Talleyrand (1754–1838). The wily French statesman majored in survival during the stormy years of the French Revolution. He hoped that bribes from U.S. envoys in the XYZ Affair might compensate for financial losses suffered while living in exile in Pennsylvania in the 1790s. (Emmet Collection, Miriam and Ira D. Wallach Division of Art, Prints, and Photographs, The New York Public Library, Astor, Lenox and Tilden Foundations)

treat neutral vessels the way neutrals permitted England to treat them—that is, "free ships" would not guarantee "free goods." Shortly thereafter, French privateers and warships began seizing American merchant vessels in the West Indies. By June 1797 the French had seized 316 ships. In addition, the five-man Directory that ruled France had refused to receive Charles C. Pinckney, the South Carolina Federalist whom Washington had sent to replace Monroe, thus presenting Adams with a complete diplomatic rupture. The new president decided on a special commission to negotiate outstanding differences with the French. To accomplish this delicate task, Adams named Pinckney, Federalist John Marshall of Virginia, and Massachusetts Republican Elbridge Gerry. Adams displayed his nonpartisanship by selecting Gerry, an old friend, only after Jefferson and Madison had declined to serve.

The three U.S. envoys arrived in Paris in October 1797. The sinuous Charles Maurice de Talleyrand-Périgord, formerly a bishop in the ancien régime, recently an exile for two years in the United States, had become French foreign minister that summer. Despite his firsthand acquaintance with Americans, Talleyrand evinced little affection for the United States, a nation of mere "fishermen and woodcutters" that should not be treated "with greater respect than [the city-states] Geneva or Genoa."

Maritime pressure offered a convenient way to persuade the Americans to acknowledge their commercial obligations to France under the treaty of 1778. The French still wanted Yankee ships to take over their carrying trade with the French West Indies, an impossible undertaking if the Americans refused to defend such commerce against the British. Talleyrand did not want open war—only "a little clandestine war, like England made on America for three years, would produce a constructive effect." The war in Europe had begun to go well again for France under the young Corsican general Napoleon Bonaparte. If Talleyrand could string out negotiations with the U.S. commission, party divisions might reappear in the United States, and France could easily make a favorable settlement. Or so Talleyrand hoped.

Three French agents, later identified in dispatches as X, Y, and Z, soon approached the commissioners. The message, although indirect, seemed unmistakable. If the Americans expected serious and favorable negotiations, they should pay "something for the pocket" to Talleyrand and arrange for a large loan to the French government. To the first request, Pinckney made his celebrated reply: "No; no; not a sixpence." This initial attempt at bribery did not terminate negotiations. Conversations continued throughout the autumn and into the new year. Talleyrand's methods were common enough in Europe. The Americans refused to pay because they had no instructions, not solely because they were indignant. Gradually, however, they lost patience. In January 1798, Marshall drew up a memorial, signed by Gerry and Pinckney, which recounted all American grievances against France, including the personal indignities that French agents gratuitously inflicted on the American commissioners. Talleyrand made no reply. The French issued new and harsher decrees that made a neutral cargo liable to capture if any part of it had British origins. Marshall and Pinckney asked for their passports, although Gerry, a native of Marblehead, did linger another three months in a futile attempt to negotiate.

Rumors of French insolence filtered back to the United States in early 1798. After receiving the first dispatches, Adams went before Congress on March 19. Announcing that his peace overtures had been refused, the president asked for authority to arm merchant ships and for other defensive measures. Jeffersonian Republicans smelled a Federalist trap. The House of Representatives demanded all relevant diplomatic correspondence. Adams, ignoring Washington's refusal in the case of Jay's Treaty, sent all dispatches to the House, substituting the letters X, Y, and Z for the real names of Talleyrand's highwaymen. The country was soon aflame. Alexander Hamilton denounced France as "the most flagitious, despotic and vindictive government that ever disgraced the annals of mankind," and crowds hailed John Marshall as a triumphant hero on his return. Even the dour Adams aroused cheers when he promised Congress in June that he would never "send another minister to France without assurance that he will be received, respected, and honored as the representative of a great, free, powerful, and independent nation."

In summer 1798 Congress passed measures that amounted to "quasi-war." It declared all French treaties null and void, created a Navy Department, funded the construction of new warships, and increased the regular army. George Washington came out of retirement to lead the new forces, although effective command, at Washington's request, rested in the hands of the Inspector General Alexander Hamilton. Jeffersonians saw the army, in conjunction with the new Alien and Sedition Laws directed against pro-French radicals, as suppression of political opposition. Nonetheless, Adams did not request, nor did Congress authorize, a declaration of war. The American navy received orders only to retaliate against hostile French warships and privateers. The quasi-war lasted more than two years, during which the U.S. Navy captured some eighty-five French vessels. The new frigates performed brilliantly and helped to deter the French from widening hostilities. Adams correctly perceived that France, bogged down in campaigns in Europe and Egypt, would not respond with full-scale war or invasion. Adams lost interest in the army because "there is no more prospect of seeing a French army here, than there is in Heaven."

Federalist partisans were more bellicose. Secretary of War James McHenry voiced exaggerated fears that the French might "convoy an army of ten thousand blacks and people of colour in vessels seized from our own citizens." This force might land on the defenseless parts of South Carolina or Virginia and spark a slave insurrection, he warned. Hamilton (whose boundless ambitions Adams attributed to a "superabundance of secretions") became particularly fascinated by a grand scheme whereby the United States would undertake a joint expedition with Britain against both Spain and France in the Americas, thus securing the liberation of all Latin America, the acquisition of the Floridas and Louisiana for the United States, and military glory for Hamilton. The idea of a British alliance intrigued Secretary Pickering, Treasury Secretary Oliver Wolcott, and other high Federalists.

The proposal fizzled. Adams, suspicious of any scheme connected with Hamilton, rejected a "knavish war" that would "fill me with disgust and abhorrence." The British, too, balked at aiding a new revolution, even one aimed at reducing French and Spanish power in the New World. Enough Anglo-American cooperation did occur during the quasi-war to call it the "first rapprochement."

The individual most responsible for stopping full-scale war, ironically enough, was the same Talleyrand who had initiated the crisis. Once he learned about the American outrage against his bribery attempt, Talleyrand made it known throughout the summer and fall of 1798 that France wanted peace. He promised that any new envoy sent to make peace would "undoubtedly be received with the respect due to the representative of a free, independent, and powerful nation." Adams had spoken those precise words before Congress in June 1798. To emphasize such assurances, the French repealed their decrees against American shipping and reined in their privateers.

Adams took the chance for peace. He had received reports from his son John Quincy Adams, now American minister to Prussia, affirming that France was not bluffing and "a negotiation might be risked." The president deliberated in private, shunned his cabinet, and, on February 18, 1799, sent a message to the Senate nominating William Vans Murray as minister plenipotentiary to France. Abigail Adams wrote from Massachusetts: "It comes so sudden, was a measure so unexpected, that the whole community were [*sic*] like a flock of frightened pigeons." She correctly ranked it as "a master stroke of policy."

Federalist partisans, their appetites whetted for war with France, threatened to block Murray's confirmation until Adams also nominated Chief Justice Oliver Ellsworth and William R. Davie of North Carolina, both Federalists, as additional plenipotentiaries. Secretary of State Pickering managed to delay departure of the three negotiators for several months. Adams eventually fired him. The president understood that his decision meant political suicide, but he persisted anyway. Abigail wrote of her husband: "He has sustained the whole force of an unpopular measure which he knew would . . . shower down upon his head a torrent of invective." Years later Adams himself declared: "I desire no other inscription over my gravestone than: 'Here lies John Adams, who took upon himself the responsibility of the peace with France in the year 1800.' "

The American commissioners arrived in Paris in March 1800. Politics had again shifted in France. Napoleon Bonaparte had returned from Egypt, seized power, and had become first consul. Joseph Bonaparte, the future king of Spain, took charge of talks with the Americans. The new leadership had begun to think seriously of reconstituting France's empire in North America, which Talleyrand hoped would become "a wall of brass forever impenetrable to the combined efforts of England and America." Such plans required peace with Europe, and especially reconciliation with the United States. Napoleon's great victory at Marengo in June 1800 made a European settlement possible by assuring French control of territory in Italy, which Spain might accept in lieu of Louisiana. Only one day after the Franco-American Treaty of Mortefontaine, the French and Spanish, on October 1, 1800, concluded secret arrangements whereby Napoleon promised Spain the Italian Kingdom of Tuscany in exchange for Louisiana. Although the American negotiators did not know about this Treaty of San Ildefonso, the French desire for Louisiana played an important, if silent, role in the Franco-American accord.

The Treaty of Mortefontaine amounted to a horse trade. The U.S. negotiators had presented two basic demands: The French must nullify the 1778 treaties and pay $20 million in compensation for illegal seizures of American cargoes. America, the French retorted, had itself invalidated the 1778 treaties by conceding maritime rights to the British in Jay's Treaty; thus French prizes after 1795 were not illegal. The logjam broke when the Americans agreed to assume the claims of their own citizens, whereupon the French abrogated all previous treaties. Napoleon then suggested the insertion of a statement reaffirming neutral rights as enumerated in the 1778 alliance. The Americans, seeing no entangling commitments, agreed. The formal signing of the treaty came after a deer hunt and huge banquet echoing with toasts to Franco-American harmony. Napoleon, that "most skillful self possest [*sic*] Fencing master," was trying to lull the Americans until his plans for Louisiana jelled.

The peace of Mortefontaine, followed by Thomas Jefferson's victory in the election of 1800, ended the Federalist era in American diplomacy. The administrations of Washington and Adams, despite internal debate and external pressures, pursued a consistent foreign policy. Seeking to maintain independence and honor and to expand trade and territorial boundaries, the young republic at times seemed to veer in a pro-French direction and then tilted toward the British. At every juncture, however, Washington and Adams escaped the European maelstrom by allying with "neither John Bull nor Louis Baboon." Like Jay's Treaty, the peace of Mortefontaine avoided a war that hotheaded partisans had craved. Jefferson's inaugural address seemed to promise continuity. "We are all Federalists; we are all Republicans," he said. Slightly amending Washington's advice, the former Francophile pledged "peace, commerce, and honest friendship with all nations, entangling alliances with none."

The Louisiana Purchase

The new president showed an intense interest in expansion westward. A few months after his inauguration Jefferson told fellow Virginian James Monroe: "It is impossible not to look forward to distant times when our rapid multiplication will expand beyond those limits, & cover the whole northern if not the southern continent." Jefferson primarily eyed the Mississippi Valley, but his vision also embraced the Pacific coast, the Floridas, Cuba, and a Central American canal. So long as Spain occupied America's borderlands, standing like a "huge, helpless, and profitable whale," Jefferson advised patience. When Spain encouraged trans-Appalachian pioneers to settle in Louisiana as Spanish citizens, Jefferson hoped that "a hundred thousand of our inhabitants" would do so, thereby acquiring Spanish lands peacefully, "peice by peice [*sic*]."

Then came rumors in summer 1801 about Spain's retrocession of Louisiana to France, along with news that England and France had made peace. Soon French ships were carrying an army to the New World, commanded by Napoleon's brother-in-law, Victor Emmanuel Leclerc, with orders to put down the black rebellion led by Toussaint L'Ouverture on Hispaniola (the island shared by Haiti and Santo Domingo in the Caribbean) and then, presumably, to occupy New Orleans, Louisiana. Seeing Haiti "more as a threat to Southern slavery than as a beacon of freedom," Jefferson initially encouraged the French "to reduce Toussaint" but grew alarmed at the size of the French forces and then realized that "St. Domingo delays their taking possession of Louisiana." Even worse, Napoleonic control of New Orleans and the Mississippi might provoke western farmers to wage war or secede from the Union. Rumors circulated that western settlers were like "a large combustible mass[:] they want only a spark to set them on fire." Indeed, the "jealousies and apprehensions" arising from a "French neighborhood" prompted Jefferson to consider a veritable revolution in foreign policy. Writing in April 1802 to Minister Robert

Livingston in Paris, the president warned that the day France took possession of New Orleans "we must marry ourselves to the British fleet and nation."

The threatened Anglo-American alliance made little impact on France during 1802. Talleyrand baldly denied the existence of a retrocession treaty for several months, and then he refused to consider Livingston's offer to purchase New Orleans and West Florida. Napoleon, bent on reviving a grand French empire in America, redoubled his efforts to acquire the Floridas from Spain.

On October 16, 1802, the Spanish suddenly withdrew the American right of deposit at New Orleans, in direct violation of Pinckney's Treaty. Most Americans suspected Napoleon's hand in the plot. The riflemen of Kentucky and Tennessee "already *talk of war*" and "*kick up a dust*" to seize New Orleans. Some Federalists proposed war to embarrass Jefferson. "We should annex . . . all the territory east of the Mississippia [*sic*], New Orleans included," urged Hamilton. To calm the growing clamor, Jefferson, in January 1803, nominated James Monroe as special envoy to France and Spain, empowered to assist Livingston in purchasing New Orleans and Florida for $10 million. The former governor of Virginia reportedly had "*carte blanche*" and would go to London if "badly received in Paris." Congress provided additional diplomatic muscle by authorizing the president to call some 80,000 militia members into federal service. Monroe finally arrived in Paris on April 12, 1803. The previous day Talleyrand had astonished Livingston by offering to sell all of Louisiana to the United States for $15 million.

"Unforeseen and unexpected circumstances" caused Napoleon to sell. The French failure in Haiti loomed large, as Leclerc's 30,000-man army disintegrated from guerrilla attacks and yellow fever. When Bonaparte learned in January that his brother-in-law had also succumbed to fever, he burst out: "Damn sugar, damn coffee, damn colonies." Napoleon's scheme of empire envisaged Louisiana as the source of supply for the sugar and coffee plantations of Haiti, but without Haiti, Louisiana became a liability. In the event of war, England could easily overrun Louisiana, and Napoleon was already thinking of war. The sale price would fill French coffers in preparation for the next campaigns and at the same time eliminate American hostility.

The negotiations did not take long. "They ask of me a town . . . and I give them an empire," said Napoleon. Instead of paying $10 million for New Orleans, Monroe and Livingstone pledged $15 million for New Orleans and an empire "of so great an extent" that lay to the west of the Mississippi, including 50,000 new citizens of French-Spanish descent and about 150,000 Indians. The treaty, signed on April 30, 1803, stipulated that the United States received Louisiana on the same terms that Spain had retroceded the territory to France. Livingston, wondering about West Florida, asked what the precise boundaries were. Talleyrand replied vaguely: "You have made a noble bargain for yourselves, and I suppose you will make the most of it." This enigmatic remark provided the basis for future American claims to Spanish territory in Florida and Texas. In fact, acquiring some 828,000 square miles of a "new, immense, unbounded world" at three cents an acre seemed an enormous achievement. Bonaparte remarked: "This accession of territory affirms forever the power of the United States, and I have just given England a maritime rival that sooner or later will lay low her pride."

The Senate still had to approve the treaty. Some Federalists voiced opposition. "We are to give money of which we have too little for land of which we already have too much," bewailed one Bostonian. Federalist senator John Quincy Adams questioned whether the Constitution, under the treaty power, permitted the incorporation of 50,000 Creoles into the Union without their consent. The president, however, told Madison that "the less we say about constitutional difficulties respecting Louisiana the better, and that what is necessary for surmounting them must be done sub silentio." The purchase eventually passed the Senate 24 to 7 in October. The formal transfer of territory came at noon on December 20, 1803, in the Place d'Armée in New Orleans. As the French flag fluttered down and the Stars and Stripes climbed upward, the United States officially doubled its territorial domain.

The Spanish borderlands continued to attract attention for the next several years. Claiming that Louisiana included West Florida, Jefferson sent troops in 1804 to the border area where American residents greatly outnumbered Spaniards and French. Only concern for his reputation caused the president to back away from war. Jefferson's subsequent attempt in 1806 to bribe Napoleon into forcing Spain to sell Florida prompted one critic to charge "base prostration of the national character to excite one nation by money to bully another nation out of its property."

Other Americans probed the Spanish empire to the west. In 1806–1807 an American military officer, Lieutenant Zebulon M. Pike, led a cartographic expedition up the Arkansas River into Spanish territory, failed to climb the mountain peak that bears his name, and was temporarily detained by Spanish troops for violating Spanish sovereignty. Pike later published an account of his travels that extolled the furs, precious minerals, and commercial attractions of Spanish territory, thus envisioning what became the Santa Fe Trail of the 1820s. At this time, too, Aaron Burr and sixty followers went down the Mississippi on flatboats, ostensibly to capture Texas from the Spanish, but more likely to set Burr up as the emperor of a secessionist Louisiana. Whatever the purpose of Burr's conspiracy, Jefferson had his former vice president arrested and took special care to keep the peace with Spain.

The most enduring example of Jefferson's western vision was his sponsorship of the Lewis and Clark Expedition (May 14, 1804–September 23, 1806). Conceived by Jefferson even before he bought Louisiana, the trek was intended to find water routes, to map the region, and to develop fur trade with the Indians. Leaving St. Louis, the "Corps of Discovery" went up the Missouri, crossed the Continental Divide, and followed the Snake and Columbia rivers to the Pacific. Lewis and Clark returned along the same route, reaching St. Louis in September 1806. This epic exploration helped the United States lay claim to lands in future negotiating, stimulated interest in the rich furs and abundant fauna of the Rocky Mountains, and suggested wrongly that the Missouri-Columbia route formed a convenient waterway for trade with China. John Jacob Astor chartered his American Fur Company in 1808, and with Jefferson's encouragement, Astor projected a line of fortified posts from St. Louis to the Pacific. Only Astoria, at the mouth of the Columbia River, was completed by the outbreak of war in 1812.

The acquisition of continental empire also planted "the seeds of extinction" for Indian culture because, as Jefferson noted, if Native Americans did not "willingly

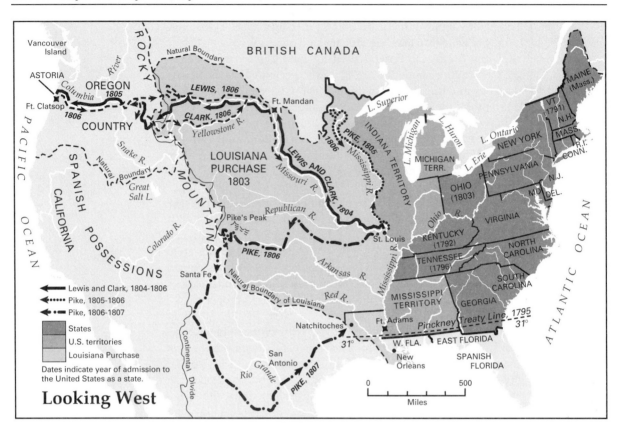

Lewis and Clark, 1804–1806
Pike, 1805–1806
Pike, 1806–1807

States
U.S. territories
Louisiana Purchase

Dates indicate year of admission to
the United States as a state.

Looking West

abandon traditional ways, take up the plough, and eventually melt into the larger white population," he would banish them to the trans-Mississippi region. Jefferson's imperial vision anticipated a loose confederation of possibly two republics, divided at the Mississippi, sharing a common language and tradition, shutting out Britain, Spain, and Native Americans. "The future inhabitants of the Atlantic and Mississippi States will be our sons," he wrote. As one biographer puts it, Jefferson thought of the West much as "modern optimists think of technology, as almost endlessly renewable and boundlessly prolific," a "fountain of youth" that made "republicanism immune to the national aging process, at least for the remainder of the century." At the same time, what Jefferson called "an empire for liberty" also implanted slavery in much of the Louisiana territory.

The expansionist president also wanted to protect American commerce on the high seas. Jefferson eagerly employed the U.S. Navy in the Mediterranean to protect trade against the depredations of the Barbary states—Algiers, Tripoli, Tunis, and Morocco—which practiced piracy. The war with Tripoli lasted for years. A squadron consisting of the flagship *Constitution,* the frigate *Philadelphia,* and smaller vessels performed creditably under the command of the feisty Commodore Edward Preble. In October 1803 the *Philadelphia* ran aground while chasing pirates outside the harbor of Tripoli. The captain of the ill-fated ship surrendered. A few months later,

Stephen Decatur (1779–1820) Battles Muslims. This popular engraving shows two American heroes and two Muslim enemies during the Barbary War of 1804. Stephen Decatur aims his pistol at a Tripolitan officer who had just killed his brother. An American sailor is shielding Decatur from a Muslim sailor about to slash Decatur with his sword. According to the historian Robert J. Allison, this engraving reflects the negative cultural images Americans had of the Muslim world in the eighteenth and nineteenth centuries—"where honest commerce was perverted into piracy by avaricious deys and pashas" and "women were debased in harems and seraglios, the victims of unrestrained sexual power." (U.S. Naval History Center)

Lieutenant Stephen Decatur heroically slipped into Tripoli harbor and burned the American frigate. In summer 1804 Preble's guns began to bombard the walled city, and in early 1805 a contingent of seven U.S. marines and assorted soldiers of fortune, led by Consul William Eaton, marched from Egypt across the Libyan desert and captured the port of Derna on the shores of Tripoli. The pasha of Tripoli cut a deal in June 1805, freeing all American captives for $60,000 in ransom. This extended encounter with the Barbary states accentuated the prevailing American perception of the Muslim world, as conveyed by captivity narratives, poems, and other contemporary writings—an image that emphasized the political and moral depravity of despotic Oriental power. Americans had to wait until after the War of 1812 when two navy squadrons finally put an end to Barbary piracy. Nonetheless, Jefferson's vigorous defense of American rights in the Mediterranean helped set the United States on a course of projecting its naval presence throughout the world.

Blockades, Neutral Trade, and Impressment, 1803–1807

Some two weeks after selling Louisiana to the Americans in spring 1803, Napoleon renewed the war with England. It raged for twelve years, spreading over much of the world and ending only with the Congress of Vienna (September 1814–June 1815) and Bonaparte's lonely exile to St. Helena in the south Atlantic. The war transformed the United States into the world's largest neutral carrier. American shipping expanded at a rate of 70,000 tons annually, particularly between the West Indies and French and Spanish ports on the European continent. Because such direct trade violated Britain's arbitrary Rule of 1756 (which decreed that trade not

"John Bull Taking a Lunch."
The Englishman enjoys a French
warship for lunch. In a study of
Republican rhetoric in 1811–1812,
the scholars Ronald L. Hatzenbuehler and Robert L. Ivie have
shown that congressional "war
hawks" projected a diabolic image
of John Bull, depicting the
covetous British "trampling on
America's rights and wresting independence from its citizens in order to sate a bestial appetite for
control of world commerce."
(Library of Congress)

open to a nation in time of peace could not be opened in time of war), American merchants usually "broke" the voyage by stopping at a U.S. port and paying duties on the cargo, thus converting it to "free goods." The voyage would then continue until the "neutralized cargo" reached France or Spain. This lucrative reexport trade soared from $13 million in 1803 to $36 million in 1804 to $53 million in 1805.

For more than two years neither the British nor the French interfered seriously with American commerce. Indeed, British Admiralty courts had not disputed the legality of the "broken voyage." But on October 21, 1805, Lord Horatio Nelson's thick-hulled ships smashed the combined French and Spanish fleets off Trafalgar, thus establishing England's overwhelming control of the seas. Two months later Napoleon crushed the Russian and Austrian armies at Austerlitz, making him master of Europe. A commercial struggle ensued between "one nation bestriding the continent of Europe like a Colossus, and another roaming unbridled on the ocean." In the ensuing web of blockades and counterblockades, America's neutral trade became inextricably ensnared.

The British decision in the *Essex* case, in May 1805, spelled trouble. British warships had captured the American merchant brig *Essex,* en route to Havana, Cuba, from Barcelona, after it had "broken" the voyage in Salem, Massachusetts. The British Admiralty judge ruled that the *Essex* had not paid bona fide duties on its cargo. Thereafter American shippers had to prove that importation of enemy goods into the United States was not merely a legal subterfuge to bypass the Rule of 1756. Under the new doctrine of the "continuous" voyage, trade carried by a neutral between a belligerent colonial port and home port violated British maritime regulations. Soon British cruisers lurked outside American harbors, practically blockading the coastline.

The British followed with an order in council of May 1806 calling for a complete blockade of Napoleonic Europe, from Brest to the Elbe River. Americans angrily denounced this "paper blockade" because British cruisers did not actually deny access to enemy ports. Napoleon retaliated in November with his Berlin Decree, which created a paper blockade of the British Isles by declaring that any ship that had previously touched at a British port was a lawful prize and its cargo forfeit. The London government struck back with two more orders in council, barring all trade with ports under French jurisdiction unless that shipping first passed through a system of British controls and taxes. England was in essence telling neutrals that they could trade with the continent of Europe only if they paid tribute first. Napoleon retaliated again in the Milan Decree, which stated that any ship that submitted to visit and search by British cruisers or stopped at a British port would be treated, ipso facto, as a British ship. The French emperor was erecting his "Continental System," a gigantic attempt to ruin England's export trade by closing off all European outlets. The project never became fully effective, as Spain, Sweden, and Russia opened their ports to British goods at various intervals after 1807. Caught between French decrees and British orders in council, Yankee traders ran the risk of British seizure if they traded directly with French-controlled ports, whereas they incurred Napoleonic displeasure if they first submitted to British trade regulations.

"I consider Europe as a great mad-house," Jefferson lamented, "& in the present deranged state of their moral faculties to be pitied & avoided." In the diplomatic protests that followed, American efforts aimed more at England than at France, because British warships operating in U.S. waters more directly jeopardized American commerce. The British, so absorbed in the life-or-death struggle against Napoleon, hardly acted humbly or apologetically toward Washington. French seizures usually occurred in French ports and in the Caribbean and were often shrouded in official verbiage that smacked of misunderstanding and promised rectification. With the Americans, Napoleon was evasive but seldom arrogant.

Impressment, which exploded as an issue in the *Chesapeake* affair, helped focus resentment on England. With service on a British naval vessel resembling prison life, English seamen in increasing numbers jumped ship, took advantage of liberal American naturalization laws, and then enlisted in the American merchant marine. By 1812, according to official British claims, some 20,000 English sailors were manning U.S. vessels, so many that Jefferson suspended "all propositions respecting our non-employment of them" and let any "negotiation take a friendly nap." Since the Royal Navy required 10,000 new recruits annually to maintain full strength, the need to impress British deserters from American service became vital. In carrying out impressment, however, British captains "resorted to the scoop rather than the tweezers," and soon naturalized Americans by the hundreds were manning Royal Navy yardarms. According to U.S. figures, some 6,257 Americans suffered impressment after 1803. The British could not accept any abridgment of a practice considered imperative for maritime supremacy. Washington admitted the British right to search for contraband or enemy personnel, but denied that this right justified the impressment of U.S. citizens. "That an officer from a foreign ship," wrote Secretary of State James Madison in 1807, "should pronounce any person he pleased, on board an American ship on the high seas, not to be an American Citizen, but a British subject, & carry his interested decision . . . into execution on the spot . . . is anomalous in principle, . . . grievous in practice, and . . . abominable in abuse."

Jefferson and Madison rejected a possible solution in the Monroe-Pinkney Treaty of December 1806. Jefferson had sent William Pinkney, an able Maryland lawyer, and James Monroe to London in an attempt to settle outstanding differences with England, including impressment and "broken" voyages. Any treaty had to contain an explicit British disavowal of impressment. The British would make concessions on broken voyages and the reexport trade, but not on impressment. The most London would propose was "the strictest care . . . to preserve the citizens of the United States from any molestation or injury; and . . . prompt redress . . . of injury sustained by them." Because the British promised to mitigate in practice what they would not surrender in principle, Pinkney and Monroe signed a new accord that would give more commercial benefits than Americans had enjoyed under the expiring Jay's Treaty. Their treaty, signed on December 31, 1806, amounted to probably the best bargain that the United States could have extracted from England during the Napoleonic wars. Still, Jefferson refused to submit it to the Senate. He and Madison believed that the threat of American economic retaliation would force the British to reconsider. Like John Adams in the Model Treaty of 1776, they thought that the attractions of American commerce, plus the rightness of American principles, would cause England to mend its ways.

"Peaceable Coercion" and the War of 1812

Anglo-American relations deteriorated steadily following the abortive Monroe-Pinkney Treaty. The *Chesapeake* episode of June 1807 underscored the volatile nature of the impressment issue. "Never since the battle of Lexington," Jefferson wrote in July, "have I seen this country in such a state of exasperation." The president sought an alternative to war. As he had written in 1801, the United States could employ "peaceable coercion" to achieve its goals because American commerce was "so valuable" to European nations "that they will be glad to purchase it when the only price we ask is to do us justice." Congress thereupon passed the Embargo Act on December 22. Evenhanded in principle, the embargo, in combination with a nonimportation measure against England, primarily targeted the British. The embargo banned the export of American goods anywhere, by sea or land, although coastal trade continued with increasingly elaborate controls. Recorded American exports dropped 80 percent in 1808. The embargo effectively "stimulated manufactures, injured agriculture, and prostrated commerce."

Domestic protest erupted. Representative John Randolph, citing the loss of shipping and declining agricultural prices, charged his fellow Virginians with attempting to "cure the corns by cutting off the toes." Numerous vituperative epistles reached the White House, including one of August 1808: "Thomas Jefferson/You are the damdest/dog that God put life into/God Dam you." Such dissent, combined with widespread resistance to enforcement, caused Jeffersonians to despair. Albert Gallatin preferred "war itself than to display our impotence to enforce our laws." In New England, where Yankee merchants and sailors had long depended on commerce for their livelihood, ships rotted in harbor and weeds grew on once busy wharves. Federalists accused Jefferson of conspiring with Napoleon in initiating the embargo, and rumors circulated about secessionist conversations between New Englanders and British agents. "I did not expect a crop of so sudden and rank growth of fraud," wrote Jefferson, urging Congress to "legalize *all* means which may be necessary to obtain *its end*." On March 1, 1809, three days before Jefferson left the presidency, Congress replaced the embargo with the Non-Intercourse Act, thus freeing American exports to all ports except those controlled by England and France, and promising renewed trade with either belligerent if it respected American neutral rights.

Jefferson's embargo failed to deliver the desired diplomatic effect. London at first welcomed the measure, inasmuch as it gave British shippers a virtual monopoly over trade with Europe. Alternative markets for British goods conveniently appeared in Spain (which revolted against Napoleonic rule in 1808) and Spain's Latin American colonies. The French continued to seize American ships, even those that evaded the British blockade, claiming that such ships must be British in disguise because the embargo law prohibited their presence on the high seas. Rising food prices in England, plus the decline of manufacturing sales, might have tempted the British to appease their best trading partner if the embargo had lasted longer. Actually, the rising prices had attracted the most American violators in the last months of the embargo.

The embargo also exacerbated sectional and party differences over foreign policy. New England Federalists argued that, absent the embargo, they could freely trade with other parts of the world where British restrictions did not apply. The embargo, not London, cut commercial ties with India, the East Indies, South America, and the Mediterranean. Southern planters, however, saw their prosperity dependent on selling their produce primarily in England and on the European continent. The British closing of continental markets hurt the South, and the British market became glutted. Tobacco and cotton prices fell below what it cost southerners to raise their crops. Thus Republicans more willingly supported all "peaceable coercions" to force British concessions, and Federalists became more opposed to all restrictions on trade.

A face-saving substitute, nonintercourse actually favored the British more than the French. American ships could clear port ostensibly for a neutral destination such as Sweden but illegally take their cargo to British or Canadian ports; vessels heading for French-controlled ports still had to face British blockade ships. The new president, James Madison, nonetheless hoped to use nonintercourse to modify British policy. He found a willing collaborator in British minister David M. Erskine, the only British envoy in the early national period who developed cordial personal relations with his American hosts. At Madison's urging, Erskine recommended repeal of the orders in council, provided that the United States keep nonintercourse against France. In April 1809, Madison lifted nonintercourse against Britain on June 10, the date that England, according to the Erskine agreement, would repeal its orders in council. More than 600 American vessels laden with two years' accumulation of goods promptly set sail for British ports. Huzzas echoed from Maine to Georgia.

The joy soon whimpered away. Foreign Secretary Canning repudiated the agreement because he had ordered Erskine to demand approval for the Royal Navy to seize American ships that violated the Non-Intercourse Act. Canning, of course, allowed American ships still at sea to bring supplies to England. News of repudiation stunned Americans and angered Madison, who quickly renewed nonintercourse, but the damage had been done. "We are not so well prepared for resistance as we were one year ago," Gallatin reported. "We have wasted our resources without any national unity."

Canning aggravated matters further by replacing Erskine with Francis James ("Copenhagen") Jackson, a notorious diplomat whose mission to Denmark in 1807 had resulted in the British fleet's destruction of the Danish capital. The bumptious Briton managed to offend almost everyone in Washington, and diplomacy went nowhere. "God damn Mr. Jackson," shouted one Kentuckian, "the President ought to . . . have him kicked from town to town until he is kicked out of the country. God damn him." Madison finally declared Jackson persona non grata and London did not send a replacement for nearly two years.

When the Non-Intercourse Act expired in the spring of 1810, legislation known as Macon's Bill Number Two replaced it. The new law ostensibly removed all restrictions on American commerce, including trade with England and France; it also empowered the president to renew nonintercourse against one belligerent if the other gave up its punitive decrees. This "weird form of reverse blackmail," as the historian Garry Wills calls it, seemed to say: "We will be nice to you both until one is nice in return, upon which we will turn nasty to the other." Now came an opportunity for Napoleon who promised repeal of the Berlin and Milan decrees against American commerce, provided only that the United States "shall cause their rights

Tecumseh (1768–1813). The Shawnee chief and his brother Tenskwatawa sought but failed to block white expansion into Indian territory by forming a confederacy. During the War of 1812, Tecumseh joined the British army along the Canadian border. He died at the Battle of the Thames. (Library of Congress)

to be respected by the English." The French pledged to lift their decrees on November 1, 1810. Madison naively assumed that the French promises were genuine. On November 2, 1810, without adequate proof that Napoleon had freed American shipping (he had not), the president proclaimed nonintercourse against Britain.

The British, however, refused to be blackmailed. Not only did the British not repeal their orders in council, they enforced them even more vigorously. "The United States," wrote the new secretary of state, James Monroe, "cannot allow Great Britain to regulate their trade, nor can they be content with a trade to Great Britain only. . . . The United States are, therefore, reduced to the dilemma either of abandoning their commerce, or of resorting to other means more likely to obtain a respect for their rights."

Disputes with Native Americans on the frontier also exacerbated Anglo-American acrimony. Beginning in 1806 two remarkable Shawnees, Tecumseh and Tenskwatawa, took advantage of a nativist religious revival to organize a Pan-Indian movement against further white expansion. When the U.S. government purchased 2.5 million acres of Indian land in the Treaty of Fort Wayne in 1809, Tecumseh claimed the sale invalid. He pointedly asked Governor William Henry Harrison: "How can we have confidence in the white people when Jesus Christ came upon earth you kill'd and nail'd him on a cross?" Frontier leaders were quick to attribute conspiratorial designs to the British in Canada, where Tecumseh's followers received food and shelter (but not guns and ammunition, as Americans alleged). On November 7, 1811, an armed clash occurred at Tippecanoe Creek in what is now Indiana. U.S. forces under Harrison barely defeated a superior Indian concentration. Americans simply assumed that the British were stirring up the tribes, which they were not doing. In Congress and in the West people talked of taking Canada. As member of Congress from Kentucky Henry Clay put it, "Is it nothing to us to extinguish the torch that lights up savage warfare?"

The United States thus moved inexorably toward war in the winter and spring of 1812, not knowing that economic distress was finally causing Britannia to alter course. Beginning in autumn 1810, a depression hit the British, accompanied by poor harvests, unemployment, higher taxes, higher prices, and bread riots. British exports to Europe dropped by one-third from 1809 to 1811, and exports to the United States dropped by seven-eighths. Manufacturing interests put pressure on Parliament. On June 16, 1812, Britain scrapped the orders in council. Two days later, however, unaware of this significant action, Congress declared war against England.

In All the Tenses: Why War Came

The close vote for war (79 to 49 in the House, 19 to 13 in the Senate) prompted one representative to exclaim: "The suspense we are in is worse than hell!!!" Only 61 percent supported war, with most members from Pennsylvania and the South and West voting aye and most from the North and East voting nay. The vote followed partisan lines—81 percent of Republicans in both houses voted for war (98 to 23), and all Federalists voted nay (39 to 0).

Had speedier transatlantic communications existed in 1812, war might have been prevented. But it does not follow that Americans went to war for frivolous reasons. The causes of the War of 1812 were numerous, and Madison gave a reasonably accurate listing in his war message of June 1. The president placed impressment first, spotlighting those hundreds of Americans "dragged on board ships of war of a foreign nation and exposed, under the severities of their discipline, to be exiled to the most distant and deadly climes, to risk their lives in the battles of their oppressors." Second, Madison mentioned illegal depradations within sight of U.S. harbors, as well as "pretended blockades" that disregarded international law. Third, Britain's orders in council waged war on American trade in order to maintain "the monopoly which she covets for her own commerce and navigation." And last, Madison blamed the English for igniting "the warfare just renewed by the savages on one of our extensive frontiers." Privately, Madison noted that the United States had "no choice but between that [war] & the greater evil of a surrender of our sovereignty."

What about the seeming contradiction between Madison's emphasis on maritime causes and the fact that a majority of war votes came from the agrarian South and West, not from the commercially minded Northeast? Part of the apparent paradox can be explained by noting economic self-interest: the West and South were wracked by depression in 1812; eastern merchants, even with British and French depredations, were still making profits. Jeffersonian farmers and people of the frontier, many dependent on the export trade, blamed falling agricultural prices on the British blockade. As John C. Calhoun of South Carolina argued: "They are not prepared for the colonial state to which again that Power is endeavoring to reduce us."

Some scholars, echoing John Randolph, who called the war "not of defense, but of conquest, aggrandizement, and ambition," have listed a desire for territorial expansion as a major cause of the war. "War hawks" did talk of adding Canada to the American Union, but Westerners focused on Canada in part because of their belief that England was stirring up the Indians north of the Ohio River and because Canada was the only place to retaliate against British maritime practices. Representative Matthew Clay of Virginia proclaimed: "We have the Canadas as much under our command as she [Great Britain] has the ocean; and the way to conquer her on the ocean is to drive her from our land." Others urged an invasion of Canada because it had developed as an alternative source of supplies for the West Indies and as a mecca for American smugglers. Indeed, Canadian exports seemed to undermine Madison's assumption that the British Empire was "dependent on the United States for 'necessaries.' "

National honor served as another unifying force for war. Commercial coercion had not worked. Submission to the orders in council promised a return to colonial status; war seemed a better option. The real issue, wrote one Virginian in 1812, "went beyond" certain rights of commerce; "it is now clearly, positively, and directly *a question of* . . . whether the U. States are an independent nation." These younger, "energized" Republicans "ceased worrying whether war would corrupt the republic. Rather, they grew convinced that it *must* absorb the shock of violent conflict to prove its worth."

England realized too late that the United States might actually fight. Preoccupied by the war against Napoleon, the British were poorly served by Minister Augustus Foster, who fraternized too much with Federalists and did not take Madison's bellicose hints seriously. British politicians became even more distracted at the close of 1810, when the aged George III finally went incurably insane. Several months were taken up with political debate over the accession of the Prince Regent, thus delaying the decision to lift the orders against American shipping. Nonetheless, perceptive reporting by U.S. diplomats in England might have noted signs that pointed to eventual repeal. The capable William Pinkney had departed England in despair in February 1811, however, and chargé d'affaires Jonathan Russell simply discounted the effect of protests and petitions on Parliament. Russell's last dispatches, which reached the United States on May 22, 1812, held out no promise that England would repeal its decrees. Not knowing that Britain had repealed, Madison made his decision for war in defense of American commerce, honor, and sovereignty.

Why not declare war against France as well? In a preliminary vote on June 12, a Federalist proposal to place France and England on the same belligerent footing just failed to pass, 17 to 15. The suspicious Federalists subsequently charged that the declaration of war against England was made in collusion with Napoleon. Not so. Madison and his Republican colleagues saw little choice between "a ruthless tyrant, drenching Europe in blood" and "a nation of buccaneers, urged by sordid avarice." Yet a triangular war seemed out of the question. French outrages occurred in European waters. British press gangs roamed just off American shores, and British officers—not French—were allegedly stirring up the Indians. The United States could deal with Napoleon *after* it captured Canada. "As to France," the hawkish Henry Clay explained, "we have no complaint . . . but of the past. Of England we have to complain in all the tenses."

Madison welcomed the potential advantages of cobelligerency with France. Napoleon's forces could keep the British bogged down in Spain. The French invasion of Russia might bring about the full application of the Continental System, thus putting added pressure on Britain. American cruisers and privateers, meanwhile, could use French ports to refit and sell their prizes. But Madison shunned any formal alliance with France. Even in going to war with England, he tried to make the most of an independent foreign policy.

Wartime Diplomacy and the Peace of Ghent

"At the moment of the declaration of war, the President regretted the necessity which produced it, looked to its termination, and provided for it." Thus did Secretary Monroe write on learning of Britain's repeal of the orders in council. He then sent instructions to London to seek an armistice, provided that England agreed to end impressment. Hopes for a quick peace evaporated, however, when the British clung stubbornly to impressment. "The Government could not consent to suspend the exercise of a right," said Foreign Secretary Castlereagh, "upon which the naval strength of the empire mainly depends." The Americans also stood firm about impressment. Two years of war followed.

The next hint of peace came from St. Petersburg in the winter of 1812–1813. The Russian foreign minister offered mediation to U.S. envoy John Quincy Adams. Without waiting for formal British agreement, Madison appointed Federalist James Bayard and Treasury Secretary Albert Gallatin to join Adams as peace commissioners in the Russian capital. Not wanting to offend their powerful continental ally and alert to the mutual interest of Russia and the United States in defending neutral rights, the British stalled. They had no objection to treating directly with the Americans, but no one bothered to tell the three plenipotentiaries in St. Petersburg. Not until January 1814 did Castlereagh formally propose direct negotiations to the United States, and even then he remained vague as to time and place.

In North America during these months the war sputtered. Master Commandant Oliver Hazard Perry's victory on Lake Erie, the recapture of Detroit, and the death of Tecumseh in 1813 effectively foiled British and Indian efforts to roll back American expansion in the Old Northwest. Elsewhere U.S. forces found themselves constantly on the defensive. The conquest of Canada, contrary to Madison's expectation, was not accomplished with a single "rapier thrust." U.S. generals displayed incompetence, New England governors refused to release state militia for federal service, 12.7 percent of wartime recruits deserted "at least once," and the Canadians fought loyally under British command. Madison shuddered at the prospect of British reinforcements after the defeat of Napoleon. The war at sea fared better, with swift Yankee frigates winning several duels with British men-of-war, and U.S. warships and privateers capturing 1,408 British prizes. But even on the oceans British supremacy began to assert itself by 1814 against the puny American navy. The Royal Navy showed in 1814 that it could land troops almost anywhere on American shores. Little wonder, then, that Madison welcomed Castlereagh's offer to negotiate. The president shrewdly added Jonathan Russell and Henry Clay to the three peace commissioners already in Europe. The appointment of Clay, the loudest "war hawk" of all, provided insurance with Congress if the peace treaty did not obtain the war goals of 1812.

A diplomatic retreat seemed unavoidable. On June 27, 1814, just prior to the embarrassing British burning of Washington, D.C., Secretary Monroe instructed the plenipotentiaries to "omit any stipulation on the subject of impressment," if such action would facilitate a peace settlement. The U.S. peacemakers paced for six weeks in the picturesque Flemish village of Ghent in Belgium before the British delegation finally arrived in early August. Preoccupied by European negotiations at the "Great Congress" in Vienna, Castlereagh thought that news of British military successes in North America would simplify diplomacy at the "little Congress" in Ghent. Meanwhile, like thoroughbred horses, the American delegates chafed and snapped at each other. Clay's predilection for poker, brandy, and cigars irritated the acerbic Adams, whose stoic regimen commenced each dawn with an hour of Bible study. Gradually, however, Clay's affability, Gallatin's tactful urbanity, and Bayard's good-humored patriotism caused Adams to "be animated by the same desire of *harmonizing* together,"

The British, by asking for a separate Indian buffer state in the Old Northwest, some territorial additions south of the Great Lakes, and a quid pro quo for renewing American fishing rights, nearly ended negotiations at the start. Only Clay, a self-proclaimed expert at "outbragging" an opponent, thought the British were bluffing. He proved right. After a few weeks the Indian issue gradually disappeared. The British still insisted on boundary changes, direct access to the Mississippi, and compensation for fishing privileges. Next came a British demand for peace based on the war map of the moment, meaning that the English would continue to hold eastern

Maine and some territory south of the Great Lakes. The Americans insisted on the 1783 boundary. News finally reached Ghent in late October that the British invasion of the Hudson Valley had been stopped dead at Plattsburgh, New York, and an amphibious attack on Baltimore repelled. Worse yet for Britain, President Madison had rallied support by violating diplomatic etiquette and publishing the initial British peace demands. "Mr. Madison has acted most scandalously," sniffed Prime Minister Lord Liverpool.

Great Britain had a choice—continue the war or accept a peace without territorial gain. Facing complicated negotiations in Vienna, Castlereagh hoped to make a European peace "without the millstone of an American war." The British cabinet thereupon turned for advice to the Duke of Wellington, who said that he would lead His Majesty's troops in America, if ordered, but it would be better, after the defeat at Plattsburgh, to negotiate peace on the terms *status quo ante bellum*. Lord Liverpool agreed to seek peace without territorial additions. European trouble once again served the American cause.

Another month of negotiations settled all remaining questions. During this last phase the one serious disagreement arose among the American delegates. The British, still hoping for a quid pro quo in return for American fishing rights, asked for access to the Mississippi River. When Adams seemed favorably disposed, Russell accused him of trying to "barter the patriotic blood of the West for blubber, and exchange ultra-Allegheny scalps for codfish." Gallatin then suggested that any reference to the Mississippi and the fisheries be omitted from the final treaty. The British delegation agreed. And so, on the night before Christmas 1814, the treaty of peace was signed, reaffirming the *status quo ante bellum*. Adams hoped "it will be the last treaty of peace between Great Britain and the United States."

The pact elicited great rejoicing when it reached Washington. On February 11, 1815, the Senate voted approval 35 to 0, notwithstanding that the treaty addressed none of the ostensible causes of the war. Partly responsible for the euphoria was the *previous* arrival of news concerning Andrew Jackson's smashing victory over the British at New Orleans on January 8. Many Americans believed erroneously that Jackson's achievement influenced the Ghent treaty, and the Madison administration did not regret ending what had been an unpopular war in a blaze of military glory. News of Ghent and New Orleans also undermined any impact that the Hartford Convention might have had on American diplomacy. Composed of New England Federalists who opposed war against England, the Hartford Convention had sent delegates to Washington with proposals to amend the Constitution, including a sixty-day limit on embargoes and a two-thirds vote of Congress for war. Madison snubbed the New Englanders, who slunk home in disgrace.

The Legacy of an Unwon War

The Peace of Ghent marked the culmination of an important phase of American foreign relations. The United States, after 1793, had reacted to Europe's wars by trying to expand its commerce as a neutral carrier and enlarge its territory by playing on European rivalries. American diplomats sought these goals without war or European entanglements until 1812, when quarrels over neutral rights catapulted an unprepared country into a second war of independence against Great Britain. The end of that Anglo-American conflict, combined with peace in Europe, made questions of maritime rights academic. For the next thirty years or so, American relations with Europe focused mainly on the matter of territorial expansion in the Western Hemisphere.

By twentieth-century standards the War of 1812 seems inexpensive—2,260 battle deaths and $158 million in direct costs. Yet its consequences were large. James Monroe thought that "we had acquired a character and rank among other nations which we did not enjoy before. . . . We cannot go back." Albert Gallatin offered a more balanced accounting: "The War has been productive of evil & good," he wrote, "but I think the good preponderates. . . . Under our former system we were become too selfish. . . . The people . . . are more Americans: they feel & act more as a Nation." The French minister in Washington concluded that "the war has given the Americans what they so essentially lacked, a national character founded on a glory common to all."

This sense of national confidence and glory rested partly on illusion. Jackson's heroics at New Orleans caused people to forget the burning of Washington, to forget that the war was hardly a spectacular success. Many forgot the lack of preparedness. John Quincy Adams spoke only for himself in hoping that the United States would learn "caution against commencing War without a fair prospect of attaining its objects." The revulsion against the Federalists for their apparent lack of patriotic fervor provided an ominous precedent for future opponents of American wars. Forgotten, too, was the probability that, with more patience by the Madison administration, and more attentiveness to American issues by the British, the War of 1812 need never have been fought.

The naval successes of the war, if limited, had a more enduring effect, as much of the wartime navy remained in service after 1815. In the ensuing decades naval officers gained fame as advance agents of American empire. But even in naval matters Americans remembered the limits of power less than the superpatriotism of Captain Stephen Decatur's famous toast: "Our country! In her intercourse with foreign nations may she always be in the right; but our country, right or wrong."

Even if the peace settled no major issues by treaty, the United States, with its population doubling every twenty-three years, profited. In Henry Adams's words, "they gained their greatest triumph in referring all their disputes to be settled by time, the final negotiator, whose decision they could safely trust." However much the United States risked by going to war in 1812, the paradoxical effect of that war was to increase American self-confidence and to ensure European respect. The young republic still had not reached the rank of a great power by Europe's standards, but the war with England had shown that in North America the United States could not be treated like Geneva or Genoa.

Native Americans in the trans-Allegheny west came to know U.S. power only too well. The unity that Tenskwatawa and Tecumseh had worked to build collapsed when General William Henry Harrison's forces killed Tecumseh at the Battle of the Thames in 1813. In an even bloodier campaign in the South in 1814, Andrew Jackson's troops routed Creeks in the "dreadful victory" at Horseshoe Bend in present-day Alabama, where some 800 Indians perished. After Castlereagh's diplomats failed to obtain an Indian buffer state at the Ghent negotiations, Native Americans could no longer rely on British protection against white encroachment. By 1817 the U.S.

War Department reported that the Indians had "ceased to be an object of terror, and have become that of commiseration."

The legacy of 1812 significantly altered Anglo-American relations. Even if the British refused to revoke impressment in theory, war's end brought the release of hundreds of U.S. citizens from British ships and prisons. Never again would impressment disrupt Anglo-American relations. Engaged in a life-or-death struggle with Napoleon, Britain found the United States a tough adversary. As the Duke of Wellington recognized, Canada could be defended only with the greatest difficulty. Postwar British exports to America rose substantially, thus presaging a commercial interdependence that promoted peaceful Anglo-American relations. Rivalry between the two English-speaking nations did not end in 1815, of course, and Britain still stood as a barrier to U.S. expansion. So did Canada. The War of 1812 gave impetus to *Canadian* nationalism, causing American expansion to move south and west rather than north. In the West, the United States would again collide with British interests. Still, after 1815, Britain chose to settle differences with the United States at the negotiating table, not on the battlefield. When the British West Indies finally opened to American trade in 1830, an aging James Madison predicted that England could "no longer . . . continue mistress of the seas" and the "Trident must pass to this hemisphere." And so it did.

FURTHER READING FOR THE PERIOD 1789–1815

General histories include Reginald Horsman, *The Diplomacy of the New Republic, 1776–1815* (1985); Daniel G. Lang, *Foreign Policy in the Early Republic* (1985); Peggy Liss, *Atlantic Empires* (1983); Bradford Perkins, *The Creation of a Republican Empire, 1776–1865* (1993); and Marie-Jeanne Rossignol, *The Nationalist Ferment* (2004).

For George Washington and 1790s issues, see Harry Ammon, *The Genet Mission* (1973); Joyce Appleby, *Capitalism and a New Social Order* (1984); Samuel Flagg Bemis, *Jay's Treaty* (1962) and *Pinckney's Treaty* (1960); Jerald A. Combs, *The Jay Treaty* (1970); Stanley Elkins and Eric McKittrick, *The Age of Federalism* (1993); Joseph Ellis, *His Excellency* (2005) (Washington); Todd Estes, *The Jay Treaty Debate* (2006); Don Higginbottom, *George Washington* (2002); James Roger Sharp, *American Politics in the Early Republic* (1993); Scott Silverstone, *Divided Union* (2004); Robert W. Smith, *Keeping the Republic* (2004); and Matthew Spalding and Patrick J. Garrity, *A Sacred Union of Citizens* (1996) (Farewell Address).

For the Adams presidency, see Albert H. Bowman, *The Struggle for Neutrality* (1974); Ralph A. Brown, *The Presidency of John Adams* (1979); Alexander DeConde, *The Quasi-War* (1966); John P. Diggins, *John Adams* (2003); Joseph J. Ellis, *Passionate Sage* (1993); John Ferling, *Adams vs. Jefferson* (2004); Lawrence S. Kaplan, *Entangling Alliances with None* (1987); Stephen Kurtz, *The Presidency of John Adams* (1957); Philippe Roger, *The American Enemy* (2005); and William Stinchombe, *The XYZ Affair* (1981).

Jefferson and his vision of empire are studied in Joyce Appleby, *Thomas Jefferson* (2003); Alexander DeConde, *This Affair of Louisiana* (1976); Joseph J. Ellis, *American Sphinx* (1997); Lawrence S. Kaplan, *Thomas Jefferson* (2002); Peter J. Kastor, ed., *The Louisiana Purchase* (2002); Roger Kennedy, *Mr. Jefferson's Lost Cause* (2003); John Kukla, *A Wilderness So Immense* (2003); Peter Onuf, *Jefferson's Empire* (2000); Peter Onuf and Leonard Sadosky, *Jeffersonian America* (2002); Norman K. Risjord, *Thomas Jefferson* (1994); Malcolm J. Rohrbough, *The Trans-Appalachian Frontier* (1978); and Robert W. Tucker and David C. Henrickson, *Empire of Liberty* (1990).

Studies of the Lewis and Clark Expedition include Stephen E. Ambrose, *Undaunted Courage* (1996); Gunther Barth, ed., *The Lewis and Clark Expedition* (1998); Daniel Botkin, *Our Natural History* (2004); Albert Furchtwanger, *Acts of Discovery* (1999); and James P. Ronda, *Jefferson's West* (2002).

The foreign-policy ideas and record of James Madison are treated in Jack Rakove, *James Madison and the Creation of the American Republic* (2002); Robert A. Rutland, *James Madison* (1987) and *The Presidency of James Madison* (1990); and Garry Wills, *James Madison* (2002).

Issues leading to the War of 1812 are traced in Clifford L. Egan, *Neither Peace nor War* (1983); Ronald L. Hatzenbuehler and Robert L. Ivie, *Congress Declares War* (1983); Peter P. Hill, *Napoleon's Troublesome Americans* (2005); Reginald Horsman, *The Causes of the War of 1812* (1962); Bradford Perkins, *The First Rapprochement* (1955) and *Prologue to War* (1961); Burton Spivak, *Jefferson's English Crisis* (1979); J. C. A. Stagg, *Mr. Madison's War* (1983); Spencer C. Tucker and Frank T. Reuter, *Injured Honor* (1996); and Steven Watts, *The Republic Reborn* (1987).

For wartime questions and Ghent peacemaking, see Richard J. Barbuto, *Niagara 1814* (2000); Pierre Berton, *The Invasion of Canada, 1812–1813* (1980); James G. Cusick, *The Other War of 1812* (2003); Donald R. Hickey, *The War of 1812* (1989); Bradford Perkins, *Castlereagh and Adams* (1964); Richard J. Skeen, *Citizen Soldiers and the War of 1812* (1999); and Patrick C. T. White, *A Nation on Trial* (1965).

For aspects of expansionism, see Robert J. Allison, *The Crescent Obscured* (1995); James C. Bradford, ed., *Command Under Sail* (1985); Gordon S. Brown, *Toussaint's Clause* (2005); Evan Cornog, *The Birth of Empire* (1998); Tim Matthewson, *A Proslavery Foreign Policy* (2002); Frank L. Owsley, Jr., and Gene A. Smith, *Filibusters and Expansionists* (1997); Richard B. Parker, *Uncle Sam in Barbary* (2004); James P. Ronda, *Astoria and Empire* (1990); and Reginald C. Stuart, *United States Expansionism and British North America, 1775–1871* (1988).

Borderlands issues and relations with Native Americans are discussed in James F. Brooks, *Captives and Cousins* (2003); Gregory Evans Dowd, *A Spirited Resistance* (1992); John Grenier, *The First Way of War* (2005); Stephen G. Hyslop, *Bound for Santa Fe* (2002); Dorothy V. Jones, *License for Empire* (1982); James E. Lewis, Jr., *The American Union and the Problem of Neighborhood* (1998) (U.S.-Spain); John Sugden, *Tecumseh* (1998); Anthony F. C. Wallace, *Jefferson and the Indians* (2001); and David J. Weber, *The Spanish Frontier in North America* (1992) and ed., *New Spain's Far Northern Frontier* (1988).

To the biographical studies listed above and in Chapter 1, add Robert J. Allison, *Stephen Decatur* (2005); George A. Billias, *Elbridge Gerry* (1979); Ron Chernow, *Alexander Hamilton* (2004); Gerald H. Clarfield, *Timothy Pickering and the American Republic* (1981); Joseph Ellis, *Founding Brothers* (2001); Stephen Englund, *Napoleon* (2005); John L. Harper, *American Machiavelli* (2004) (Hamilton); Peter P. Hill, *William Vans Murray* (1971); Lawrence S. Kaplan, *Alexander Hamilton* (2002); Stuart Leiberger, *Founding Friendship* (1999); Melanie Randolph Miller, *Envoy to the Terror* (2005) (Gouverneur Morris); Robert W. Remini, *Henry Clay* (1991); and Martin R. Zahniser, *Charles Cotesworth Pinckney* (1967).

See also Robert L. Beisner, ed., *Guide to American Foreign Relations Since 1600* (2003).

For comprehensive coverage of foreign-relations topics, see the articles in the four-volume *Encyclopedia of U.S. Foreign Relations* (1997), edited by Bruce W. Jentleson and Thomas G. Paterson.

CHAPTER 3

Extending and Preserving the Sphere, 1815–1848

✳ *Mexican-American War on the Rio Grande, 1846*

THE MOMENTOUS ORDER to march to the Rio Grande reached General Zachary Taylor on February 3, 1846. Planning took several weeks, so the first infantry brigades did not depart Corpus Christi until March 9. The army averaged ten miles a day, through suffocating dust, across sunbaked soil, through ankle-deep sands, past holes of brackish water, into grasslands capable of supporting vegetation. Late in the morning of March 28, Taylor's army reached the north bank of the Rio Grande in disputed Texas territory. Across the 200 yards of mud-colored river stood the Mexican town of Matamoros with its garrison of 3,000 men. Taylor encamped, set up earthworks (Fort Texas), and waited. "The attitude of the Mexicans is so far decidedly hostile," Taylor informed his superiors.

The next three weeks passed nervously but peacefully. The "government" had sent Taylor's army "on purpose to bring on a war, so as to have a pretext for taking California and as much of this country as it chooses," one officer wrote in his diary. Taylor had to conduct his initial parley with the Mexicans in French because no American officer could speak Spanish and no Mexican present had mastered English. Taylor assured them that his advance to the Rio Grande was neither an invasion of Mexican soil nor a hostile act. The suspicious Mexicans reinforced their garrison with 2,000 additional troops. Then, on April 24, Major General Mariano Arista notified Taylor that hostilities had begun. Mexican cavalry, 1,600 strong, crossed the river at La Palangana, fourteen miles upstream from Matamoros. Taylor sent dragoons to investigate, but they returned having seen nothing. That same evening, April 24, Taylor ordered out another cavalry force under Captain Seth B. Thornton. This time the Americans rode into an ambush. Thornton lost eleven men. The Mexicans took the rest of his sixty-three-man contingent captive. News of the fight reached Taylor at reveille on April 26. "Hostilities may now be considered as commenced," he immediately alerted Washington, D.C. His dispatch took two weeks to reach the capital.

U.S. Forces Enter Mexico City, 1847. General Winfield Scott triumphantly parades in the plaza as an American flag flies above. One Mexican, at the left with stone in hand, did not appreciate the ceremonies. (Library of Congress)

A stiff, angular man, with sharp gray eyes set in a sad, thin face, President James K. Polk met with his cabinet on May 9. The chief executive was looking for an excuse to declare war on Mexico. Reviewing the diplomacy of the past year, which included United States annexation of Texas, suspension of relations with Mexico, and abortive attempts to solve boundary disputes and to purchase California and New Mexico, Polk self-righteously announced that "in my opinion we had ample cause of war, and that it was impossible that we could stand in *statu[s] quo,* or that I could remain silent much longer." He hoped that the Mexicans would commit an act of aggression against Taylor's army, but as yet nothing had happened. Polk's cabinet agreed that he should soon send a war message to Congress, although one member thought it better if some hostile act on the border occurred first. Polk began to compose the war message.

At six o'clock that evening news of the Rio Grande skirmish reached the White House. The cabinet hastily reconvened and reached a unanimous decision: Submit a war message as quickly as possible. All day May 10, Polk anxiously labored over his statement, conferring with cabinet colleagues, military advisers, and congressional leaders. At noon the next day the message went to Congress. "The cup of forbearance has been exhausted," Polk wrote. "After reiterated menaces, Mexico has passed the boundary of the United States, has invaded our territory and shed American blood upon American soil." War, "notwithstanding all our efforts to avoid it, exists by the act of Mexico herself." A bill accompanied the war message authorizing the president to accept militia and volunteers for military duty. The bill asked Congress to recognize that "by the act of . . . Mexico, a state of war exists between the government and the United States."

A disciplined Democratic majority responded swiftly. Debate in the House was limited to two hours. Angry Whigs asked for time to examine 144 pages of documents that Polk sent with his message. Denied. The Speaker of the House repeatedly

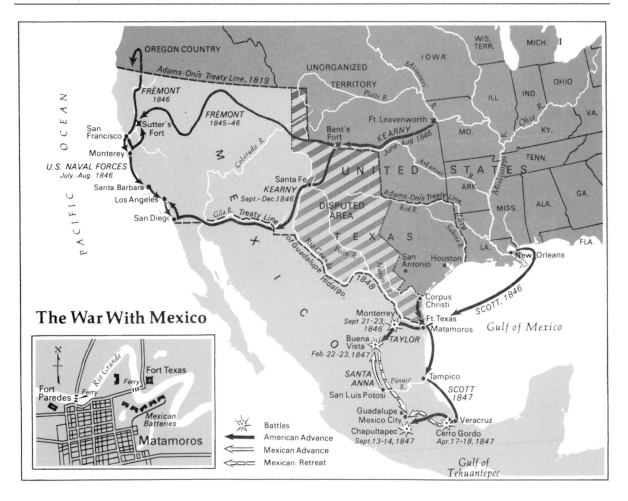

failed to recognize members who wanted to ask detailed questions. Only by demanding permission to explain why they should be excused from voting did two dissenters gain the floor and denounce Polk's war message as falsehood. The House vote of 174 to 14 represented a victory for stampede tactics. In the Senate the following day, the vote was 40 to 2. Whigs and dissident Democrats, remembering the political fate of Federalists who had opposed the War of 1812, either voted aye or did not vote. Democratic senator John C. Calhoun of South Carolina later insisted that fewer than 10 percent of his colleagues would have voted for war if Polk had presented the issue fairly. Nonetheless, Calhoun abstained when his name was called.

Thus began the War with Mexico, a conflict that lasted nearly two years and added to the United States a vast domain, which included the present-day states of New Mexico, Arizona, California, Nevada, and Utah. Contemporaries called it "Mr. Polk's War," a most appropriate appellation. Despite backing from a unanimous cabinet, the Tennesseean made the crucial decisions for war. It was Polk who unilaterally defined the geographic limits of Texas as including disputed land between the Nueces River and the Rio Grande. Polk, as commander in chief, ordered General Taylor to the Rio Grande. Polk decided that Mexico had fired the first shot. Polk presented Congress with an accomplished fact.

The presidential war did not go unchallenged. Declaring Polk's claim of Mexican aggression "in direct and notorious violation of the truth," Representative John Quincy Adams, long an advocate of expansion, stood with thirteen northern Whigs to vote against an "unrighteous" war to extend slavery. One senator called Taylor's march to the Rio Grande "an act of aggression" comparable to "pointing a pistol at another's breast." If the president can "invade a neighboring nation, whenever he shall deem it necessary to repel an invasion," Illinois Representative Abraham Lincoln warned, "you allow him to make war at pleasure." Yet Polk could get away with it because his war aims reflected the grand hopes of expansionist America.

Expanding the Sphere: Manifest Destiny

The war on the Rio Grande came at a critical juncture and dramatized the expansionist themes that dominated American foreign relations after the War of 1812. At the very time Taylor's troops were fighting Mexicans in the Southwest, Polk was quietly settling a dispute with England over the Pacific Northwest. By dividing Oregon at 49° north latitude in June 1846, Polk temporarily abated the rivalry with England over the territory and commerce of North America. Exaggerated fears of British encroachment in Texas and California had contributed to the outbreak of war against Mexico. That the United States fought Mexico and not Britain in 1846 illustrated another theme: American expansionists acted more aggressively against weaker Spaniards, Mexicans, and Indians than against the stronger British. According to the expansionist ideology, those peoples who neither improved the land they held nor developed effective political institutions had to make way for those who could. The lands Polk wanted from Mexico had sparse populations that could easily assimilate American institutions, or so he assumed. England, with greater power and similar traditions, could be a rival but not a victim. Indeed, Polk invoked the Monroe Doctrine in 1845, warning England against further expansion in North America and making explicit what had been implicit in 1823—that Europeans could not annex territory in the Western Hemisphere, but the United States could. Moreover, Polk sincerely believed that Mexico fired the first shot on the Rio Grande, just as many sincerely believed that God had destined the United States to control the entire continent. The sincerity of such beliefs did not stop expansionism from being both racist and imperialistic.

Continental expansion dominated the three decades after 1815. Having defended their territorial integrity during the second war with Great Britain, American nationalists proceeded to acquire Florida, Texas, Oregon, and the Mexican cession, some 1,263,301 square miles. Population nearly trebled, from 8,419,000 in 1815 to 22,018,000 in 1848. American commerce expanded into new channels, notably Latin America and Asia, with total exports climbing from $53 million in 1815 to $159 million in 1847. The gross output of farm production increased from $338 million in 1820 to $904 million thirty years later. Cotton production, vital to Anglo-American

Makers of American Foreign Relations, 1815–1848

Presidents	Secretaries of State
James Madison, 1809–1817	James Monroe, 1811–1817
James Monroe, 1817–1825	John Quincy Adams, 1817–1825
John Quincy Adams, 1825–1829	Henry Clay, 1825–1829
Andrew Jackson, 1829–1837	Martin Van Buren, 1829–1831
	Edward Livingston, 1831–1833
	Louis McLane, 1833–1834
Martin Van Buren, 1837–1841	John Forsyth, 1834–1841
William H. Harrison, 1841	Daniel Webster, 1841–1843
John Tyler, 1841–1845	Abel P. Upshur, 1843–1844
	John C. Calhoun, 1844–1845
James K. Polk, 1845–1849	James Buchanan, 1845–1849

relations, rose from 209,000 bales in 1815 to 2,615,000 bales in 1847. Construction of canals and railroads created a transportation and market revolution that quickened U.S. growth. It became the purpose of U.S. diplomacy during these years to facilitate this expansion. "Everyone always grows a little in this world," said Tsar Alexander I of Russia after John Quincy Adams told him of the American acquisition of West Florida.

The roots of expansion were many—historical, economic, demographic, intellectual, strategic. Much that occurred after 1815 derived from earlier decisions. Part of the rationale for acquiring East Florida in 1819 followed the example of Louisiana: Florida, just like New Orleans, might be ceded by Spain to a more dangerous neighbor, hence the argument for possessing it before England or France could grab it. Memories of the Revolution of 1776, combined with opportunities for Latin American markets, helped prompt the Monroe Doctrine of 1823. By stipulating that Europe and the Americas had distinctly different political systems, Monroe's message recalled the isolationist principles of Paine's *Common Sense* and Washington's Farewell Address.

Echoes of the past reverberated in the Anglo-American trade rivalry in Latin America and in the attempts to gain equal access to the British West Indian trade in the 1820s. An explicit reference to earlier disputes about neutral rights came in 1831 when President Andrew Jackson negotiated an agreement whereby France promised to pay an indemnity of 25 million francs for illegal seizures of American shipping in the years 1805–1812. When the French defaulted on an installment in 1834, Jackson reportedly shouted: "I know them French. They won't pay unless they are made to." The French paid the debt. Jackson's pugnacity also served notice that the United States would insist on the right to expand its carrying trade in the event of another European conflagration.

An important element in expansion after 1815 derived from the growing vision of what was possible. Despite treaties in 1818 and 1819 that established a firm claim to the Pacific coast, most Americans still thought of the Rocky Mountains as a "natural" boundary. It had taken Lewis and Clark eighteen months to travel to the Pacific from St. Louis. A sea voyage from Boston to the Pacific coast lasted six to eight months. Even the expansionist Senator Thomas Hart Benton of Missouri went on record in 1825 in favor of the Rocky Mountain limitation. "Along the back of this ridge," he intoned, "the Western limit of the republic should be drawn, and the statue of the fabled god, Terminus, should be raised upon its highest peak, never to be thrown down." Within a generation the Rocky Mountains became "less terminus than pivot to empire."

Technology shrank geography and expanded horizons. Steamboats, canals, and railroads stimulated imaginations as well as commerce. The development of high-speed printing presses gave rise in the early 1840s to mass circulation newspapers, which in turn trumpeted expansionist rhetoric to a larger foreign-policy public. Samuel F. Morse's invention of the telegraph in 1844 created "the world's first Internet." "The magnetic telegraph," boasted the editor John L. O'Sullivan in 1845, "will enable the editors of the 'San Francisco Union,' the 'Astoria Evening Post,' or the 'Nootka Morning News,' to set up in type the first half of the President's Inaugural before the echoes of the latter half shall have died away."

The same O'Sullivan, as editor of the *Democratic Review,* nurtured such writers as Herman Melville, Nathaniel Hawthorne, and Walt Whitman in creating an expansive national literature. One of his contributors, Jane McManus Storm, gave the expansionist process a name in 1845 when she proclaimed America's "manifest destiny to overspread the continent allotted by Providence for the free development of our yearly multiplying millions." Although the geographical limits of the Temple of Freedom were not always clear—the Pacific? the continent? the hemisphere?—most believers in Manifest Destiny followed John Quincy Adams's claim that the United States and North America were identical. Manifest Destiny meant republicanism, religious freedom, states' rights, free trade, inexpensive land. It appealed to the individualistic ideology of Jacksonianism—"opportunity and expansion for everyone amid minimal or no government regulation, a rhetoric of republican equality that actually masked a profoundly unequal society."

Manifest Destiny in its purest form did not envisage taking territory by force. Peaceful occupation of uninhabited wilderness, followed by self-government on the American model and eventual annexation by mutual consent—this was the ideal. Neighboring peoples of Spanish and Indian heritage, given time and the American example, might qualify for peaceful incorporation. The process seemed almost automatic. "Go to the West," said an Indiana member of Congress in 1846, and "see a young man with his mate of eighteen; and [after] a lapse of thirty years, visit him again, and instead of two, you will find twenty-two. . . . How long, under this process of multiplication, will it take to cover the continent with our posterity?"

Reality did not match the ideal, as "Polk's War" on the Rio Grande sadly attested. Racism inevitably corroded Manifest Destiny. One diplomat compared the typical Colombian to "an obedient animal that fawns when chastised," thereby reflecting the dominant racist thinking that posited Anglo-Saxon superiority as a

"Manifest Destiny." John Gast's painting captures the ebullient spirit of the trek westward. Pioneers relentlessly move on, attracting railroads and driving out Native Americans, as "Columbia" majestically pulls telegraph wires across America. (Museum of the American West collection, Autry National Center)

proven scientific fact and denigrated peoples who resisted the inexorable march of democratic institutions. Protestant missionaries who sought to assimilate Indians into white society firmly believed that "any right-thinking savage should be able to recognize the superiority of Christian society," and thus any failures in the acculturation process were attributed to the victims. Just as the negative stereotype of African Americans in the nineteenth century justified slavery in the South and unequal treatment of freedmen in the North, and as the prevailing image of the Indians as savages justified their subjugation, so too did expansionists project their notions of racial superiority against Mexicans who were allegedly too cowardly to fight or too treacherous to win if they did fight.

Indian relocation became official policy under President Andrew Jackson. Once native people lived apart from whites, Jackson believed, Indians would be "free to pursue happiness . . . under their rude institutions." In the Removal Act of 1830 Congress gave him the money and authority to impose new treaties and forcibly resettle 85,000 Indians of the five "civilized nations" from the southeastern states— Cherokee, Choctaw, Creek, Chickasaw, and Seminole—across the Mississippi. The

French visitor Alexis de Tocqueville, stopping in Memphis during the winter of 1831–1832, described Choctaws crossing the great river: "The wounded, the sick, newborn babies, and the old men on the point of death . . . the sight will never fade from my memory." Even the assimilated, self-governing Cherokees had to relocate to "the barren plains of the West" where they awaited "degradation, dispersion, and ultimate extinction." In a larger context, the government's treatment of Native Americans became "part of a global pattern of intensified conflict" during the nineteenth century wherein European-style imperialism expanded at the expense of indigenous populations, including the British subjugations of the Maori in New Zealand and the Xhosa in South Africa.

Yet most Americans viewed expansion as a natural, organic process. Americans always sought greater productivity through the cultivation of new lands. Increased population, inadequate transportation, depressed agricultural prices, and general hard times also caused periodic migrations into new areas. Whether emigrants moved into American territory beyond the Alleghenies or into fertile lands under alien rule, they retained their distinctly Yankee customs; under foreign rule, they rejected alien institutions and virtually established American "colonies." Politicians at home directed U.S. foreign policy toward the "protection" of their compatriots. Thus came the spread-eagle appeals to national prestige, the glittering description of natural resources and arable lands. As the American enclaves grew in size, so too did fears increase that some European power, probably perfidious England, would snatch the potential prize. If politicians exaggerated the extent to which England meddled in California, Oregon, and Texas, British rivalry did contribute to the expansionist momentum.

Population movements tended to come on the heels of economic downturns. The Panic of 1819, combined with Mexico's generous land policies, encouraged the first flood of immigration into Texas in the 1820s. Similarly, the severe economic depression in 1837–1842 stimulated more western farmers and southern planters to migrate westward. The population of Texas ballooned to 100,000 by 1845, and in far-off Oregon some 5,000 Americans had crossed the Rockies. As one resident of California put it: "Once let the tide of emigration flow toward California, and the American population will soon be sufficiently numerous to play the Texas game." This inexorable process of agrarian migration prompted Calhoun in 1843 to advocate a "wise and masterly inactivity" on the part of the U.S. government. Whigs especially believed that "whenever and wherever expansion came, it must be peaceful" and proceed "with the consent of the governed." Force did not seem necessary in theory.

Commercial Ambitions in the Pacific

Growing global commerce also fueled U.S. expansion. Trade with Latin America increased, and merchants plying the west coast of South America made profits that could be used to purchase the products of East Asia. "The North American road to India" was Senator Benton's description of the Columbia River during the 1840s. Whaling, salmon fisheries, furs, the fabled China trade, commercial rivalry with Britain and Russia—all were stressed from the 1820s onward by publicists seeking to colonize Oregon as a means to commercial expansion.

Just as the first settlers reached Oregon in 1843, the British, victorious in the Opium War (1839–1842), were breaking down Chinese trade barriers. By the Treaty of Nanjing in 1842, Britain forced China to open five new coastal ports (Guangzhou, Xiamen, Ningbo, Fuzhou, and Shanghai) and grant broad rights of extraterritoriality (legal trials for foreigners in special courts of their own nationality). This British success prompted Americans to obtain their own treaty for trade purposes. Already clipper ships carried cotton to China and returned with tea. Already U.S. merchants used Cantonese middlemen to sell Turkish opium in the land of Confucianism. President John Tyler entrusted Massachusetts Whig Caleb Cushing with the mission to negotiate with the Chinese. His Treaty of Wangxia (1844) gained for the United States the same rights, on an unconditional most-favored nation basis, that England had won in the Opium War. The ensuing influx of and cooperation among Yankee traders, missionaries, and diplomats created an "open door constituency" committed to "penetrating China and propagating at home a paternalistic vision . . . of defending and reforming China."

The U.S. Navy's Asiatic Squadron sometimes used force to protect the China trade in the 1840s—as "the Society for the Diffusion of Cannon Balls," in one missionary's quaint phrase. The navy's chief contribution came in the exploratory expeditions sponsored by Matthew Maury and led by Charles Wilkes. Charting coastlines, publicizing points of commercial and strategic interest, enlightening Washington about the Pacific, these naval explorers became " 'maritime frontiersmen,' mirror images of the thousands of mountain men, traders, pioneers, adventurers, and army surveyors who trekked westward to the Pacific." A key stimulus for expansion appeared with the publication in 1842 of Wilkes's *Narrative of the United States Exploring Expedition,* which provided accurate data about the Pacific coast from Vancouver Island to Baja California. Wilkes's unqualified praise for San Francisco and the Strait of Juan de Fuca contrasted sharply with his dismissal of the Columbia River, with its shifting sandbars, as a viable entrepôt. U.S. diplomats, particularly Daniel Webster, stepped up efforts thereafter to acquire one or both of these harbors. The main reason Americans pressed so hard for the triangle of Oregon between the Columbia and the strait was the need for a deepwater port. Only seven Americans lived north of the Columbia River in 1845.

Commercial empire became even more the object in Mexico's California. When a British naval officer entered San Francisco Bay in 1845, he exclaimed: "D—n it! is there nothing but Yankees here?" The Americans were connected primarily with the Boston trading company of Bryant & Sturgis. Having pioneered the otter trade in the Pacific and opened an office in Portuguese Macao, Bryant & Sturgis began in the 1820s to shift from furs to hides, which it bought cheaply from Catholic missions and rancheros. The firm established offices in Santa Barbara and Monterey. Thomas O. Larkin, later appointed the first American consul to California and a crucial figure in the diplomacy of 1845–1846, worked for Bryant & Sturgis, as did Richard Henry Dana, author of the epic narrative *Two Years Before the Mast* (1840), depicting a voyage to California around Cape Horn. Altogether, some 25,000 persons lived in California in 1845, including 800 Americans. Its link with Mexico City, more than 1,500 miles away, was weak. Overland communications were primitive, and courts, police, schools, and newspapers scarcely existed. American merchants, whalers, and sailors competed ardently with their British counterparts.

Commercial opportunities also beckoned in Hawai'i, which by the 1840s resembled New England in the mid-Pacific. After white settlers ("*haoles,*" or "men without souls") had stripped Hawai'i of its abundant sandalwood for the China trade in the 1820s, others came to save pagan souls, extract sugar cane, and kill whales. By the 1840s, Protestant missionaries, finding Hawai'i more hospitable than China, had established seventy-nine mission stations, six schools, and two printing houses to spread the gospel. In 1842 President Tyler informed Congress that U.S. stakes in Hawai'i had become so impressive that any attempt by another nation "to take possession of the islands, colonize them, and subvert the native Government" would meet U.S. opposition. Although this Tyler Doctrine endorsed Hawai'i's independence, the United States declared its special interest in the archipelago and warned other powers away.

The Pacific and beyond yielded more than profits, as mariners and missionaries brought back by the 1820s enough artifacts to start museums such as the East India Marine Society of Salem, Massachusetts. Straight-laced Yankee merchants left diaries that described "Manila girls" as the "handsomest in the world" with whom "a small puff of wind would discover their nakedness." Although apparently less interested in erotica than New Englanders, entrepreneurs in the Midwest sought to link maritime trade to agrarian migration. Farmers moving to Oregon had in mind an expanded market for their products in Asia, as did some southerners, who saw the Chinese as potential buyers of cotton and tobacco. Agrarian politicians such as Stephen Douglas embraced projects linking the Mississippi Valley with the Pacific via a transcontinental railroad. Indeed, in January 1845, Asa Whitney, a prospering New York merchant engaged in the China trade, first proposed government land grants to build a railroad from the Great Lakes to Oregon. Such schemes did not reach fruition until after the Civil War, but their existence in the 1840s testifies to the dual nature (maritime and agrarian) of continental expansion.

John Quincy Adams, the Floridas, and the Transcontinental Treaty

Following the Louisiana Purchase of 1803, American diplomats had tried to obtain Florida by arguing that it had always been a part of Louisiana. The Spanish rejected such a claim. The first U.S. bite out of the territory came in September 1810, when a group of American settlers revolted against Spanish rule, captured the fortress at Baton Rouge, and proclaimed the "Republic of West Florida." A blue woolen flag with a single silver star replaced the Bourbon banner. Worried about "the uncontrolled current of a revolutionary impulse," Madison annexed West Florida by proclamation and sent troops to the Pearl River in October. During the War of 1812, American soldiers occupied all of West Florida to the Perdido River—the only tangible addition of territory resulting from that war.

It fell to the Monroe administration (1817–1825) and Secretary of State John Quincy Adams to complete the absorption. Spanish minister Don Luis de Onís proved himself a dogged, skillful advocate of a hopeless cause. Adams took the diplomatic offensive, arguing that Spain should cede East Florida because Spanish authorities had not prevented Indians from raiding American territory (as required by

John Quincy Adams (1767–1848). This portrait of the famed diplomat, secretary of state, president, and congressman from Massachusetts demonstrates well his austere and gloomy countenance. Ralph Waldo Emerson noted that Adams "must have sulphuric acid in his tea." (National Portrait Gallery, Smithsonian Institution/Art Resource, N.Y.)

Pinckney's Treaty of 1795). Adams also blamed the Spanish for not returning thousands of escaped slaves and for allegedly assisting British forces during the War of 1812. Indeed, a continuing alliance between fugitive blacks and Seminoles, as well as a "Negro fort" on the Apalachicola River, made the acquisition of Florida imperative for those Americans who could not "tolerate a southern sanctuary from slavery." Faced with revolts in its South American empire, Spain wanted a promise from the United States neither to assist the revolutionaries nor to recognize their declared independence. Madrid also instructed Onís to settle the disputed western boundary of Louisiana, and only to cede Florida in exchange for the best frontier he could get. Adams urged that the boundary be set well southwest at the Rio Grande, or at least the Colorado River of Texas. Onís grudgingly proposed the Mermentau and Calcasieu rivers in the middle of present-day Louisiana. The negotiators were far apart. "There had never been a negotiation," Adams wrote gloomily, with "so little prospect that the parties would ever come to an understanding."

The man who would break the impasse, General Andrew Jackson, bivouacked with 4,800 troops at Big Creek, near the Georgia-Florida boundary in early 1818. Ostensibly under orders to pursue and punish Seminole Indians and runaway slaves who had been using Spanish Florida as a base from which to raid U.S. settlements, Jackson had suggested secretly to Monroe that "the whole of East Florida [be] seized and held as indemnity for the outrages of Spain upon the property of our Citizens." Whether or not Monroe or Secretary of War John C. Calhoun explicitly approved Jackson's proposal, neither man ever told Jackson *not* to cross the border. To the pugnacious Tennessean, this silence from Washington constituted tacit agreement that the Spanish were every bit as much the enemy as were the Seminoles and "Black Indians."

"Old Hickory" burst across the border in late March 1818. On April 6 the Spanish garrison at St. Marks surrendered, and inside Jackson found "the noted Scotch villain Arbuthnot." Alexander Arbuthnot, in actuality, was a kindly, seventy-year-old Scots trader from Nassau whose scrupulously honest commercial dealings with the Indians had annoyed his profit-minded superiors in England. Convinced that Arbuthnot was in cahoots with the Seminoles, Jackson plunged into the tropical swamps looking for the main Indian camp. He found the camp but not the Indians. He seized another Englishman, Robert C. Ambrister, formerly of the British Royal Colonial Marines. Returning to St. Marks, Jackson convened a court-martial, hanged Arbuthnot, and shot Ambrister, thereby administering American "justice" on Spanish soil to two British subjects. Pensacola capitulated on May 28, whereupon "Old Hickory" promptly replaced the Spanish governor with one of his own colonels and declared in force the revenue laws of the United States, all of which he justified as "absolutely necessary to put down the Indian war." In two short months, Jackson had occupied every important Spanish post in Florida except St. Augustine.

Learning of Jackson's deeds, Onís roused Secretary Adams from his morning Bible study and demanded an indemnity, as well as punishment of Jackson. Calhoun and other cabinet members suggested a court-martial for the rambunctious general. Monroe quietly agreed to return the captured posts to Spain. But he did not censure Jackson and even offered to falsify some of the general's dispatches so that the invasion would appear in a more favorable light. Congress launched an investigation. Only Adams stoutly defended Jackson, saying that "everything" he did "was *defensive.*"

When the British did not protest the deaths of Arbuthnot and Ambrister, Monroe gave his secretary of state full backing. Avoiding any "appearance of truckling to Spain," Adams drew up a memorable reply to Onís's demands for censure and indemnity. If Spain could not restrain its Indians, the United States would in self-defense. Adams boldly claimed that the right of defensive invasion was "engraved in adamant on the common sense of mankind." Charging the Spanish with "impotence" rather than perfidy, the secretary demanded that Spain must either "place a force in Florida adequate at once to the protection of her territory and to the fulfillment of her engagements, or cede to the United States a province, of which she retains nothing but the nominal possession, but which is, in fact, a derelict, open to the occupancy of every enemy, civilized or savage, of the United States." Onís's superiors in Madrid reacted to Jackson's forays with instructions to cede Florida quickly and retreat to the best possible boundary between Louisiana and Mexico.

Further negotiations completed the Adams-Onís Treaty (or Transcontinental Treaty), signed in Washington on February 22, 1819. The United States acquired East Florida and a new boundary line that began at the mouth of the Sabine River, moved stairstep fashion along various rivers in a northwesterly direction to the forty-second parallel, and then went straight west to the Pacific. The secretary of state pushed the boundary to the Pacific entirely on his own. In return for these gains, Adams surrendered vague U.S. claims to Texas arising from the Louisiana Purchase. In fact, Onís had instructions to retreat even on the Sabine boundary, but Monroe thought Florida more important than Texas and did not press the matter. The United States also agreed to assume the claims of its own citizens against Spain, some $5 million resulting from Franco-Spanish seizures of U.S. shipping during the undeclared war of 1798–1800. The Transcontinental Treaty said nothing about recognition of Spain's rebellious colonies. Adams staunchly resisted any hand-tying nonrecognition pledge. Minor disputes delayed ratifications until 1821.

The importance of the Adams-Onís Treaty lay in what it foreshadowed. Just as in his diplomacy with England in the Convention of 1818, Adams was projecting a continental, even larger, vision. It did not matter if he and Onís were drawing lines across deserts that did not exist or around mountains that were not where maps said they should be. Adams was projecting an expansive vision of the United States that anticipated the railroad and other future technologies. "Americans," Onís wrote prophetically, "believe that their dominion is destined to extend, now to the Isthmus of Panama, and hereafter over all the regions of the New World." They "consider themselves superior to the rest of mankind."

More ominous was the way in which Jackson's invasion of Florida had buttressed diplomacy. Spain's willingness to yield Florida, combined with Britain's refusal to question the executions of Ambrister and Arbuthnot, minimized diplomatic repercussions. Nevertheless, as the congressional investigation revealed, Monroe and Jackson had virtually waged war without the approval of Congress. Because Monroe had apparently pledged that Jackson would not seize any Spanish forts if he crossed the border in pursuit of Seminoles, Henry Clay urged Congress to "assert our constitutional powers, and vindicate the instrument from military violation." Nonetheless, on February 8, 1819, after a twenty-seven-day debate, the four congressional resolutions condemning Jackson went down to defeat by comfortable margins. Appreciative that the headstrong general had facilitated expansion of the national domain, Congress accepted a precedent of unilateral executive military action that would repeat itself often in American history. By endorsing the administration's undeclared war, Congress voted to acquiesce in its own subordination in the checks-and-balances system of U.S. governance.

The Monroe Doctrine Targets Europe and the Western Hemisphere

The next notable milestone for expansion came with the Monroe Doctrine of 1823. At first glance, that statement of American diplomatic principles appears entirely anti-imperialist in intent—a warning to reactionary Europe not to interfere with revolutions in the New World, a gesture of solidarity with the newly independent republics to the south. Monroe's declaration was indeed a warning and a gesture, but its motives were hardly selfless. In saying "Thou Shalt Not" to Europe, James Monroe and John Quincy Adams carefully exempted the United States. By facilitating commercial expansion into Latin America and landed expansion across the North American continent, the Monroe Doctrine became "an official declaration fencing in the 'western hemisphere' as a United States sphere of influence."

The Latin American revolutions (1808–1822) had a magnetic effect on the United States. The exploits of such Latin American leaders as Simón Bolívar, José San Martín, and Bernardo O'Higgins rekindled memories of 1776. Henry Clay eloquently proposed an inter-American "counterpoise" to monarchical Europe, "a rallying point" of freedom that would inspire "the friends of Liberty throughout the world."

That the United States did not immediately recognize the Latin American republics owed mainly to the calculating diplomacy of John Quincy Adams. Cynical and cautious, Adams "wished well" to the new nations but doubted that they could "establish free or liberal institutions of government. . . . Arbitrary power, military and ecclesiastical, was stamped upon . . . all their institutions." Adams carefully avoided recognition, thereby easing negotiations with Spain over the Transcontinental Treaty. After signing, he worried that Onís would jettison the treaty if the United States recognized the new Latin American states. Adams also warned that meddling in independence struggles might mean that the United States "would no longer be the ruler of her own spirit." So the secretary of state proclaimed on July 4, 1821: "Wherever the standard of freedom and independence has or shall be unfurled, there will her [the U.S.] heart, her benedictions, and her prayers be. But she goes not abroad in search of monsters to destroy." Not until spring 1822, after the expulsion of Spanish armies from the New World, and following a sharp rise in U.S. trade with Latin America, did President Monroe extend formal recognition to the new governments of La Plata, Peru, Colombia, and Mexico. Both Monroe and Adams feared the continued "intrigues of foreign powers" and "subserviency to *European* interests."

European threats loomed. Following Napoleon's final defeat, European statesmen had endeavored to restore order and legitimacy to an international system thrown out of kilter by the French Revolution and the conquests of Bonaparte. Conservatism became the watchword, and by the Treaty of Paris of 1815 the members of the Quadruple Alliance (Austria, Prussia, Russia, and Britain) bound themselves to future diplomatic congresses for the maintenance of peace and the status quo. A penitent France formally joined the "Concert of Europe" in 1818, and the Quadruple Alliance turned into the Quintuple Alliance. The allies also organized in 1815 the new Holy Alliance. By 1819–1820 the Austrian foreign minister, Prince Klemens von Metternich, enthusiastically supported by Tsar Alexander I of Russia, had transformed both alliances into instruments for suppressing revolutions. At the Congress of Troppau in 1820 the Allies agreed that if internal revolutions posed threats to neighboring states, "the powers bind themselves, by peaceful means, or if need be by arms, to bring back the guilty State into the bosom of the Great Alliance."

In 1821, Austrian armies put down uprisings in Naples and Piedmont. The following year a French army marched across the Pyrenees in support of Spain's unstable Ferdinand VII, who was then resisting a liberal constitutionalist government. The Allies also gave diplomatic support to Ottoman Turkey in its attempt to snuff out a national revolution in Greece. With Americans particularly incensed at the betrayal of freedom in Greece, Adams feared that any gesture to the Greeks would get the United States "encumbered with a quarrel with all of Europe."

British diplomacy during these years played an ambivalent role. Foreign Secretary Castlereagh wanted very much to preserve the grand coalition that had defeated Napoleon. The British had little sympathy for revolution. Confident of the stability of their own political institutions, and guarded by the English Channel and the Royal Navy, many Britons considered the use of French and Austrian troops to suppress foreign revolts as upsetting the balance of power. When the Congress of Verona (1822) sanctioned the deployment of French military forces in Spain, something the British had fought the bitter Peninsular War (1809–1814) to prevent, England's withdrawal from the Holy Alliance became inevitable. Castlereagh's successor, George Canning, promised a return to isolation from continental entanglements.

Also influencing Canning was Great Britain's position "at the top of the wheel of fortune." Enjoying global economic hegemony and naval supremacy, the British eyed ever-expanding commercial opportunities—and threats to them. British merchants had captured the lion's share of trade with rebellious Spanish ports in the New World. These lucrative commercial dealings, however, had not overcome London's antipathy to revolution so as to bring about formal recognition, although the British did fear that return of Spanish America to Ferdinand VII might curtail British trade. As Canning later boasted, "I resolved that if France had Spain, it should not be Spain 'with the Indies.' I called the New World into existence to redress the balance of the old."

Canning's opposition to any restoration in Latin America led, in August 1823, to a remarkable conversation with U.S. minister Richard Rush. In discussing French armies in Spain, Rush casually mentioned that the British should never permit France to interfere with the independence of Latin America or to gain territory there by conquest or cession. Canning listened intently. What, he asked Rush, would the U.S. government say to going hand in hand with England in such a policy? No concerted action would be necessary; if they simply told the French that the United States and Britain held the same opinions, would that not deter them? Both nations would also disavow any aim of obtaining territories for themselves. Intrigued but cautious, Rush referred the matter to Washington, D.C.

Rush's dispatch arrived in early October and sparked one of the most momentous discussions in American history. Monroe sought the advice of Thomas Jefferson and James Madison. These two elder Virginians agreed with the president that he should accept the British proposal. "Great Britain," Jefferson wrote, "can do us the most harm of any one, or all on earth; and with her on our side we need not fear the whole world." Concurring with Jefferson, Madison even suggested a joint statement on behalf of Greek independence. Armed with these opinions, Monroe called a cabinet meeting on November 7, fully prepared to embrace British cooperation.

Adams, however, fought vigorously for a unilateral course. Adams did not trust the British. Hoping to compete successfully for Latin American markets, and not wanting to tie U.S. hands in some future acquisition of, say, Texas or Cuba, the secretary of state argued that it would be more dignified to make an independent declaration to the Holy Alliance than "to come in as a cockboat in the wake of the British man-of-war." In this and subsequent meetings Adams gradually won Monroe over. U.S. leaders did not know that Canning, on October 9, had made an agreement with the French, the so-called Polignac Memorandum, whereby the French disclaimed "any intention or desire" to act against the former Spanish colonies in Latin America. News also arrived of the French capture of Cadiz, Spain, along with rumors that a French fleet might soon embark for the New World. Monroe worried that if "the allied powers . . . succeeded with the colonies[,] they would . . . invade us." Adams remained optimistic. Citing competing national interests within the Holy Alliance, especially England's stake in Latin America, he no more believed "that the Holy Allies will restore the Spanish dominion on the American continent than that the Chimborazo [a mountain in Ecuador] will sink beneath the ocean." Adams won his point, and Monroe followed his advice.

Next came the official declaration. Monroe's original draft included a ringing indictment of the French intervention in Spain and a statement favoring the independence of revolutionary Greece. Adams opposed both points. However much he deplored events in Spain and Greece, the secretary advocated isolation from European embroilments. He urged the president "to make an American cause and adhere inflexibly to that." Monroe excised the offending passages. The Monroe Doctrine then became part of the president's message to Congress of December 2, 1823. It contained three essential points: noncolonization, "hands off" the New World, and American noninvolvement in European quarrels.

Noncolonization focused specifically on Russia and responded to the tsar's announcement in 1821 that Russian dominion extended southward from Alaska along the Pacific to the fifty-first parallel. Adams had protested to the Russian minister in summer 1823, so Monroe simply reiterated the axiom that "the American continents, by the free and independent condition which they have assumed and maintain, are henceforth not to be considered as subjects for future colonization by any European powers." By implication, the noncolonization principle also applied to England and the Holy Alliance.

Monroe's second principle, "hands off," posited the notion of two different worlds. He observed that the monarchical system of the Old World "is essentially different from that of America" and warned that "any attempt" by the European powers to "extend their system to any portion of this hemisphere" would be regarded as "dangerous to our peace and safety" and "unfriendly" to the United States. As for the final principle, abstention, Monroe echoed Washington's Farewell Address: "In the wars of the European powers in matters relating to themselves we have never taken any part, nor does it comport with our policy to do so."

An implicit corollary to the Monroe Doctrine, although not mentioned in the address, was the principle of "no transfer." Earlier that same year, in response to reports that Britain might negotiate the cession of Cuba from Spain, Adams had informed both the Spaniards and the Cubans that the United States opposed British annexation. "Cuba," Adams wrote in April 1823, "forcibly disjoined from its own unnatural connection with Spain, and incapable of self-support, can only gravitate towards the North American Union, which by the same law of nature cannot cast her off from its bosom." Thus, in the context of Adams's concern over Cuba, the noncolonization principle in the Monroe Doctrine also warned Spain against transferring its colony to England or to any other European power.

The immediate effect of Monroe's message was hardly earthshaking. Brave words, after all, would not prevent the dismemberment of Latin America. The Polignac Memorandum and the British navy actually took care of such a contingency. The Holy Allies sneered, calling Monroe's principles "haughty," "arrogant," "blustering," and "monstrous." Realizing that Monroe and Adams might steal his thunder and turn Latin gratitude into Yankee trade opportunities, Canning rushed copies of the Polignac Memorandum to Latin American capitals to show that England, not the upstart Yankees, had thwarted any possible intervention. Latin Americans at first received the Monroe Doctrine cordially. When Washington refused to negotiate military alliances with Colombia and Brazil, however, disillusionment quickly set in. At home, most Americans applauded Monroe's message for its "explicit and manly tone," which "has evidently found in every bosom a chord which vibrates in strict unison." In France, the Marquis de Lafayette called it "the best little bit of paper that God ever permitted any man to give to the World."

Adams knew that the United States lacked the power to back up the words with deeds. Later generations talked less about matching commitment and power and more about Monroe's words as justifying U.S. expansion in the name of hemispheric solidarity. Indeed, from the beginning, Monroe's message—"a vague statement of policy, a lecture, a doctrine, an ideal"—pledged the United States "only to its own self-interest."

Trade, Canada, and Other Anglo-American Intersections

For years after the Monroe Doctrine, because of commercial rivalry in Latin America, squabbles over West Indian trade, politics in Canada, boundary disputes, and British attempts to suppress the international slave trade, most Americans continued to regard Britain as *the* principal threat to the national interest. As co-occupant of the North American continent, supreme naval power in the world, and commercial giant, only England could block U.S. expansion.

Still, just as in the 1790s, the intertwining of the two economies lessened the odds that "some tempest may suddenly arise." In 1825, for example, the United States exported $37 million in goods to England, out of total exports valued at $91 million; by 1839 the figures stood at $57 million and $112 million. The burgeoning British textile industry came to depend on American cotton. Imports from Britain during the 1820s and 1830s fluctuated between one-half and one-third of total U.S. imports. In 1825, 18 percent of total British exports went to the United States; in 1840, 10 percent. In those same years England received 13 percent and 27 percent of its total imports from America.

These figures, combined with the British decision in 1830 to open the West Indies to direct trade with the United States, reflected a growing British trend toward free trade, which in the 1840s meant dismantling imperial "preferences," repealing protective tariffs, and concentrating on manufactured exports. Anglo-American economic interdependence acted as a brake against military hostilities. Despite commercial rivalry, Britons and Yankees sometimes cooperated to reduce costs. In faraway ports such as Singapore and Hong Kong, U.S. merchants relied on British bills of exchange and letters of credit and on the services of British agents. "Wherever English enterprise goes, ours is quickly alongside it," remarked an American diplomat who understood both the competitive and cooperative features of the relationship.

The years immediately following the War of 1812 marked a high point in Anglo-American relations, thanks largely to the conciliatory diplomacy of John Quincy Adams and Lord Castlereagh. After signing the Treaty of Ghent, Adams, Albert Gallatin, and Henry Clay went directly to London and negotiated a commercial treaty with the British Board of Trade in 1815. A reciprocal trade agreement, it repeated the trade terms of Jay's Treaty. The accord also forbade discriminatory duties by either country against the other, thus tacitly conceding the failure of Jefferson's "peaceable coercions." The accord said nothing about impressment or neutral rights. The two nations renewed this commercial convention in 1818 for ten more years.

War's end also found the British and Americans engaged in feverish warship construction on the Great Lakes. Confident that the United States could build vessels quickly in a crisis, the Monroe administration proposed a standstill agreement to the British. Much to the dismay of the Canadians, Castlereagh agreed. By the Rush-Bagot agreement, negotiated in Washington in April 1817, each country pledged to maintain not more than one armed ship on Lake Champlain, another on Lake Ontario, and two on all the other Great Lakes. The Rush-Bagot accord applied only to warships and left land fortifications intact. Although the "unguarded frontier" between Canada and the United States did not become reality until the Treaty of Washington in 1871, the Rush-Bagot agreement ranks as one of the world's first successful disarmament treaties.

The Convention of 1818, negotiated in London by Richard Rush and Albert Gallatin, dealt with the fisheries and the northwestern boundary. In an effort to settle the vaguely defined limits of the Louisiana Purchase, the Americans initially proposed to extend the boundary westward from Lake of the Woods to the Pacific

Ocean along the line of 49° north latitude. Because Britain refused to abandon its claims to the Columbia River Basin, the convention stipulated that the boundary should run from Lake of the Woods to the "Stony Mountains" along the forty-ninth parallel. Beyond the Rockies, for a period of ten years, subject to renewal, the Oregon territory should remain "free and open" to both British and American citizens. As for the vexatious matter of the Atlantic fisheries, the 1818 agreement won confirmation of the "liberty" to fish "for ever" along specific stretches of the Newfoundland and Labrador coasts, as well as to dry and cure fish along other areas of the same coastline. Secretary Adams accepted the agreement as vindication of his family's honor. Not for nothing was the motto on the Adams family seal "We will fish and hunt as heretofore."

After the Monroe Doctrine, Canning hoped to minimize friction with Washington. "Let us hasten settlement, if we can," he wrote, "but let us postpone the day of difference, if it must come." Yet a series of crises disrupted relations. Most important was the Canadian rebellion of 1837, led by William Lyon Mackenzie. Some Americans cheered the Canadian quest for self-government and volunteered. Coming a year after the Texas war for independence, the Canadian rebellion also revived expansionist visions of 1812. Rensselaer Van Rensselaer, son of an American general, tried to become a Canadian version of Sam Houston, leading Canadian rebels and American sympathizers on raids into Canada from New York.

In December 1837 pro-British Canadians struck Van Rensselaer's stronghold on Navy Island in the Niagara River, hoping to capture the rebel supply ship *Caroline*. The troops crossed to the American shore, found the forty-five-ton *Caroline*, set it afire, and cast it adrift to sink a short distance above the great falls. During the fracas an American, Amos Durfee, died. Durfee's body was displayed before 3,000 mourners at Buffalo city hall. Angry demonstrators in Lewiston, New York, made a bonfire of books by British authors. In May 1838 some Americans boarded the Canadian steamboat *Sir Robert Peel,* plying the St. Lawrence River. They burned and looted the vessel, shouting "Remember the *Caroline!*" Raids and counterraids continued through 1838. President Martin Van Buren sent General Winfield Scott to the New York–Ontario border to restore quiet. Scott brooked no nonsense. "Except if it be over my body," he shouted to an unruly crowd, "you shall not pass this line—you shall not embark." When Mackenzie and Van Rensselaer fled to the American border, local authorities quickly arrested them, and the rebellion petered out.

Agitation spread to northern Maine in February 1839. The vast timberlands spanning the Maine–New Brunswick border had long provoked diplomatic dispute because of cartographic "doubts" in the 1783 peace treaty. In the mid-1830s, settlers moved to the fertile Aroostook Valley. Rival claims and occasional brawls ensued. Soon axe-wielding lumberjacks became embroiled in the "Aroostook War." Maine mobilized its militia, as did New Brunswick, and Congress appropriated some $10 million for defense. It seemed an opportunity to whip the "Warriors of Waterloo." As the "Maine Battle Song" had it: "Britannia shall not rule the Maine, / Nor shall she rule the water; / They've sung that song full long enough, / Much longer than they oughter." The "war" did not last long. After a few tense weeks the British minister and Secretary of State John Forsyth negotiated a temporary armistice pending a final boundary settlement. The only American death came at

Daniel Webster (1782–1852).
A famed constitutional lawyer from Massachusetts, Webster served as a member of Congress (1823–1827), a U.S. senator (1827–1841), and secretary of state (1841–1843). He helped settle the northeastern boundary dispute. As a senator again in 1845–1850, he opposed the acquisition of Texas and the War with Mexico. From 1850 until his death, this imposing political figure sat once more as secretary of state. (National Portrait Gallery, Smithsonian Institution/Art Resource, N.Y.)

the very end when a Maine militiaman, firing his musket in celebration of the peace, accidentally killed a farmer working his field.

Any possibility that Americans would forget the *Caroline* affair soon disappeared in November 1840, when a Canadian grocer named Alexander McLeod allegedly bragged that he personally had killed Amos Durfee. New York State authorities quickly arrested McLeod and charged him with murder and arson. British foreign secretary Lord Palmerston fulminated that McLeod's execution "would produce . . . a war of retaliation and vengeance." Anglo-American amity nonetheless survived this crisis. McLeod produced credible witnesses who swore that he had not participated in the *Caroline* raid. The jurors believed the witnesses, and McLeod went free.

Within a month of McLeod's acquittal, another crisis erupted. In November 1841, a cargo of slaves being transported from Hampton Roads to New Orleans mutinied and took control of the American vessel *Creole,* killing one white man. The slaves sought refuge at Nassau in the Bahamas, where British authorities liberated all but the actual murderers. Southerners demanded retribution. The Supreme Court recently had passed judgment on the similar case of the Spanish slaver *Amistad,* in which fifty-three African captives killed the captain and crew in Cuban waters in 1839 and then attempted unsuccessfully to sail to Africa. U.S. authorities seized the *Amistad* off Long Island and jailed the Africans in New Haven, Connecticut. Despite Spain's demand for the return of "property" under existing treaties, John Quincy Adams, acting as a private attorney with strong backing from northern abolitionists, won freedom for the *Amistad* blacks on the basis of their natural rights as "kidnapped Africans" since Spain had outlawed the African slave trade in 1820. Nonetheless, the *Creole* affair seemed more explosive because it involved legal American slaves freed by the British, whose efforts to suppress the international slave trade often collided with America's refusal to permit its vessels to be searched. Southern outrage at the loss of honor and slaves forced Secretary Webster to demand the return of *Creole* mutineers to stand trial. As the U.S. minister to France pointedly asked: Who made John Bull the "great Prefect of police on the ocean?"

Thus did a long list of troubles beset Anglo-American relations in 1842. The northeastern boundary remained in contest. Britain had not apologized for the *Caroline* affair. British interest in Oregon and Texas worried Americans, who disliked British snobbery. British visitors, most notably Charles Dickens, wrote scathingly of American manners and morals. But the time seemed ripe for the settlement of many of these issues. A new Tory government took office in September 1841, and Lord Aberdeen, a conciliatory protégé of Castlereagh, replaced the cantankerous Palmerston at the Foreign Office. Aberdeen appointed as a special envoy to Washington the accommodating Lord Ashburton, who had opposed British maritime restrictions before the War of 1812. Beetle-browed Daniel Webster reciprocated Ashburton's amicability. Indeed, Webster had long acted as the American legal agent for Ashburton's banking firm, often earning a good salary through British commissions. Three years earlier the erudite and eloquent orator, then at the peak of his political career, had toured England, dined with Queen Victoria, and won wide acclaim. The two diplomats met leisurely in summer 1842, feasted on Maine salmon, Virginia terrapin, Maryland crabs, and Chesapeake duck, and produced the Webster-Ashburton Treaty, signed and approved in August.

The Anglo-American agreement drew a new Maine boundary. Far enough south to permit a British military road between New Brunswick and Quebec, the border was still considerably north of Britain's maximum demand. The United States received approximately 7,000 of the 12,000 square miles under dispute. Farther west Webster won most of the contested territory near the headwaters of the Connecticut River, as well as a favorable boundary from Lake Superior to Lake of the Woods. Included in the latter acquisition was the valuable iron ore of the Mesabi Range in Minnesota. Although not part of the treaty per se, notes expressing mutual regrets over the *Caroline* and *Creole* affairs were exchanged by the diplomats, and in 1853 a joint claims commission awarded $110,330 to owners of the freed slaves.

Webster's discussions with Ashburton seemed simple compared with his subsequent diplomacy with Maine and Massachusetts. The Bay State had retained half ownership in Maine's public domain after the latter had become a separate state in 1820, and so Webster enticed both states to approve the new boundary through dubious cartographic persuasion. One of Webster's friends was Jared Sparks, a historian who later became president of Harvard. Sparks had been researching the diplomacy of the American Revolution in the British archives, and he told Webster he had seen the original map on which Benjamin Franklin had drawn a strong red line delineating the northeast boundary. From memory Sparks reproduced the line on a nineteenth-century map, and it corresponded closely to British claims. A second map turned up, older but still not genuine, also supporting the British position. Accepting both spurious maps as authentic, Webster sent Sparks to Augusta and Boston with this new "evidence" to persuade local officials to accept the treaty before the British reneged. Webster also offered each state $150,000. Maine and Massachusetts quickly endorsed the treaty.

The original maps used in the 1782 peace negotiations actually did have lines that supported American boundary claims. Palmerston had found one such authentic map in 1839 but said nothing. A second map showed up in the Jay family papers in 1843. But the lines on these maps seemed preliminary rather than definitive, as Webster later recognized, not at all "drawn for the purpose of shewing [*sic*] on the map, a boundary which had been agreed on." Thus, by reasonable compromise, "a good and wise measure," in Ashburton's words, did 3,207,680 acres of Maine woodland become part of Canada.

Contest Over Oregon

The Webster-Ashburton negotiations did not settle the question of the "Oregon country"—that great wilderness west of the Rocky Mountains and between the forty-second parallel in the South and 54°40 in the North. Webster proposed yielding territory north of the Columbia River if the British would, first, offer a tract of land adjoining the Strait of Juan de Fuca, which Webster believed had the best deepwater ports in the disputed territory, and, second, persuade Mexico to sell Upper California. Ashburton declined.

That same year, 1842, saw the beginning of "Oregon fever," as farmers began to arrive in the lush Willamette Valley. Oregon suddenly became controversial. In 1843 the Senate called for forts along the Oregon route, but the House demurred.

When rumors leaked of Webster's offer to surrender some of Oregon, numerous "Oregon conventions" met, especially in the Midwest, to reassert America's claim to 54°40. "Thirty thousand rifles in Oregon will annihilate the Hudson's Bay Company," bellowed Thomas Hart Benton. The Democratic party platform of 1844 called for the "reoccupation" of Oregon, and the party's candidate, James K. Polk, vowed to effect it. At stake was not only the fate of U.S. citizens living in the contested lands but also ports for ships plying waters to Asian markets, especially after the Treaty of Wangxia opened more of China to U.S. vessels.

In actuality, war over Oregon lacked urgency. The American population in Oregon, increasing every year, still numbered only 5,000 people in 1845, and all but a handful lived south of the Columbia River. In contrast, the 700-odd trappers and traders associated with the Hudson's Bay Company all lived north of the river. Four times, in 1818, 1824, 1826, and 1844, the British had proposed the Columbia as the boundary. Each time the United States had countered with 49°. The dispute centered on the triangle northwest of the Columbia, including the deepwater Strait of Juan de Fuca. Notwithstanding shouts of "Fifty-four forty or fight," only a minority of the Democratic party, mainly Midwesterners, seemed eager to challenge England. Southern Democrats cared more for Texas than for Oregon. A few Whigs, such as Webster, wanted Pacific ports but not at the risk of war. Even though Polk had won election on an expansionist platform, the new president had ample opportunity to settle the Oregon boundary through diplomacy.

Polk began badly. Asserting full U.S. claims, he announced in his inaugural address that the American title to the whole of Oregon was "clear and unquestionable." This claim raised British hackles. Polk, it seems, was talking more for domestic consumption, for in July Secretary of State James Buchanan proposed the forty-ninth parallel as a fair compromise. Buchanan's offer, however, did not include free navigation of the Columbia River, and this omission, coupled with Polk's earlier blustering about 54°40, caused British minister Richard Pakenham to reject the proposal. Polk waited several weeks. Then, on August 30, despite tensions with Mexico over Texas, he withdrew his offer and reasserted American claims to 54°40.

Polk increased the pressure in his annual message to Congress of December 1845. Again claiming all of Oregon, he urged giving Britain the necessary year's notice for ending joint occupation and hinted at military measures to protect Americans in Oregon. Polk also cited the Monroe Doctrine: "The United States cannot in silence permit any European interference on the North American continent, and should any such interference be attempted [the United States] will be ready to resist it at any and all hazards." Polk was pointedly warning Britain.

For the next five months Polk remained publicly adamant for 54°40. Twice London offered to arbitrate; each time Washington refused. Lord Aberdeen already had begun a propaganda campaign in the London *Times* designed to prepare public opinion for the loss of the Columbia River triangle. It helped when the Hudson's Bay Company, with American settlers flooding into the Willamette Valley, decided in 1845 to abandon "trapped-out" southern Oregon and move its main depot from the Columbia River north to Vancouver Island. Still, the foreign secretary threatened offensive military preparations in Canada, including the immediate dispatch of "thirty sail of the line." In late February 1846, Polk replied that if the British proposed "extending the boundary to the Pacific by the forty-ninth parallel and the Strait of Fuca," he would send the proposition to the Senate, "though with reluctance."

The British proposal dutifully arrived in early June. Before signing the treaty, however, Polk submitted it to the Senate for *previous* advice, thus placing the onus for the settlement squarely on the Senate and camouflaging his own retreat from 54°40. The Senate advised Polk, by a vote of 38 to 12, to accept the British offer. On June 15, 1846, the president formally signed the treaty, which the Senate then approved, 41 to 14. Compromise came so willingly, of course, because war with Mexico had begun some six weeks earlier.

The Texas Revolution and Annexation

The acquisition of Texas pushed the United States and Mexico toward war. The United States had confirmed Spanish claims to this northernmost province of Mexico in the Adams-Onís Treaty of 1819, but the self-denial was only temporary. After Mexico won independence from Spain in 1821, two U.S. envoys attempted to purchase the area. The first, South Carolinian Joel Poinsett, involved himself in local politics in the late 1820s and tried to work through friendly liberals in the Mexican congress. His successor, Anthony Butler, an unscrupulous crony of Andrew Jackson, tried bribery. Both efforts came to naught. As with Oregon and Florida, transborder migration became the chief engine of U.S. expansion.

Large-scale American settlement did not begin until the 1820s. Spanish authorities, in 1821, hoping to build up Texas as a buffer against U.S. expansion, had encouraged immigration through generous grants of land. Moses Austin and his son Stephen became the first empresarios by pledging to bring in 300 families, who, in turn, would swear allegiance to Spain and the Catholic faith. The new Mexican government confirmed these grants and issued others. Within a decade, some 20,000 Americans had crossed into Texas seeking homesteads—more people than had settled in the previous three centuries. Most of the "G.T.T." (Gone to Texas) were slaveholders seeking the fertile delta soil along the Gulf coast to grow cotton. Mexican inhabitants soon discerned American racial prejudice.

Friction occurred. The newcomers, required by law to become Roman Catholics and Mexican citizens, remained predominantly Protestant and never ceased to think of themselves as Americans. Sporadic trouble erupted over immigration, tariffs, slavery, and Mexican army garrisons. Finally, General Antonio López de Santa Anna seized dictatorial power in 1834 and established a strong centralized government in Mexico City. Regarding this change as a violation of their rights under the Mexican Constitution of 1824, American settlers resisted. By autumn 1835, Texans had skirmished with local Mexican soldiers, set up a provisional government, and begun raising a rebel army under Sam Houston.

Santa Anna responded by leading a large force north across the Rio Grande. At the old Alamo mission in San Antonio, some 200 Texans stood off 1,800 Mexicans for nearly two weeks. Then, on March 6, 1836, Santa Anna's forces broke through the Alamo's defenses and killed every resister, including the legendary Davy Crockett and James Bowie. Three weeks later another Texan force surrendered at Goliad. The Mexicans promptly executed more than three hundred. These atrocities

Stephen F. Austin (1793–1836). Born in Virginia, educated in Connecticut and Kentucky, Austin grew up in Missouri, with its polyglot population of Indians, French, Spaniards, Anglo-Americans, and African Americans. As the founder of Anglo-American Texas, Austin speculated in land, displaced Native Americans, introduced slavery, learned Spanish, became a loyal Mexican citizen, and rebelled only when Santa Anna drastically limited Texas self-government. (Courtesy, Center for American History, University of Texas at Austin. Prints and Photographs Collection, CN01436)

enraged North Americans, hundreds of whom joined Sam Houston's army, which retreated eastward. The showdown came on April 21, 1836, when Houston's force, now numbering 800, turned and attacked the Mexican military near the San Jacinto River. Yelling "Remember the Alamo," the Texans charged across an open field, and routed the Mexicans, killing about 630 and capturing Santa Anna. Houston thereupon extracted a treaty from the Mexican leader that recognized Texas's independence and set a southern and western boundary at the Rio Grande. Mexico repudiated this agreement after Santa Anna's release, but the Battle of San Jacinto ensured Texas's independence.

Texas sought immediate annexation to the United States—"as a bride adorned for her espousals," in Houston's words. His good friend President Jackson certainly desired Texas, but by 1836 annexation had become a political taboo. The problem was slavery. Fervent continentalists such as John Quincy Adams saw as never before that expansion westward also meant the expansion of slavery. The balance in 1836 stood at thirteen slave states and thirteen free states. An alert politician, "Old Hickory" tiptoed. Not until eleven months after San Jacinto did Jackson even recognize Texas's independence. Jackson's successor, Martin Van Buren, also spurned annexation "out of deference to the [anti-slavery] prejudices of the North." Annexation slumbered until 1843, when unpopular President John Tyler seized on Texas as a vehicle for lifting his political fortunes. He successfully negotiated an annexation treaty with the Texans and submitted it to the Senate in April 1844.

Tyler, and later Polk, urged support for the absorption of Texas by playing on fears of British intrusion. To block American expansion, the British extended diplomatic recognition in 1840 to "the Band of outlaws who occupy Texas." Further, Texas could offer an alternative supply of cotton for England's textile factories. A low-tariff Lone Star Republic might grow into a large British market and, by example, stimulate southern states to push harder in Washington for tariff reduction. Certain Britishers also tried to persuade Texas to abolish slavery, a prospect that Texan leaders manipulated to gain British support against Mexico. England did arrange a truce between Mexico and Texas in 1842, and two years later Lord Aberdeen suggested an international agreement whereby Mexico would extend diplomatic recognition to Texas, and England, France, and the United States would guarantee the independence and existing borders of both Texas and Mexico. Mexico stubbornly refused any dealings with Texas. Not until May 1845, after a resolution for annexation had already passed the U.S. Congress, did Mexico agree to recognize Texas. Too late.

Such British maneuvers alarmed U.S. expansionists. The Tyler administration might have achieved annexation in 1844 had not Secretary of State John C. Calhoun injudiciously boasted that annexation would guard against the danger of abolition of slavery under British tutelage and extolled slavery as "essential to the peace, safety, and prosperity" of the South. He made pseudoscientific arguments that offended the British far less than they antagonized abolitionists and free soilers in the North. When the Senate voted on June 8, 1844, the tally was 35 to 16, a two-thirds majority *against* annexation.

Texas became central to the 1844 presidential campaign. Nominating James K. Polk of Tennessee, the Democrats fervently embraced expansion. The party platform promised the "reoccupation of Oregon and the re-annexation of Texas," implying that somehow the United States once owned Texas. The Whigs nominated Henry Clay, who warned that "Annexation and war with Mexico are identical." After a fierce campaign, Polk won by a margin of 170 to 105 in the Electoral College. Although people at the time considered the Democratic victory a mandate for expansion, other factors, including an abolitionist third-party candidate who took votes from Clay in the decisive state of New York, help explain Polk's victory. Thus, in one of the rare presidential elections in which foreign-policy issues predominated, voters had elected the candidate who would bring war. If Clay had won in 1844, he almost certainly would have kept peace with Mexico.

Even before Polk took office, the annexationists acted. The lame-duck Tyler suggested annexation by joint resolution (simple majorities of both houses). Opponents howled, demanding a two-thirds vote for a treaty in the Senate. Critics called it "an undisguised usurpation of power" and a "monstrous trap." But the annexationists had the votes—120 to 98 in the House, 27 to 25 in the Senate—and on March 1, 1845, Tyler signed the fateful measure. Five days later the Mexican envoy in Washington asked for his passport and went home.

Polk did not inherit an inevitable conflict with Mexico. Rather, the president made decisions and carried them out in ways that exacerbated already existing tension and made war difficult to avoid. Mexico had promised to sever diplomatic relations if the United States annexed Texas, but Polk compounded the problem by supporting Texas's flimsy claim to the Rio Grande as its boundary. Except for Santa Anna's treaty in 1836, the Nueces River had always stood as the accepted boundary, and Texas made no subsequent move to occupy the disputed territory south of Corpus Christi. During the negotiations to complete annexation in summer 1845, however, Polk's emissaries apparently urged Texas president Anson Jones to seize all territory to the Rio Grande. Polk also ordered U.S. military and naval forces to respond to any Mexican retaliation. At this time, too, the president sent secret orders to Commodore John D. Sloat of the Pacific Squadron to capture the main ports of California in the event that Mexico attacked Texas. Whether Polk actively sought to provoke war or merely used force to buttress diplomacy, his unilateral decisions disregarded Mexican sensibilities and ignored congressional prerogatives.

When Mexico did not retaliate, Polk again tried diplomacy. He had received word from the U.S. consul in Mexico City that the government, although furious at annexation, did not want war and would receive a special emissary to discuss Texas. Polk sent John Slidell, a Louisiana Democrat, as a full minister plenipotentiary empowered to negotiate issues other than Texas. California now loomed larger in Polk's mind than Texas. No sooner had the president instructed Slidell to purchase New Mexico and California for $25 million than a report arrived from Consul Thomas Larkin in Monterey describing in lurid terms British machinations to turn California into a protectorate. This misinformation prompted Polk to conclude that "Texas must immediately become American or [it] will soon be British." He thus instructed Larkin to inspire Californians "with a jealousy of European dominion and to arouse in their bosoms that love of liberty and independence so natural to the American Continent." These same orders also reached Lieutenant John C. Frémont, head of a U.S. Army exploring party in eastern California, who interpreted the instructions as

a command to foment insurrection among American settlers. This Frémont proceeded to do in the summer of 1846, vowing that "we must be first."

Despite Polk's optimism, the Slidell mission failed. Mexican officials refused to
receive the envoy because his title of minister plenipotentiary suggested prior acceptance of Texas's annexation. Even if Slidell had made the monetary offer for California, no Mexican leader could sell territory to the United States without inviting
charges of treason. Any offer to purchase California, coming so closely on the heels
of Texas's annexation, seemed out of the question. War seemed preferable. "Nothing is to be done with these people," Slidell arrogantly reported, "until they have
been chastised."

Polk responded in January 1846 by ordering General Taylor south from Corpus
Christi to occupy the left bank of the Rio Grande. Even though Polk initially regarded this action as added pressure on Mexico to negotiate, Mexicans interpreted
it as aggression. Taylor blockaded Matamoros, itself an act of war under international
law. The Mexicans retaliated. The first clash occurred on April 24, and Polk could
present Congress with a fait accompli.

The War with Mexico and the Treaty of Guadalupe Hidalgo

Polk gambled on a short war. California and the Rio Grande boundary were his
principal objectives, and he was willing to explore diplomatic alternatives. Shortly
after hostilities broke out, the president conferred with an emissary of Santa Anna,
then in exile in Cuba. Santa Anna promised that if the United States helped him return to Mexico he would help Polk get the territory he desired. After apparently
agreeing to terms, Santa Anna in August 1846 slipped through the U.S. naval blockade and landed at Veracruz. A revolution propitiously occurred in Mexico City making Santa Anna president. Instead of making peace, however, the self-proclaimed
Napoleon of the West marched his army north to fight General Taylor. Only belatedly did Polk understand that he had been conned.

Another diplomatic opportunity presented itself in November 1846 in the persons of Moses Y. Beach and Jane McManus Storm. Beach, a Democratic editor and
chief drumbeater for Manifest Destiny, had contacts in the Mexican army and the
Mexican Catholic hierarchy. He persuaded Polk to appoint him a confidential agent
to Mexico, empowered to negotiate a peace that would include, in addition to Texas
and California, the right to build a canal across the Isthmus of Tehuantepec. Beach
then journeyed to Veracruz and Mexico City, accompanied by Storm, the "manifest
destiny" advocate whose friendships with prominent Texans, fluency in Spanish, and
personal contacts with the Polk administration made her "the author of the entire
episode." Storm gained fame as publicist, lobbyist, political fixer, and participant in
various expansionist projects from the 1830s to the 1860s. Once in Mexico City,
however, she and Beach rashly joined a clerical uprising against Santa Anna. The rebellion collapsed, along with hopes for a quick peace. The two Americans fled to
the cover of U.S. forces in Tampico.

President Polk finally decided in spring 1847 to send an accredited State Department representative along with General Winfield Scott's army. He selected Nicholas P. Trist, chief clerk of the department, a man of impeccable Democratic credentials, who could also keep a watchful eye on the politically ambitious Scott, a Whig. Polk immediately regretted his choice. When Trist reached the U.S. army, he quarreled furiously with the "utterly incompetent" Scott, who resented Trist's power to decide when hostilities should cease. The two men did not speak to one another for six weeks, communicating only through vituperative letters. Then Trist fell ill, and Scott chivalrously sent a box of guava marmalade to speed his recovery. Almost overnight the two prickly prima donnas resolved to work together.

By this time, September 1847, Scott's troops had battered their way to Mexico City, and the diplomat and warrior sought peace with any Mexican faction that would negotiate. Polk, angry that Trist had forwarded to Washington a Mexican peace proposal that still insisted on the Nueces as the Texas boundary, summarily recalled his unruly representative. The president now seemed in no hurry to end the war. Military successes had made it possible to obtain more territory than he had originally coveted—perhaps Lower as well as Upper California, the Isthmus of Tehuantepec, and Mexico's northern provinces. Polk even contemplated the absorption of all Mexico. Some expansionists depicted the "spoils of war" in gendered terms, arguing that soldiers could intermarry with Mexican women and thus "regenerate" Mexico by "gradually infusing vigor into the race."

Trist now took an extraordinary step. He refused his own recall. Trist believed deeply in the promise of Manifest Destiny, "confident that Mexico, left to herself, would someday enter the temple of freedom." But such a process could not be hurried. Reconciliation had to come first. Any peace that demanded too much would violate this canon. Even before he received his recall notice, Trist had begun to treat with a moderate faction that had come to power. These Mexicans urged him to remain. Scott concurred. Trist thereupon informed Polk, in a bristling sixty-five-page letter, that he was continuing peace talks under his original instructions. Polk grew splenetic. "I have never in my life felt so indignant," he told his diary.

Trist concluded his peace treaty, signed on February 2, 1848, at Guadalupe Hidalgo, near Mexico City. Mexico ceded California and New Mexico and confirmed the annexation of Texas with the Rio Grande as the boundary. In return, the United States paid $15 million and assumed the claims of U.S. citizens totaling another $3.25 million. The president reluctantly submitted the accord to the Senate, notwithstanding that "Mr. Trist has acted very badly." The territorial gains comprised all Polk had empowered Slidell to obtain in his 1845–1846 mission. "If I were now to reject a treaty," Polk explained, "made upon my own terms . . . the probability is that Congress would not grant either men or money to prosecute the war." The Whig-dominated Senate had just passed a resolution praising Taylor's victories in "a war unnecessarily and unconstitutionally begun by the President of the United States." Despite their distaste for territory by conquest, as one Whig noted, the choice was "between the continuance of an expensive & unfortunate war & a *bad* treaty—the people want peace." The treaty thereupon passed the Senate, 38 to 14, on March 10, 1848.

Abraham Lincoln (1809–1865). As a one-term Whig member of Congress from Illinois, Lincoln strongly opposed the extension of slavery into new territories and called war with Mexico a "war of conquest." Lincoln dismissed Polk's attempt to blame the war on Mexico as the "half insane mumbling of a fever-dream." This 1846 daguerreotype photo by N. H. Shepherd is the earliest known of Lincoln. (Library of Congress)

War with Mexico swelled the membership of pacifist organizations such as the American Peace Society, which offered a $500 prize for the best essay analyzing the war. Yet the antiwar forces in Congress, consisting largely of Whigs and Calhoun Democrats, made little impact. Opponents at first criticized the questionable way in which Polk had begun the war, and they later rallied against any administration effort to take "All Mexico." Polk struck back at his critics by suggesting that they were aiding the enemy, citing the Constitution's definition of treason. Few opponents voted against military supplies. As one Whig phrased it: "We support the war, though we condemn those who have brought us into it." A war, right or wrong, which Congress had voted for, had to be upheld.

The Wilmot Proviso sparked the most ominous debates of the war. Attached as a rider to the war appropriation bill of August 1846 by Democrat David Wilmot of Pennsylvania, the proviso held that no territory acquired from Mexico should be open to slavery. Its supporters consisted almost exclusively of northerners, and a coalition of Southern Whigs and administration Democrats sufficed to defeat it. Nonetheless, the Wilmot Proviso was introduced again and again, never passing but arousing increasingly partisan emotions and causing southerners such as Calhoun to despair for the Union.

The Lessons and Costs of Expansion, 1815–1848

The United States gained more than 50,000 square miles of territory in the war against Mexico. Polk did not obtain "All Mexico," but he had taken what he wanted: Texas and California. The casualties: 1,721 Americans killed in battle and 11,550 deaths from other causes, mainly disease. At least 50,000 Mexicans died.

The war brought other ugly consequences not so easily quantified. The arrogant rationalizations for expansion appalled an old Jeffersonian such as Albert Gallatin, who noted: "All these allegations of superiority of race and destiny neither require nor deserve any answer; they are pretences [*sic*] . . . to disguise ambitions, cupidity, or silly vanity." John C. Calhoun had warned in 1847 that "Mexico is to us the forbidden fruit" because "eating it" would "subject our institutions . . . to political death." Debates over the Wilmot Proviso raised the all-important question whether the new territories would become free or slave. It took two more decades and a bloody civil war to answer the question. In fact, the issue of race in the 1850s blocked additional acquisitions in the Caribbean or Pacific. Such potential prizes as Cuba or Hawai'i had racially mixed populations and thus seemed less adaptable to American settlers and institutions than did the less populated prairies of North America.

The American Indian became a casualty of westward expansion. "Land enough—Land enough! Make way, I say, for the young American Buffalo!" shouted one fervent orator in 1844. Native Americans had to give way. While white Americans in the 1820s and 1830s settled fertile lands in Texas and Oregon, other farmers were encroaching on Indian lands east of the Mississippi. Despite treaties, the federal government removed most Native Americans in the Old Northwest and Southwest to new reservations in Oklahoma and Missouri. It became a brutal process—a "trail of tears." Forced to march thousands of miles, robbed by federal

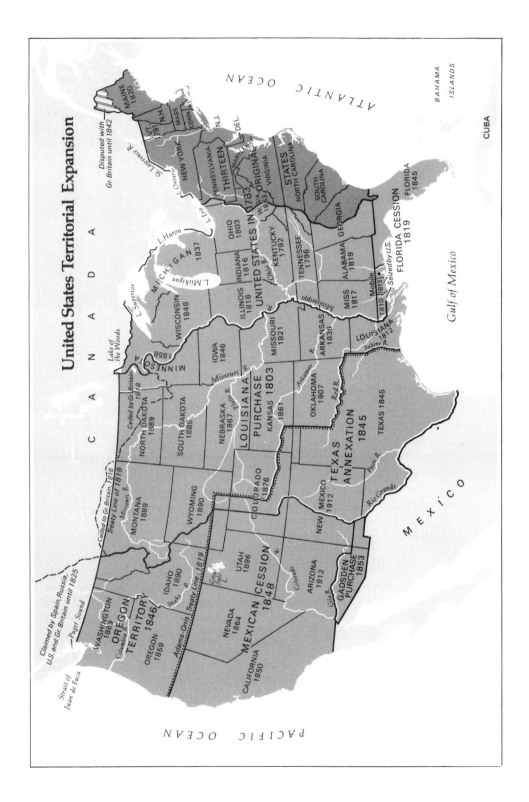

United States Territorial Expansion

"The Trail of Tears." Robert Lindneux's poignant painting of Indian removal illustrates a tragic consequence of U.S. expansion. Of the 100,000 Indians transported beyond the Mississippi between 1824 and 1845, one-fourth to one-third died during or shortly after the forced marches. (From the original oil painting at Woolaroc Museum, Bartlesville, Oklahoma)

and state officials, ravaged by disease, some resisted, as evidenced the guerrilla warfare waged by the Seminoles in the Everglades for nearly a decade. The Seminole War finally ended in 1842 with the order: "Find the enemy, capture, or exterminate." In the case of the Creeks, the population in 1860 comprised only 40 percent of what it had been thirty years earlier. Other Indians suffered similar losses. The roughly 486,000 Native Americans beyond the Mississippi would feel the crunch of empire after 1848.

Defeated Mexico relinquished more than half of its national territory and saw large amounts of real estate, foodstuffs, art treasures, and livestock destroyed by the invading armies. A Mexican scholar, Jorge Castañeda, has suggested that Mexico, by waging war rather than ceding half the national patrimony to John Slidell, ultimately kept Sonora, Chihuahua, and Baja California from becoming American, and thus "fighting and losing proved to be a better deal than selling and perhaps losing far more."

The invaders treated Mexicans as they did the Indians—as racial inferiors. General John Quitman called Mexico's 8 million inhabitants "beasts of burden, with as little intellect as the asses whose burdens they share." The multiracial, multicultural Hispanic "frontier of inclusion" that had welcomed American settlers gave way to an Anglo-American "frontier of exclusion." Mexicans who had lived in Texas lost most of their lands through fraud and outright confiscation, and the *corridos* (folk ballads) of the border region excoriated the Texas Rangers as *"los tejanos sangrientes"* ("bloody Texans")—killers of Mexicans who "spared neither age nor sex in their terrible fury." Tumultuous Mexico had to endure another twenty-five years of rebellion, civil war, and European intervention before attaining a degree of national unity under the authoritarian regime of Porfirio Díaz. The war increased the disparity in size, power, and population between the United States and Mexico, creating long-standing attitudes of suspicion, distrust, and prejudice on both sides of the border.

The success of continental expansion left one obvious imprint on the United States—that of increased power. No country had grown so fast as the United States, "the *wunderkind* nation of the nineteenth century." No longer "a low-rung power with little international clout," the United States had become dominant within the hemisphere, as evidenced by the growth of the Monroe Doctrine. President Monroe had hurled his defiant message in 1823 without the power to enforce it. When Britain seized the Falkland Islands in 1833 and the French bombarded Mexican ports in 1838, U.S. leaders did nothing. In 1842, however, President Tyler specifically warned England and France against annexing Hawai'i. Three years later Polk arrogantly invoked the Monroe Doctrine in proclaiming U.S. rights to Texas, California, and Oregon. As U.S. power continued to increase after 1848, as economic interests began to focus on the Caribbean and the possibility of an isthmian canal, U.S. diplomats would repeatedly invoke the Monroe Doctrine. The same mixture of motives that operated in the 1820s would continue—namely, a studied desire to forestall European interference, combined with a wish to extend U.S. influence throughout the hemisphere.

Polk told one member of Congress in 1846 that "the only way to treat John Bull was to look him straight in the eye." Polk's confrontational style seemed successful with both Britain and Mexico. Polk himself thought the war had boosted national prestige abroad by demonstrating that a democracy could prosecute a foreign war "with all the vigor" usually associated with "more arbitrary forms of government." As for the Tennessean's "lessons" for subsequent generations, Theodore Roosevelt considered Polk a model for reasserting strong executive leadership in foreign policy. So did Harry S. Truman. Polls of historians continue to rank Polk among the top ten presidents.

In fact, Polk was lucky. Unlike John Quincy Adams, whose forceful diplomacy against Spain and the Holy Alliance rested on a shrewd understanding of international power realities, Polk moved inexpertly against Mexico and Britain. Regarding Oregon, his initial call for 54°40 unnecessarily heightened tensions on both sides of the Atlantic and prevented any settlement until spring 1846. Given the concurrent crisis with Mexico, such a delay invited the disastrous possibility of a war on two fronts. British conciliation owed more to troubles at home—potato famine in Ireland, political turmoil over repeal of the Corn Laws—than to U.S. bravado. Aberdeen's sobering presence also helped. Had Palmerston become foreign secretary, Polk's "eyeball" tactics might have meant war. In the context of American immigration into the Pacific Northwest in 1844–1846, Calhoun's policy of "masterly inactivity" almost certainly would have produced a favorable settlement without risking war. Polk did not know what Castlereagh said a generation earlier: "You will conquer Oregon in your bedchambers."

"Masterly inactivity" might have worked with Mexico as well. Polk did not want war so much as he desired the fruits of war. He wanted California, New Mexico, and the Rio Grande boundary; and he hurried because he suspected British intrigues. Keeping Taylor's army at Corpus Christi would have protected Texas with little provocation to Mexico. Negotiations could resume when emotions cooled. As for California, Polk should have understood, after a careful reading of all diplomatic correspondence, that England had no serious intention of seizing that lucrative prize.

The president might have waited to see if the influx of American settlers would make California another Texas or Oregon. Annexation might have come peacefully during some subsequent European crisis such as the Crimean War. As it turned out, Polk's decision for war in the spring of 1846 was reckless while tensions with England remained so acute. War risked all the expansionist goals. A major Mexican victory might have brought a European loan to Mexico, military stalemate, and possible British mediation. He might have lost California. Polk was also lucky in Trist's treaty. Insistence on "All Mexico" might have led to the kind of protracted guerrilla war against U.S. occupation forces that Mexicans waged against French armies twenty years later (see Chapter 4). Overall, if Polk truly believed in Manifest Destiny, he should not have risked what Americans had long deemed inevitable. But because Polk ultimately succeeded in pushing American borders to the Pacific, the blemishes in his diplomatic record will probably continue to be covered with the cosmetic cream of national celebration.

FURTHER READING FOR THE PERIOD 1815–1848

For Manifest Destiny and expansionism, see Evan Cornog, *The Birth of Empire* (1998); Amy S. Greenberg, *Manifest Manhood and the Antebellum American Empire* (2005); Thomas R. Hietala, *Manifest Design* (2003); Reginald Horsman, *Race and Manifest Destiny* (1981); Howard Jones, *Mutiny on the* Amistad (1987); Robert F. May, *Manifest Destiny's Underworld* (2002); Frederick Merk, *Manifest Destiny and Mission in American History* (1963); Christopher Morris and Sam W. Haynes, eds., *Manifest Destiny and Empire* (1997); Michael A. Morrison, *Slavery and the American West* (1997); Gregory H. Nobles, *American Frontiers* (1997); Richard Slotkin, *Regeneration Through Violence* (1996); Anders Stephanson, *Manifest Destiny* (1995); William Earl Weeks, *Building the Continental Empire* (1996); Edward L. Widmer, *Young America* (1999); and Valarie H. Ziegler, *The Advocates of Peace in Antebellum America* (1992).

Leaders in this period are featured in John Buchanan, *Jackson's Way* (2001); Andrew Burstein, *The Passions of Andrew Jackson* (2003); Greg Cantrell, *Stephen F. Austin* (1999); Noble E. Cunningham, *The Presidency of James Monroe* (1996); William Dusinberre, *Slavemaster President* (2003) (Polk); John Eisenhower, *Agent of Destiny* (1997) (Scott); Sam W. Haynes, *James K. Polk and the Expansionist Impulse* (2002); Linda S. Hudson, *Mistress of Manifest Destiny* (2001) (Storm); Timothy D. Johnson, *Winfield Scott* (1998); Thomas Leonard, *James K. Polk* (2000); Willard C. Lunder, *Lewis Cass and the Politics of Moderation* (1996); John Niven, *John C. Calhoun and the Price of Union* (1988); Norma Lois Peterson, *The Presidencies of William Henry Harrison and John Tyler* (1989); Robert Remini, *Andrew Jackson and the Course of American Freedom* (1981) and *Henry Clay* (1991); and Major L. Wilson, *The Presidency of Martin Van Buren* (1984). For John Quincy Adams and Daniel Webster, see below.

For the U.S. Navy and explorations, see Kenneth J. Hagan, *This People's Navy* (1991); John H. Schroeder, *Shaping a Maritime Empire* (1985); Gene A. Smith, *Thomas ap Catesby Jones* (2000); and Herman Viola and Carolyn Margolis, eds., *Magnificent Voyages* (1985).

John Quincy Adams is treated in Samuel Flagg Bemis, *John Quincy Adams and the Foundations of American Foreign Policy* (1949); James E. Lewis, *John Quincy Adams* (2001); Robert P. Remini, *John Quincy Adams* (2003); and William E. Weeks, *John Quincy Adams and American Global Empire* (1992).

For the Floridas, the Adams-Onís Treaty, Latin America, and the Monroe Doctrine, see Philip C. Brooks, *Diplomacy and the Borderlands* (1939) (Adams-Onís); David S. Hendler and Jeane T. Hendler, *Old Hickory's War* (2003); John J. Johnson, *A Hemisphere Apart* (1990); Lester D. Langley, *The Americas in the Age of Revolution* (1996); James E. Lewis, *American Union and the Problem of Neighborhood* (1998); John Missall and Mary Lou Missall, *The Seminole Wars* (2004); and Gretchen Murphy, *Hemispheric Imaginings* (2005).

Daniel Webster is studied in Irving Bartlett, *Daniel Webster* (1978); Maurice G. Baxter, *One and Inseparable* (1984); and Robert Remini, *Daniel Webster* (1997).

Anglo-American issues, including Oregon and Canada, appear in Francis A. Carroll, *A Good and Wise Measure* (2001); Howard Jones, *To the Webster-Ashburton Treaty* (1977); Howard Jones and Donald Rakestraw, *Prologue to Manifest Destiny* (1997); Kenneth R. Stevens, *Border Diplomacy* (1989); and Reginald C. Stuart, *United States Expansionism and British North America, 1775–1871* (1988).

Texas, California, the War with Mexico, and President Polk are explored in Paul H. Bergeron, *The Presidency of James K. Polk* (1987); H. W. Brands, *Lone Star Nation* (2005); Michael Costeloe, *The Central Republic in Mexico, 1935-1846* (2002); William C. Davis, *Three Roads to the Alamo* (1998); John D. Eisenhower, *So Far from God* (1989) (War with Mexico); Richard Francaviglia and Douglas W. Richmond, eds., *Dueling Eagles* (2000); Donald S. Frazier, ed., *The United States and Mexico at War* (1999); Neal Harlow, *California Conquered* (1982); Robert W. Johannsen, *To the Halls of Montezuma* (1985); Jonathan W. Jordan, *Lone Star Navy* (2005); Dean Mahin, *Olive Branch and Sword* (1997); James F. McCaffrey, *Army of Manifest Destiny* (1992); Anna K. Nelson, *Secret Agents* (1988); Wallace Ohrt, *Defiant Peacemaker* (1998) (Trist); David M. Pletcher, *The Diplomacy of Annexation* (1973); Pedro Santoni, *Mexicans at Arms* (1996); John H. Schroeder, *Mr. Polk's War* (1973); and Richard B. Winders, *Mr. Polk's Army* (1997).

For encounters with Asia—especially China—see Jacques M. Downs, *The Golden Ghetto* (1997) (U.S.-China); Jonathan Goldstein et al., eds., *America Views China* (1991); Michael Hunt, *The Making of a Special Relationship* (1983); and John C. Perry, *Facing West* (1994).

See also Robert L. Beisner, ed., *Guide to American Foreign Relations Since 1600* (2003).

For comprehensive coverage of foreign-relations topics, see the articles in the four-volume *Encyclopedia of U.S. Foreign Relations* (1997), edited by Bruce W. Jentleson and Thomas G. Paterson.

CHAPTER 4

Expansionism, Sectionalism, and Civil War, 1848–1865

✳ William Walker and Filibustering in Central America, 1855–1860

"THERE ARE BUT a few men now living who occupy so much of the public mind as Gen. William Walker," a Kentucky newspaper proclaimed in 1858. "[He] is, indeed, the hero of the time." In the decade before the Civil War, this unprepossessing Tennesseean, "standing barely five feet four in his boots" and weighing only 115 pounds, gained notoriety as the most successful of American filibusters, those soldiers of fortune who attempted to grab territories through unauthorized and illegal attacks on sovereign nations. Walker won renown as the "grey-eyed man of destiny" because he allegedly fulfilled the prophecy that a "grey-eyed" man of the Anglo-Saxon race would rescue the indigenous peoples of Nicaragua from Spanish oppression.

This self-styled "regenerator of Central America" earned a physician's degree from the University of Pennsylvania, studied medicine in Paris, and edited a New Orleans newspaper before embarking on imperial schemes in Mexico and Nicaragua. Lured to California in 1850 by the gold rush, Walker hatched plans for an invasion of Baja California. Barely thirty years old in 1853, this soft-spoken young man marched forty-five companions into Mexican lands, captured the capital of La Paz, and declared himself president of a new republic. In little time, however, the invasion collapsed from faulty organization and discontent among Walker's followers. Arrested for violating U.S. neutrality laws, Walker won acquittal from an admiring San Francisco jury.

Walker next eyed Nicaragua, a country often mentioned as a route for an Isthmian canal. Hardly the agent of benevolent democratic Manifest Destiny that his admirers attempted to portray, he became a "freckle-faced despot" who sought to subjugate Nicaragua in 1855, 1857, 1858, and 1860. In contrast to travel writers

William Walker (1824–1860). The most infamous of American filibusters terrorized Latin American nations, ruled Nicaragua for a short time, and flouted U.S. law—all by the age of thirty-six. He fell before a firing squad and remains buried in an unmarked grave in Honduras. The journalist Horace Greeley called him the "Don Quixote of Central America." (National Portrait Gallery, Smithsonian Institution/Art Resource, N.Y.)

who extolled Nicaragua's fertile lands and scantily clad "señoritas" with "big lustrous eyes," Walker plundered and killed. In the first expedition, leading fifty-seven men ("immortals") whom he described as "tired of the humdrum of common life," he joined one side in a civil war, won promotion to commander in chief, and seized the presidency for himself. Apparently influenced by a visit from Louisiana's proslavery politician Pierre Soulé, Walker decreed the legal return of slavery. The U.S. minister in Nicaragua, North Carolina slaveholder John Hill Wheeler, abetted Walker because he believed that the "cotton, sugar, rice, corn, cocoa, indigo, etc., can never be developed without slave labor." Walker dreamed beyond Nicaragua: He wanted to build a Central American federation and then invade Cuba. Wheeler urged diplomatic recognition, hailing Walker as the vanguard of a superior white race that would "purify" the supposedly degenerate Nicaraguans, who would become "Americanized by the industrious and interprizing [*sic*] from the North." Reluctant at first to approve "a violent occupation of power, . . . as yet unsanctioned by . . . the people of Nicaragua," President Franklin Pierce officially recognized Walker's regime in 1856.

But Walker soon wobbled. He alienated Nicaraguans through pillaging and dictatorial orders, and his soldiers fell victim to frequent drunkenness and disease. When he brutally sacked the city of Granada in November 1856, he discouraged such potential recruits as future Confederate general P. G. T. Beauregard, who

"The Filibuster Polka."   This sheet music from 1852 is one example of how filibustering became part of popular culture in the decade before the Civil War. (Courtesy of the Music Division, Library of Congress)

rejected such "Vandalism [as] unworthy of the American character." Walker then antagonized the railroad magnate Cornelius Vanderbilt, whose Accessory Transit Company carried 2,000 Americans per month across the waist of Nicaragua and then, by steamship, to California. The powerful Vanderbilt backed Honduras, Guatemala, El Salvador, and Costa Rica when they took up arms against the intruding adventurer. As the tide turned, proslavery sympathizers blamed "black republicanism" of "the North" for the flow of arms and gold to Walker's opponents. In May 1857 the filibuster fled to the United States, claiming that he had been betrayed "for the paltry profits of a railroad company."

Walker returned to Nicaragua in November 1857, but marines from the U.S.S. *Wabash* forced his surrender. The "lion-hearted devil," when captured, "wept like a child" and eventually escaped prosecution. Walker's third effort, in 1858, ended ingloriously near British Honduras, where his ship ran aground on a coral reef. A British naval vessel returned the filibusters to the United States. Still claiming to be president of Nicaragua, the irrepressible Walker headed for his adopted country once again in spring 1860. This time he invaded Honduras first. Honduran troops inflicted heavy casualties, and Walker soon surrendered. "Will the South stand by and permit him to be shot down like a dog?" exhorted one southern woman. "If so, let her renounce her reputation for chivalry, valor, policy, or pride!" Such appeals went unheeded, and Walker died before a Honduran firing squad on September 12, 1860.

During his heyday Walker became a cultural "icon," as evidenced by the hit musical, *Nicaragua, or General Walker's Victory* at New York's Pardy's National Theater in

1856. Newspapers across the country reported his exploits. He became the subject of poems, novels, and songs. More than a century later in the Hollywood film *Walker* (1988), actor Ed Harris's performance in the title role reminded viewers of Lieutenant Colonel Oliver North, a Reagan-era American who also meddled in Nicaragua. In the end Walker symbolized for many the survival of slavery and the southern way of life. In his quest for glory and adventure, Walker mastered the rhetoric of southern expansion, especially in his presidential decree reinstituting slavery in Nicaragua in 1856, an alleged act of "benevolence and philanthropy" for "inferior" blacks, "half-castes," and Indians. Southern "fire-eaters" took heart, thinking it easier to implant slavery in the tropics than in contested Kansas. Hindered by northern opponents from territorial gains through diplomacy or war, the ardent defenders of the "peculiar institution" turned to the illegal machinations of the filibusters. They would also opt for secession and civil war in 1861.

Sectionalism and Sputtering Expansionism

As Walker's fate indicated, the momentum of American expansionism sputtered after the War with Mexico. Despite boasts that not even the Roman Empire had "an ambition for aggrandizement so marked as that which has characterized the American people," Manifest Destiny became less manifest in the 1850s. Tough talk about annexing Canada subsided. Even in Latin America, an area of prime focus, expansionist schemes went awry. Attempts to grab Cuba collapsed. Notions of planting an American colony in slaveholding Brazil enjoyed some currency after an exploration inspired by Lieutenant Matthew F. Maury, but nothing came of the scheme. Washington did persuade Mexico to negotiate the Gadsden Purchase of 1853, which added 29,640 square miles at a cost of $10 million for a potential railroad route to the Pacific—the only land acquired in the period from 1848 to the end of the Civil War.

Expansion faltered because of the heated sectional debates over chattel slavery that drew the nation into the Civil War. Divisive debates over slavery soured northern appetites for Latin American lands, where the black servitude might flourish and slave states might arise to vote with the South. After defeating such restrictions as the Wilmot Proviso, many southerners continued the cry for empire, hoping to enhance their declining political status and defend slavery, "the cornerstone of their way of life." In contrast, northerners such as the Illinois attorney Abraham Lincoln claimed slavery "deprives our republican example of its just influence in the world—enables the enemies of free institutions to taunt us as hypocrites." Divided at home by insistent northern abolitionists and southern "fire-eaters," the United States lacked a consensus to undertake further bold ventures in international affairs. Intensely preoccupied by domestic disputes over slavery, Americans gave less and less attention to foreign-policy questions.

Some Americans tried to harmonize sectional discord by trumpeting the nationalistic "Young America" movement. They hailed the revolutions of 1848 in Europe as evidence of New World, republican influence on the Old, and applauded heroic leaders whose short-lived rebellions against entrenched monarchies kindled American sympathies. Orators proclaimed the "young Giant of the West," standing in the "full flush of exulting manhood," whose "onward progress" the "worn-out Powers of the Old World may not hope either to restrain or impede."

Makers of American Foreign Relations, 1848–1865

Presidents	Secretaries of State
James K. Polk, 1845–1849	James Buchanan, 1845–1849
Zachary Taylor, 1849–1850	John M. Clayton, 1849–1850
Millard Fillmore, 1850–1853	Daniel Webster, 1850–1852
	Edward Everett, 1852–1853
Franklin Pierce, 1853–1857	William L. Marcy, 1853–1857
James Buchanan, 1857–1861	Lewis Cass, 1857–1860
	Jeremiah S. Black, 1860–1861
Abraham Lincoln, 1861–1865	William H. Seward, 1861–1869

In 1850 the Whig secretary of state Daniel Webster lectured the Hapsburg government, claiming that, compared to the mighty United States, Austria was "but a patch on the earth's surface." Webster wanted his rebuke to those who crushed the Hungarian revolution to "touch the national pride, and make a man feel *sheepish* and look *silly* who would speak of disunion." When Lajos Kossuth, the leader of the failed Hungarian Revolution, excited the United States in 1851–1852 during a rousing visit, Webster once again stirred nationalist sentiment by rejoicing "to see our American model upon the lower Danube." Nonetheless, the secretary privately vowed to "have ears more deaf than adders" if Kossuth asked for U.S. intervention on behalf of Hungary. In the 1852 Democratic party platform, the rallying cry was "Young America." The following year, "Young America" advocate and Democratic secretary of state William Marcy ordered a new dress code for U.S. diplomats—the "simple dress of an American citizen" to reflect "republican institutions."

"Young America" tried, in effect, to pour "the old wine of Jefferson and Jackson—a broad, nationally based republicanism of slavery and territorial aggrandizement—into new bottles." Claiming that "the more degrees of latitude and longitude embraced beneath our Constitution, the better," enthusiasts such as Democratic Senator Stephen A. Douglas of Illinois urged Democrats and Young Americans to "come together upon the basis of *entire silence on the slavery question.*" Yet the hope that expansion would subsume sectional differences over slavery proved illusory. Popular sovereignty, wherein settlers themselves voted whether territories should be free or slave, as in the Kansas-Nebraska Act of 1854, seemed a contradiction in terms—in Abraham Lincoln's view, a "deceitful pretense for the benefit of slavery." To many opponents, "Young America" expansionists were hypocrites who claimed to champion liberty abroad but permitted slavery to crawl "like a slimy reptile . . . to defile a second Eden."

Most scholars rate American political leaders between the 1840s and 1860s as mediocre. The presidents and secretaries of state conducted a blustering foreign policy, often playing to domestic political currents through bombastic rhetoric. Although both James Buchanan and Lewis Cass had extensive service as diplomats in

Europe, neither had acquired much finesse. An opponent mocked Stephen Douglas for thinking "he can bestride the continent with one foot on the shore of the Atlantic, the other on the Pacific. But he can't do it. . . . His legs are too short." Inept leaders muddled relations, crudely grasped at an elusive Cuba, permitted filibusters to alienate Latin America, squabbled clumsily with Britain in Central America, meddled in European revolutions, followed the British in humiliating the Chinese, and gave half-hearted attention to Japan after "opening" it. President Lincoln and his expansionist secretary of state, William H. Seward, certainly raised the level of competence in Washington, for the duo did manage to win the Civil War, contain it as a "localized" conflict, and avoid the world war it might have become. In doing so they preserved American power, thereby permitting the United States to resume its expansionist course after the fratricidal conflict.

The South's Dream of Empire

Many southern leaders tried to exploit Manifest Destiny for territorial conquest in the Caribbean. They failed largely because they provoked domestic opposition by insisting that slavery be permitted in new lands. At the same time, some northern expansionists, such as Seward—then senator from New York—hoped that the abolition of slavery would eliminate northern opposition to expansion into the Caribbean and Mexico. Paradoxically, Southern expansionists sought a larger empire for the United States while they denigrated the supremacy of the federal government itself. "You are looking toward Mexico, Nicaragua, and Brazil," one northern representative lectured his southern colleagues, "while you are not sure you will have a government to which these could be ceded."

For southerners, expansion seemed essential. Since the Missouri Compromise of 1820, they had witnessed a profound shift in political and economic balance to the North. Under the Compromise of 1850, California would enter the Union as a free state, and the rest of the Mexican cession could determine whether it wished to be slave or free (the concept of "popular sovereignty"). A strong majority of southern members of Congress voted against the compromise bill.

Fearing that slavery could not adapt to the arid regions of the West, southern expansionists looked elsewhere. Tropical states where black slaves could toil under white mastery had long piqued the southern imagination, but now, in the 1850s, the matter became urgent. Shouting the message were such belligerent voices as those of James D. B. DeBow, in his widely read *DeBow's Review,* and the Knights of the Golden Circle, a secret society of several thousand members pledged to tropical expansion. The Gulf of Mexico, DeBow opined, comprised the "great *Southern sea.*" Even after the Kansas-Nebraska Act in 1854 opened the territories to slavery through popular sovereignty, expansionists preferred Central America, Mexico, and Cuba, where the South could acquire "more power & influence than would a dozen wild deserts" in the American West. "I want them all for the same reason—for the planting or spreading of slavery," a Mississippi senator declared.

Diplomacy could not satisfy southern desires quickly enough, so many southerners supported the filibusters. Although often backed by financial interests in New York, and cheered by the penny press, most filibuster bands originated in New

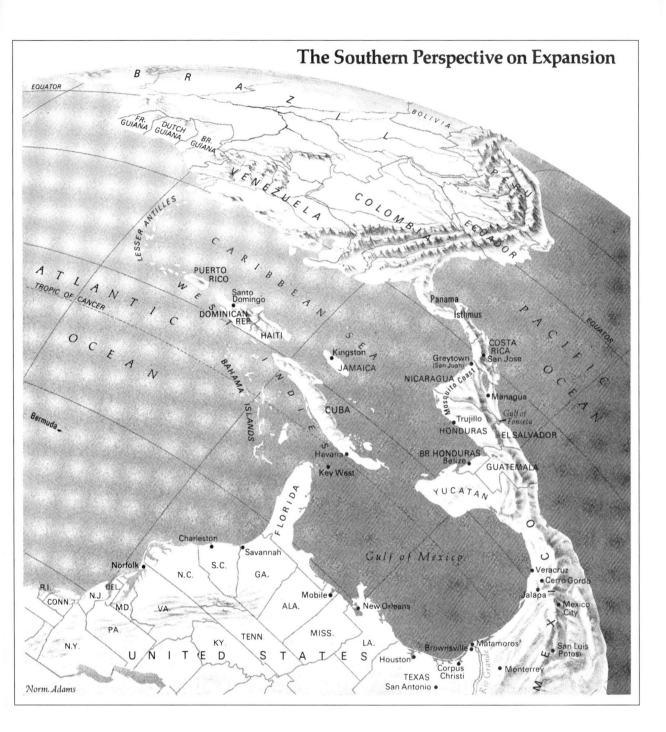

The Southern Perspective on Expansion

Norm. Adams

Orleans, became thoroughly "southern" in goals and personnel, and employed the rhetoric of Manifest Destiny for sectional purposes. Narciso López, John A. Quitman, and William Walker led the ill-fated ventures.

Venezuelan by birth, General Narciso López had careers as a Spanish military officer and Cuban businessman before his attempted invasion of Cuba in 1849. Married into a proslave aristocratic Cuban family, he vowed to save the island from the perfidies of imperial Spain. He wished to free Cuba and annex it to the United States. Using New York City and New Orleans as bases, López enlisted veterans from the War with Mexico, promising them "plunder, women, drink, and tobacco," plus a $1,000 bonus and 160 acres of Cuban land if the expedition succeeded. López gathered several hundred mercenaries at Round Island, off the Louisiana coast, but in September 1849 the U.S. Navy foiled his plans.

López reached for support elsewhere in the South. He won over southern expansionists such as John A. Quitman, the governor of Mississippi (1850–1851); the editor of the *New Orleans Delta,* Laurence J. Sigur, a former senator and cotton planter from Mississippi, John Henderson; and editor John L. O'Sullivan of Manifest Destiny fame. In May 1850, disguised as emigrants to California, the López filibusters departed New Orleans for Cuba. Upon landing, they suffered sixty-six casualties to superior Spanish forces and attracted little Cuban support. López and most of his followers fled to Key West with a Spanish warship in hot pursuit. López, Quitman, Henderson, Sigur, and O'Sullivan, among others, stood trial in New Orleans for violating the Neutrality Act of 1818, which forbade military operations from American soil against countries at peace with the United States. Southern juries acquitted them.

López launched another attack against Cuba in August 1851 with 500 "freebooters, pirates, and plunderers." Federal officials in New Orleans obligingly looked the other way. The mustachioed López invoked American icons, telling his followers: "We are sons of Washington . . . come to free a people" and "to add another glorious star . . . over 'The land of the Free.'" This time Spanish authorities captured most of his ragtag army. Tried by a military court, López and fifty of his mercenaries were executed.

Undeterred by the López debacle, DeBow insisted that the American "lust for dominion" over Cuba remained unquenched. An angry mob broke into the Spanish consulate in New Orleans, defaced portraits of the Spanish queen, and shredded the Spanish flag. Secretary of State Daniel Webster apologized and paid Spain $25,000 in damages. Quitman, who had resigned his governorship in 1851 because of the filibustering flap, feared that Spain might free slaves in Cuba. Only filibustering could avert "Africanization" and guarantee "safety to the South & her institutions." The filibusters could conquer Cuba, proclaim an independent republic on the Texas model, prevent emancipation, and insist on slave status as a condition of annexation to the United States. When a Cuban group offered Quitman "all of the powers and attributes of dictatorship," he organized an expedition of 3,000 men, but financial shortages, lack of support in Cuba, and warnings that President Franklin Pierce would thwart any expedition forced Quitman to abandon the filibuster in April 1855.

Among those who supported Walker, Lopez, and other filibusters were the redoubtable journalist Jane McManus Storm and her new husband, the Texas entrepreneur William Cazneau. Motivated less by proslavery sentiment than by a "Young America" vision of liberating the tropics, the Cazneaus mixed profits with patriotism. Land deals in Mexico, silver mines in Nicaragua, propaganda tracts for the New York Cuban Council—all were prelude to their special plans for the Dominican Republic. Through his wife's contacts with Secretary of State Marcy, William Cazneau wangled an appointment in 1854 as a commissioner to investigate trade opportunities. The Cazneaus described the country's resources in glowing terms, recommending immediate diplomatic recognition and acquisition of the strategic harbor of Samaná Bay. They also saw the Dominican Republic as a potential haven for emancipated slaves. When the British and French consuls tried to block Cazneau's negotiations, he protested their interference with President Monroe's "principles of 1823." Nonetheless, the Dominicans, following British advice, rejected Cazneau's treaty. Recalled in late 1854, the Cazneaus embarked on a second Dominican mission in 1859–1860. Because of Washington's preoccupation with the sectional crisis, however, their pleas for a "free commercial entrepôt at the gates of the Gulf of Mexico and the Caribbean Sea" and their warnings that the debt-ridden Dominican government might seek reannexation to Spain brought no official response.

The Cuba–United States Nexus

The Caribbean island of Cuba lay too close to the United States to escape expansionist urges. The U.S. minister to England boomed: "We want Cuba, Sir, and we must have it." One southerner waxed erotic: "The Queen of the Antilles [Cuba] . . . sits on her throne, upon the silver waves, breathing her spicy, tropic breath, and pouting her rosy, sugared lips. Who can object? None. She is of age—take her, Uncle Sam."

Spain once called Cuba the "Ever Faithful Isle" because it did not revolt against Madrid in the stormy decades of the early nineteenth century. After 1818, with the opening of the island to world trade, a Cuba-U.S. commercial nexus began to replace the connection with Spain. As the British novelist Anthony Trollope wrote from Cuba in 1859: "Havana will soon become as much American as New Orleans." Cuba's rich sugar production attracted North American entrepreneurs, slaveholders, engineers, and machinists. The new order also included the growth of Protestantism in the predominantly Catholic island.

Slave revolts in the 1830s and 1840s, as well as anticolonial rebellions in the following decade, aroused North Americans, especially southerners who feared the abolition of slavery (45 percent of the island's population of 1 million were slaves). A corrupt and inept Spanish administration exacerbated Cuba's plight and tugged at North American sympathies. Expansionists believed that inevitably, by "natural growth," Cuba would be taken under their eagle's outstretched wings. Or, to use a metaphor of the times: "The fruit will ripen, and fall from the parent stem." In Cuba itself, members of the Creole elite (Spaniards born in Cuba) increasingly made the case for annexation because, as part of the United States, their sugar would get preferential treatment and "their slave property would become secure."

In 1848 President Polk contemplated purchasing Cuba from Spain for $100 million. But Spain's refusal and the adamant opposition of France and Britain blocked him. Whig President Zachary Taylor and his successor Millard Fillmore had little interest in purchasing Cuba and worked to prevent filibustering. In 1852 Britain and France proposed a three-power statement to disavow "all intention of obtaining possession" of Cuba. Unwilling to sign such a self-denying agreement, Fillmore replied that "this question would fall like a bomb in the midst of the electoral agitation for the presidency" and divide North from South. Secretary of State Edward Everett disavowed any desire to "covet" Cuba, but the status of the island was nonetheless "mainly an American question." By quoting Washington's Farewell Address and Jefferson's aversion to "entangling alliances," Everett shunned a pact with European nations. Most important, the United States would not permit the transfer of Cuba to any other power.

President Pierce did covet Cuba. Backed by the expansionists Secretary of State William L. Marcy, minister to Britain James Buchanan, minister to Spain Pierre Soulé, and minister to France John Y. Mason, Pierce played to the Cuban fancies of southern Democrats. Born in France, schooled as a lawyer, and elected U.S. senator from Louisiana, the impetuous Soulé became a central figure in the North American quest for Cuba. Soon after his arrival in Madrid, Soulé wounded the French ambassador in a duel. Fearful that "the fruit [Cuba] might become spoiled" through slave rebellion if Uncle Sam waited too long to pick it, this misplaced "diplomat" constantly irritated Spanish court officials. Marcy had instructed Soulé to inquire discreetly about a possible Spanish sale of Cuba. "Discreetly," however, did not exist in Soulé's vocabulary.

In February 1854, Havana authorities seized the American merchant ship *Black Warrior* for allegedly violating port regulations. President Pierce demanded a $100,000 indemnity and heated up American fevers for revenge by sending a belligerent anti-Spanish message to Congress. Pierce thus fed Soulé's intemperance. The haughty envoy demanded an apology for this affront to the U.S. flag. The Spanish agreed to restore the ship to its owner and pay a smaller indemnity, even though Marcy found the Spanish reply full of "evasions."

The *Black Warrior* affair soon became overshadowed by a new, rash attempt to annex Cuba. Because Spanish authorities had ended the slave trade and were allegedly arming free blacks to defend against filibusters, panicky U.S. consuls in Cuba predicted "a disastrous bloody war of the races." Marcy thereupon instructed Soulé in April 1854 to try to buy Cuba for $130 million or less. Failing that, "you will then direct your efforts to the next desirable object which is to detach that island from the Spanish dominion and from all dependence on any European power." Then, in August, the secretary told Soulé to meet with ministers Buchanan and Mason to discuss annexation. The three expansionists relished the chance; they met in October in Belgium where they created the confidential document known as the Ostend Manifesto. The three emissaries recommended the purchase of Cuba for no more than $120 million. But if Madrid refused to sell, "we shall be justified in wresting it from Spain" to prevent Cuba from becoming a "second St. Domingo, with all its attendant horrors to the white race."

The manifesto arrived in Washington on Election Day, November 1854, and was leaked to the press. Democrats had just suffered losses in midterm elections, which they blamed on opposition to the Kansas-Nebraska Act. Critics of the Kansas-Nebraska Act now accused the Pierce administration of propagating a slave conspiracy to annex Cuba, characterizing the manifesto as "the highwayman's plea, that might makes right." Grasping for a scapegoat, Pierce and Marcy reprimanded Soulé, who resigned in indignation. The indefatigable Marcy then instructed Soulé's successor to encourage Spain to grant independence to Cuba. Madrid again refused.

One author of the Ostend Manifesto, James Buchanan, became president in 1857. "If I can . . . add Cuba to the Union, I shall be willing to give up the ghost," he remarked. In December 1858, "Old Buck" praised the commercial and strategic virtues of Cuba, urged its purchase, and asked Congress to appropriate a large sum for this purpose. The Senate Foreign Relations Committee then issued a favorable report that declared the "law of our national existence is growth. We cannot if we would, disobey it." If the United States did not act, a European power might. The report also recommended $30 million—some of it no doubt for bribes of Spanish public officials. But antislavery Republicans blocked action on what one Ohioan called a bill to add 750,000 "niggers" to the United States. A slow learner, Buchanan futilely appealed to Congress to pass the "Thirty Million Dollar Bill" in his annual messages of 1859 and 1860. Abraham Lincoln's election as president in 1860 frustrated any further attempts to embrace Cuba.

Openings to East Asia

As southerners dreamed of Caribbean empires to the south, so did other Americans gaze westward across the Pacific. With California firmly a part of the Union in 1850, strengthening links with Asia seemed a logical progression. With new and faster steamships, the valuable ports of San Diego and San Francisco, already existing commercial and missionary ties, prospects of a canal across Central America and a transcontinental railroad to reduce travel time, the population of California ballooning because of the gold rush of 1849—with all of these changes and aspirations, American interest in Asia flamed anew after 1848. Lieutenant John Rodgers, who headed a U.S. surveying expedition to the northern Pacific Ocean in 1853–1856, predicted lucrative trade with the Chinese: The prospects "are so vast as to dazzle sober calculation."

This interest in Asia was nothing new. The first American ship to China sailed in the 1780s, and U.S. merchants and missionaries had been active for decades. Caleb Cushing, the first American commissioner to China, had secured trading privileges in five Chinese ports in 1844. By the early 1850s Americans carried about one-third of Chinese trade with the West. Not yet a major player in Asian politics, the United States usually trailed behind the British, who were not averse to using military force to build up imperial privileges, as in the Opium War. The Americans, complained a Chinese official, "do no more than follow in England's wake and utilize her strength." Although the United States did not gobble up territory as did Britain (India), the Netherlands (East Indies), and Portugal (Macao), Asians could only view Americans as another nation of grasping foreigners who denied them their sovereignty and dignity.

The Asian Frontier

Matthew C. Perry (1794–1858). This career naval officer was born in Newport, Rhode Island. One U.S. sailor noticed that Japanese artists always began their portraits of Americans by drawing a large nose and then sketching other features around it, as suggested by this Japanese rendition of Perry. (Honolulu Academy of Arts, Gift of Mrs. Walter F. Dillingham in memory of Alice Perry Grew, 1960 [2732.1])

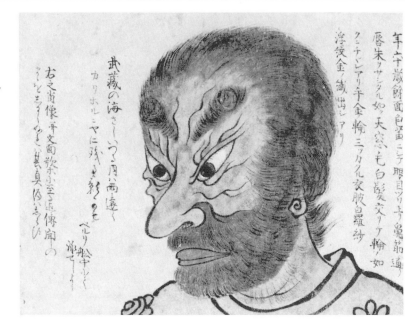

The most important American initiative came with the "opening" of Japan in 1853–1854. Except for a single port, Nagasaki, where the Dutch traded, few westerners were welcome in a Japan governed by feudal lords bent on maintaining their isolation from "barbarian" whites. U.S. commodore James Biddle had tried to open negotiations with this "double-bolted" land in 1846, only to have Japanese officials treat him rudely and warn him "never again to appear on the Japanese coast." Seven years later, in July 1853, Commodore Matthew C. Perry sailed into Tokyo Bay with an armada of "black ships" that included two coal-powered, steam-driven side-wheelers. Awed by smoke-belching warships they had never seen before, the Japanese feared invasion by "barbarians . . . in floating volcanoes."

President Fillmore had given Perry the specific task of "opening" Japan to westerners. Instructed to obtain a treaty that would grant the United States trading and coaling stations and promise the safe treatment of shipwrecked American sailors, Perry handed Japanese officials a presidential message. "Our steamships can go from California to Japan in eighteen days," Fillmore's letter boasted. "I am desirous that our two countries should trade with each other." The Japanese grudgingly accepted the impertinent letter "in opposition to Japanese law" and asked Perry to "depart." The commodore promised to return the next year with all of his ships "and probably more." Perry's next visit in March 1854 found the Japanese more courteous. Banquets, sumo wrestlers, and an American minstrel entertained guests and hosts. The Americans set up for the curious Japanese a quarter-scale railroad train and a telegraph system. Perry also gave his hosts a bound history of the War with Mexico, 100 gallons of Kentucky bourbon whiskey, and four volumes of John James Audubon's *Birds of America*.

The resulting Treaty of Kanagawa, signed on March 31, 1854, guaranteed protection for shipwrecked seamen, opened two ports for obtaining coal and other supplies, and established consular privileges at those ports. Yet the two ports, Shimoda and Hakodate, were relatively inaccessible and unimportant. In fact, the treaty contained no binding commitment for beginning trade. Thus Perry had "opened" Japan only slightly. When Perry returned to the United States in April 1855, the New York Chamber of Commerce nonetheless presented him with a 381-piece silver dinner service, and Congress voted him a bonus of $20,000. The Senate approved the treaty unanimously.

Perry saw his Japan expedition as but one step toward a U.S. empire in the Pacific. He wished to seize Okinawa and the Bonin Islands as coaling stations for a projected Pacific steamship line. He envisaged American settlement on the "magnificent island" of Formosa (Taiwan), and he urged U.S. military intervention in the internal affairs of Asian states because of the "responsibilities with which our growing wealth and power must inevitably fasten upon us." He wanted to "extend the advantages of our national friendship and protection" to Siam, Indochina, and the East Indies. Eventually, Perry prophesied, the American people would "extend their dominion and their power, until they shall have brought within their mighty embrace the Islands of the great Pacific, and place the Saxon race upon the eastern shores of Asia."

For the moment, Perry's grandiose vision fell short. In Japan, where Townsend Harris went as consul to capitalize on the commodore's treaty, the gains were modest. Isolated at the post of Shimoda, Harris patiently waited for an opportunity to negotiate a genuine commercial treaty. Lacking the naval power exerted by the westerners in China and displayed by Perry in 1854, Harris could not threaten Japanese leaders but pressed his case in another classic example of "personal diplomacy." In 1858 his tenacity paid off in a treaty wherein Japan opened other ports, provided for freedom of trade, and created a tariff schedule. The next year Harris became minister to Japan and established an American legation in Tokyo. The intrepid diplomat did not gain lasting fame until a century later when John Wayne portrayed him in the motion picture *The Barbarian and the Geisha* (1958).

Despite these evidences of U.S. engagement in the 1850s, "Asia remained an abstract idea, a distant area that was only one part of a worldwide commercial empire." The euphoria following Perry's drama soon evaporated. The State Department gave little guidance to its representatives in Asia, who often acted on their own. In 1856, for example, Commodore James Armstrong's warships destroyed five Chinese forts near Guangzhou (Canton) after a cannon fired on an American vessel. President Franklin Pierce subsequently reprimanded the naval officer. As another example of America's secondary interest in Asia, Rodgers of the North Pacific Surveying Expedition found on returning to San Francisco in 1856 that he could not complete his survey of trade routes because his funds had run out. Two years later, following a civil war called the Taiping Rebellion, France and Britain further gouged China by opening ten new treaty ports, whereupon the United States, by a form of "hitchhiking imperialism," gained access to these ports in the dictated treaty of Tianjin (Tientsin). The Civil War prevented further commercial expansion.

Anglo-American Détente, an Isthmian Canal, and Central America

Great Britain kept a worried eye on U.S. attempts, official and unofficial, to expand in the Caribbean and Central America. At the close of the War with Mexico, Anglo-American relations seemed tranquil. Earlier compromises over the Maine and Oregon boundaries had diminished the danger of war, and the growth of Anglo-American trade had resumed after a decade of sluggishness. By the 1850s the United States supplied Britain with 50 percent of its imports and 80 percent of its raw cotton, the basis of England's largest export industry. Forty percent of all U.S. imports came from England, and America's expanding economy attracted British capital, especially during the railroad building boom of the 1840s. "Increased Commercial Intercourse may add to the Links of mutual Interest," Lord Palmerston observed. But he also warned that commercial links can snap "under the Pressure of National Passions."

A treaty negotiated with New Granada (later Colombia) in 1846 granted the United States transit rights across the Isthmus of Panama, a promising railroad and canal route. Alarmed by this intrusion in the Caribbean, the British struck back. In January 1848 they seized a Nicaraguan town, which they renamed Greytown. This port controlled the most technologically feasible transisthmian canal route. When added to the British protectorate over the Mosquito Indians inhabiting Nicaragua's eastern coast, possession of Belize (later British Honduras) and the Bay Islands, and the Royal naval base at Jamaica, Greytown gave Britain a potentially dominant position in Central America.

That same month John Marshall discovered gold at Sutter's Mill in California. The great gold rush soon swelled California's population by 100,000 and led to admission of the Golden State to the Union in 1850. Most of the "forty-niners" reached San Francisco by steamship. The trip included arduous overland travel through Nicaragua or Panama. Construction of an isthmian canal or railway now became a matter of urgency, although the British presence in Central America precluded unilateral U.S. action. Whig secretary of state John M. Clayton therefore proposed "a great highway" across the isthmus, "to be dedicated especially by Great Britain and the United States, to the equal benefit and advantage of all nations of the world." Foreign Secretary Palmerston told Clayton that Britain had "no selfish or exclusive views" about the isthmus. Like Clayton, he hoped "that any undertaking of this sort . . . should be generally open to and available to all the nations of the world." To confirm this understanding, he sent Sir Henry Bulwer to Washington in 1849. The Clayton-Bulwer Treaty of April 19, 1850, stipulated that neither country alone would ever monopolize or fortify a canal in Central America, and that neither would "colonize, or assume, or exercise any dominion over . . . any part of Central America."

The isthmian canal would have to await the twentieth century, but American enterprise soon began to saturate Central America. Cornelius Vanderbilt organized an interoceanic steamship and railroad connection through Nicaragua, and other entrepreneurs completed a railroad across Panama in 1855. But the flag did not follow investors into Central America. The deepening domestic crisis over slavery prevented Presidents Pierce and Buchanan from doing much more than nip verbally at the heels of the gradually retreating British. For his part, Palmerston continued to berate the "vulgar minded Bullies" of North America, from whom "nothing is gained by submission to Insult & wrong." When a Greytown mob assaulted an American diplomat in 1854, Pierce ordered the U.S.S. *Cyane* to bombard the "pretended community" of "outlaws" and "savages." The British quietly let the matter drop.

The costly Crimean War (1854–1856), which pitted England and France against Russia, made a showdown with the United States over Central America unlikely. When the English government sent agents to the United States to recruit soldiers, Secretary Marcy sent them packing for violating U.S. neutrality laws. Palmerston thereupon urged "some little Flourish" addressed to the "free, enlightened and Generous Race . . . of the great North American Union" as a means of dampening Marcy's "Bunkum vapouring." Marcy eased matters by negotiating a long-desired reciprocity treaty in 1854. A crisis over American fishing rights and navigation of the St. Lawrence River also prompted London to send the governor-general of Canada, Lord Elgin, to negotiate with Marcy. "Lord Elgin pretends to drink immensely," his secretary recorded, "but I watched him [at a party], and I don't believe he drank a glass between two and twelve. He is the most thorough *diplomat* possible." In the ensuing Marcy-Elgin Treaty of June 5, 1854, Americans could navigate the St. Lawrence without restriction and fish within three miles of British North America, and Canadians could send duty-free a wide variety of agricultural products into the United States. U.S. consul Israel Andrews thought reciprocity might lead to U.S.-Canadian "convergence" wherein "under different governments we shall be one people, laboring hand in hand to accomplish the high destiny of the North American continent." The Marcy-Elgin Treaty, like the Webster-Ashburton Treaty and the Oregon settlement, contributed to tranquility along the northern border of the United States.

That Anglo-American relations in the 1850s ended with a whimper and not a bang owed mainly to the worsening American crisis over the expansion of slavery. A British reappraisal following the Crimean War also facilitated Anglo-American détente. Always the bellwether of official British opinion, Palmerston wrote in 1857, in regard to Central America, that the Yankees "are on the Spot, strong, deeply interested in the matter, totally unscrupulous and dishonest and determined. . . . We are far away, weak from Distance, controlled by the Indifference of the Nation . . . and by its Strong commercial Interest in maintaining Peace with the United States." When he became prime minister in June 1859, Palmerston relinquished the Bay Islands to Honduras and the Mosquito Coast to Nicaragua. The new foreign secretary, Lord Malmesbury, allowed that "all the Southern part of North America must come under this Government of the United States; that he had no objection to what seemed the inevitable course of things."

The American Civil War and International Relations

On April 12, 1861, at Charleston, South Carolina, Confederate forces opened fire on the federal garrison barricaded in Fort Sumter. With this defiant act the rebellious South forced Abraham Lincoln to choose between secession and civil war.

William H. Seward (1801–1872). Union College graduate, U.S. senator (1849–1861), and secretary of state (1861–1869), Seward spent the Civil War years trying to preserve the Union by keeping the European powers neutral. (Houghton Mifflin Company)

Sworn to defend the Constitution, the new Republican president called for 75,000 militiamen to suppress the insurrection.

For support, Lincoln leaned on a fractious cabinet of politically ambitious men, headed by a secretary of state who thought himself far abler than his chief. Willing to act as prime minister to a hesitant president, William Henry Seward concocted plans to "wrap the world in flames" in order to melt domestic disunity in the furnace of foreign war. On April 1 he sent Lincoln "Some Thoughts for the President's Consideration," which proposed hostility or war against Britain, France, Russia, and Spain. The next day Seward responded to Spain's reannexation of the Dominican Republic with a threat of war. Spain ignored him, while Lincoln said he would formulate policy with the "advice of all the Cabinet."

Scarcely deterred, Seward challenged Britain's interpretation of international maritime law. He persuaded Lincoln to proclaim a blockade of the southern ports as a matter of domestic policy. Britain quite properly interpreted the Union blockade as the act of a nation at war and recognized the belligerent status of the Confederacy. With equal logic, Confederate president Jefferson Davis met Lincoln's blockade by calling for privateers, a historic mode of American naval warfare.

In the 1856 Declaration of Paris following the Crimean War, Britain and France had codified the rules of maritime warfare and outlawed privateering. The United States had refused to sign away a favorite naval strategy, but the Confederacy's resort to privateering impelled Seward to inform the British minister, Lord Richard Lyons, that he wished belatedly to initial the covenant. Lyons noted Washington's inability to obligate the South. To Seward's claim that the South had no independent status, Lyons coolly replied: "Very well. If they are not independent then the President's proclamation of blockade is not binding. A blockade . . . applies only to two nations at war." Seward retorted: "Europe must interpret the law our way or we'll declare war." The secretary's truculence caused Palmerston to see him as a "vapouring, blustering, ignorant Man" who "may drive us into a quarrel without intending it."

Seward spoke from weakness, and the British knew it. Even with twice the population of the South, the North faced the difficult military task of subduing 9 million hostile people and sealing off innumerable harbors strung along a 3,500-mile coastline. To blockade this coast, the U.S. Navy could muster only forty-two operational warships. To win, Confederate armies needed only to hold out long enough to force the North to conclude that the costs of conquering the South were too high. British officials, especially Lyons, thought it unlikely that Lincoln could preserve the Union against such odds.

The economic balance sheet also seemed to favor the South. Prior to the Civil War, British subjects invested widely in American securities, sent at least 25 percent of their annual exports to the United States, and depended on America for 55 percent of all foodstuffs imported each year. But these economic ties favoring the industrial North and farming West paled beside the South's share of three quarters of the British market for raw cotton, the staple undergirding an industrial and commercial empire employing between 4 and 5 million people. Stop the cotton trade and England's economy would allegedly collapse. One southern politician bragged that "foreign nations cannot exist without the cotton produced by slave labor in the Southern states."

President Jefferson Davis moved quickly. In March he dispatched three ministers to Europe to seek full diplomatic recognition, or even intervention, in exchange for an uninterrupted supply of cotton, free trade with the Confederacy, and expansion of European power throughout the Western Hemisphere. To parry this diplomatic thrust, Seward sped Charles Francis Adams to London. The son of the author of the Monroe Doctrine and grandson of the diplomat who had negotiated the 1783 peace with England, Adams ultimately softened Seward's bombastic language without deviating from the secretary's goals. Especially effective with British foreign secretary Russell, Adams came across as "equally cold: formal, diplomatic, and almost equally British. A diamond come to cut a diamond."

"King Cotton Bound; or, the Modern Prometheus." In Greek mythology, Prometheus was the creator and savior of humankind whom Zeus chained to a mountain peak. In this rendition by the British humor magazine, *Punch,* the northern eagle picks at the Confederate "King Cotton," manacled by the naval blockade. In the end, northern exports of wheat ("King Corn") to Britain proved more important than southern cotton. (*Punch,* 1861)

Adams arrived in London on May 14, 1861, dismayed to learn that England had recognized Confederate belligerency. Russell had received but not officially met with Confederate commissioners. Adams thought of severing diplomatic relations, but rejected such action as the "extreme of shallowness and folly," because a war with England, added to the Civil War, "would grind us all into rags in America." Nonetheless, Seward drafted a hostile dispatch for Adams, threatening to declare war if Britain recognized Confederate independence, only to have Lincoln pencil out the most bellicose phrases and send it for Adams's guidance rather than as an ultimatum. Reverses at the front rendered the secretary's threats of war with Europe ridiculous. On July 21, 1861, at Manassas Junction, Virginia, Confederate troops stampeded a Union army into full retreat north.

The summer and fall of 1861 brought more bad news. In England James D. Bulloch, head of the Confederacy's overseas secret service, contracted for the construction of two sloops. Disguised as merchant ships until their departure from British waters to circumvent neutrality laws, the *Florida* and *Alabama* soon played havoc with northern commerce. In August the *Bermuda,* a blockade runner laden with war matériel for Savannah, dashed from the Thames. To exploit these favorable events, President Davis sent two fresh ministers to Europe, the aristocratic James M. Mason of Virginia and John Slidell, formerly Polk's emissary to Mexico in 1845. On October 11, they boarded the Confederate steamer *Nashville* at Charleston to begin their journey.

Hoping to cross the Atlantic under a neutral flag, Mason and Slidell transferred to the British mail steamer *Trent* in Havana. U.S. Navy captain Charles Wilkes then intercepted the *Trent* as it left Cuban waters on November 8, 1861. Since the British vessel carried Confederate mail, Wilkes could have seized it as a prize. Instead, he hauled Mason and Slidell aboard the U.S.S. *San Jacinto* and allowed the *Trent* to continue its voyage, an act reminiscent of British impressment before the War of 1812. Ecstatic Americans cheered Wilkes, and Congress voted him a gold medal. Lincoln himself feared Mason and Slidell might become "white elephants" but doubted he could free the prisoners without a public backlash.

News of Wilkes's deed reached London on November 27, igniting a panic on the stock exchange. The British government instructed Lyons to demand the release of Mason and Slidell and a formal apology "for the insult offered to the British flag." Prince Albert, a staunch advocate of Anglo-American peace, devised a loophole allowing the U.S. government, if it wished, to deny that Wilkes had acted under instructions, "or, if he did, that he misapprehended them." Russell then directed Lyons "to abstain from anything like menace" and "to be rather easy about the apology."

As the watered-down ultimatum crossed the Atlantic, British officials tempered their enthusiasm for war because of the vulnerability of Canada. They also feared marauding Yankee cruisers that might prey on British shipping. Albert's death on December 14 further sobered the national mood. Russell advised restraint:"I do not think the country [Britain] would approve an immediate declaration of war." Lord Lyons made "the pill as easy to swallow as possible" when he delivered Russell's demands on December 19. Pressure mounted for U.S. capitulation. From London, Charles Francis Adams warned of implacable British determination to free Mason and Slidell. Seeing the folly of "two wars . . . at a time," Lincoln and Seward thereupon decided to defuse the crisis. Seward's reply to Lyons defended Wilkes's right to stop, search, and seize the *Trent* but admitted that Wilkes had erred in not taking the vessel into port for hearings before a legal tribunal. The secretary thus disavowed Wilkes, congratulated the British for accepting U.S. views on impressment, and "cheerfully liberated" the two Confederates. Clever or not, Seward's settlement of the *Trent* affair "further embittered the opinion of this people toward Great Britain," the Mexican envoy Matías Romero reported from Washington. War, he predicted, "is not a remote possibility."

Just prior to the *Trent* crisis, Britain, France, and Spain had landed troops at Veracruz, Mexico, ostensibly to compel payment on a $65 million foreign debt. Seward acknowledged the right of the powers to collect debts forcibly, provided they did not harbor political or territorial ambitions in Mexico. U.S. fears of European plots against Latin America were realistic. In early 1862, Prime Minister Palmerston thought a European monarch in Mexico City "would be a great blessing" and "would also stop the North Americans . . . in their absorption of Mexico."

In April 1862, Britain and Spain settled their Mexican debts and withdrew from the joint venture. French troops continued their march westward toward Mexico City, where Napoleon III hoped to install a puppet government under Archduke Ferdinand Maximilian, brother of the Austrian emperor. Fierce Mexican resistance delayed French occupation of the capital city until June 1863. This entrapment forced Napoleon to follow Britain's lead in Civil War diplomacy, despite his own bias in favor of the South. Seward and Lincoln watched these machinations without protest. Why "gasconade about Mexico," Seward explained, "when we are engaged in a struggle for our own life?"

British "Lookers On" Across the Atlantic

In 1862, along the southern coast, the Union's tightening blockade locked up Confederate privateers and harassed neutral shipping. In Tennessee an unknown general, Ulysses S. Grant, chased the rebels from Forts Donelson and Henry. Admiral David G. Farragut captured New Orleans in April, opening the Mississippi River to a campaign that would finally sever Texas, Arkansas, and Louisiana from the Confederacy. Union general George B. McClellan faltered outside Richmond in July 1862, just as Virginia's Robert E. Lee pulled back after the bloodletting at Antietam two months later. The British government watched and waited. London prudently acquiesced in the Union blockade, accumulating precedents useful for future conflicts when once again England would be a belligerent and the United States neutral.

Cotton did not drive British policy—at least not at first. England did not initially crave raw cotton. The bumper American crop of 1860 provided 1.6 million bales for the saturated Lancashire mills in 1861. Anticipating an early end to the Civil War, British cotton manufacturers complacently counted on their stockpiled raw cotton to carry them through a short-term crisis. As the military deadlock deepened in 1862, the textile producers developed alternative sources, notably in Egypt and India. These new fields began to yield amply by 1863. In France, Napoleon's insistence on following British policy toward the Civil War prevented the Confederacy from capitalizing on discontent in the French cotton industry.

The South fared better in maritime Liverpool. Contemptuous of the queen's neutrality proclamation, Liverpool shipping interests sought to recoup from the costly disruption of trade with the Confederacy by building blockade runners, commerce raiders, and rams for the South's agent James D. Bulloch. Of 2,742 blockade runs attempted during the war, steam-driven runners completed 2,525, or 92 percent, mainly during the ineffective first year of the blockade. Greed for profits, moreover, induced many southern shippers to import luxury items rather than military matériel, thus wasting precious cargo space and scarce southern capital.

Commerce raiders posed a greater threat. Bulloch contracted for these vessels and disguised them as cargo ships during construction in order to circumvent British neutrality, which forbade outfitting warships for either belligerent. In March 1862 the *Oreto,* renamed *Florida* once at sea, slipped from Liverpool. Adams protested and demanded that Russell detain a larger second vessel then nearing completion. On July 31, Russell's reluctant order to seize the ship arrived a day after the *Alabama* had sailed. Under the command of the South's most gifted naval officer, Raphael Semmes, the eight-gun raider sank nineteen Union merchant vessels in its first three months at sea. Together with the *Florida* and lesser raiders, it preyed on Union commerce worldwide, driving northern merchants to flags of foreign registry.

Two months after the *Alabama*'s escape, impressed by the Confederate victory at the Second Battle of Bull Run, Russell proposed to Palmerston an Anglo-French mediation "with a view to the recognition of the independence of the Confederates." Cotton shortages added impetus to Russell's proposal, and William E. Gladstone, a member of the cabinet, declared publicly that Jefferson Davis had "made a nation." News of Lee's reversal at Antietam in September finally inclined Palmerston to "continue to be lookers on till the war shall have taken a more decided turn." This repudiation on October 22, 1862, of both mediation and recognition of Confederate independence remained British policy until the end of the war.

Lincoln did all he could to ensure continued European neutrality. Convinced that no "European Power would dare to recognize and aid the Southern Confederacy if it became clear that the Confederacy stands for slavery and the Union for freedom," he issued the Emancipation Proclamation on September 22. This historic gesture set January 1, 1863, as the date for freedom of slaves in areas not controlled by the Union—in short, only in districts still in rebellion. At first Palmerston dismissed the proclamation as "trash." Within months, however, Adams's son Henry reported that the Emancipation Proclamation "created an almost convulsive reaction in our favor."

As 1863 opened, a Polish uprising against Russian rule threatened to disrupt the critical European balance of power. Charles Francis Adams welcomed such continental distractions and waited impatiently for Union victories to give him diplomatic clout. Then in July came the good news: The northern armies held at Gettysburg, and Grant won control of the Mississippi River at Vicksburg.

As Confederate bonds plummeted on the London market, Adams pressed Lord Russell to seize two ironclad, steam-driven vessels nearing completion at the Laird yards in Liverpool. These shallow-draft warships mounted seven-foot iron rams, theoretically an ideal weapon for piercing the wooden hulls of the Union's blockaders. Bulloch had ordered the Laird rams but so cleverly covered his tracks that the pasha of Egypt seemed their legal owner. Since the rams lacked guns and the Crown lacked proof of Confederate ownership, Russell's law officers could not find them in violation of British neutrality. Russell, however, dared not disregard Adams's increasingly shrill warnings. Nor was it in Britain's national interest to encourage the precedent of weak naval powers constructing warships in neutral shipyards during wartime. On September 3, 1863, he prudently detained the rams, telling Palmerston that "neutral hostility should not be allowed to go on without some attempt to stop it."

Northern morale received a boost from the visit of the Russian Baltic and Pacific squadrons to New York and San Francisco in September and October of 1863. Fearful of war with England over Poland, Russia sent its ships in the hope that they could operate against the Royal Navy from ice-free American ports. As Russian sailors marched down Broadway, northerners wishfully interpreted the visit as a sign of St. Petersburg's support for their cause. Secretary of the Navy Gideon Welles mistakenly thought "our Russian friends are rendering us a great service."

In 1863, too, the troops of Napoleon III finally fought their way into Mexico City. In July, the victorious French emperor proclaimed a Mexican monarchy under Austrian archduke Maximilian. Seward refused recognition to Maximilian when the aspiring royal arrived in Mexico in July 1864. By then General William T. Sherman was marching through Georgia. The apparently inevitable Union triumph would place a huge army and one of the world's largest navies along the border of Napoleon's puppet state. Napoleon began to scale down his commitment, intending to remove all but 20,000 French troops from Mexico by 1867. He also curried favor with Washington by directing Maximilian not to receive Confederate ministers, and he seized two Confederate rams under construction at Nantes in May 1864. A month later the U.S.S. *Kearsarge* sank the C.S.S. *Alabama* within sight of Cherbourg.

The diplomatic and naval isolation of the Confederacy became complete. "King Cotton" had failed. Confederate diplomacy, lacking decisive support from the battlefield, did not win European capitals to its cause. The "War Between the States" had remained just that.

War as Catalyst

When the Civil War finally ended at Appomattox in April 1865, more than 600,000 Americans lay dead, and hundreds of thousands nursed disfiguring wounds. The war cost at least $20 billion in destroyed property and expenditures. The American merchant marine lay in shambles. U.S. commerce was badly disrupted. The eleven Confederate states suffered heavy economic losses, as a dislocated population and labor force, including 4 million former slaves, worked in denuded agricultural fields and burned-out cities. Although the Union became whole once again, regional bitterness persisted. The necessity of postwar reconstruction suggested that sectionalism would continue to impede U.S. expansion abroad.

Countervailing evidence, however, indicated that the expansionism that had slowed in the 1850s would enjoy a rebirth. The United States, after all, had become an economic power before the Civil War. Although overall trade had stalled, northern commerce in grain with England expanded greatly during the war, and prospects for a renewal of the cotton trade were good. Even during the French occupation of Mexico (1862–1867), U.S. investors expanded into mining, petroleum, and agriculture south of the border.

During the war northern politicians established high tariffs to protect their own manufacturers, stabilized the banking system, passed the Homestead Act to settle western lands, and provided for the construction of a transcontinental railroad. Large federal expenditures of about $2 million a day generated capital accumulation and stimulated some industries. The Civil War thus helped spur the American "industrial revolution" of the late nineteenth century, which increasingly shifted the character of the nation's foreign trade from agricultural to industrial goods. An economic and political "colossus . . . has been created on the other side of the Atlantic," a French observer noted in 1866, so that "within thirty years North America will be a rival to Europe, competing with her in everything."

The victory of Republican principles elevated America's international status. Despite taunts about the American "smashup" from foreign critics, the Lincoln administration had won the war, freed the slaves, and preserved federal institutions. None other than the European socialist Karl Marx congratulated Lincoln on delivering "the Union from this curse and shame" of slavery. Indeed, as one historian has noted: "Before 1861 the two words 'United States' were generally regarded as a plural noun: 'The United States *are* a republic.' The war marked the transition of the United States to a singular noun." Simply put, "the vision of a voluntary union of the states" had given way to "the imperatives of nation and empire, from which there could be no withdrawal."

Once freed from the constraints of war, Secretary Seward envisioned a larger U.S. empire. A noted expansionist before the Civil War, Seward in 1865 turned his attention southward, intent on driving the French and Maximilian from Mexico, annexing territories, expanding trade, and building naval bases in the Caribbean. Santo Domingo, which Spain ruled from 1861 to mid-1865, became one of Seward's first targets. Moreover, Lincoln's diplomatic recognition of the free black countries of Haiti and Liberia in 1861, heretofore blocked by southern opposition, suggested that racism might prove less inhibiting to American expansion after the war.

The British in particular had good reason to be wary. Northerners angrily remembered the marauding *Alabama* and the seeming British tolerance of southern secession. Also, Anglo-American competition in Central America and the Caribbean joined competition in the Pacific and Asia to propel London and Washington along a contentious course. The Marcy-Elgin reciprocity agreement of 1854 was abrogated in 1866. A new generation of Anglophobes vowed to twist the British lion's tail, with some insisting that London cede Canada to atone for its sins. Indeed, to blunt U.S. advances, the formation of the Dominion of Canada, accomplished in 1867, may have been the "most tangible international repercussion of the American Civil War."

The British nonetheless carried away from the contest some welcome precedents in international law. While the Confederacy relied futilely on such honored American policies as embargoes and the destruction of commerce, the Lincoln administration reversed the traditional U.S. view of neutral rights and adopted what had been the British position. Seward insisted that the war was a *domestic* conflict, yet the United States declared a paper-thin blockade under *international* law. Such behavior violated international law, for blockades must be effective. Seward even reversed the hallowed American doctrine that neutral shipping was immune to capture when traveling between neutral ports, regardless of the ultimate destination of the cargo. In 1863 he implicitly approved the capture of the *Peterhoff*, a British steamer loaded with Confederate goods en route to Matamoros, Mexico, suggesting that the cargo's ultimate destination made the voyage "continuous." During the period of American neutrality in the First World War (1914–1917), the British dusted off their history tomes and reminded Washington of Seward's Civil War policies. The legacy of the Civil War had a long reach indeed.

FURTHER READING FOR THE PERIOD 1848–1865

For the 1850s, Latin America, and the coming of the Civil War, see Frederick M. Binder, *James Buchanan and the American Empire* (1994); James C. Bradford, ed., *Captains of the Old Steam Navy* (1986) (U.S. Navy); Charles H. Brown, *Agents of Manifest Destiny* (1980) (filibusters); E. Bradford Burns, *Patriarch and Folk* (1991) (Nicaragua); Tom Chaffin, *Fatal Glory* (1996) (López); Don E. Fehrenbacher, *The Slaveholding Republic* (2001); John E. Findling, *Close Neighbors, Distant Friends* (1987) (Central America); William H. Freehling, *The Road to Disunion* (1990); Brady Harrison, *Agent of Empire* (2005) (Walker); Michael F. Holt, *The Rise and Fall of the Whig Party* (1999); Mark A. Lause, *Young America* (2005); Rodrigo Lazo, *Writing to Cuba* (2005); Luis Martínez-Fernández, *Torn Between Empires* (1994) (Spanish Caribbean); Robert E. May, *The Southern Dream of a Caribbean Empire, 1854–1861* (2002), *John A. Quitman* (1985), and *Manifest Destiny's Underworld* (2002); Michael A. Morrison, *Slavery and the American West* (1997); Louis A. Pérez, Jr., *Cuba and the United States* (1997); Thomas D. Schoonover, *The United States in Central America* (1991); John Schroeder, *Shaping a Maritime Empire* (1985) (U.S. Navy); and James T. Wall, *Manifest Destiny Denied* (1982).

For key characters, see K. Jack Bauer, *Zachary Taylor* (1985); Linda S. Hudson, *Mistress of Manifest Destiny* (2001) (Jane Storm Cazneau); Robert W. Johannsen, *Stephen A. Douglas* (1973); William C. Klunder, *Lewis Cass and the Politics of Moderation* (1996); John Niven, *Gideon Welles* (1973); and Ernest N. Paolino, *The Foundations of the American Empire* (1973) (Seward).

For Japan and Asian issues, see Peter Duus, *The Japanese Discovery of America* (1996); Fumiko Fujita, *American Pioneers and the Japanese Frontier* (1994); Arrell M. Gibson, *Yankees in Paradise* (1993); Gerald S. Graham, *The China Station* (1978); Joseph Henning, *Outposts of Civilization* (2000); Curtis T. Henson Jr., *Commissioners and Commodores* (1982); Michael Hunt, *The Making of a Special Relationship* (1983) (China); Walter LaFeber, *The Clash* (1997); Walter A. McDougall, *Let the Sea Make a Noise* (1993); William McOmie, *The Opening of Japan, 1853–1855* (2004); Robert A. Rosenstone, *Mirror in the Shrine* (1988) (Japan); John Schroeder, *Matthew Calbraith Perry* (2001); and Peter Booth Wiley, *Yankees in the Land of the Gods* (1991) (Perry).

Anglo-Canadian-American relations are examined in Martin Crawford, *The Anglo-American Crisis of the Mid-Nineteenth Century* (1987); Wilbur D. Jones, *The American Problem in British Diplomacy* (1974); Reginald C.

Stuart, *United States Expansionism and British North America, 1775–1871* (1988); and Donald Warner, *The Idea of Continental Union* (1960) (annexation of Canada).

For European questions, see Henry Blumenthal, *France and the United States* (1970); Alan Dowty, *The Limits of American Isolation* (1971) (Crimean War); James A. Field, Jr., *America and the Mediterranean World, 1776–1882* (1969); Normal Saul, *Distant Friends* (1991) (Russia); and Donald M. Spencer, *Louis Kossuth and Young America* (1977).

For Union and Confederate foreign policies, especially naval issues and maritime rights, see works cited above and Eugene H. Berwanger, *The British Foreign Service and the American Civil War* (1994); R. J. M. Blackett, *Divided Hearts* (2001); David W. Blight, *Race and Reunion* (2001) and *Beyond the Battlefield* (2002); Gabor S. Boritt, ed., *Why the Confederacy Lost* (1992); Adrian Cook, *The* Alabama *Claims* (1975); David P. Crook, *Diplomacy During the American Civil War* (1975) and *The North, the South, and the Powers, 1861–1865* (1974); David H. Donald, *Lincoln* (1995) and ed., *Why the North Won the Civil War* (1996); Norman B. Ferris, *The* Trent *Affair* (1977) and *Desperate Diplomacy: William H. Seward's Foreign Policy, 1861* (1975); Gary Gallagher, *The Confederate War* (1997); Charles M. Hubbard, *The Burden of Confederate Diplomacy* (1998); Brian Jenkins, *Britain and the War for the Union* (1974–1980); Howard Jones, *Union in Peril* (1992) and *Abraham Lincoln and a New Birth of Freedom* (1999); Dean B. Mahin, *One War at a Time* (1999); James M. McPherson, *Battle Cry of Freedom* (1989) and *Ordeal by Fire* (1982); Frank J. Merli, *Great Britain and the Confederate Navy* (1970) and *The* Alabama, *British Neutrality, and the American Civil War* (2004); Warren F. Spencer, *The Confederate Navy in Europe* (1983); Emory M. Thomas, *The Confederate Nation, 1861–1865* (1979); and Gordon H. Warren, *Fountain of Discontent* (1981) (*Trent*).

For Mexico and the French intervention, see Alfred J. Hanna and Kathryn A. Hanna, *Napoleon III and Mexico* (1971); John M. Hart, *Empire and Revolution* (2002); Donathon C. Olliff, *Reforma Mexico and the United States* (1981); and Thomas D. Schoonover, *Dollars over Dominion* (1978).

See also Robert L. Beisner, ed., *Guide to American Foreign Relations Since 1600* (2003).

For comprehensive coverage of foreign-relations topics, see the articles in the four-volume *Encyclopedia of U.S. Foreign Relations* (1997), edited by Bruce W. Jentleson and Thomas G. Paterson.

CHAPTER  5

Global Rivalry and Regional Power, 1865–1895

※ The Foiled Grab of the Dominican Republic, 1869–1870

PRESIDENT ULYSSES S. GRANT salivated over his pet project as he visited the elegant Washington home of the chair of the Senate Foreign Relations Committee, Charles Sumner. The flattery of senatorial egos sometimes brought fruitful results, and in this case Grant sought a two-thirds vote. On that evening in January 1870, Sumner was entertaining two politicos when Grant appeared, uninvited and unexpected. Awkward moments passed before the president revealed his mission. Would the Massachusetts senator support an annexation treaty for the Dominican Republic? Grant only briefly sketched his case for this imperialistic scheme. "Mr. President," said Sumner, "I am an Administration man, and whatever you will do will always find in me the most careful and candid consideration." The president left, satisfied that this polite remark signaled senatorial backing for the project. An American land grab seemed imminent—or so Grant thought.

The Dominican Republic had a stormy history. Formerly part of both the French and the Spanish empires, the Dominicans declared independence from Spain in 1821 only to be occupied by neighboring Haiti from 1822 to 1844. República Dominicana then won its independence, but from 1861 to 1865 Spain reestablished rule over the strife-torn nation. Often known at the time by the name of its capital, Santo Domingo, the Dominican Republic suffered rule by the unscrupulous. Dominican president Buenaventura Báez, "an active intriguer of sinister talents," seemed eager to sell his country.

The Dominican Republic had long held the eye of U.S. expansionists. The U.S. Navy coveted the harbor at Samaná Bay, a choice strategic site in the Caribbean. The country's raw materials, especially timber and minerals, attracted foreign entrepreneurs; others thought of Santo Domingo as a potential sanitarium for isthmian

114

Annexation Demonstration, Dominican Republic. James Taylor's watercolor of a Dominican rally in favor of the nation's annexation to the United States captured the moment but did not move the question. (Library of Congress)

canal workers struck by yellow fever. Yet, as expansionists warned, Europeans might thwart the "inevitable destiny" that "territorial fruits" would gravitate to the United States.

In July 1869, Grant's personal secretary, General Orville Babcock, had visited this "Gibraltar of the New World." Later exposed as a member of the Whiskey Ring, which defrauded the U.S. Treasury of millions of dollars, Babcock was also looking for personal profit. He befriended William and Jane Storm Cazneau and Joseph Fabens, American speculators and sometime diplomatic agents who owned key Dominican mines, banks, and port facilities, including the frontage to Samaná Bay. The trio also represented a steamship company that sought traffic between New York and the island. With the Cazneaus and Fabens in the wings, and warning that any attack "upon Dominicans . . . will be considered an act of hostility" to the United States, Babcock and Báez struck a deal in two treaties signed on November 29, 1869. In the first, the United States agreed to annex the Dominican Republic and assume its national debt of $1.5 million. The second treaty promised that if the U.S. Senate refused to take all of the country, Washington could buy Samaná Bay for $2 million.

Grant began to lobby for annexation. His visit to Sumner's house was a calculated step to build support. Yet the independent-minded Sumner remained noncommittal for months. The more Sumner and his colleagues heard, the more they recoiled from the untidy affair. When the U.S. Navy intervened to prevent rebels from toppling Báez, Republican senator Carl Schurz of Missouri claimed that Grant usurped the warmaking power of Congress. Babcock, moreover, had acted as a presidential agent, not as an accredited diplomat. Along with Fabens and the Cazneaus,

Charles Sumner (1811–1874). Harvard graduate, lawyer, abolitionist, critic of the War with Mexico, senator from Massachusetts, and chair of the Foreign Relations Committee (1861–1871), the strong-willed Sumner blocked attempts to annex the Dominican Republic and harassed England over the *Alabama* claims. (National Portrait Gallery, Smithsonian Institution/Art Resource, N.Y.)

he saw a lucrative opportunity and had enthralled the gullible Grant with a best-case Dominican scenario. Finally, Haiti seemed poised to invade Santo Domingo, especially when Grant talked loosely about purchasing "that island." Sumner grumbled about these unsavory facts. Other skeptics sniffed another scandal like that which had tarnished the Alaska purchase in 1867.

Grant redoubled his efforts. He warned reluctant cabinet members to back the treaty or resign. The secretary of state, Hamilton Fish, threatened to quit, but a sense of loyalty and Grant's personal appeal kept him at his post. Fish opposed annexation but favored same form of a "protectorate." He could not persuade the stubborn president, who seemed bent on total victory or total defeat. On March 15, 1870, the Foreign Relations Committee, by a 5 to 2 vote, with Sumner in the lead, disapproved the treaty. Days later, Sumner proposed instead a "free confederacy" in the West Indies where the "black race should predominate" under U.S. protection.

Annexationists countered that the absorption would ensure a steady flow of raw materials to the United States. Displaying pieces of Dominican hemp, two senators performed an impromptu tug-of-war to demonstrate the fiber's strength. Another predicted that the spindles of New England textile mills would whirl once the Dominicans began to buy American cotton goods. Anti-imperialists retorted that the Dominican populace consisted of two-thirds "native African" and one-third "Spanish Creole," a mixture "still more barbaric and savage than the pure African"; that annexation would spur the building of a larger navy, which would in turn entangle the United States in foreign troubles; that Americans were acting too much like colonizing Europeans; and that Congress had a constitutional duty to check such presidential excesses.

To regain the offensive, Grant on May 31 sent a special message to Congress extolling the virtues of the tiny island nation. It read like an expansionist's shopping list: raw materials, excellent harbors, a naval base, national security, a market for American products, and a site from which to quash the revolution raging in Cuba. Without evidence, the president claimed that "a first class European power stands ready now to offer $2,000,000 for Samaná Bay," thus violating the Monroe Doctrine. He even reported a farcical plebiscite in which the Dominicans registered their support for selling themselves to the United States by the rigged vote of 15,169 to 11.

Personalities exacerbated the issue. The plainspoken Grant had an almost visceral loathing for the urbane Sumner. Unenthusiastic about Grant's nomination in 1868, Sumner had opposed some of the president's appointees and belonged to the radical wing of the Republican party—a faction to which Grant never warmed. Grant also felt betrayed, remembering when Sumner had apparently given his word of support. Babcock called Sumner a "liar and coward" and "poor *sexless* fool." The senator, for his part, had little respect for the intellectually inferior Grant and probably felt pique at not being named secretary of state. Sumner's explosive temper, florid rhetoric, and intellectual certitude sparked obstinacy, anger, and contempt in Grant. The Dominican treaty brought these personal antagonisms to the forefront.

In June, the Senate voted 28 to 28 on the treaty, well short of the two-thirds vote required for approval. The president and loyal Republicans vowed to strip Sumner of his leadership of the Foreign Relations Committee. Sumner lost support among his colleagues when he refused even to approve a commission to study Dominican annexation. The senator denounced it as a trick, a "dance of blood," in his dramatic "Naboth's Vineyard" speech (referring to the biblical story of King Ahab, who coveted his neighbor's vineyard). Sumner scorned the Cazneaus and Fabens as "political jockeys" who had "seduced" Babcock. Santo Domingo, he insisted, belonged to the "colored" Dominicans and "our duty is as plain as the Ten Commandments. Kindness, beneficence, assistance, aid, help, protection, all that is implied in good neighborhood, these we must give freely, bountifully, but their independence is as sacred to them as ours is to us."

The Senate nonetheless voted 32 to 9 to establish the commission (it issued a favorable report in early 1871). Many senators voted aye because the commission provided a face-saving device for Grant and a rebuke to the carping Sumner. In March 1871, the Republican caucus voted 26 to 21 to remove Sumner altogether from the Foreign Relations Committee. Sumner, ill and irascible, still savored his victory over the Dominican annexation.

The Culture of Expansionism and Imperialism

The foiled grab of Santo Domingo, coming so soon after the Civil War, suggests that the sectional conflict only briefly interrupted the continuity of expansion. To be sure, most Americans in the late 1860s were not thinking about foreign-policy issues, preoccupied as they were with healing the wounds of war, reconstructing a fractured nation, and settling the trans-Mississippi West. And, although the soaring oratory of "Manifest Destiny" sounded again through the late nineteenth century, the United States lacked well-defined, sustained foreign "policies" and seemed ambivalent about overseas expansion in an era of "imperial understretch." As the Dominican episode illustrates, domestic politics, personal whims and antagonisms, and tensions between the executive and legislative branches could intrude. Fierce anti-imperialist sentiment also warned that overseas empire would undermine institutions at home, invite perpetual war, and violate such honored traditions as self-determination. Unable to work its will in some parts of the world, U.S. power largely confined itself to the Western Hemisphere and parts of the Pacific.

Still, the direction of U.S. foreign policy after the Civil War quickly became unmistakable: Americans intended to exert their influence beyond the continental United States. The more concerted, less restrained, and less erratic foreign policy that emerged in the 1890s consummated an imperial trend evident intermittently but persistently since the 1860s—"an accumulation of calculated decisions." Before the Civil War, American expansion had both commercial and territorial goals. The commercial expansion became global and largely maritime; the territorial expansion was regional and limited to areas contiguous to the United States. After the Civil War as Secretary of State James G. Blaine put it, the United States showed more interest in the annexation of trade than in the annexation of territory.

Although most Americans applauded economic expansion, many felt uneasy with overseas imperialism—the imposition of control over other peoples, denying them the freedom to make their own choices, undermining their sovereignty. The critical factor in empire-building was power—the power to make others move the way the imperial state dictated. Imperialism took several forms, both formal (annexation, colonialism, or military occupation) and informal (the threat of intervention or economic or political manipulation). For example, economic domination of a country through trade and investment constituted informal imperialism, even though Washington did not officially annex the territory and make it a colony. The United States never formally acquired the Dominican Republic, but by the twentieth century, after years of private American economic expansion into the island, it had become subservient to the United States and hence part of the informal U.S. empire. Imperialism differed from expansionism. The latter referred only to the outward movement of goods, dollars, ships, people, and ideas. In the period after the Civil War, the United States was demonstrably expansionist. In some instances, this expansion became imperialism.

An intertwined set of ideas infused post–Civil War expansion: nationalism, capitalism, exceptionalism, Social Darwinism, paternalism, and the categorization of foreigners in dismissive age-, race-, and gender-based language. Fear also influenced American attitudes toward the world and "the Other"—fear of revolutionary disorder, fear of economic depression, fear of racial and ethnic mixing, fear of women's emancipation, fear of a closed frontier, fear of declining international stature. To assuage these fears, it seemed necessary to remake other societies in the image of the United States.

A reinvigorated nationalism fueled the expansionist impulse. After the Civil War, national leaders sought to narrow sectional divisions. The 1876 centennial celebration emphasized national unity. Confederate and Union soldiers met on former battlefields to exchange flags. New patriotic associations emerged to champion nationalism: Colonial Dames of America (1890), Daughters of the American Revolution (1890), and Society of Colonial Wars (1893). World's fairs such as Chicago's Columbian Exposition of 1893 aimed to "teach . . . the world, what a young republic . . . has done in its brief past, is doing in the present, and hopes to do in the greater future for its people and for mankind." Americans thought themselves a special people, even God-favored, whose industrial power would soon surpass Great Britain's. As emissaries of Christ, representatives of the Young Women's Christian Association helped indigenous women in India and China, for example, by trying to end such practices as footbinding, child marriage, and suttee (widow immolation). Reformers in the Women's Christian Temperance Union (WCTU) spread the gospel in "heathen" lands and competed against other Anglo-Saxons who exported another "kind of American dream"—alcoholic beverages.

The prevalence of Social Darwinist thought—that by the natural order of things some people were meant to survive and others to fail—encouraged notions of racial and national superiority. In their sense of racial hierarchy, Americans placed "uncivilized" people of black color and Indians at the bottom. Slightly lower on the ladder, Americans ranked European peoples—"aggressive" Germans followed by "peasant" Slavs, "sentimental" French and Italians, and "Shylock" Jews. The middle rank comprised Latinos, the Spanish-speaking peoples of Latin America. Often disparaging Latinos as "dagoes" and "half-castes" unable to govern themselves, North American imperialists also portrayed Latin Americans as distressed damsels in need of manly rescue, as sister republics amenable to avuncular advice, and as squabbling

"The Mexican Wild Man."   Among the exhibits at American fairs were "freak shows," where people of color from abroad were displayed in exaggerated ways to suggest exotic, untamed, and uncivilized characteristics. Sometimes whites dressed up in animal skins as "wild men" and "wild women." Here, George Stall does so in the early 1890s. Such images reflected negative American views of foreign peoples of color and helped condition the environment in which U.S. leaders made decisions. (Photo by Charles Eisenmann, Special Collections Research Center, Syracuse University Library)

children requiring paternalistic supervision. Also in middle rank stood the peoples of East Asia, the "Orientals" or "Mongolians" whom Americans perceived as crafty, inscrutable, somnolent, and immoral, albeit in the case of the Japanese sometimes capable of regeneration with outside assistance.

A masculine ethos also shaped American conceptions of foreigners. Words such as "manliness" and "weakling" coursed through the language of American leaders. The naval historian Theodore Roosevelt often described other nations as too weak and effeminate, in contrast to a virile Uncle Sam, to cope with the imperatives of world politics. The gendered imagery joined race thinking to place women, people of color, and nations weaker than the United States lowest in the hierarchy of power, and, hence, in a dependent status justifying American hegemony.

The magazine *National Geographic* chronicled with photographs America's growing overseas interests. The editors chose pictures that underscored American ethnocentric notions about foreigners. Even when smiling faces predominated, the image reflected that of strange, exotic, premodern people who had not yet become "Western." Emphasizing this perspective, *National Geographic* regularly carried photographs of bare-breasted women. Fairs, too, stereotyped other peoples as falling short of "civilized." Not only did fair managers tout the technological wonders of "Western civilization," but anthropologists at the New Orleans fair of 1884 displayed the smaller skulls of "primitive races" next to larger skulls of "more advanced races," thus suggesting the need for "nurturing and protection" from Anglo-Saxon civilization. At the 1895 Atlanta and 1897 Nashville fairs, exhibits of Cubans and Mexicans in native village settings stood next to bearded women and the world's fattest man.

Religious zeal also gave impetus to imperialist attitudes. "A hundred thousand heathen a day are dying without hope because we are not there teaching the Gospel to them," exhorted the traveling secretary of the Student Volunteer Movement, founded by college students in the 1880s. However benevolent their intentions, missionaries often carried chauvinistic prejudices abroad, as indicated by one missionary "Mother Goose" rhyme: "Ten little heathen standing in a line;/One went to mission school, then there were but nine. . . . /Three little heathen didn't know what to do;/One learned our language, then there were two./Two little heathen couldn't have any fun/One gave up idols, then there was but one./One little heathen standing all alone;/He learned to love our flag, then there were none."

The multiple arguments for expansion seemed all the more urgent when Americans anticipated the closing of the frontier at home. In 1893 Professor Frederick Jackson Turner postulated his thesis that an ever-expanding continental frontier had shaped the American character. The "frontier has gone," wrote Turner, "and with its going has closed the first period of American history." Nonetheless, "American energy will continually demand a wider field for its exercise" elsewhere, perhaps overseas. The dying frontier did regenerate itself, figuratively speaking, in Europe when Colonel William F. ("Buffalo Bill") Cody brought his famed Wild West Show to England, France, Germany, Spain, Italy, and Austria-Hungary, beginning in 1887. Replete with bronco-riding, steer-roping, trick shooting, and a reenactment of General Custer's Last Stand, the stylized pageant celebrated the defeat of the primitives and "glorified the march of civilization across the American landscape" wherein the dignified, buckskin-clad Cody comported himself like "a knight of the plains" with "a chivalric past."

Of course, the Turner thesis that American distinctiveness derived from exploiting "virgin soil" in "unoccupied territory" downplayed the significance of Native Americans. So too did official policy work to remove Indians in the post–Civil War era, pushing tribes into smaller reservations, taking lands for the railroad, killing buffalo, fighting military campaigns against the Sioux, Nez Percé, and Utes in the 1870s and against the Apache a decade later. The Indians' victory over General George A. Custer's troops at the Little Big Horn in Montana in 1876 proved similar to temporary Zulu success against British forces in South Africa in 1879—minor reverses in the inexorable contest between "western powers and less technologically developed peoples." By 1868 the Supreme Court ruled that Congress could override old treaties by passing new statutes without the consent of the Indians. The Dawes Severalty Act of 1887 ended communal ownership of Indian lands and granted land allotments to individual Native American families, promising citizenship to those who accepted allotments. Thus did the government pursue a "clear pattern of colonialism toward Native Americans" by the 1890s that set a "precedent for imperialist domination" of Filipinos and other peoples after the Spanish-American-Cuban-Filipino War.

Economic Expansion and International Rivalry

The dynamics of the international system favored the United States. Victorian England, heretofore the dominant power, started to suffer relative decline. In the 1870s, European imperialists began to carve up Asia and Africa into colonies and exclusive spheres of influence. When the U.S. economy, unburdened by large defense expenditures, surged after the Civil War and passed Britain as the world's foremost industrial power by the early 1890s, it seemed imperative that Washington should compete or be left behind.

When nationalistic Americans boasted about their country, they especially celebrated its economic achievements. After the Civil War, railroads created a coast-to-coast marketplace. Bold entrepreneurs such as John D. Rockefeller and Andrew Carnegie built huge corporations whose assets and incomes dwarfed those of many of the world's nations. In the process of industrialization, inventors such as Thomas Edison and George Westinghouse pioneered whole new enterprises—in their case, electricity. The spread of the telegraph and telephone linked Americans together in a national communications network. Sprawling, busy cities became the centers of rapidly expanding manufacturing production. The federal government, through subsidies, land grants, loans, tariffs, and tax relief, stimulated the growth of American business. Not all went well, of course. Major depressions in 1873–1878 and 1893–1897, the financial insolvency of railroads, farm indebtedness, inhumane working conditions, child labor, political corruption, business abuses, discriminatory wages favoring men over women, and the failure of consumption to keep pace with production tarnished the American record. Still, the United States by 1900 had become an economic giant surpassing Great Britain and Germany. From the early 1870s to 1900 the gross national product more than doubled.

Foreign trade helped to spur this growth. The U.S. "feeds and clothes Europe," a Frenchman wrote in 1876, "it feeds us grain and salt and dresses us in cotton; it gives us half the tobacco we need." Exports expanded from $234 million in 1865 to $1.5 billion in 1900. Although exports of manufactured items increased, agricultural goods (cereals, cotton, meat, and dairy products) accounted for about three-quarters of the total in 1870 and about two-thirds in 1900. From 1874 until 1934, with the one exception of 1888, the United States enjoyed a favorable balance of trade (exports exceeded imports).

Growing American productive efficiency, a decline in prices, the high quality of American products, and improvements in transportation (steamships and the Suez Canal) help explain this impressive upturn in foreign trade. In 1866, through the persevering efforts of Cyrus Field, an underwater transatlantic cable linked European and American telegraph networks. James A. Scrymser connected the U.S. telegraph system with Latin America, first wiring Florida to Havana, Cuba, and then, in 1881, Galveston, Texas, to Mexico City. By 1883 Americans could communicate directly with Brazil; in 1890 Scrymser's lines reached Chile. By hooking into British cables, Americans could "talk" with Asian cities as well. Transfer of information that had once taken days and weeks could now flow around the world in hours. Business leaders, diplomats, naval officers, and journalists worked the new communications system to seize opportunities. Reporter Nellie Bly's celebrated trip around the world in seventy-two days in 1890 showed how much technology had shrunk the globe.

Although exports represented only 6 to 7 percent of the gross national product, American prosperity and key segments of the economy came to rely on foreign sales. It became popular to think that surplus production, or the "glut," had to be exported to avert economic calamity at home. Otherwise, the economist David A.

Wells warned, "we are certain to be smothered in our own grease." The glut thesis appealed particularly to farmers, for the domestic marketplace could not absorb their bounty. Producers of cotton, tobacco, and wheat counted on foreign markets. Over half of the cotton crop was exported each year, and wheat growers in the period 1873–1882 received about a third of their gross annual income from exports. Wisconsin cheesemakers shipped to Britain; meat companies sold refrigerated beef in Europe; and Quaker oats became an international food. To sell American grain in Asia, James J. Hill of the Great Northern Railroad distributed cookbooks translated into several languages.

John D. Rockefeller's Standard Oil also sold abroad, notably in Germany, England, Cuba, and Mexico. "Even the sacred lamps over the Prophet's tomb at Mecca," one U.S. diplomat bragged in 1879, "are fed with oil from Pennsylvania." Cyrus McCormick of International Harvester sent his "reaper kings" into Russian fields, and by the turn of the century his company's foreign sales accounted for about 20 percent of its business. Metal-products firms such as National Cash Register and Remington became active globally. Alexander Graham Bell and Thomas Edison collaborated in 1880 to install England's first telephone system. U.S. entrepreneurs also planted a huge banana industry—an "empire in green and gold"—in the Caribbean and Central America after the Civil War, culminating in the merger of the United Fruit Company in 1899, whose steamships and railroads soon controlled 90 percent of the banana market in the United States. As the trademark "Made in America" came to signify superior products at affordable prices, Europeans prophesied the "Americanization of the world." Thus did one British journalist gripe that the average Briton "rises in the morning from his New England sheets," shaves with a "Yankee safety razor, pulls on his Boston boots over his socks from North Carolina, slips his Waltham or Waterbury watch in his pocket," sits at his office on "a Nebraska swivel chair, before a Michigan roll-top desk," and writes letters on a "Syracuse typewriter, signing them with a New York fountain pen."

Official Washington subsidized exhibitions in foreign trade fairs and assisted business in other ways to expand abroad. Consular officials prepared reports on commercial prospects, and naval officers scouted markets and protected merchants. The government provided help in expanding the telegraph, negotiated reciprocity treaties to open trade doors, and kept up the drumbeat of patriotic rhetoric about the wonders of the export market.

Until the 1890s, however, economic expansion derived primarily from the activities of private companies and individuals, not from governmental policies. Washington so neglected the merchant marine that by 1900 American ships carried only 10 percent of U.S. trade. The diplomatic corps and consular service were besmirched by the spoils system; too many political hacks rather than professionals filled their ranks. Washington also maintained a high-tariff policy, with rates reaching a peak in the 1890 McKinley Tariff (average duties of 49 percent). This exclusionist policy may have slowed the pace of economic expansion by stimulating foreign retaliatory tariffs against U.S. products. Americans could nonetheless successfully pursue protection at home and commercial expansion abroad because England, still the world's leading economic power, maintained a liberal trade strategy and welcomed U.S. exports.

ZULULAND.

COPYRIGHT 1892, BY THE SINGER MANUFACTURING CO.

Singer Sewing Machine in Zululand. The Singer Manufacturing Company distributed this promotional postcard at the 1893 Columbian Exposition in Chicago. Three-quarters of all sewing machines sold in world markets were Singers. This machine was sold in South Africa, where, the company advised, the "Zulus are a fine warlike people" moving toward "civilization" with Singer's help. (Neg. #WHi [X3] 48814, Wisconsin Historical Society)

How significant were foreign commerce and investments ($700 million in 1897) to the U.S. economy? The statistics presented above tell only part of the story. The rest lies in perception. Prominent Americans *believed* that the economic health of the nation depended on selling their surplus production in foreign markets. During depressions especially, goods stacked up at home could be peddled abroad, thus stimulating the American economy. Hypothetically, even if only 1 percent of American goods sold abroad and exports represented only 1 percent of the gross national product, foreign trade would be inescapably intertwined with foreign policy and thus a factor of importance. Anticipating conflicts and wars, the navy's policy board in 1890 concluded: "In the adjustment of our trade with a neighbor we are certain to reach out and obstruct the interest of foreign nations." And even if all the efforts to expand trade delivered minimal results, the quest itself would necessitate naval and diplomatic activity.

Why did American leaders believe foreign trade so important? First, exports meant profits—the pocketbook issue. Second, exports might relieve social unrest at home caused by overproduction and unemployment. Third, economic ties could lead to political influence (as in Hawai'i and Mexico) without the formal necessity of military occupation and management. Fourth, foreign trade, hand in hand with religious missionary work, could promote "civilization" and human uplift. Fifth, economic expansion helped spread the American way of life, creating a more hospitable world. Sixth, foreign trade, if it conquered new markets abroad and helped bring prosperity to the United States, enhanced national pride at a time of international rivalry. Trade, then, held an importance beyond statistics. It became an intricate part of American "greatness" because leaders believed it vital to the national interest.

The New Navy

In the late nineteenth century a popular doctrine gradually took hold: To protect overseas commerce, deemed vital to America's well-being, the nation had to build a larger navy. In popular terms, the navy acted as "the pioneer of commerce." To fuel and repair ships in distant waters, naval stations and colonies had to be added. To ensure that foreigners did not endanger American merchants, property, investments, and trade, U.S. warships had to go on patrol, ready to use force to protect U.S. interests in an era of intense international rivalry. As one naval officer put it bluntly: "The man-of-war precedes the merchantman and impresses rude people." Since the end of the War of 1812, the United States had been stationing warships in Latin America, Africa, and Asia to protect the American merchant marine and merchants. New to the 1880s and 1890s was the shrinking theater of free operations, as European imperialists seized colonies and closed out other foreigners. For the U.S. Navy, then, the next enemy might be an imperial European navy rather than a truculent "mob" in an Asian port. New strategies and technologies seemed imperative.

By European standards, American military power before the 1890s was meager. The army demobilized after the Civil War, then killed or tamed Indians on the frontier under a strategy of "annihilation," and shrank to fewer than 30,000 troops. The navy concentrated on defending the long American coastline and protecting American life and property abroad. For these tasks, U.S. forces seemed adequate. The European powers, feuding in the Old World, did not threaten America. Even the most bellicose European militarist would have been deterred by the difficulties of transporting forces across the Atlantic and then supplying them in the United States, whose tremendous size and fiercely independent population could swallow alien armies. The navy could punish unarmed peoples, chase pirates, protect missionaries and traders, and chart unexplored regions. Without faraway fueling stations for taking on coal, a navy of long-range, steam-driven, blue-water vessels did not make much sense. The brown-water ships designed for coastal defense and riverine operations seemed adequate.

In the 1880s and 1890s, as U.S. expansionism accelerated and overseas commitments increased, young naval officers joined politicians, shipbuilders, armaments manufacturers, and commercial expansionists to lobby for an expanded fleet. The navy had not kept pace with European technological advances in hulls, engines, and guns. Dominated by the political spoils system, government-operated shipyards had become corrupt and inefficient. Naval leaders pressed for improvements. As the Europeans built fast, heavily armed, well-armored battleships, America's slower, wooden cruisers and gunboats became obsolete—mere floating museums, snickered European officers.

Rear Admiral Stephen B. Luce, father of the modern U.S. Navy, became an effective naval politician. He founded the Naval War College in 1884, instilled greater professionalism, and encouraged officers such as Captain Alfred T. Mahan to disseminate their ideas. Mahan earned an international reputation for popularizing the relationship between a navy and expansion. An instructor at the Naval War College, Mahan published his lectures in 1890 as *The Influence of Sea Power Upon History*. Not only did British, German, and Japanese leaders read the book, but it also became a treasured volume in the libraries of American imperialists such as Henry Cabot Lodge and Theodore Roosevelt. A nation's greatness depended on its sea power, Mahan argued. Victory in war and a vigorous foreign trade, two measurements of greatness, depended on an efficient and strong navy. Ships of war, in turn, required fueling stations and colonies, which would further enhance foreign commerce and national power.

During the 1880s, the U.S. Navy evolved from sail-driven and wooden-hull ships to steam-powered and steel-clad vessels. Its mission ultimately shifted from coastal defense to command of the seas. In 1883 Congress funded the *Atlanta, Boston,* and *Chicago*—steel-hull, steam-powered cruisers. By 1889, funding for thirty more vessels, including the battleship *Maine,* was approved. With Secretary of the Navy Benjamin F. Tracy (1889–1893) urging seagoing battleships for this "New Navy," the fast armor-plated *Oregon, Indiana, Massachusetts,* and *Iowa* soon joined the fleet bearing the names of states to rally public support for naval expansion. The sleek battleship designs with armored turrets and jutting guns so impressed the editors of *Scientific American* that they reproduced them in seventeen cover engravings in 1887, thus projecting what has been called "battleship envy." In the process, the government, military, and industry forged a partnership that would grow through the twentieth century.

By 1893 the navy ranked seventh in the world. These "New Navy" ships would spearhead the imperialist ventures of the 1890s: the *Boston* and its crew helped attach Hawai'i to the United States; the destruction of the *Maine* in the harbor of Havana helped move the United States toward war with Spain; the 14,000-mile race of the battleship *Oregon* from the Pacific coast to Cuba in 1898 fired desire for a canal across Central America; and the cruiser *Olympia* carried Commodore George Dewey into Manila Bay to help seize the Philippines from Spain.

Secretary William H. Seward Eyes the Future

As secretary of state from 1861 to 1869, William Henry Seward connected prewar and postwar expansionism. Until 1865 he had to prevent European powers from interfering in the Civil War (see Chapter 4). Thereafter this confident Republican leader avidly redirected foreign policy toward his vision of a coordinated empire tied together by superior U.S. institutions and commerce. Latin America, the Pacific islands, Asia, and Canada, Seward prophesied, would eventually gravitate toward the United States because of the contagion of American greatness. He believed that "commerce has largely taken the place of war" and that trade would produce "influence" and bind distant areas together. Surplus American meats, cereals, and cotton goods would flow to overseas markets, accompanied by "the Bible, the Printing Press, the Ballot Box, and the Steam Engine," Seward boasted. His blueprint for empire rested on improved foreign trade, immigration to provide cheap labor for American factories, high tariffs to protect industry, liberal federal land policies to open the American West to economic development, globe-circling telegraph systems, transcontinental railroads, a Central American canal, and annexation of non-contiguous territories.

In 1865 Seward began negotiations with Denmark to purchase the Danish West Indies (Virgin Islands), potential naval stations for defending the Caribbean and Gulf. Seward promised $7.5 million for two of the islands, St. Thomas and St. John, in a treaty signed in October 1867. When a hurricane and tidal wave wracked St. Thomas, critics poked fun at Seward's "footholds." The accord also reached the Senate at the very time that President Andrew Johnson faced impeachment. Incoming President Grant shelved the treaty, and the Virgin Islanders had to wait until 1917 for American annexation.

Seward also wanted a piece of the Dominican Republic. In 1866 he offered $2 million for Samaná Bay, but the proposed deal languished until he left office. Seward's vision encompassed Haiti (which he thought of annexing outright), some small Spanish, French, and Dutch islands in the Caribbean, revolution-torn Cuba, Iceland and Greenland (both of which he hoped to buy), Honduras's Tigre Island, and Hawai'i, fast becoming Americanized as more sugar was planted and more churches built. Seward's imperialist ambitions went unfulfilled in his day, except for two real estate transactions. One minor acquisition occurred in August 1867 when Captain William Reynolds of the U.S.S. *Lackawanna* formally claimed the Midway Islands, some 1,000 miles northwest of Hawai'i. Most Americans never knew about these tiny imperial outposts until the great American-Japanese naval battle there in 1942.

More significant and controversial was Seward's purchase of Alaska. Russia had put Alaska up for sale because it no longer remained profitable as colonial property, and because the tsar feared that Britain would seize the undefended territory in a future war. Edouard de Stoeckl, the Russian diplomat who negotiated the transfer, noted: "In American eyes this continent is their patrimony. Their destiny (manifest destiny as they call it) is to always expand." American fur traders, whalers, and fishermen had been exploiting the area's natural resources for decades. Why not cultivate a "friend" and sell the 591,000 square miles (twice the size of Texas) to the

Makers of American Foreign Relations, 1865–1895

Presidents	Secretaries of State
Andrew Johnson, 1865–1869	William H. Seward, 1861–1869
Ulysses S. Grant, 1869–1877	Elihu B. Washburne, 1869
	Hamilton Fish, 1869–1877
Rutherford B. Hayes, 1877–1881	William M. Evarts, 1877–1881
James A. Garfield, 1881	James G. Blaine, 1881
Chester A. Arthur, 1881–1885	Frederick T. Freylinghuysen, 1881–1885
Grover Cleveland, 1885–1889	Thomas F. Bayard, 1885–1889
Benjamin Harrison, 1889–1893	James G. Blaine, 1889–1892
	John W. Foster, 1892–1893
Grover Cleveland, 1893–1897	Walter Q. Gresham, 1893–1895
	Richard Olney, 1895–1897

United States? Seward moved quickly. "Why wait until tomorrow, Mr. Stoeckl? Let us make the treaty tonight," he said.

The cabinet and president remained largely ignorant of the talks until Seward produced a hastily drawn treaty and a bill for $7.2 million—no small sum in March 1867. Although the editor Horace Greeley joked about "Walrussia" as a worthless acquisition, Seward astutely won over Charles Sumner, who applauded Alaska's commercial potential and natural resources. Sumner's influence; a vigorous propaganda program, in which Seward compared Alaska to the Louisiana Purchase; the Russian minister's hiring of lobbyists and distributing $100,000 in bribes to key members of Congress; and the exhilaration over expanding American boundaries—all combined to carry the treaty through the Senate only ten days after it was signed. The House stalled fifteen months before voting the funds, but by then Seward had already raised the Stars and Stripes over his imperial catch.

Seward acquired fewer territories than he desired, largely because of domestic obstacles. A Republican supporter of Democratic President Johnson, Seward evinced little sympathy for the plight of freed blacks in the South. Angry Radical Republicans called for Seward's ouster from the cabinet and helped block his imperialistic schemes. Some people soured on expansion because of the corruption attending the annexation of Alaska. Reconstruction, railroad growth, an inflated economy, landless freedmen, a recalcitrant South—such issues compelled many Americans to look inward and to skimp on foreign adventures that cost money. Seward could only lament "how sadly domestic disturbances of ours demoralize the National ambition."

The secretary's ambition misfired, too, because articulate anti-imperialists such as Senator Justin Morrill (Vermont), the author Mark Twain, and the editor E. L. Godkin spoke out. They called for the development of America's existing lands and for showcasing domestic reforms as the best way to persuade other people to adopt U.S. institutions. Whereas some imperialists were racists who wanted to subjugate "inferior" people, some anti-imperialists, such as Godkin, opposed the annexation of the Dominican Republic because thousands of Catholic, Spanish-speaking blacks might seek U.S. citizenship. Other anti-imperialists insisted that colonialism violated the principle of self-government and increased the threat of foreign wars. Such dissent helped thwart Seward's efforts to create a larger empire. He moved too fast for most Americans.

Great Britain, Canada, and North American Disputes

Anglo-American tensions, so evident during the Civil War, persisted in the 1865–1895 period. Union leaders remained irate over Britain's alleged bias toward the South, especially the outfitting of Confederate vessels in British ports. At war's end, Seward filed damage claims, even proposing at one point that Britain cede to the United States British Columbia or the Bahama Islands in lieu of a cash settlement. Canadians and Americans squabbled over the Fenian raids, tariffs, boundaries, fishing rights in the North Atlantic, and seal hunting. The neighbors to the north bristled at arrogant predictions that the United States would one day absorb Canada.

Although annexationist rhetoric echoed throughout the United States, only the hottest heads urged force to attach Canada to the Union. Pure Manifest Destiny doctrine, after all, prescribed patience until the inevitable "Americanization" of Canadians. And while Americans were busy settling their own West, there seemed no hurry. Even though "twisting the Lion's tail" proved popular politics in the United States, few politicians wanted British naval assaults on American shores.

The resistance of infant Canadian nationalism also foiled expansion northward. Canadian nationalists such as John A. Macdonald actually saw themselves as British North Americans, who disapproved of the political scandals, racial and ethnic prejudices, and flashy materialism of Gilded Age America. Macdonald became his nation's first prime minister when the Dominion of Canada came into being in 1867 as a confederation of provinces. Free homesteads under the Dominion Lands Act of 1872 and construction of the Canadian Pacific Railway facilitated settlement of Canada's prairie provinces and ensured that the dominant culture would remain "Protestant, conservative, and very British." Hard times in the 1880s revived discussions about commercial union, or a common market, but higher U.S. tariffs caused such ideas to "blaze, crackle, and go out with a stink," as Macdonald put it. By century's end, Americans had come to see Canada less as "a northern enemy base" and more as "a brother government soon to adopt the republican principles America held dear."

Despite these longer trends, Anglo-Canadian-American relations see-sawed from crisis to crisis. In 1866, armed forces of the Fenian Brotherhood, Irish-American militants pledged to win Irish independence from Britain, attacked Canada from Vermont. Seward wanted Canada, but not through such methods. He sent troops to the border to squelch further skirmishes. Canada soon became entangled in another Anglo-American dispute: the question of the English-built Confederate ships (especially the *Alabama*) that had disrupted Union shipping during the Civil War. The irrepressible Charles Sumner added the naval damages to indirect damages by claiming that British aid had prolonged the war by two years; he totaled up a bill of $2.125 billion. Some Americans thought the transfer of Canada to the United States would erase the debt. A Joint High Commission eventually negotiated the Washington Treaty in May 1871 wherein the British expressed regret for the actions of British-built Confederate raiders, and the signatories agreed to establish a tribunal in Geneva, Switzerland, to determine damages and claims. That arbitral commission's decision came in December 1872: Britain must pay the United States $15.5 million. "As the price of conciliating the United States, and protecting British naval interests," one historian has written, "it was a bargain."

Another longstanding dispute proved more rancorous—the rights of American fishermen in North Atlantic waters. The Washington Treaty gave permission to Yankee fishermen to cast their nets in Canadian waters and allowed Canadians to fish the coastal regions of the United States above 39° north latitude. Macdonald grumbled that the British were conceding too much to the Americans. But the prime minister recognized Canadian weakness—the federation had not yet "hardened from gristle into bone." In 1877 a fisheries commission ruled that the United States should pay $5.5 million for the privilege of fishing in Canadian waters. The United States paid, but in 1885 it reactivated the fish war by unilaterally abrogating that part of the Washington Treaty dealing with fishing rights. The Canadians thereupon began seizing American vessels. A British diplomat denounced Americans as "a bunch of dishonest tricksters." An Anglo-American fisheries treaty of 1888 failed to pass the Senate. Then British minister Sir Lionel Sackville-West committed a sin of the first order for a diplomat. When a Republican pretending to be a former Englishman asked Sackville-West whether he should vote in 1888 for the Republican candidate Benjamin Harrison or the Democrat Grover Cleveland, the careless diplomat recommended Cleveland as more friendly to Britain. Gleeful Republicans printed and distributed copies of Sackville-West's indiscreet letter. Cleveland sent Sackville-West packing just before the president lost his reelection bid. The prime minister, Lord Salisbury, pointedly did not send a new envoy until March of the next year.

Anglo-American rivalry next flared over seals in the Bering Sea near Alaska. Most of the seal herds lived in the Pribilof Islands near the Aleutians. American law forbade the killing of female or young seals and limited the slaughter of males. Yet foreign hunters slaughtered at will when the animals wandered on the high seas in search of food. In 1889 President Harrison warned Canadians against "pelagic" sealing (killing animals in ocean waters). When U.S. cutters seized several Canadian sealing boats in international waters, the British sent four warships to the disputed region. In 1891 diplomats struck a temporary agreement halting pelagic sealing for a year and eventually placed these matters before an arbitral tribunal. In 1893 the arbiters permitted pelagic sealing within prescribed limits. The furry mammals continued their numerical decline until 1911, when the United States, Britain, Russia, and Japan finally banned pelagic sealing altogether and limited land kills. The seal population soon rejuvenated, thus marking an early example of U.S. and international environmental regulation.

Americans in Asia: China, Japan, and Korea

With its vast territory, huge population, and tributary states, China attracted foreigners eager to sell, buy, invest, convert, and dominate. Although some Chinese leaders considered Americans less bullying than British gunboat diplomatists, the Chinese viewed all westerners as "barbarians." Indeed, the United States demanded the same privileges China granted to other nations: open ports, low tariffs, protection for missionaries, and exemption of foreigners from Chinese legal jurisdiction. Before the 1890s the United States largely followed the British lead by practicing "hitchhiking" diplomacy; they seized opportunities created by the guns of other westerners to expand trade and missionary work. The Asiatic Squadron, for example, cruised the seas and visited ports to protect American lives and commerce.

In 1870, fifty American companies operated in China but this number dropped to thirty-one a decade later. U.S. exports to China slumped to $1 million in 1880; and although they rose to $15 million in 1900, trade with China claimed a minuscule part of American overseas commerce. Cotton goods and kerosene constituted the largest exports. Cheap, coarse cloth from U.S. mills soon undercut finer British textiles and came to dominate the Chinese market and to account for about half of the American industry's foreign sales. Kerosene also became big business in China; Standard Oil of New York advertised widely and introduced small, inexpensive

"Pacific Chivalry." How Californians handled the Chinese. The historian David M. Pletcher has written that increased contact with Chinese immigrants after the 1840s created a stereotype in which the "heathen Chinee" were seen as "backward, unreliable, deceitful, and immoral, perhaps not even human." (*Harper's Weekly,* 1869)

lamps. U.S. investments in China remained modest, growing to less than $20 million by 1900.

Protestant missionaries, another American presence in China since the 1830s, steadily expanded their work, moving from treaty ports to the interior. By 1889 500 of them, mostly women, carried Christian teachings to "the heathen Chinee." They not only gained converts; they also helped promote American products simply by using them in front of curious Chinese. In some cases, religious missionaries and economic expansionists joined hands, as when Singer executives and missionaries championed the "civilizing medium" of the sewing machine. "Fancy what would happen to the cotton trade if every Chinese wore a shirt!" remarked Charles Denby, who represented the State Department in China in 1885–1898. "Well, the missionaries are teaching them to wear shirts."

Between 1850 and 1900 about half a million Chinese, mostly males, emigrated to the United States. They mined, built railroads, farmed, and laundered. By the mid-1870s about 150,000 Chinese resided in the United States, with the largest number in the San Francisco area. Wherever they settled, the Chinese formed close-knit communities, or "Chinatowns." Many joined secret societies and maintained their cultural identity. Sinophobia on the West Coast wreaked hatreds and violence on the expatriate Chinese and created laws to exclude Asian immigrants. Americans in California spawned myths about filthy, rat-eating, opium-drunk "coolies" who threatened American culture by refusing to assimilate. White laborers complained that Chinese workers ate little and depressed wages. Anti-Chinese violence flared through the 1860s and 1870s; riots rocked Los Angeles in 1870 and San Francisco seven years later. In October 1880, 3,000 white men attacked the Chinese district in Denver, killing one resident, beating others, destroying property.

Five years later at Rock Springs, in the Wyoming Territory, white miners invaded Chinatown during labor and ethnic unrest in the area. The Chinese workers fled, but many were shot; others burned to death in fires set to raze the Chinese community. At least twenty-five mutilated Chinese bodies lay in the debris. The

Chinese minister to the United States called the local judicial proceedings, in which all rioters won acquittal, a "burlesque." President Cleveland, who dispatched federal troops to restore order, deemed the result a "ghastly mockery of justice." Congress eventually paid an indemnity of $148,000 to Chinese who had lost property.

Washington strongly lectured the western states against violence but informed Chinese diplomats that the federal government had no legal jurisdiction. At the same time, U.S. officials demanded that Beijing protect Americans in China where missionaries bore the brunt of nativist hostility and violence. By undermining the authority of local elites and by seeking Christian converts who fractured the local society, missionaries became subversive "foreign devils" around whom circled myths about exotic sexual and medical practices. Antimissionary riots erupted in the 1880s and 1890s, prompting more appeals for official U.S. protection.

Washington and Beijing at first tried to reduce friction. Anson Burlingame, U.S. minister to China (1861–1867), went to work for the Chinese government after his retirement with an assignment to reduce western intrusions. With Secretary Seward he negotiated the 1868 Burlingame Treaty, providing for free immigration between the two nations and the stationing of Chinese consuls in the United States (to look after Chinese subjects). Seward welcomed the pact as a step toward improved trade.

Sinophobic politicians from the West lobbied hard to restrict Chinese immigration. A new treaty negotiated with China in 1880 permitted the United States to suspend, but not prohibit, Chinese immigration. Two years later Congress suspended Chinese immigration for ten years and denied Chinese immigrants U.S. citizenship. Congress renewed these provisions again and again. China could neither protect its people in the United States nor challenge American immigration policy.

In 1863–1864, despite the Civil War, the U.S. Navy deployed one armed warship alongside British, French, and Dutch vessels to punish the Japanese for their antiforeign riots and harassment of merchant ships. At Shimonoseki this firepower destroyed forts and boats, opening the strait to trade once again. Internally divided and militarily weak, the Japanese could not resist the $3 million indemnity forced on them by the Western powers. Then, in the Convention of 1866, Japan reluctantly bestowed low tariffs on Western imports. By the late 1890s, America's trade with Japan surpassed its trade with China but still constituted only about 2 percent of total U.S. foreign commerce. Soon the Japanese consciously adopted a policy of "westernization" (which included learning American baseball), persuading some Americans that, unlike the Chinese, they had become "civilized."

Korea became one of Japan's victims. This kingdom, called the "hermit nation" because of its self-imposed isolation, remained technically a tributary state that relied on China to handle its external relations. But China's weakness left Korea vulnerable to the predatory Japanese and westerners, including the French, who used gunboats in the 1860s to punish Korea's mistreatment of missionaries. Secretary Seward hoped to trade with the kingdom, but the fate of the merchant ship *General Sherman* revealed obstacles. In 1866, without Korean permission, the trading schooner pushed upriver. Its captain became embroiled in a dispute with villagers, who burned the ship and killed all aboard. The following year, Commodore Robert W. Shufeldt recommended a punitive force to teach Korea the lesson "taught to other Eastern nations, that it can no longer maintain that contemptuous exclusiveness." A mission in

1871, headed by the U.S. minister to China and buttressed by five warships, sought not only to deal with the *General Sherman* incident but also to establish commercial relations and to guarantee the protection of shipwrecked Americans. When the fleet sailed up the Han River, Koreans fired on the advance party, whereupon American guns bombarded their forts, killing at least 300 defenders. "Every urchin in our kingdom [will] spit at and curse you," said the Koreans as they again rejected any treaty.

Japan battered Korea's gates open by imposing a treaty in 1876 that recognized Korean independence from China. The Chinese then encouraged Western contacts with Korea to thwart the Japanese—"to play off the foreign enemies one against the other." In 1882 a Korean-American treaty provided for American diplomatic representation and trade relations; the Treaty of Chemulpo passed the Senate the following year. Throughout the 1880s American entrepreneurs built trade links; even Thomas Edison signed a contract for the installation of electric lights in the royal residence. For the United States, however, Korea constituted a peripheral interest that Washington could not prevent from moving into Japan's orbit. In the Sino-Japanese War of 1894–1895 Japanese forces crushed the Chinese, as Washington remained neutral. Americans, including missionaries, tended to favor a Japanese triumph to force China into the modern age. Victorious Japan soon dominated Korea, and China became all the more vulnerable to Western and Japanese imperialists. In the late 1890s, to protect their interests in China, Americans turned to the Open Door policy (see Chapter 6).

Pacific Prizes: Hawai'i and Samoa

Hawai'i, that commercial and naval jewel of eight major islands in the Pacific, was linked in the American mind to Asia. They beckoned as exotic stations on the way to Asian markets. The undeveloped port of Pearl Harbor was an admiral's dream, and American missionaries accumulated converts and property. Although not yet ready to annex the islands, Washington repeatedly warned others not to do so. In 1875, a reciprocity treaty transformed Hawai'i into "an economic and eventually a political satellite." With Hawaiian sugar now entering the United States duty free, Claus Spreckels of California became "His Royal Saccharinity" as he bought up plantations, imported Chinese and Japanese labor, and disfigured the landscape through massive hydraulic projects. After Secretary Blaine instructed the British in 1881 to stay out of Hawai'i as "essentially a part of the American system of states," American residents organized secret clubs and military units to contest the government of King Kalakaua. In 1887, the conspirators forced the native monarch to accept the so-called Bayonet Constitution, which granted foreigners the right to vote and shifted authority from the throne to the legislature. That same year, the United States gained naval rights to Pearl Harbor.

Reflecting the longstanding American interest in Hawai'i, Secretary Blaine noted that "Hawaii may come up for decision at any unexpected hour, and I hope we shall be prepared to decide it in the affirmative." Like the expansionists of the 1840s, Americans hurried the hour. The McKinley Tariff of 1890 eliminated Hawaiian sugar's favored status in the United States by admitting all foreign sugar duty free and provided a bounty of two cents a pound to domestic U.S. growers. Sugar shipments to the United States soon declined. Hawaiian producers screamed in economic pain and plotted revolution against Queen Lili'uokalani, who became monarch in 1891. Organized into the subversive Annexation Club, influential white American lawyers, merchants, and sugar planters, many of them the sons of Protestant missionaries, plotted revolution. One of them, Sanford B. Dole, who became Hawai'i's first president, called the queen inept and corrupt because he feared that as a Hawaiian nationalist she would roll back the political power of the *haole* (foreigners). At the root of the conspiracy, of course, lay the desire to annex Hawai'i to the United States so that Hawaiian sugar would be classified as domestic rather than foreign.

On January 16, 1893, the conspirators bloodlessly toppled the queen and proclaimed a provisional government. Surrendering in protest to the "superior force" of the United States, Queen Lili'uokalani endured confinement for several months. The revolution could not have succeeded without the assistance of U.S. minister John L. Stevens and the men of the U.S.S. *Boston*. An active partisan for annexation, Stevens sent 164 armed bluejackets into Honolulu. They did not bivouac near American property to protect it, the announced pretext for landing, but quickly deployed near the monarch's palace. Brandishing Gatling guns, the troops by their very presence forced the queen to give up. Stevens recognized the provisional government, declared a U.S. protectorate, and announced that the "Hawaiian pear is now fully ripe, and this is the golden hour for the United States to pluck it." Native Hawaiians, comprising 53 percent of the population, never voted on joining the United States.

Harrison quickly signed a treaty of annexation with a "Hawaiian" commission (four Americans and one Englishman). Before the Senate could act, Grover Cleveland had replaced Harrison in the White House. Cleveland soon withdrew the treaty and ordered an investigation. It confirmed that most native Hawaiians opposed the coup and that Minister Stevens and the revolutionary leaders had "determined on annexation to the United States, and agreed on the part each was to act to the very end." Although a commercial expansionist, Cleveland worried what southern Democrats would think of incorporating a multiracial population in the Union, among other issues. The president thus killed the treaty, but he did not restore the queen, who urged beheading the usurpers and confiscating their property. The white leaders in Hawai'i had to wait for a more friendly president and for more propitious world events for the United States to annex the islands (see Chapter 6).

International rivalry increased throughout the Pacific. Germany, Britain, and the United States collided in Samoa, a group of fourteen volcanic islands lying 4,000 miles from San Francisco. American whalers had long been stopping there, and in 1839 Charles Wilkes of the U.S. Navy had surveyed the islands. After the Civil War, nationals of the three great powers scrambled for privileges and exploited the chaotic tribal politics of the islets. At stake were coconut plantations, national pride, and coaling stations. In 1872 a tribal chief granted the United States naval rights at Pago Pago, the "most perfect land-locked harbor . . . in the Pacific." This pact died because the Senate took no action. In 1878 U.S. agents for the Central Polynesian Land and Commercial Company accompanied the Samoan chief Le Mamea to Washington and negotiated a new treaty. It gave Americans privileges at Pago Pago and provided for U.S. good offices in disputes between Samoa and outside nations.

Queen Lili'uokalani of Hawai'i (1838–1917). This Hawaiian nationalist sought to stem the growing economic and political power of foreigners. Eager to take Hawai'i back for her people when she inherited the throne in 1891, she could not prevent the white Annexation Club's conspiracy to overthrow her in 1893. Hawai'i, which the United States had recognized as an independent nation in 1849, became a U.S. territory on July 7, 1898, and a state on August 21, 1959. (Library of Congress)

In 1885–1886, after years of German "calculated hostility," Secretary of State Thomas F. Bayard launched a more active diplomacy toward Samoa. He protested that Germany aimed at "the virtual displacement of the United States" from its "preferred status" as "benevolent protector" in Samoa. In 1887 Bayard convened a three-power Washington Conference, but it could not reach agreement. When Germany landed marines on Samoa, Washington dispatched a warship. German chancellor Otto von Bismarck vowed to "show sharp teeth." Eager for a "bit of a spar with Germany," Theodore Roosevelt admitted that the Germans might burn New York City. In early 1889 Congress authorized half a million dollars to protect Americans and their Samoan property and another $100,000 to build a naval station at Pago Pago. Whether boldness or bluff, this action prodded Bismarck to settle. A typhoon that devastated Samoa and sank all German and American warships also facilitated peace.

At the Berlin Conference of 1889, the three powers carved Samoa into a tripartite protectorate (the United States got Pago Pago) and forced an unpopular king on the Samoans. The writer Robert Louis Stevenson, a prominent resident of the islands, protested this violation of native sovereignty, this "Triple-Headed Ass." Ten years later, in the aftermath of the Spanish-American-Cuban-Filipino War, the United States and Germany formally partitioned Samoa into colonies, with Britain compensated by other Pacific acquisitions.

Eyeing Africa

Before the Civil War, American ships and merchant traders frequented Africa's coast. But conflict disrupted old trading patterns, lower transportation costs made European goods less expensive in African markets, and discriminatory trade practices stymied Yankee competition. As a result, the American presence on the continent shrank in the late nineteenth century. American adventurers, explorers, mining engineers, and traders, and a few naval officers dispatched to identify prospects for foreign commerce, kept some U.S. interest in Africa alive. But official Washington took few steps to advance U.S. interests in the vast land that the European powers were rushing to carve up.

American tobacco, kerosene, and rum nevertheless continued to claim a good share of African markets. Zanzibar preferred American cotton goods; in exchange, East African gum copal and ivory were shipped to New England factories. When, in the early 1880s, tribal warfare in Tanganyika interrupted the ivory trade, Connecticut plants had to shut down. In West Africa, where many consular agents had long handled American commercial interests, British tariffs hurt U.S. trade—for example, tobacco and rum on the Gold Coast and Sierra Leone. Higher tariffs in French West Africa also undercut American commerce. By 1900, U.S. trade with the continent had become inconsequential.

Americans nonetheless became fascinated with black Africa because individuals bent on adventure, fame, and wealth popularized it. Foremost among them was Henry M. Stanley, an immigrant from Wales who claimed U.S. citizenship. While working for the *New York Herald*, Stanley was sent to Africa and to find Dr. David Livingstone, the missionary-explorer who in 1866 had disappeared into central Africa in search of the Nile's source. Stanley arrived in Zanzibar in 1871 and cabled

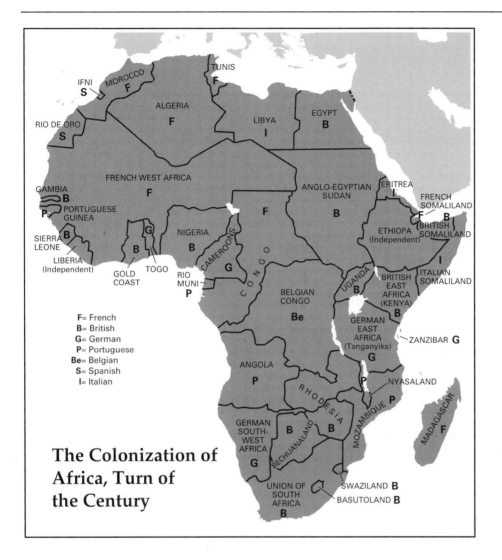

F= French
B= British
G= German
P= Portuguese
Be= Belgian
S= Spanish
I= Italian

The Colonization of Africa, Turn of the Century

dramatic stories about Africa. With an American flag at the head of his large expedition, he cut across Tanganyika and found Livingstone, who appreciated Stanley's supplies and medicine but insisted on looking for the great river's headwaters. Three years later Stanley led another venture into the African interior; in his 999-day trek through the wilderness he mapped the territory, disparaged natives as "woolyheaded rabble . . . uncurbed by the hand of law," and made the Congo Basin and himself internationally famous. Congress even voted him a resolution of thanks.

King Leopold II of Belgium saw in Stanley an instrument to bring his small nation a large empire. Unable to compete with the more powerful European imperialists, Leopold formed an organization whose announced philanthropic purpose was to end the slave trade and protect legitimate commerce, but whose real objective was an imperial foothold for Belgium in the Congo. The king hired Stanley, who negotiated with African leaders in the region to gain their allegiance to the international organization. Leopold also employed Henry S. Sanford, a U.S. minister to Belgium who sought personal gain from free trade in the region. Working to thwart the encroaching Europeans, Sanford lobbied in Washington until the United States in 1884 recognized the *Association Internationale du Congo* as sovereign over the area.

An international dispute erupted, for other European nations claimed parts of the Congo. To head off a clash, the European rivals convened in Berlin in fall 1884. Washington sent two delegates, one of them Sanford; Stanley advised the U.S. diplomats. The conferees signed an agreement that recognized the international association's (and hence Leopold's) authority over the Congo and ensured an open trade door. The new president, Grover Cleveland, shunning entanglements with Europeans, withdrew the accord from the Senate. Still, the United States abided by its terms and in 1890 sent representatives to another Congo conference. This time, the conferees in Brussels closed the commercial door by permitting Leopold to levy import duties in the Congo ostensibly to eradicate the slave trade. Having inadvertently helped the Belgian monarch take over a million and a half square miles of African territory and create "a gigantic trading monopoly behind a smokescreen of philanthropy and altruism," the United States ratified the accord two years later.

American Christian missionaries also entered Africa. By 1900 the American Board of Commissioners for Foreign Missions had built schools, hospitals, and a seminary for training an African clergy. Its missionaries established stations in South Africa, Mozambique, and Angola, and translated the Bible into Zulu. Baptists sought converts in Nigeria, and Lutherans opened missions in Madagascar. The African Methodist Episcopal Church, a major black church in the United States, sought converts in Liberia, Sierra Leone, and South Africa. In the 1890s, one of its bishops, the black nationalist Henry Turner, urged segregated and disenfranchised American blacks to emigrate to Africa—"a place of refuge . . . from the horrors of American prejudice." Hundreds of African Americans heeded his call. Most white Americans, ignorant of African diversity, viewed the continent through a racist prism: Big-game hunter Theodore Roosevelt denigrated Africans as "ape-like naked savages, who dwell in the woods and prey on creatures not much wilder or lower than themselves."

American prospectors and mining engineers flocked to the gold and diamond regions of South Africa. One fortune seeker, Jerome L. Babe, arrived in 1870 and invented a screening apparatus for diamond mining. A self-taught engineer from Kentucky, Hamilton Smith wrote glowing reports on gold that attracted large investments from the European bank of Rothschild. More than eighty Americans became Egyptian mercenaries in the 1870s. With no connection to the U.S. government, these Civil War veterans "infused American democratic attitudes into the Egyptian army" at the military academy and around bivouac campfires. Indeed, the leader of an Egyptian rebellion in 1882 attended a reception at the U.S. consulate in Cairo celebrating George Washington's birthday. To prevent the loss of the Suez Canal, however, Britain quelled the nationalist revolt and militarily occupied Egypt.

Americans knew more about Liberia than about any other African area. Settled in 1821 and governed by American blacks under the auspices of the American Colonization Society, Liberia suffered internal strife and French and British nibblings at its territory. The United States, in 1875 and again in 1879, displayed its warships to help the Americo-Liberians quash rebellions by indigenous Africans. In the 1880s and 1890s British and French forces coerced Liberia into ceding land. Calling Liberia "an offshoot of our own system," President Cleveland declared that the United States had a "moral right and duty" to protect Liberia. Although Washington refused to employ its meager power to halt imperial ambitions, its patronage, however minimal, may have forestalled full-scale European domination of that African nation.

With the United States as an interested observer, whites carved up Africa—the British took Egypt, Sierra Leone, and the Gold Coast; the Germans feasted on Tanganyika and Southwest Africa; the French grabbed Tunis and West Africa; the Portuguese absorbed Angola and Mozambique; and the Belgians gained the Congo. By 1895 Europeans had partitioned most of Africa. As at the Berlin conference more than a decade earlier, U.S. officials constantly reminded the imperialists to keep the doors open to honor the principle of equal trade opportunity.

Latin America Moves into the Yankee Vortex

During this period the United States was more active in Latin America than in any other part of the world. Americans challenged European interests, expanded trade and investment links, intervened in inter-American disputes, deployed warships in troubled waters to "show the flag," tried to annex territories, sought canal routes across Central America, lectured everybody about the supremacy of the Monroe Doctrine, and organized the Pan American movement.

When the French in 1861 intervened militarily in Mexico and placed the young Archduke Ferdinand Maximilian of Austria on a Mexican throne, the intrusion seemed to hurl a blatant challenge at the Monroe Doctrine. Seward first sent arms to the forces of former Mexican president Benito Juárez. After the Civil War, President Johnson ordered 52,000 American soldiers to Texas, where they buttressed Washington's diplomatic demands for a French exit. In early 1866 Seward firmly asked Napoleon III when the French military would withdraw. Facing opposition at home and Prussian competition in Europe, harassed by guerrillas in Mexico, and confronted by a noisy, well-armed United States, the emperor decided to recall his troops. The abandoned "archdupe" Maximilian fell in 1867 before a Mexican firing squad. Americans believed, much too simply, that they had forced France out and that the Monroe Doctrine had gained new vigor.

A quite different challenge sprang from Cuba, the Spanish colony that many North Americans believed would one day become part of the U.S. empire. From 1868 to 1878, a Creole-led rebellion bloodied the island. With annexationist sentiment strong among the Creoles, they petitioned Washington for admission to the Union. During the Ten Years' War, U.S. officials rejected Cuban independence, urged Spain to introduce reforms, and considered buying the island. With Secretary Fish disparaging the rebels, President Grant denounced any recognition of Cuban independence as impractical and indefensible. The Creoles' defense of slavery posed a major obstacle, as anti-imperialists claimed it was impossible to "make citizens" of

James G. Blaine (1830–1893). Republican representative and senator from Maine and secretary of state (1881, 1889–1892), Blaine expanded U.S. interests in Latin America. Blaine regarded Latin Americans as Washington's "younger sisters . . . a race . . . of hot temper, quick to take affront, ready to avenge a wrong whether real or fancied." (Library of Congress)

"ignorant Catholic Spanish Negroes." Someday, Fish remarked in 1869, Spanish rule would collapse and "civilized nations" would "all be glad that we should interpose and regulate the control of the Island."

The *Virginius* affair of 1873 entangled the United States in the rebellion. That Cuban-owned, gun-running vessel was captured by the Spanish, who shot as "pirates" fifty-three of the passengers and crewmen, some of them U.S. citizens. As Americans shouted for revenge, the levelheaded Fish demanded and received an apology and indemnity from Madrid of $80,000. In view of the "hundreds of thousands of children who might have been made orphans, in an *unnecessary* war undertaken for a dishonest vessel," Fish worked "to avoid the terrible evil." Cuba continued to bleed until 1878, when the rebellion ended and slavery was abolished. From then until 1895, when a new revolution erupted, islanders and exiles still cried for *Cuba Libre.*

Cubans turned more and more toward U.S. markets and capital when beet-sugar growers in Europe cut into Cuban sales and threw the island economy into chaos. North American investors, such as the Boston banker Edwin Atkins, seized opportunities to buy properties across Cuba, displacing planters of the Creole elite. Cubans also played the American game of baseball, forming their first professional league in 1878. Expatriates in Tampa and Key West donated baseball gate receipts to the cause of Cuban independence. Further evidence of cultural fusion became evident in the flow of people back and forth between Cuba and the United States. Wealthy Creoles sent their children to American colleges, married North American spouses, took North American names, and jettisoned Catholicism for Protestant denominations.

Growing economic interests in the hemisphere seemed to promise what James G. Blaine called "a commercial empire that legitimately belongs to us." U.S. investments in and trade with Latin American countries expanded dramatically—in Cuba (sugar and mines), Guatemala (the United States handled 64 percent of the country's trade by 1885), and Mexico (railroads and mines). In Mexico North American elites "tested a variety of approaches they have since used to extend their power and influence around the globe." Much of Mexico was "pulled into the Yankee vortex," as U.S. industrialists and financiers formed partnerships with local notables, pioneered cooperative arrangements with multinational firms, constructed railroads, dug copper ore, bought large tracts of land, developed ports, and meddled in Mexican politics. Helped to power by U.S. arms and dollars, the long and stable regime of Mexican dictator Porfirio Díaz (1876–1910) invited American capital and technology in the belief that it would "modernize and transform their country." By the 1890s, the United States was buying 75 percent of Mexico's exports and supplying about 50 percent of its imports. U.S. citizens had invested some $250 million in all of Latin America by 1890. Still, the region took just 5 percent of total American exports that year. Most U.S. trade remained with Europe. Yet for countries like Cuba and Mexico such links became vital and brought the United States into the internal affairs of these countries. Economic interests also drew the United States into a Brazilian civil war in 1893–1894, where Washington sent the South Atlantic Squadron to break a rebel blockade of Rio de Janeiro.

Central America attracted considerable U.S. interest because of prospects for an isthmian canal linking the Pacific Ocean and the Gulf of Mexico. The gala opening of the Suez Canal in 1869 spurred American canal enthusiasts, most notably the irascible Senator John Tyler Morgan of Alabama, an ardent expansionist who hoped to convert "the Gulf of Mexico into an American Mediterranean and Mobile into a flourishing international port." Panama and Nicaragua seemed possible sites. The problem was the Clayton-Bulwer Treaty (1850), which mandated joint U.S.-British control over any Central American canal. When President Rutherford Hayes learned in 1880 that Ferdinand de Lesseps, builder of the Suez Canal, would attempt to construct a canal through Panama, he sent two warships to demonstrate U.S. concern. "A canal under American control, or no canal," exclaimed Hayes, who called a completed canal "virtually a part of the coastline of the United States."

In 1881 Secretary Blaine denounced the Clayton-Bulwer Treaty, claiming that the United States "will not consent to perpetuate any treaty that impeaches our right and long-established claim to priority on the American continent." Three years later, in overt violation of Clayton-Bulwer, the United States signed a canal treaty with Nicaragua, although President Cleveland withdrew the offending pact when he took office. The movement led by naval officers, business leaders, and diplomats for an exclusive U.S. canal had begun nonetheless. In Panama in 1873 and 1885, U.S. troops went ashore to protect American property threatened by civil war. In the latter year a warship under the command of Alfred Thayer Mahan displayed U.S. power to Guatemala, whose invasion of El Salvador threatened James A. Scrymser's Central and South American Telegraph Company.

The convocation of the first Pan American Conference in Washington in 1889 bore further witness to the growing U.S. influence in Latin America. The glittering event attracted representatives from seventeen countries. After a tour of industrial sites in forty-one cities, the conferees assembled in Washington to hear Secretary Blaine's appeal for "enlightened and enlarged intercourse." Unlike similar conclaves in the twentieth century, the United States could not dictate the results. Opposed to hemispheric union because the "Yankees consider the Americas their own and view the remaining nations as children under their tutelage," Argentina saw Pan Americanism as a U.S. ruse to gain commercial domination. Although the conferees rejected Blaine's proposals for a low-tariff zone and for compulsory arbitration of political disputes, they did organize the Pan American Union and encouraged reciprocity treaties to expand hemispheric trade. The conference also promoted inter-American steamship lines and railroads and established machinery to discuss commercial questions.

The Pan American Union amounted to little in its early days. Its most conspicuous impact occurred on the Washington landscape, where, with major financial help from the steel baron Andrew Carnegie, the Pan American Union put up an impressive building in the nation's capital. Pan Americanism did not mean hemispheric unity; rather it represented growing U.S. influence among neighbors to the south. For that reason European powers eyed the new organization with suspicion.

Crises with Chile in 1891 and with Venezuela in 1895 (see Chapter 6) demonstrated U.S. determination to dominate the Western Hemisphere. Chilean-American relations steadily deteriorated, in part because the United States had clumsily attempted to end the War of the Pacific (1879–1883), in which Chile battled Bolivia and Peru to win nitrate-rich territory. When civil war ripped through Chile in early 1891, Washington backed the sitting government, which had tried to assume dictatorial powers. The U.S. Navy seized arms purchased in the United States and destined for the rebels. When the victorious revolutionary Congressionalists took office, President Benjamin Harrison at first withheld recognition, vowing to "instruct them" on "how to use victory with dignity and moderation." To make matters worse, Washington suspected that Britain, ever the competitor in Latin America, was cementing close ties with the new Chilean regime.

An incident in October 1891, after the end of the civil war, nearly exploded into a Chilean-American war. At Valparaiso, a major port for North American traders, one of the ships of the Pacific Squadron, the heavily armed *Baltimore,* anchored in the harbor. Commanded by Captain Winfield S. Schley, the ship had orders to protect American interests during the civil war. On October 16 its crew went ashore on liberty. The exuberant sailors gave local taverns and brothels considerable business. Outside the True Blue Saloon, rum-drunk Americans and anti-Yankee Chileans quarreled, fists flew, and knives slashed. Two Americans died, others suffered wounds, and some were arrested.

President Harrison reacted angrily to this affront to the American uniform. Captain Robley D. ("Fighting Bob") Evans of the *Yorktown* warned Chileans that "if they could not control their people," he would "shoot any and every man who insulted me or my men or my flag in any way." After a change in the Chilean cabinet in early 1892, the cautious South Americans expressed regret and paid an indemnity of $75,000 in gold. The Yankee Goliath had taught "the snarling whelps of the Pacific that we cannot be snapped at with impunity," and Latin Americans had to wonder what Pan Americanism really meant. Advocates of the expanding U.S. Navy cheered the "victory" over Chile, but a British official thought the incident created a "passionate sense of hatred toward the United States, which will take a long time to remove."

Senator George Shoup of Iowa drew a different lesson from the Chilean episode: "The American Republic will stand no more nonsense from any power, big or little." Indeed, by the mid-1890s, the United States had become far more self-confident and certainly cockier than it had been in 1865, and far more willing to exert its growing power, especially in Latin America. The anti-imperialist sentiments that had spoiled earlier imperial ventures had weakened by the 1890s, undercut by chauvinistic nationalism, international rivalry, the glut thesis, the depression of the 1890s, and the relentless U.S. expansion that had put Iowa farmers' cereals in England, missionaries in China, Wild West shows in Europe, cans of Armour corned beef in India, Singer sewing machines in the Caroline Islands, McCormick reapers in Russia, warships in Korea and Brazil, explorers in Africa, sugar growers in Hawai'i, baseball in Cuba, mining companies in Mexico, rollicking sailors in Chile, and Nellie Bly girdling the globe. All demonstrated the transformation of the United States from a regional to a global power.

FURTHER READING FOR THE PERIOD 1865–1895

General and presidential studies include Robert L. Beisner, *From the Old Diplomacy to the New* (1986); Edward J. Blum, *Reforging the White Republic* (2005); Charles W. Calhoun, ed., *The Gilded Age* (1995); Walter LaFeber, *The American Search for Opportunity, 1865–1913* (1993) and *The New Empire,* new ed. (1998); Henry E. Mattox, *The Twilight of Amateur Diplomacy* (1989) (foreign service); David M. Pletcher, *The Diplomacy of Involvement* (2001) and *The Diplomacy of Trade and Investment* (1998); William A. Williams, *The Roots of the Modern American Empire* (1969) and *The Tragedy of American Diplomacy* (1962); Fareed Zakaria, *From Wealth to Power* (1998); and Warren Zimmermann, *First Great Triumph* (2002).

For explanations of shifting power in the international system of the late nineteenth century and for comparative studies, see Philip Darby, *Three Faces of Imperialism* (1987); Aaron L. Friedberg, *The Weary Titan* (1988); Paul Kennedy, *The Rise and Fall of the Great Powers* (1987); and Anne Orde, *The Eclipse of Great Britain* (1996).

Biographical studies include Edward P. Crapol, *James G. Blaine* (2000); Joseph A. Fry, *Henry S. Sanford* (1982) and *John Tyler Morgan and the Search for Southern Automony* (1992); Henry F. Graff, *Grover Cleveland* (2002); David Healy, *James G. Blaine and Latin America* (2001); Ernest N. Paolino, *The Foundations of the American Empire* (1973) (Seward); and Gene E. Smith, *Grant* (2001).

For cultural and ideological influences, including American images of foreign peoples, see Nancy Boyd, *Emissaries* (1996) (YWCA); Holly Edwards, *Noble Dreams, Wicked Plans* (2000) (Orientalism); John Eperges, *The Imperialist Imaginary* (2004); Patricia Hill, *The World Their Household* (1985) (women missionaries); Matthew Frye Jacobson, *Barbarian Virtues* (2000); Amy Kaplan, *The Anarchy of Empire in the Making of U.S. Culture* (2002); R. Kroes et al., eds., *Cultural Transformations and Receptions* (1993); Eric T. L. Love, *Race Over Empire* (2004); Catherine A. Lutz and Jane L. Collins, *Reading* National Geographic (1993); Emily S. Rosenberg, *Spreading the American Dream* (1982); Robert W. Rydell, *All the World's a Fair* (1985), ed., *Fair Representations* (1994), and *World of Fairs* (1993); Robert W. Rydell and David Spurr, *Buffalo Bill in Bologna: The Americanization of the World, 1869–1922* (2005); David Spurr, *The Rhetoric of Empire* (1993); and Ian Tyrrell, *Women's World/Women's Empire* (1991) (WTCU).

Economic questions are treated in William H. Becker, *The Dynamics of Business-Government Relations* (1982); Vincent P. Carosso, *The Morgans* (1987); David A. Lake, *Power, Protection, and Free Trade* (1988); and Mira Wilkins, *The Emergence of the Multinational Enterprise* (1970).

The transformation of the U.S. Navy is discussed in Frederick C. Drake, *The Empire of the Seas* (1984) (Shufeldt); Kenneth J. Hagan, *American Gunboat Diplomacy and the Old Navy, 1877–1889* (1973), ed., *In Peace and War* (1984), and *This People's Navy* (1991); David F. Long, *Gold Braid and Foreign Relations* (1988); Robert Seager, *Alfred Thayer Mahan* (1977); and Mark R. Shulman, *Navalism and the Emergence of American Sea Power* (1995).

For the Great Britain–Canada–U.S. relationship, see Adrian Cook, *The* Alabama *Claims* (1975); Edward P. Crapol, *America for Americans* (1973); John M. Findlay and Ken S. Coates, eds., *Parallel Destinies* (2002); W. S. Neidhardt, *Fenianism in North America* (1975); Richard A. Preston, *The Defense of the Undefended Border* (1977); and Reginald C. Stuart, *United States Expansionism and British North America, 1775–1871* (1988).

U.S. relations with Latin America are discussed in Richard H. Bradford, *The* Virginius *Affair* (1980); Joyce S. Goldberg, *The* Baltimore *Affair* (1986); John Mason Hart, *Empire and Revolution* (2002) (Mexico); Virginia Scott Jenkins, *Bananas* (2000); Luis Martínez-Fernández, *Torn Between Empires* (1994) (Spanish Caribbean); Louis A. Pérez Jr., *Cuba and the United States* (1997) and *Cuba Between Empires* (1982); W. Dirk Raat, *Mexico and the United States* (1992); Ramón E. Ruíz, *The People of Sonora and Yankee Capitalists* (1988); Thomas D. Schoonover, *Dollars Over Dominion* (1978) (Mexico) and *The United States in Central America, 1860–1911* (1991); Lars Schoultz, *Beneath the United States* (1998); Joseph Smith, *Illusions of Conflict: Anglo-American Diplomacy Toward Latin America, 1865–1896* (1979); and Steven C. Topik, *Trade and Gunboats* (1996) (Brazil).

For Hawai'i, see Helena G. Allen, *Sanford Ballard Dole* (1988) and *The Betrayal of Queen Liliuokalani* (1982); Ralph S. Kuykendall, *The Hawaiian Kingdom, 1874–1893* (1967); John E. Van Sant, *Pacific Pioneers* (2000); and Noenoe Silva, *Aloha Betrayed* (2004).

For Asian-American relations, see David L. Anderson, *Imperialism and Idealism* (1985); W. G. Beasley, *Japan Encounters the Barbarians* (1995); Jerome Ch'en, *China and the West* (1979); Wayne Flynt and Gerald W. Berkeley, *Taking Christianity to China* (1997); Gael Graham, *Gender, Culture, and Christianity* (1995) (missionaries in China); Jack L. Hammersmith, *Spoilsman in a "Flowery Fairyland"* (1998); Joseph Henning, *Outposts of Civilization* (2000) (Japan); James Huffman, *A Yankee in Meiji Japan* (2003); Michael H. Hunt, *The Making of a Special Relationship* (1983) (China); Paul M. Kennedy, *The Samoan Tangle* (1974); Walter La Feber, *The Clash* (1997); Yun-Bok Lee, *Diplomatic Relations Between the United States and Korea, 1866–1887* (1970); Charles J. McClain, *In Search of Equality* (1994) (Chinese in United States); Craig Storti, *Incident at Bitter Creek* (1991); and Shih-shan Henry Tsai, *China and the Overseas Chinese in the United States, 1868–1911* (1983).

Alaska and Russian-American relations are discussed in James T. Gay, *American Fur Seal Diplomacy* (1987); Paul S. Holbo, *Tarnished Expansion* (1983); Ronald J. Jensen, *The Alaska Purchase and Russian-American Relations* (1975); Howard I. Kushner, *Conflict on the Northwest Coast* (1975); and Norman E. Saul, *Concord & Conflict* (1996).

U.S. interest in Africa is studied in Peter Duignan and L. H. Gann, *The United States and Africa* (1987); James L. Newman, *Imperial Footprints* (2004) (Henry M. Stanley); Thomas Pakenham, *The Scramble for Africa* (1991); Lamin Sanneh, *Abolitionists Abroad* (1999); Elliott P. Skinner, *African Americans and U.S. Policy Toward Africa, 1850–1924* (1992); and Walter L. Williams, *Black Americans and the Evangelization of Africa, 1877–1900* (1982).

See also Robert L. Beisner, ed., *Guide to American Foreign Relations Since 1600* (2003).

For comprehensive coverage of foreign-relations topics, see the articles in the four-volume *Encyclopedia of U.S. Foreign Relations* (1997), edited by Bruce W. Jentleson and Thomas G. Paterson.

CHAPTER  6

Imperialist Leap, 1895–1900

DIPLOMATIC CROSSROAD

✳ *The* Maine, *McKinley, and War, 1898*

THE SLEEK U.S. BATTLESHIP *Maine* steamed into Havana harbor on January 25, 1898. "A beautiful sight," reported the American consul-general Fitzhugh Lee, who had requested the visit ostensibly to protect Americans living in war-torn Cuba. Spain was then in its third year of attempting to suppress Cuban rebels fighting for national independence. The *Maine* was to stay three weeks and then depart for New Orleans in time for Mardi Gras. But at 9:40 P.M. on February 15, a "dull sullen" roar followed by massive explosions ripped through the 6,700-ton ship, killing 266 Americans. President William McKinley, who had been taking drugs to sleep, awoke an hour before dawn for a phone call from Secretary of the Navy John D. Long. "The *Maine* blown up! The *Maine* blown up!" the stunned president kept muttering. Even though "the country was not ready" for it, the war with Spain that McKinley was laboring so hard to avoid would occur within three months.

McKinley ordered an official investigation of the *Maine* disaster and tried to gain time. With no evidence but with considerable emotion, many Americans assumed that the *Maine* had been "sunk by an act of dirty treachery on the part of the Spaniards." In early March U.S. Minister Stewart L. Woodford protested strongly to the Spanish about the *Maine*. "End it at once—*end it at once—end it at once!*" he exhorted Madrid regarding the war in Cuba. On March 6 the president met with Joe Cannon, chair of the House Appropriations Committee, and asked for $50 million for war preparedness. Congress enthusiastically obliged three days later.

In mid-March Senator Redfield Proctor of Vermont, a friend of McKinley reportedly opposed to war, graphically told his colleagues about his recent visit to Cuba. He recounted ugly stories about the forced concentration of Cubans into fortified camps: "Torn from their homes, with foul earth, foul air, foul water, and foul food or none, what wonder that one-half died and one-quarter of the living are so diseased that they cannot be saved?" Shortly after this moving speech, which convinced many members of Congress and business leaders that Spain could not restore order to Cuba, the U.S. court of inquiry on the *Maine* concluded that an external

143

U.S.S. *Maine* Entering Havana Harbor. The gleaming white battleship, commanded by Captain Charles Sigsbee, arrived in Havana on January 25, 1898, ostensibly to protect American citizens caught up in the Cuban rebellion against Spanish rule. Because a few sailors had been swept overboard and drowned on earlier missions, the *Maine* had the reputation of being a "Jonah" or "Hoodoo" ship. (Courtesy National Archives—SC-94543)

mine of unknown origin had destroyed the vessel. A Spanish commission at about the same time attributed the disaster to an internal explosion. (More than a century later, after several more investigations, experts still disagree whether the *Maine* blew up because of "a coal bunker fire" or from an "undership mine.") In 1898 vocal Americans pinned "the crime" squarely on Spain. "Remember the *Maine,* to hell with Spain" became a popular slogan.

A decorated veteran of the Civil War, President McKinley once asserted: "I have been through one war; I have seen the dead piled up, and I do not want to see another." He quietly explored the possibility of purchasing Cuba for $300 million—or some other means "by which Spain can part with Cuba without loss of respect and with certainty of American control." But a jingo frenzy had seized Congress. Interventionist critics increasingly questioned the president's manhood, claiming, as did Assistant Secretary of the Navy Theodore Roosevelt, that he "had no more backbone than a chocolate eclair." One member of Congress called McKinley's policies on Cuba "lame, halting, and impotent," while another claimed: "He wobbles, he waits, he hesitates. He changes his mind." Following one stormy Senate session, Vice President Garrett Hobart warned: "They will act without you if you do not act at once." "Say no more," McKinley responded.

On March 27, the president cabled his demands to Madrid: an armistice, Cuban-Spanish negotiations to secure a peace, McKinley's arbitration of the conflict if there was no peace by October, termination of the forced concentration policy, and relief aid to the Cubans. Implicit was the demand that Spain grant Cuba its independence under U.S. supervision. As a last-ditch effort to avoid American military intervention, the scheme had little chance of success. The Cubans had already vowed to accept "nothing short of absolute independence." Hoping to elicit European backing, Madrid's answer held some promise: Spain had already ended concentration, would launch reforms, and would accept an armistice if the rebels did so first. Yet by refusing McKinley's mediation and Cuban independence, the Spanish reply fell short. McKinley began to compose a war message in early April. On April 9, Spain declared a unilateral suspension of hostilities "for such a length of time" as the Spanish commander "may think prudent." The declaration still sidestepped Cuban independence and U.S. mediation. Any chance of European support for Spain faded when the British told Washington that they would "be guided [on Cuban issues] by the wishes of the president." On April 11, McKinley asked Congress for authority to use armed force to end the Cuban war. Since neither Cubans nor Spaniards could stem the blood-letting, Americans would do so because of the "cause of humanity" and the "very serious injury to the commerce, trade, and business of our people, and the wanton destruction of property." Conspicuously, he made no mention of Cuban independence, defining the U.S. purpose as "forcible intervention . . . as a neutral to stop the war." At the very end of the message, McKinley asked Congress to give "your just and careful attention" to news of Spain's recently offered armistice.

As Congress debated, McKinley beat back a Senate attempt to recognize the rebels. He strongly believed that Cuba needed American tutelage to prepare for self-government. And he wanted a Cuba subservient to the United States. Congress did endorse the Teller Amendment, which disclaimed any U.S. intent to annex the island. Even Teddy Roosevelt supported the amendment lest "it seem that we are merely engaged in a land-grabbing war." On April 19 Congress proclaimed Cuba's independence (without recognizing the Cuban junta), demanded Spain's evacuation from the island, and directed the president to use force to secure these goals. Spain broke diplomatic relations on April 21. The next day U.S. warships began to blockade Cuba; Spain declared war on April 24. Congress issued its own declaration the next day.

Because of the Teller Amendment, the choice for war seemed selfless and humane, and for many Americans it undoubtedly was. But the decision had more complex motives. McKinley cited humanitarian concern, property, commerce, and the removal of a threat. Politics also mattered. Senator Henry Cabot Lodge told the White House that "if the war in Cuba drags on . . . we [Republicans] shall go down to the greatest defeat ever known." Important business leaders, initially hesitant, shifted in March and April to demand an end to Cuban disorder. Farmers and entrepreneurs ogling overseas markets thought a U.S. victory over Spain might open new trade doors by eliminating a colonial power. Republican senator George F. Hoar of Massachusetts, later an anti-imperialist, could not "look idly on while hundreds of thousands of innocent human beings . . . die of hunger close to our doors.

William McKinley (1843–1901). In one of his last speeches before his death in 1901, McKinley peered into the next century: "How near one to the other is every part of the world. Modern inventions have brought into close relations widely separated peoples . . . distances have been effaced. . . . The world's products are being exchanged as never before . . . isolation is no longer possible or desirable." (Library of Congress)

If there is ever to be a war it should be to prevent such things." Another senator claimed that "any sort of war is better than a rotting peace that eats out the core and heart of the manhood of this country." Christian missionaries dreamed of new opportunities to convert the "uncivilized." Imperialists hoped that war would add new territories to the United States and encourage the growth of a larger navy.

Emotional nationalism also made an impact. The *Maine* ignited what one educator called the "formidable inflammability of our multitudinous population." Imperialist senator Albert Beveridge waxed ebullient: "At last, God's hour has struck. The American people go forth in a warfare holier than liberty—holy as humanity." Excited statements by people such as Roosevelt, who regarded war as a sport, stirred martial fevers. War would repudiate those "old women of both sexes, shrieking cockatoos" who made virile men "wonder whether" they lived "in a free country or not." Newspapers of the "yellow press" variety, such as William Randolph Hearst's *New York Journal,* sensationalized stories of Spanish lust and atrocities. The American public, already steeped in a brash nationalism and prepared by earlier diplomatic triumphs, reacted favorably to the hyperbole.

Both Washington and Madrid had tried diplomacy without success. McKinley wanted "peace" and independence for Cuba under U.S. tutelage. The first Spain could not deliver because the Cuban rebels sensed victory and complete independence. The second Spain could not grant immediately because ultranationalists might overthrow the Bourbon constitutional monarchy. When Spain promised to fight the war more humanely and grant autonomy, McKinley and Congress wanted more, and they believed they had the right and duty to judge the affairs of Spain and Cuba.

Well-meaning or not, American meddling prevented Cubans and Spaniards from settling their own affairs. Dispatching the *Maine* and asking Congress for $50 million probably encouraged the Cuban rebels to resist any compromise. McKinley could have given Spain more breathing space. Spain, after all, did grant partial autonomy, which ultimately might have led to Cuban independence. Some critics said the president should have recognized the Cuban insurgents and covertly aided them. American materiél, not men, might have liberated Cuba from Spanish rule. By April 1898, one U.S. official concluded that Spain had become "absolutely hopeless, . . . exhausted financially and physically, while the Cubans are stronger." McKinley chose war reluctantly only after trying other options. That he adamantly refused to recognize the insurgency indicates also that he did not endorse outright Cuban independence. He probably had two goals in 1898: to remove Spain from Cuba and to control Cuba in some manner yet ill defined. When the Spanish balked at a sale and both belligerents rejected compromise, McKinley chose war—the only means to oust Spain *and* to control Cuba. A new and enlarged American empire was about to be created.

The Venezuela Crisis of 1895

Three years earlier, during the administration of an avowedly anti-imperialist president, a seemingly insignificant cartographic controversy in South America had served as a catalyst for empire. In July 1895, Secretary of State Richard Olney personally delivered a 12,000-word draft document to President Grover Cleveland on the Venezuelan boundary dispute. Deeming it "the best thing of its kind I ever read,"

"The Real British Lion." A popular American depiction of the British global presence during the crisis over Venezuela. A few years later, President Cleveland himself recalled British behavior as "mean and hoggish." (*New York Evening World,* 1895)

the president directed Olney to send the document to London, which he did on July 20.

What became known as Olney's "twenty-inch gun" was aimed at Great Britain, which had long haggled with Venezuela over its boundary with British Guiana. The British drew a line in the 1840s, but nobody liked it. In the 1880s, the discovery of gold in the region in question raised the stakes. Since the 1870s Venezuela had remonstrated against Britain's alleged violation of the Monroe Doctrine. Washington repeatedly asked the British to submit the issue to arbitration but met constant rebuff. London's latest refusal in December 1894 led to Olney's "twenty-inch gun" answer.

The Venezuelans had hired William L. Scruggs, a former U.S. minister to Caracas, to propagandize their case before the American public. His widely circulated pamphlet *British Aggression in Venezuela, or the Monroe Doctrine on Trial* (1895) stirred considerable sympathy for the South American nation. Stereotypes soon congealed: The land-grabbing British were robbing a poor hemispheric friend of the United States. A unanimous congressional resolution of February 1894, calling for arbitration, underscored growing U.S. concern. Cleveland's Democratic party had lost badly in the 1894 elections, and Republicans were attacking his administration as cowardly for not annexing Hawai'i. Bold action might recoup Democratic losses. As one Democrat advised Cleveland, "Turn this Venezuelan question up or down, North, South, East or West, and it is a 'winner.' "

The global imperial competition of the 1890s also pushed the president toward action. The British, already holding large stakes in Latin America, seemed intent on enlarging them. Like the French intervention in Mexico a generation earlier, London's claim against Venezuela became a symbol of European intrusion into the hemisphere. The economic depression of the 1890s also caused concern. Many Americans, including Cleveland, thought that overproduction had caused the slump and that expanding foreign trade could cure it. The National Association of Manufacturers, organized in 1895 to encourage exports, chose Caracas for its first overseas display of U.S. products. Might the British close this potential new market?

Cleveland also disliked bullies. He had already rejected Hawaiian annexation in part because he thought Americans had bullied the Hawaiians. Now the British were arrogantly slapping the Venezuelans. Defense of the Monroe Doctrine became his and Olney's maxim. In unvarnished language, the "twenty-inch gun" of July 20, 1895, warned that European partition of Africa should not repeat itself in Latin America. The "safety," "honor," and "welfare" of the United States were at stake, and the Monroe Doctrine stipulated that "any permanent political union between a European and an American state [was] unnatural and inexpedient." The Cleveland-Olney message stressed that Latin American countries "are friends and allies, commercially and politically, of the United States. To allow the subjugation of any one of them by a European power . . . signifies the loss of all the advantages incident to their natural relations with us." The forceful overriding theme of the note boldly addressed an international audience. "To-day the United States is practically sovereign on this continent, and its fiat is law upon the subjects to which it confines its interposition." And more: The United States's "infinite resources combined with its isolated position render it master of the situation and practically invulnerable as against any or all other powers." Finally, the message demanded arbitration and requested a British answer before Cleveland's annual message to Congress in December.

British prime minister Lord Salisbury received the missive with some surprise and sent it to the Foreign Office for study. Distracted by crises especially in Africa, Salisbury saw no urgency. In the late nineteenth century Anglophobic bombast was not unusual, especially before U.S. elections. Thus the British reply did not arrive until after Cleveland's annual message, which was actually quite tame on Venezuela. Salisbury's note, which smacked of the "peremptory schoolmaster trying—with faded patience—to correct the ignorance of dullards in Washington," denied the applicability of the Monroe Doctrine and dismissed any U.S. interest in the controversy.

On reading the note, Cleveland became "mad clean through." His special message to Congress on December 17 rang the alarm bell: England must arbitrate; the United States would create an investigating commission to set the true boundary line; then American action would follow. The message seemed an ultimatum, with the danger of war lurking throughout. Congress quickly voted funds for the commission. Republicans and Democrats rallied behind the president, and New York City police commissioner Theodore Roosevelt boomed: "Let the fight come if it must; . . . we would take Canada." With Irish-Americans volunteering to fight their ancient foe, the British ambassador reported: "Nothing is heard but the voice of the Jingo bellowing defiance to England."

War fevers cooled rapidly in early 1896. Many business leaders grew alarmed when the stock market plummeted, in part because British investors were pulling out. The *New York World* put out a special Christmas issue under the headline "PEACE AND GOOD WILL," suggesting the irrationality of war with Britain, a country so close in race, language, and culture. Even the U.S. ambassador in London feared the president had been "too *precipitate*" in joining "the camp of aggressiveness." But Cleveland never wanted war. He wanted peace on his terms.

What followed seemed anticlimactic. The British cabinet in early January 1896 decided to seek an "honourable settlement" with the United States. Facing a new dispute with Germany over South Africa, England needed friends, not enemies.

Formal talks continued until November 1896, when London and Washington agreed to set up a five-person arbitration board to define the boundary. Finally, in October 1899, that tribunal rejected the extreme claims of either party and generally followed the original line from the 1840s. The mouth of the Orinoco went to Venezuela, which came out of the dispute rather well, considering that neither the United States nor Britain cared much about Venezuela's national interest. In fact, both parties excluded Venezuela's duly accredited minister in Washington from the talks. Lobbyist William Scruggs complained that the United States sought to "*bull-doze* Venezuela." He had it right, but Washington's "sledgehammer subtlety" targeted others besides that South American nation. The overweening theme of the "twenty-inch gun" merits repeating: "To-day the United States is practically sovereign on this continent, and its fiat is law upon the subjects to which it confines its interposition."

Men of Empire

The Venezuelan crisis and the war with Spain punctuated an era of imperialist competition when, as one senator grandly put it: "The great nations are rapidly absorbing . . . all the waste areas of the earth . . . for civilization and the advancement of the race." Cleveland and McKinley helped move the United States toward world-power status. As examples of forceful, even aggressive, diplomacy, both events accelerated important trends. Besides ignoring the rights and sensibilities of small countries, both episodes revealed a United States more certain about the components of its "policy" and more willing to confront rivals. Both episodes stimulated what critics at the time called "jingoism." The Monroe Doctrine gained new status as a warning to European nations to curb their activities in the Western Hemisphere. Just as Cleveland went to the brink of war over Venezuela without consulting Congress, so McKinley, despite a jingo Congress and inflamed public opinion, reinforced presidential control over foreign policy.

In both crises Latin Americans learned again that the United States sought supremacy in the Western Hemisphere and would intervene when it saw fit. The Venezuela crisis and the outbreak of revolution in Cuba in 1895 intensified North American interest in the Caribbean, a significant dimension of which was economic. Coinciding with a severe economic depression at home, the potential loss

Makers of American Foreign Relations, 1895–1900

Presidents	Secretaries of State
Grover Cleveland, 1893–1897	Walter Q. Gresham, 1893–1895
	Richard Olney, 1895–1897
William McKinley, 1897–1901	John Sherman, 1897–1898
	William R. Day, 1898
	John Hay, 1898–1905

of markets in Venezuela and Cuba brought more attention to the theory of over-production as a cause of depression, which exports could allegedly cure. Commercial expansion received another boost.

The discord over Venezuela also helped foster Anglo-American rapprochement. Cooperation and mutual interest increasingly characterized relations thereafter between Washington and London. British diplomats cultivated U.S. friendship as a possible counterweight to growing German power, and Britain's support over Cuba and its subsequent deference regarding the Caribbean facilitated the emerging entente.

The chief way the United States could manage events in that area was through naval power. The Venezuelan crisis, joined by crises in Asia and the belief that naval construction would employ those idled by the depression, stimulated additional naval expansion. The Navy Act of 1896, for example, provided for three new battleships and ten new torpedo boats, several of which contributed to naval victories over Spain two years later.

By the end of the decade the United States had gained new U.S. colonies in the Pacific, Asia, and the Caribbean, a protectorate over Cuba, and Europe's recognition of U.S. hegemony in the Caribbean. By 1900, too, the United States had pledged to preserve the "Open Door" in China; its navy had just annihilated the Spanish fleet and ranked sixth in the world; and its export trade had grown to $1.5 billion. Steel and iron production almost equaled that of Britain and Germany combined. The postwar acquisition of new colonies suggests that *only then,* about 1898, did the United States become an imperialist world power. Having taken halting steps toward a larger empire before the depression of the 1890s, the United States then took the leap.

Theodore Roosevelt described the anti-imperialists in 1897 as "men of a bygone age" and "provincials." Indeed, anti-imperialism waned through the late nineteenth century. Increasing numbers of educated, economically comfortable Americans made the case for formal empire (colonies or protectorates) or informal empire (commercial domination). Naval officers, diplomats, politicians, farmers, skilled artisans, business leaders, and clergy made up what political scientists call the "foreign-policy public." Having access to lecterns to disperse their ideas, this "elite" helped move America to war and empire. Neither "public opinion" nor the jingoistic "yellow press" in the 1890s compelled the United States to war. Rather, two key elements stand out: a McKinley administration very much in charge of its diplomacy through skillful maneuvering, and a majoritarian view within the articulate "foreign-policy public" in favor of a vigorous outward thrust.

Analysis of the phrase "public opinion" helps explain the *hows* as distinct from the *whys* of decisionmaking. One often hears that "the man in the street" influenced a leader to follow a certain course of action. But "public opinion" did not comprise a unified, identifiable group speaking with one voice. Further, political leaders and other articulate, knowledgeable people often shaped the "public opinion" they wanted to hear by their very handling of events and their control over information—that is, leaders *led*. Social-science studies demonstrate that in the 1890s the people who counted, the people who expressed their opinion publicly in order to influence policy, numbered no more than 1.5 million to 3 million, or between 10 and 20 percent of the voting public. These upper- and middle-income groups, educated, active politically, constituted the "foreign-policy public." The "public opinion" the president heard in the 1890s did not come from the "people," but rather from a small, articulate segment alert to foreign-policy issues. Although this educated public counted anti-imperialists among them, the "foreign-policy public" leaned heavily toward the side of imperialism.

The president often dominates policymaking, even thwarting the advice of the "foreign-policy public" itself. President Cleveland, for example, successfully resisted pressure to annex Hawai'i and withdrew the treaty from the Senate, and he never let Congress or influential public opinion shape policy toward the Venezuelan crisis. Clamorous jingoes and a sensationalist press intruded in the 1890s, but the initiative in foreign affairs, unlike in the 1860s and 1870s, remained largely in executive hands, with Cleveland and McKinley "unabashed in their resistance" to "public opinion." In most historical periods, the public *reacts* to *immediate* events; the executive *acts* and *manages* with *long-term* policy considerations.

Cleveland and McKinley Confront *Cuba Libre,* 1895–1898

The year 1895 brought momentous events. The Venezuelan crisis, Japan's defeat of China in the Sino-Japanese War, and the outbreak of revolution in Cuba—all carried profound meaning for U.S. foreign relations. The sugar-rich island of Cuba, following its unsuccessful war for independence (1868–1878), suffered political repression and poverty. From 1880 to 1895, the Cuban national hero José Martí plotted from exile in the United States. In 1892 he organized the Cuban Revolutionary party, using U.S. territory to recruit men and money. Martí's opportunity came when Cuba's economy fell victim in 1894 to a new U.S. tariff, which raised duties on imported sugar and hence reduced Cuban sugar shipments to the United States. On February 24, 1895, with cries of *"Cuba Libre,"* the rebels opened their drive for independence.

Cuban revolutionaries kept a cautious eye on the United States, well known for its relentless interest in their nation's destiny. José Martí's fifteen-year stay in the United States had turned him into a critic of what he called "the monster,"—an "aggressive" and "avaricious" nation "full of hate" and "widespread spiritual coarseness." He asked rhetorically: "Once the United States is in Cuba, who will drive them out?" On May 19 Martí died in battle.

Cuban and Spanish military strategies produced destruction and death. Led by General Máximo Gómez, the *insurrectos* burned cane fields, blew up mills, and disrupted railroads, with the goal of rendering Cuba an economic liability to Spain. Spain, in turn, vowed to "use up the last peseta in her treasury and sacrifice the last of her sons" to retain Cuba. Although outnumbered (about 30,000 Cuban troops fought 200,000 Spanish) and lacking adequate supplies, the insurgents, with the sympathy of the populace, wore the Spanish down through guerrilla tactics. By late 1896 rebels controlled about two-thirds of the island, with the Spanish concentrated in coastal and urban enclaves. That year, to break the rebel stronghold in the rural areas, Governor-General Valeriano y Nicolau Weyler instituted the brutal reconcentration program. He divided the island into districts and then herded one-half million Cubans into unsanitary fortified camps, where perhaps 200,000 people soon died. Weyler's soldiers regarded any Cubans outside the camps as rebels and hence targets for death; they also killed livestock, destroyed crops, and polluted water sources. This effort to starve the insurgents, combined with the rebels' destructive behavior, made a shambles of Cuba's society and economy.

The Cleveland administration could have recognized Cuban belligerency. But such an act, Olney noted, would relieve Spain of any responsibility for paying claims filed by Americans for properties destroyed in Cuba. Cleveland and Olney found recognition of Cuban independence even less appetizing, for they believed the Cubans ("the most inhumane and barbarous cutthroats in the world") incapable of self-government and feared anarchy and even racial war. Olney toyed with buying the island at one point. The Cleveland administration settled on hostility to the revolution and pressure on Spain to grant some autonomy. Lecturing to a foreign government seemed to work in the Venezuelan crisis; perhaps it would work with Cuba.

Prodded by a Republican Congress and by Spanish obstinacy in refusing reforms and adhering to force, Olney sent a note to Spain in April 1896. He urged a political solution that would leave "Spain her rights of sovereignty . . . yet secure to the [Cubans] all such rights and powers of local self-government as they [could] ask." Spain should initiate reforms short of independence. When Spain rejected Olney's advice, the Cleveland administration seemed stymied. It did not desire war, but it meant to protect U.S. interests. Congress kept asking for firm action. And in Havana, hotheaded Consul-General Fitzhugh Lee clamored for U.S. annexation. Cleveland did not feel he could fire Lee, nephew of General Robert E. Lee, because the incumbent president needed political friends at a time when Democrats were dumping him in favor of William Jennings Bryan. Consul-General Lee also warned that "there may be a revolution within a revolution," noting that Cuban insurgents vowed to redistribute property, which U.S. officials (and Creole elites) would not tolerate. It further nettled Cleveland and Olney that Spain had approached the courts of Europe for diplomatic support, with the argument that the Monroe Doctrine threatened all European powers.

British ambassador to Spain H. Drummond Wolff accurately claimed that for Cuba the United States wanted "peace with commerce." In December 1896, Cleveland reported that neither the Spanish nor the Cuban rebels had established their authority over the island. Americans felt a humanitarian concern, he said, and their trade and investments ("pecuniary interest") faced destruction. Further, the United States had to police the coastline to intercept unlawful expeditions. Spain must grant "home rule," but not independence, to "fertile and rich" Cuba to end the bloodshed and devastation. Otherwise, having thus far acted with "restraint," Washington might abandon its "expectant attitude." But Cleveland had more bark than bite. Through Olney he successfully buried a Senate resolution urging recognition of Cuban independence and acknowledged limited Spanish reforms of February 1897. Thereafter he bequeathed Cuba to the incoming McKinley administration.

President William McKinley had defeated William Jennings Bryan in the election of 1896. The teetotaling Ohioan seemed a stable, dignified figure in a time of crisis. He projected deep religious conviction, personal warmth, sincerity, party loy-

Uncle Sam—"All That You Need Is Backbone." This cartoon depicts a tall, erect Uncle Sam shoving a rifle down President McKinley's coat to provide him with a backbone. As the historian Kristin Hoganson points out in *Fighting for American Manhood* (1998), expansionist critics of McKinley often accused the president of being weak, flabby, and vacillating because he did not immediately leap into war with Spain. (*Chicago Chronicle,* in *Cartoons of the War of 1898 with Spain,* Chicago, 1898)

alty, and support for expansion abroad. Yet McKinley often gave the appearance of being a pliant follower, a mindless flunky of the political bosses. Cartoonists often depicted him in women's dress and called him a "goody-goody" man. Such an image was created in large part by bellicose imperialists who believed that McKinley was not moving fast enough. Certainly a party regular and friend of large corporations, the president was no lackey. A manager of diplomacy, who wanted a settlement of the Cuban question without U.S. military intervention, McKinley acted as his own man.

McKinley shared America's image of itself as an expanding, virile nation of superior institutions and as a major power in Latin America. He agreed that the United States must have a large navy, overseas commerce, and foreign bases. As a tariff specialist who wanted America to export its surplus, he favored high tariffs on manufactured goods, low tariffs on raw materials, and reciprocity agreements. The Republican party platform of 1896 overflowed with expansionist rhetoric. It urged American control of Hawai'i, a Nicaraguan canal run by the United States, an enlarged navy, purchase of the Virgin Islands, and Cuban independence. Before inauguration, however, McKinley quietly joined Cleveland in sidetracking a Senate resolution for recognition of Cuba. He wanted a free hand, and he did not believe that Cubans could govern themselves. His inaugural address vacuously urged peace, never mentioning the Cuban crisis.

Beginning in March 1897, resolutions on Cuba sprang up repeatedly, but McKinley managed to kill them. He did satisfy imperialists by sending a Hawaiian annexation treaty to the Senate. In June, Madrid received a nonpublic American rebuke for Weyler's uncivilized warfare and for his disruption of the Cuban economy. Spain, however, showed no signs of tempering its military response to the insurrection. U.S. citizens languished in Spanish jails; American property continued to be razed. In July, McKinley instructed Minister Woodford to demand that the Spanish stop the fighting. Increasingly convinced that the Cuban *insurrectos* would not compromise, the president implored Spain to grant autonomy. A new Spanish government soon moderated policy by offering Cuba a substantial degree of self-government. Even more, it removed the hated Weyler and promised to end reconcentration. Such reforms actually encouraged intransigence, as Cuban leaders saw them as "a sign of Spain's weakening power and an indication that the end is not far off."

McKinley's annual message to Congress in December discussed the Cuban insurrection at great length. Voicing the "gravest apprehension," McKinley rejected annexation as "criminal aggression." He opposed recognition of belligerency, because the rebels hardly constituted a government worthy of recognition. And he ruled out intervention as premature while Spain traveled the "honorable paths" of reform. Asking for patience, he promised to keep open all policy options, including intervention "with force."

By mid-January it became apparent that Spanish reforms had not moderated the crisis; in fact, insurgents, conservatives, and the Spanish army all denounced them. After antireform Spaniards rioted in Havana, McKinley sent the *Maine*. On February 9, the State Department received a copy of a private letter written in late 1897 by the Spanish minister to the United States Enrique Dupuy de Lôme. Intercepted by a rebel sympathizer who forwarded it to the Cuban junta in New York City, the letter was published that same day by William Randolph Hearst's flamboyant *New York Journal* under a banner headline: "Worst Insult to the United States in its History." De Lôme had labeled McKinley "weak," a "bidder for the admiration of the crowd," and a "would-be politician." McKinley particularly resented another statement—that Spain did not take its reform proposals seriously and would persist in fighting to defeat the rebels. Spain, it appeared, could not be trusted. De Lôme's hasty recall hardly salved the hurt. Less than a week later the *Maine* blew up, setting in motion events and decisions that led to war and overseas empire for the United States.

The Spanish-American-Cuban-Filipino War

Americans enlisted in what they trumpeted as a glorious expedition to demonstrate U.S. right and might. They were cocky. Theodore Roosevelt, who resigned as assistant secretary of the navy to lead the flashy but overrated Rough Riders, said that it was not much of a war but it was the best Americans had. It was a short war, ending August 12, but 5,462 Americans died in it—only 379 of them in combat. Most met death from malaria and yellow fever. Camera operators for Thomas Edison and Biograph shot "moving pictures" of the war, as crowds flocked to see flickering images of battleships at sea, the wreck of the *Maine,* and triumphant victory parades.

"Cuba Reconciling the North and South." Captain Fritz W. Guerin's 1898 photograph depicted nationalism in the Spanish-American-Cuban-Filipino War. Golden-haired Cuba, liberated from her chains by her North American heroes, oversees the reconciliation of the Union and Confederacy in a splashy display of patriotism. (Library of Congress)

Led by officers seasoned in the Civil War and in campaigns against Native Americans, the new imperial fighters embarked from Florida in mid-June. Seventeen thousand men, clutching their Krag-Jörgensen rifles, landed on Cuban soil unopposed because Cuban insurgents had driven Spanish troops into the cities. Cubans and Americans cooperated warily. Yet the big news had already arrived from the Philippine Islands, Spain's major colony in Asia. Only days after the U.S. declaration of war, Commodore George Dewey sailed his Asiatic Squadron from Hong Kong to Manila Bay, where he smashed the Spanish fleet with the loss of one sailor. Slipping by the Spanish guns at Corregidor, Dewey entered the bay at night. Early in the morning of May 1, with the laconic order, "You may fire when ready, Gridley," his flagship *Olympia* began to demolish the ten incompetently handled Spanish ships. Some people, ignorant of American interests in the Pacific, wondered how a war to liberate Cuba saw its first action in Asia. Naval officials had pinpointed the Philippines in contingency plans as early as 1896. Often credited alone with ordering Dewey on February 25, 1898, to attack Manila if war broke out, Assistant Secretary of the Navy Theodore Roosevelt actually set in motion preexisting war plans already known and approved by the president.

By late June, U.S. troops in Cuba had advanced toward Santiago. Joined by experienced Cuban rebels, the North Americans on July 1 battled for San Juan Hill. American forces, spearheaded by the Rough Riders and the black soldiers of the Ninth Cavalry, finally captured the strategic promontory overlooking Santiago after suffering heavy casualties. Two days later the Spanish fleet, penned in Santiago harbor for weeks by U.S. warships, made a desperate daylight break for open sea.

U.S. vessels hurried to sink the helpless Spanish craft, which went down with 323 dead. Its fleet destroyed, Spain surrendered—but only to the Americans. Cubans were forbidden from entering towns and cities to celebrate.

U.S. troops also invaded another Spanish colony, Puerto Rico, which expansionists such as Roosevelt coveted as a Caribbean base that might help protect a Central American canal. In nineteen days General Nelson A. Miles, losing only three soldiers, captured the sugar- and coffee-exporting island. At least at first, the Puerto Rican elite welcomed their new North American masters as an improvement over their Spanish rulers.

Manila capitulated in mid-August, after the Spanish put up token resistance in a deal with Dewey that kept Filipino nationalist Emilio Aguinaldo from the walled city. Washington soon ordered Aguinaldo and other Filipino rebels, who had fought against the Spanish for independence since 1896, to remain outside the capital and to recognize the authority of the United States.

In July, to ensure uninterrupted reinforcement of Dewey, the United States officially absorbed Hawai'i, where ships took on coal en route to Manila. From 1893 to 1897, when Cleveland refused annexation, politics in Hawai'i had changed little. The white revolutionaries clung to power. After negotiating a new treaty with the white-led Hawaiian government, McKinley adopted the ploy of asking for a joint resolution. On July 7, 1898, Congress passed the resolution for annexation by a majority vote, thereby formally attaching the strategically and commercially important islands to the United States. Annexation was "not a change" but "a consummation," said McKinley.

Peace and Empire: The Debate in the United States

Spain sued for peace, and on August 12 the belligerents proclaimed an armistice. To negotiate with the Spanish in Paris, McKinley appointed a "peace commission" loaded with imperialists and headed by Secretary of State William R. Day, friend and follower of the president's wishes. After McKinley tested public opinion by touring the Midwest, he demanded all of the Philippines, the island of Guam in the Marianas, and Puerto Rico, as well as independence for Cuba. Articulate Filipinos pleaded for their country's freedom but met a stern U.S. rebuff. Spanish diplomats accepted this American land grab and the U.S. offer of $20 million in compensation. In early December, U.S. delegates walked out of the elegant French conference room with the Philippines, Puerto Rico, and Guam.

Anti-imperialists howled in protest. They had organized the Anti-Imperialist League in Boston in November 1898 and counted among their number such unlikely bedfellows as the steel magnate Andrew Carnegie, the labor leader Samuel Gompers, the agrarian spokesman William Jennings Bryan, the Massachusetts senator George Hoar, Harvard president Charles W. Eliot, and the humorist Mark Twain—people who had often disagreed on domestic issues. Hoar, the most outspoken senator against the treaty, had voted for war and annexation of Hawai'i. An expansionist, Carnegie apparently would accept colonies if they could be taken without force. He even offered to write a personal check for $20 million to buy the independence of the Philippines. But the anti-imperialists could not overcome the *fait accompli*, possession and occupation of territory, handed them by McKinley. After all, argued the president, could America really let loose of this real estate so nobly taken in battle?

The anti-imperialists denounced the thesis that greatness lay in colonies. Some of them wanted trade too, but not at the cost of subjugating other peoples. Quoting the Declaration of Independence and Washington's Farewell Address, these critics recalled America's tradition of self-government and *continental* expansion. Some anti-imperialists insisted that serious domestic problems demanded attention. The racist South Carolina representative "Pitchfork" Ben Tillman opposed annexing ten million "barbarians of the lowest type." Mark Twain wrote a scathing parody of the "Battle Hymn of the Republic": "Mine eyes have seen the orgy of the launching of the Sword;/He is searching out the hoardings where the strangers' wealth is stored;/He has loosed his fateful lightning, and with woe and death has scored;/His lust is marching on."

Prominent women also joined the debate, hoping to build a distinct foreign-policy constituency out of existing networks of women's clubs and organizations. The New Hampshire pacifist Lucia True Ames Mead pronounced it immoral for "any nation . . . which buys or takes by conquest another people . . . without promise of granting them independence." The social reformer Jane Addams saw children playing war games in the streets of Chicago. The kids were *not freeing Cubans,* she protested, but rather *slaying Spaniards* in their not-so-innocent play. Although unsuccessful in the fight against empire, tens of thousands of women became activists over the next decade.

The imperialists, led by Roosevelt and McKinley, and backed strongly by business leaders, engaged their opponents in vigorous debate in early 1899. These empire builders stressed pragmatic considerations, although they communicated common ideas of racial superiority and national destiny. "We are a conquering race," boasted Senator Albert Beveridge, and "we must obey our blood and occupy new markets, and, if necessary, new lands." The Philippines provided stepping-stones to the rich China market and strategic ports for the expanding navy that protected American commerce. International competition also dictated that the United States keep the fruits of victory, argued the imperialists; otherwise, a menacing Germany or expansionist Japan might pick up what America discarded. Few believed that the United States should relinquish territory acquired through blood. To the charge that no one had asked the Filipinos if they desired annexation to the United States, Roosevelt delighted in telling Democratic anti-imperialists that Thomas Jefferson took Louisiana without a vote by its inhabitants. McKinley put it simply: "Duty determines destiny."

Pro-imperialist Senator Lodge described the treaty fight in the Senate as the "closest, most bitter, and most exciting struggle." Shortly before the vote, word reached Washington that Filipino insurrectionists and American soldiers had begun to fight. The news apparently stimulated support for the Treaty of Paris. Democrats tended to be anti-imperialists and Republicans imperialists, yet enough of the former endorsed the treaty on February 6, 1899, to pass it by a bare two-thirds vote,

Emilio Aguinaldo (1869–1964). Of mixed Chinese and Tagalog ancestry, this Filipino nationalist was exiled by the Spanish from his country in 1897. He returned with American forces and later clashed with them when he declared independence for the Philippines. Captured in 1901, he then declared allegiance to the United States. During World War II, however, he favored the Japanese, who occupied the islands, and American authorities briefly imprisoned him in 1945 when they reestablished U.S. power over Manila. (Library of Congress)

57 to 27. William Jennings Bryan, believing that rejection of the treaty would prolong the war and that the Philippines could be freed after terminating the hostilities with Spain, urged an aye vote on his anti-imperialist friends. The Republicans probably had enough votes in reserve to pass the treaty even if Bryan had opposed it.

Imperial Collisions in Asia: The Philippine Insurrection and the Open Door in China

Controlling, protecting, and expanding the enlarged U.S. empire became a major chore. The Filipinos proved the most obstructionist. By the end of the war, Aguinaldo and rebel forces controlled most of the islands, having routed the Spanish and driven them into Manila. Aguinaldo believed that American leaders, including Dewey, had promised his country independence if he joined U.S. forces in defeating the Spanish. Ordered out of Manila by U.S. authorities after the Spanish-American armistice, he and his cohorts had to endure racial insults, as American soldiers considered the Filipinos inferior, the equivalent of Indians and blacks at home. The Treaty of Paris angered the Filipinos, as did McKinley's decree asserting the supreme authority of the United States in the Philippines. In open defiance of Washington, Aguinaldo and other prominent Filipinos organized a government at Malolos, wrote a constitution, and proclaimed the Philippine Republic in late January 1899.

McKinley believed his new subjects to be ill-fitted for self-government. In February 1899 the Filipinos began fighting better-armed American troops. After bloody struggles, Aguinaldo was captured in March 1901. Before the insurrection collapsed in 1902, some 4,165 Americans and more than 200,000 Filipinos died. One hundred twenty-five thousand American troops quelled the insurrection, which cost the United States at least $160 million. In Batangas province south of Manila, General J. Franklin Bell drove insurrectionists into the hills and killed their livestock. Then malaria-transmitting mosquitoes infected people instead of cattle. The result: an epidemiological catastrophe wherein the Batangas population declined by 90,000 over a six-year period. The Harvard philosopher William James denounced Filipino pacification as "the big, hollow, resounding, corrupting, sophisticating, confusing torrent of brutal momentum and irrationality that brings forth fruits like this!"

This savage contest saw both sides commit atrocities. After Filipinos massacred an American regiment on Samar and stuffed molasses into disemboweled corpses to attract ants, General Jacob Smith told his officers: "I wish you to kill and burn, the more you kill and burn the better you will please me." U.S. soldiers burned *barrios* to the ground, placing villagers in reconcentration camps like those that had defaced Cuba. To get information, Americans administered the "water cure," forcing prisoners to swallow gallons of water and then punching the swollen stomach to empty it quickly. Racist notions of white superiority surfaced. "Civilize 'em with a Krag" went a popular army song, as one officer urged the same "remedial measures that proved successful with the Apaches." The civil governor of the Philippines from 1901 to 1904, William Howard Taft, put it less crudely when he described the American mission: to "teach those people individual liberty, which shall lift them up to a point of civilization . . . and which shall make them rise to call the name of the

William Howard Taft (1857–1930) and Animal. The first U.S. civil governor of the Philippines, Taft weighed more than 300 pounds. He once proudly reported to Washington that he had ridden twenty-five miles to a high mountain spot. Secretary of War Elihu Root replied: "HOW IS HORSE?" (U.S. Army Military History Institute)

United States blessed." In fact, Taft administered a sedition act that censored newspapers and jailed dissenters. For years, the Moros would not submit to American rule. One military expert predicted that "the Moro question will eventually be settled in the same manner as the Indian question, that is by gradual extermination." In a June 1913 battle on the island of Jolo, U.S. forces killed 500 Moros. The army's premier "guerrilla warrior," General John J. Pershing, called that bloody encounter "the fiercest [fighting] I have ever seen."

The carrot joined the stick to pacify the Philippines. Local self-government, social reforms, and American schools, which taught Filipinos of all social classes English and arithmetic, helped win over elites and key minorities. A general amnesty proclaimed by President Theodore Roosevelt on July 4, 1902, also encouraged accommodation. By restricting suffrage at the outset to Filipinos with wealth, education, and previous government service, U.S. administrators successfully wooed Filipino elites, including former revolutionaries. American roads, bridges, port improvements, and sanitation projects soon followed. At the St. Louis World's Fair in 1904, a thousand Filipinos were put on display as "living exhibits," and photographs and dioramas depicted their "rapid social, educational and sanitary development" under "the kindly tutelage of the United States." By 1911, Cebu City could boast telephone service, English-language newspapers, Fords and Buicks, movie houses, and a baseball park, but "the poor are still poor," as one Cebuano put it. The Jones Act of 1916 promised eventual Philippine independence. It did not occur until 1946.

The proximity of the Philippines to China whetted commercial appetites. In early 1898 business leaders organized the American Asiatic Association to stimulate, protect, and enlarge U.S. interests in China. Treasury official Frank Vanderlip typically lauded the Philippines as the "pickets of the Pacific, standing guard at the entrances to trade with the millions of China." Although China attracted only 2 percent of U.S. foreign commerce, American traders had long dreamed of an unbounded China market, and missionaries romanticized a Christian kingdom. These dreams spurred action, and during the 1890s the United States, despite limited power, sought to defend its Asian interests, real and imagined.

In that decade imperial powers and Japan were dividing China, rendered helpless in 1895 after the Sino-Japanese War, into exclusive spheres of influence. The McKinley administration in early 1898 watched anxiously as Germany grabbed Jiaozhou (Kiaochow) and Russia gained a lease at Port Arthur on the Liaodong Peninsula. France, already ensconced in Indochina, leased Guangzhou Bay in southern China in April. Japan already had footholds in Formosa and Korea. The British in March 1898 suggested a joint Anglo-American declaration on behalf of equal commercial opportunity in China. Distracted by the Cuban crisis, Washington gave little attention to the request. Britain, which already had Hong Kong, then forced China to give up part of the Shandong Peninsula.

American interests in China seemed threatened. The American Asiatic Association and missionary groups appealed to Washington for help. Drawing on recommendations from William W. Rockhill, adviser on Asian policy, who in turn consulted his British friend and officer of the Chinese customs service, Alfred Hippisley, Secretary of State John Hay tried words. Hay sent an "Open Door" note on September 6, 1899, to Japan, Germany, Russia, Britain, France, and Italy, asking them to respect equal trade opportunity for all nations in their spheres. It was, of course, a traditional American principle. Noncommittal replies trickled back, but Hay read into them what he wanted and proclaimed definitive acceptance of the Open Door proposal.

Although frail, the Open Door policy carried meaning. Despite less leverage than the other imperialists, Americans discerned a delicate balance of power in Asia that the United States could upset. Excluding American commerce altogether from China might cause Washington to tip that balance by joining one of the powers against the others. A world war might erupt from competition in Asia. Americans hoped the Open Door policy would serve their goals in an area where they had little military power. The United States wanted the commercial advantages without having to employ military force, as it did in Latin America. The policy did not always work, but it fixed itself in the American mind as a guiding principle for Chinese affairs.

The Open Door note notwithstanding, the Manchu dynasty (1644–1912) neared death, unable to cope with the foreign intruders. Resentful nationalistic Chinese, led by a secret society called *Yihequan* ("Boxers"), undertook in 1900 to throw out the imperialist aggressors. The Boxers murdered hundreds of Christian missionaries and their Chinese converts and laid siege to the foreign legations in Beijing (Peking). To head off a complete gouging of China by vengeful imperialists, McKinley sent 2,500 American troops to Beijing from the Philippines to join 15,500 soldiers from other nations to lift the siege. Hay then issued another Open Door note on July 3, 1900. He redefined U.S. policy as the protection of American life and property, maintenance of "equal and impartial trade," and preservation of China's "territorial and administrative entity." In short, keep the trade door open by keeping China intact.

Certainly these actions did not save China, which had to pay more than $300 million for the Boxers' damages. Thereafter Washington buttressed its support for the Open Door by increasing the Asiatic Squadron to forty-eight warships and earmarking army forces in the Philippines for future emergency deployment in China. Even Buffalo Bill Cody extended America's frontier to China by reenacting the suppression of the Boxer Rebellion in his Wild West Show to depict the "triumph of Christian civilization over paganism."

The Elbows of a World Power, 1895–1900

Venezuela, Cuba, Hawai'i, the Philippines, Open Door notes—an unprecedented set of commitments brought new responsibilities for the United States. Symbolic of this thrust to world-power status was the ascendancy of the imperialists' imperialist, Theodore Roosevelt, to the presidency in 1901. TR warned Americans to avoid "slothful ease and ignoble peace." Never "shrink from the hard contests"; "let us therefore boldly face the life of strife." Indeed, many diplomats regarded the 1890s as a testing time when the United States met the international challenge and rightfully asserted its place as a major world power. Europeans watched anxiously. Some, especially Germans, spoke of the "American peril." The United States, European leaders pointed out, had become a factor in the "balance of power." With whom would the nation ally itself?

The odds seemed to favor Britain, although the Anglo-American courtship would be prolonged and marriage something for the future. Ever since the eyeopening Venezuelan crisis, the British had applauded Washington for "entering the lists and sharing the task which might have proved too heavy for us alone." Looking for support against an expansionist Germany, John Bull thought Uncle Sam a fit partner. During the Spanish-American-Cuban-Filipino War the British conspicuously tilted toward the American side and encouraged the subsequent absorption of Spanish colonies. U.S. leaders, in turn, compared the British suppression of the Boers in South Africa (1899–1902) with their own war against the Filipinos, saying that both peoples were equally "incapable of statehood." Articulate Americans welcomed Britain's implicit acceptance of their imperialism. "Germany, and not England, is the power with whom we are apt to have trouble over the Monroe Doctrine," wrote Roosevelt in 1898.

Britain still ranked first in naval power, but the United States stood sixth by 1900. In 1898 alone, spurred by the war with Spain, the United States added 128 vessels to its navy, at a cost of $18 million. As one scholar put it: "Every nation elbows other nations to-day." The steel magnate Andrew Carnegie boasted that "the old nations of the earth creep at a snail's pace," but the United States "thunders past with the rush of the express." Southern racists and northern imperialists now had something in common: the need to keep inferior peoples in their place. Befitting their new imperial status, U.S. leaders often used gendered and age-based language that presumed superiority over peoples deemed "emotional, irrational, irresponsible, unbusinesslike, unstable, childlike." If Americans played "the part of China, and [were] content to rot by inches in ignoble ease within our borders," warned Roosevelt, they will "go down before other nations which have not lost the manly and adventurous qualities." Imperial annexation, bragged Senator Beveridge in 1900, "means opportunity for all the glorious young manhood of the republic, the most virile, ambitious, impatient, militant manhood the world has ever seen."

The events of the 1895–1900 period further altered the process of decision-making. Both Cleveland and McKinley conducted their own foreign policies, often thwarting or manipulating Congress. Woodrow Wilson, then president of Princeton University, later noted that 1898 had "changed the balance of powers. Foreign questions became leading questions again. . . . Our President must always, henceforth, be one of the great powers of the world." From "a provincial huddle of petty sovereignties held together by a rope of sand," one editor exulted, "we rise to the dignity and prowess of an imperial republic incomparably greater than Rome."

Indeed, the allure of empire seemed to offer an exceptionalist mission for the "most merciful of the world's great race of administrators," that of "teaching the world how to govern dependent peoples through uplift, assimilation, and eventual self-government." Thus did the optimistic leaders of the "new world power" after 1900 see themselves as reforming an international system that seemed to be "working in their favor." After 1900 the task of managing the expansive empire and the global responsibilities that came with it preoccupied U.S. leaders.

FURTHER READING FOR THE PERIOD 1895–1900

For the 1890s push for empire and the coming and waging of the Spanish-American-Cuban-Filipino War, see Ada Ferrer, *Insurgent Cuba* (1999); Linda Guerra, *The Myth of José Martí* (2005); Robert E. Hannigan, *The New World Power* (2002); Kenneth E. Hendrickson, Jr., *The Spanish-American War* (2003); Sylvia Hilton and S. J. Ickringell, eds., *European Perceptions of the Spanish-American War* (1999); Kristin L. Hoganson, *Fighting for American Manhood* (1998); John L. Offner, *An Unwanted War* (1992); Louis A. Pérez Jr., *The War of 1898* (1998), *Cuba and the United States* (1997), and *Cuba Between Empires, 1878–1902* (1983); Peggy Samuels and Harold Samuels, *Remembering the Maine* (1995); Thomas Schoonover, *Uncle Sam's War and the Origins of Globalization* (2003); Angel Smith and Emma Davila-Cox, eds., *The Crisis of 1898* (1999); and Warren Zimmermann, *First Great Triumph* (2002).

For U.S. leaders, see H. W. Brands, *T.R.* (1997); Kathleen Dalton, *Theodore Roosevelt* (2002); and H. Wayne Morgan, *William McKinley and His America* (1963).

Anti-imperialism is treated in Robert L. Beisner, *Twelve Against Empire* (1968); Amy Kaplan, *The Anarchy of Empire in the Making of U.S. Culture* (2002); and Frank Ninkovich, *The United States and Imperialism* (2001).

The Open Door policy and Asia are discussed in Paul A. Cohen, *History in Three Keys* (1997) (Boxers); Michael Hunt, *Frontier Defense and the Open Door* (1973) and *The Making of a Special Relationship* (1983); Thomas McCormick, *China Market* (1967); and Marilyn Blatt Young, *The Rhetoric of Empire* (1968).

The Philippine rebellion and the American debate receive scrutiny in Vincent Cirillo, *Bullets and Bacilli* (2004); Michael Cullinane, *Illustrado Politics* (2005); Brian M. Linn, *The Philippine War* (2000); Glenn A. May, *Social Engineering in the Philippines* (1980); Stuart C. Miller, *"Benevolent Assimilation"* (1982); Resil B. Mojares, *The War Against the Americans* (1999); Daniel B. Schirmer, *Republic or Empire* (1972); Angel Velasco Shaw and Luis Francia, eds., *Vestiges of War* (1999); and Richard E. Welch, *Response to Imperialism* (1979).

For the Venezuelan crisis and Anglo-American relations, see Judith Ewell, *Venezuela and the United States* (1996); Richard B. Mulanax, *The Boer War in American Politics and Diplomacy* (1994); Thomas J. Noer, *Briton, Boer, and Yankee* (1978); Bradford Perkins, *The Great Rapprochement* (1968); and Joseph Smith, *Illusions of Conflict* (1979).

See also Robert L. Beisner, ed., *Guide to American Foreign Relations Since 1600* (2003).

For comprehensive coverage of foreign-relations topics, see the articles in the four-volume *Encyclopedia of U.S. Foreign Relations* (1997), edited by Bruce W. Jentleson and Thomas G. Paterson.

CHAPTER 7

Managing, Policing, and Extending the Empire, 1900–1914

✳ *Severing Panama from Colombia for the Canal, 1903*

"REVOLUTION IMMINENT" WARNED the cable from Colón, a normally quiet Colombian seaport on the Atlantic side of Panama. Acting Secretary of State Francis B. Loomis quickly fired off an inquiry to the U.S. consul at Panama City, on the Pacific slope: "Uprising on Isthmus reported. Keep Department promptly and fully informed." The response came back in four hours: "No uprising yet. Reported will be in the night." Loomis's anxiety soon increased when he learned that troops of the Colombian government had landed in Colón.

In Washington, D.C., it was now 8:20 P.M., November 3, 1903. As far as Loomis knew, a revolution had not yet broken out on the isthmus. Nonetheless, he hurriedly drafted instructions for the consuls at Panama and Colón. "Act promptly" to convey to the commanding officer of the U.S.S. *Nashville* this order: "Make every effort to prevent [Colombian] Government troops at Colón from proceeding to Panama [City]." Loomis agonized for another hour. Finally, a new cable arrived: "Uprising occurred to-night . . . no bloodshed. . . . Government will be organized to-night." Loomis had done his part in the scheme to acquire a canal controlled by the United States.

November 3 was far more hectic for the conspirators in Panama. A tiny band of Panamanians and Americans living on the isthmus had actively plotted revolution since August, when the Colombian congress rejected the treaty that would have permitted the United States to construct an isthmian canal. By late October, they had become convinced that the North American colossus, frustrated in its overtures to Colombia, would lend them moral and physical support. Confident that U.S. naval vessels would be at hand, they selected November 4 for their coup d'état. To their dismay, however, the Colombian steamer *Cartagena* disembarked about 400 troops at Colón early on November 3. Because Washington's order to prevent the

"The Thirteenth Labor of Hercules." With this official poster by Perham Nahl, the Panama-Pacific Exposition in San Francisco in 1915 celebrated the opening of the Panama Canal. The artist commemorates the ten-year construction project using symbols that reflect the era's themes of empire-building and male hegemony: A powerful, muscular Hercules (the United States) forcibly parts the land (a yielding Panama) to make space for the canal. (Library of Congress)

"landing of any armed force . . . at Colón" had not reached him, Commander John Hubbard of the *Nashville* did not interfere.

Forced to improvise, the conspirators deviously separated the Colombian commanding general from his troops, lured him aboard a train, and sped him across the isthmus to Panama City, where they arrested their guest, formed a provisional government, and paraded before a cheering crowd at the Cathedral Plaza. Back in Colón, the insurgents gave the colonel in charge $8,000 in gold, whereupon he ordered his remaining troops aboard a departing steamer. The U.S. consul at Panama City cabled: "Quiet prevails." At noon the next day, Secretary of State John Hay officially recognized the sovereign Republic of Panama.

The new Panamanian government appointed as its minister plenipotentiary a Frenchman, Philippe Bunau-Varilla, an engineer of an earlier failed Panama canal project. With Gallic flourish, Bunau-Varilla congratulated Secretary Hay for rescuing Panama "from the barbarism of unnecessary and wasteful civil wars to consecrate it to the destiny assigned to it by Providence, the service of humanity, and the progress of civilization." On November 18, 1903, less than two weeks after U.S. recognition of Panama, Hay and Bunau-Varilla signed a new treaty by which the United States would build, fortify, and operate a canal linking the Atlantic and Pacific oceans. Washington also guaranteed the "independence of the Republic in Panama," thereby ensuring against any retaliation from Colombia.

Theodore Roosevelt the Pirate. The Colombian minister called the United States a "pirate." When Roosevelt asked about legal precedents for his Panama policy, Attorney General Philander C. Knox replied, "Oh, Mr. President, do not let so great an achievement suffer from any taint of legality." (Frank Nankivell, Swann Collection of Caricature and Cartoon)

Hay had at last achieved a goal set by his chief, President Theodore Roosevelt, several years earlier. If an unfortified, neutral canal had existed in Central America during the recent war with Spain, Roosevelt had argued, the United States would have spent the war in "wild panic," fearful that the Spanish fleet would slip through the waterway and rush to the Philippines to attack Commodore Dewey. "Better to have no canal at all, than not give us the power to control it in time of war," Roosevelt concluded.

The Clayton-Bulwer Treaty of 1850, stipulating joint Anglo-American control of any isthmian canal, seemed to block the way. In December 1898, flushed with victory over Spain, President William McKinley had directed Secretary Hay to modify that agreement. The ensuing Hay-Pauncefote Treaty of February 1900 permitted the United States to build a canal but forbade its fortification, much to the dismay of Roosevelt who spearheaded an attack that defeated the treaty in the Senate. On November 18, 1901, with Roosevelt now president, Hay and Pauncefote signed a satisfactory new pact.

Then began the complex process of determining the route. The decisive criterion—cost—seemed exorbitant for Panama because of the New Panama Canal Company, a French-chartered firm that held the Colombian concession for canal rights. The company estimated its assets at $109 million—machinery, property, and excavated soil left by the defunct de Lesseps organization in 1888. Purchase of the company's rights and holdings would make a Panama canal prohibitively expensive if technologically easier. For these reasons, plus travel accounts that depicted Panama as "a hideous dung heap of physical and moral degradation," the House passed the Hepburn Bill in January 1902 authorizing a canal through Nicaragua.

The New Panama Canal Company's American lawyer, William Nelson Cromwell, schemed to sell the assets of his French client for the highest possible price. Lobbying hard, Bunau-Varilla even exposed the unsuitability of Nicaraguan terrain by deluging Congress with Nicaraguan postage stamps that depicted a belching volcano. The company also lowered its price to $40 million. Guided by Roosevelt and Cromwell, Congress reversed itself and chose the Panama route. The State Department soon opened negotiations with Colombia. The annual rent became a stumbling block, which Hay removed only by delivering an ultimatum to the Colombian chargé d'affaires, Tomás Herrán, in January 1903. On January 22 he and Hay signed a treaty granting Colombia an initial payment of $10 million and $250,000 annually. The United States would control the six-mile-wide canal zone for one hundred years, renewable at the "sole and absolute option" of the North American republic.

The U.S. Senate approved the Hay-Herrán Treaty on March 17, 1903, but the Colombian government attempted to extract a $10 million payment from the New Panama Canal Company for selling its assets to the U.S. government. Cromwell promptly cried foul, whereupon Hay bluntly announced that any payment to Colombia was "not permissible." The Colombians next tried to raise the initial American cash payment from $10 million to $15 million. Roosevelt exploded against "those contemptible little creatures in Bogotá." TR's intransigence and Hay's extraordinary intercession on behalf of a privately owned foreign corporation so angered the Colombian congress that it unanimously defeated the treaty on August 12, 1903.

Panama Canal. The U.S.S. *Ohio* passes through the Culebra Cut (now called the Gaillard Cut) of the Panama Canal about a year after the canal opened to traffic—both warships and commercial vessels. (Library of Congress)

Roosevelt was already pondering undiplomatic alternatives. In June the ubiquitous Cromwell had met with Roosevelt and then planted a story in the *New York World* reporting that, if Colombia rejected the treaty, Panama would secede and grant "absolute sovereignty over the Canal Zone," and that "President Roosevelt is said to strongly favor this plan." By now the president was privately castigating Colombia for its "squalid savagery . . . dismal ignorance, cruelty, treachery, greed, and utter vanity."

Roosevelt now considered seizure of Panama by force or instant recognition and support for any revolutionary regime in Panama. The president inclined sharply toward the latter course after a meeting with Bunau-Varilla on October 10, during which the Frenchman predicted an uprising. When Bunau-Varilla asked what the United States would do, TR replied: "Colombia by her action has forfeited any claim upon the U.S." One week later, on October 16, Secretary Hay informed Bunau-Varilla that American naval vessels were heading toward the isthmus. Calculating the steaming time, Bunau-Varilla cabled his fellow plotters on the isthmus that warships would arrive by November 2. Early that evening the U.S.S. *Nashville* dropped anchor at Colón as predicted. As a Colombian diplomat rightfully complained, "The Americans are against us. What can we do against the American Navy?"

Roosevelt urged swift ratification of the Hay–Bunau-Varilla Treaty, claiming that Colombia had forced him "to take decisive steps to bring to an end a condition of affairs which had become intolerable." When critics complained about his "Bowery-boy" behavior toward Colombia, Roosevelt denounced the "small body of shrill eunuchs who consistently oppose" his "righteous" policies. On February 23, 1904, the Senate approved the treaty by a vote of 66 to 14. The treaty granted the United States "power and authority" within the zone "in perpetuity" as "if it were the sovereign of the territory." Later, in 1911, TR reportedly boasted that "I took the Canal Zone and let Congress debate; and while the debate goes on the Canal does also."

Construction began in mid-1904, and the fifty-mile-long canal opened on August 15, 1914. During the first year of operation alone, 1,058 merchant vessels slid through the locks, while the Atlantic and Pacific fleets of the U.S. Navy freely exchanged ships. In 1922 the United States paid "conscience money" or "canalimony" of $25 million to Colombia but did not formally apologize for having taken the canal zone. Despite critics, most Americans have applauded Roosevelt's bold venture against Colombia. The canal, Woodrow Wilson later asserted, shifted "the center of gravity of the world."

The Conservative Shapers of Empire

The taking of Panama symbolized the new activism characteristic of American foreign policy after 1898, and construction of the canal ensured virtual U.S. hegemony over Latin America. It also intensified Washington's participation in the global contest for empire among the great powers. "The United States will be attacked as soon as you are about to complete the canal," Germany's Kaiser Wilhelm II predicted in 1907, identifying Japan as the most likely culprit. Britain, which had the power to challenge U.S. preeminence in the hemisphere, chose to acquiesce in the face of a growing threat from Germany. In turn, the vigorous German Empire, having expanded its markets and investments in Central and South America to more than 2 billion marks by 1900, seemed "desirous of obtaining a foothold in the Western Hemisphere," noted the General Board of the U.S. Navy. Revolutionary upheavals in Russia, China, and Mexico produced further shifting in the international balance of power. As European alliances consolidated and lurched toward a world war, TR and his successors had to defend, develop, and enlarge the new U.S. empire in an era of tumultuous transformation.

Makers of American Foreign Relations, 1900–1914

Presidents	Secretaries of State
Theodore Roosevelt, 1901–1909	John Hay, 1898–1905
	Elihu Root, 1905–1909
	Robert Bacon, 1909
William Howard Taft, 1909–1913	Philander C. Knox, 1909–1913
Woodrow Wilson, 1913–1921	William Jennings Bryan, 1913–1915

In the late nineteenth century, Roosevelt corresponded regularly with Alfred Thayer Mahan, the navalist who tirelessly touted the strategic advantages of a canal. During the war of 1898, the warship *Oregon* dashed at full speed from San Francisco around South America to Cuba in time to help destroy the Spanish fleet off Santiago. The race of more than 14,000 miles fired American imaginations, but it also consumed sixty-eight days and underscored the need for an interoceanic canal across Central America.

Roosevelt's sense of isthmian strategic necessity reflected a broad worldview he shared with many "progressives" in the early twentieth century. A conservative patrician reformer, he "feared that unrest caused by social and economic inequities would impair the nation's strength and efficiency." With similar danger lurking in unrest abroad, he sought U.S. influence to create order on a global scale through "proper policing." Imbibing Darwinist doctrines of "natural selection," Roosevelt proclaimed "our duty toward the people living in barbarism to see that they are freed from their chains, and we can free them only by destroying barbarism itself." Anglo-Saxon superiority was best expressed in war, he said. Not all Progressive-era reformers joined TR in advocating a vigorous activism abroad. Wisconsin's Senator Robert M. La Follette, for example, opposed imperialism and contended that the same corporate monopolists they battled at home were dragging the United States into perpetual intervention overseas. Activists in women's organizations bemoaned the "present intoxication with the hashish of conquest" as they urged "women's values" on a male government so as to rein in the "champing steeds" of militarism and empire.

Roosevelt vigorously debated his critics. Exuberant and calculating, he centralized foreign-policy decisionmaking, frequently bypassed Congress, and believed "the people" too ignorant about foreign affairs to guide an informed president like himself. Nonetheless, he kept favorite journalists and other "intelligent observers sufficiently enlightened to prevent their going wrong." Seeking world stability, Roosevelt advocated "multiplying the methods and chances of honorably avoiding war in the event of controversy." TR disliked pomp and ceremony and once broke up a state luncheon by demonstrating jujitsu holds on the Swiss minister. "The biggest matters," this progenitor of the imperial presidency later wrote, "I managed without consultation with anyone."

Roosevelt and other shapers of American foreign policy before World War I were members of an American quasi-aristocracy who moved comfortably in the affluent, cosmopolitan society of the Atlantic seaboard. Roosevelt, a graduate of Harvard College and prolific author, had served as assistant secretary of the navy and governor of New York. His successor, Ohioan William Howard Taft, a graduate of Yale, had served as a federal circuit court judge, governor of the Philippines (1901–1904), and secretary of war (1904–1908). Woodrow Wilson earned a Ph.D. from Johns Hopkins, wrote books on government and history, presided over Princeton, and governed New Jersey before entering the White House. Each president believed that "we owe to our less fortunate [international] neighbors" the same "neighborly feeling and aid that a successful man in a community owes to his less fortunate fellow citizens."

Their secretaries of state, with one exception, belonged to the same elite. John Hay, secretary from 1898 to 1905, was educated at Brown University. A poet, novelist, biographer, and editor, the wealthy Hay had served as Lincoln's personal secretary during the Civil War and later as McKinley's ambassador to Great Britain. His successor, Elihu Root (1905–1909), graduated from Hamilton College, took a law degree at New York University, and became one of America's most successful corporation lawyers. As secretary of war from 1899 to 1904, he created mechanisms, such as the Platt Amendment for Cuba, for managing the American empire. Like TR, he believed that the "main object of diplomacy is to keep the country out of trouble." Philander C. Knox (1909–1913) followed Root. A corporation lawyer, Knox served as attorney general and U.S. senator before heading the State Department. He liked to play golf at Chevy Chase, spend summers with his trotters at his Valley Forge Farms estate, and delegate departmental work to subordinates. He advocated "dollar diplomacy" to stabilize revolution-prone areas—that is, using private financiers and business leaders to promote foreign policy, and using diplomacy to promote American commerce and investment abroad. As his *second* secretary of state President Wilson named New Yorker Robert Lansing (1915–1920), a graduate of Amherst College, son-in-law of a former secretary of state, and practitioner of international law. Reserved and conservative, Lansing also abhorred disorder in the U.S. sphere of Latin America.

William Jennings Bryan, Wilson's *first* appointment (1913–1915), lacked such conservative elite status. The "boy orator" of Nebraska could mesmerize crowds but could not win a presidential election in 1896, 1900, and 1908. The "Great Commoner" languished for years as the most prominent has-been of the Democratic party until Wilson named him secretary of state as a reward for support at the convention of 1912. The president let Bryan appoint "deserving Democrats" to diplomatic posts, but Wilson bypassed him in most important diplomatic decisions, even to the point of composing overseas cables on his own White House typewriter.

The conservative managers of American foreign policy believed that a major component of national power was a prosperous, expanding economy invigorated by a healthy foreign trade. The principle of the "Open Door"—to keep open trade and investment opportunities—became a governing tenet voiced globally, if often tarnished in application. In 1900 Americans exported goods valued at $1.5 billion. By 1914 that figure stood at $2.5 billion. Exports to Latin America increased markedly from $132 million at the turn of the century to $309 million in 1914. Investments there in sugar, transportation, and banking shot up. By 1913 the United Fruit Company, the banana empire, had some 130,000 acres in cultivation in Central America, a fleet of freighters, and political influence as well. By 1914 U.S. entrepreneurs dominated nickel mining in Canada and sugar production in Cuba, and total investments abroad equaled $3.5 billion.

But those statistics meant more than fat pocketbooks. Americans believed that economic expansion also carried abroad positive values of industriousness, honesty, morality, and private initiative. Thus Yale University-in-China and the Young Men's Christian Association (YMCA) joined Standard Oil Company and Singer Sewing in China as advance agents of civilization. And Taft said about the Chinese: "The more civilized they become the more active their industries, the wealthier they become, and the better market they will become for us." President Wilson, adding missionary paternalism to the quest for order, said simply that he would "teach the

South American Republics to elect good men." Not all Americans were seen as benevolent. One Venezuelan writer characterized "Yanquis" as "rough and obtuse Calibans, swollen by brutal appetites, the enemies of idealism, furiously enamored of the dollar," whiskey-soaked sots, "overwhelming, fierce, [and] clownish." Whatever their intentions, American efforts to shape the lives of other peoples while denying any desire to dominate brought mixed results.

Cuba Under the Platt Amendment

In December 1898, President McKinley promised "free and independent" status for Cuba once the U.S. occupation had established "complete tranquility" and a "stable government." To accelerate Cuban democracy and stability, he appointed General Leonard Wood the military governor of the island. A Harvard graduate with a degree in medicine, Wood favored outright annexation of Cuba, but he loyally carried out the administration's policy of patrician tutelage. During his tenure (1899–1902), he worked to eradicate yellow fever, Americanize education, construct highways, and formulate an electoral law. He even added "before" and "after" photos of public toilets in his reports. "When money can be borrowed at a reasonable rate of interest and when capital is willing to invest in the Island," the general predicted, "a condition of stability will have been reached." Only the North Americans had the resources to reconstruct war-ravaged Cuba. Those Cuban elites who spoke English and knew American ways could serve as local managers, traders, agents, and advisers. The occupation thus stressed English in public schools because "the Cuban people will never understand the people of the United States until they appreciate our institutions."

Secretary of War Elihu Root sought a Cuban-American political relationship that would weather the storms of independence. Working closely with Senator Orville Platt, Root fashioned the Platt Amendment to the Army Appropriation Bill of 1901. By the amendment's terms, Cuba could not make a treaty with any nation that might impair its independence. Should Cuban independence ever be threatened, or should Cuba fail to protect "life, property, and individual liberty," Washington had the right to intervene. For these purposes, Cuba would cede to the United States "lands necessary for coaling or naval stations."

Cubans protested. On Good Friday 1901, Havana's *La Discusión* carried a cartoon of "The Cuban Calvary" depicting the Cuban people as Christ and Senator Platt as a Roman soldier. Root piously denied any "intermeddling or interference with the affairs of a Cuban government," but Wood privately conceded that "little or no independence [was] left Cuba under the Platt Amendment." A reluctant Cuban convention adopted the measure as an amendment to the new constitution on June 12, 1901, and the two governments signed a treaty embodying the Platt Amendment on May 22, 1903. That same year the U.S. Navy constructed a naval base at Guantánamo Bay; "Gitmo," as the marines christened it, was leased to the United States in perpetuity for a small annual fee. With North American investments pouring into capital-starved Cuba, extending control over sugar, tobacco, mining, transportation, utilities, and cattle ranching, the Reciprocity Treaty of 1902 permitted Cuban products to enter the United States at specially reduced tariff rates, thereby further interlocking the two economies.

The first president of the Republic of Cuba, Tomás Estrada Palma, acted "more plattish than Platt himself" until discontented Cuban nationalists revolted. In September 1906, the U.S. consul general in Havana reported Estrada Palma's inability to "protect life and property." "I am so angry with that infernal little Cuban republic," exploded Roosevelt, "that I would like to wipe its people off the face of the earth." All he wanted was that the Cubans "should behave themselves." Into this turmoil stepped the portly secretary of war, William Howard Taft, sent by TR to mediate between the warring factions. Estrada Palma resigned, permitting Taft to establish a new government with himself as governor. He returned home in mid-October, leaving behind a government headed by an American civilian, administered by U.S. Army officers, and backed by 5,000 American soldiers. For twenty-eight months Governor Charles E. Magoon attempted to reinstate Leonard Wood's electoral and humanitarian reforms, while Roosevelt worried that "those ridiculous dagoes would flare up over some totally unexpected trouble and start to cutting one another's throats."

Under his successor Taft, and under Taft's successor Woodrow Wilson, U.S. policy toward Cuba reflexively supported existing governments, by force if necessary. No serious effort was made to reform Cuba in the North American image. Through "dollar diplomacy," Washington sought order in Cuban politics and security for investments and commerce, particularly in sugar. The $50 million invested by Americans in 1896 jumped to $220 million in 1913. By 1920 American-owned mills produced about half of Cuba's sugar. Exports to the United States in 1900 equaled $31 million, by 1914 $131 million, and by 1920 $722 million, thus confirming the Cuban patriot José Martí's dictum that "*el pueblo que compra, manda*" ("the country which buys, commands"). U.S. entrepreneurs helped establish missionary schools that, in effect, trained Cubans for employment in North American companies. When revolution threatened, as in May 1912 and February 1917, marines went ashore. After Havana followed Washington's lead and declared war against Germany in April 1917, some 2,500 American troops went to the island, ostensibly to protect the sugar plantations that helped feed the Allied armies.

The Constable of the Caribbean

In his first annual message, on December 3, 1901, President Roosevelt called the Monroe Doctrine "a guarantee of the commercial independence of the Americas." The United States, however, as protector of that independence, would "not guarantee any state against punishment if it misconducts itself, provided that punishment does not take the form of the acquisition of territory by any non-American power." If a Western Hemispheric country misbehaved toward a European nation, Roosevelt would "let the European country spank it."

The president was thinking principally of Germany and Venezuela. The flamboyant Venezuelan dictator Cipriano Castro had perpetually deferred payment on $12.5 million in bonds held by European investors. In December 1902, after clearing the way with Washington, Germany and Britain delivered an ultimatum demanding immediate settlement of their claims, seized several Venezuelan vessels, bombarded two forts, and blockaded all ports. To all of this Roosevelt initially acquiesced. In mid-January 1903, however, the German navy bombarded two more forts. This time the president delivered a quiet warning to desist. He also sent Admiral George Dewey on naval maneuvers in the Caribbean, which were intended as "an object lesson to the Kaiser." Impressed by the U.S. reaction, the kaiser replaced his ill-informed ambassador with Hermann Speck von Sternberg, an old friend of Roosevelt. The president urged on him a quick settlement. Thereupon, Britain and Germany in February lifted the blockade and submitted the dispute to the Permanent Court at The Hague. Speck von Sternberg averred that the kaiser "would no more think of violating that [Monroe] doctrine than he would of colonizing the moon." When the Hague arbiters found in favor of Germany and England in early 1904, a State Department official complained that this decision put "a premium on violence" and made likely similar European interventions in the future.

TR also fretted about the Dominican Republic, revolution-torn since 1899. "I have about the same desire to annex it," Roosevelt said privately, "as a gorged boa constrictor might have to swallow a porcupine wrong-end to." An American firm claimed damages of several million dollars, and European creditors demanded action by their governments. The president prayed that the Dominicans "would behave so that I would not have to act in any way." By spring 1904 he thought he might have to do "what a policeman has to do." On December 6, 1904, Roosevelt described to Congress his conception of the United States as hemispheric policeman. "Chronic wrongdoing, or an impotence which results in a general loosening of the ties of civilized society," he proclaimed, may "ultimately require intervention by some civilized nation, and in the Western Hemisphere the adherence of the United States to the Monroe Doctrine may force the United States, however reluctantly . . . to the exercise of an international police power." James Monroe "certainly would no longer recognize" his own doctrine because TR had transformed the ban on European meddling into a brash promise of U.S. hegemony over the Americas.

The Rough Rider soon donned his constable's badge. He assigned a U.S. collector of Dominican customs. "The Constitution," Roosevelt later explained, "did not explicitly give me the power to bring about the necessary agreement with Santo Domingo," but it did "not forbid me." Yet "policing" and "civilizing" the Dominican Republic by presidential order provoked nationalist resentment, as Dominicans soon quieted "their children with the threat 'There comes an American. Keep quiet or he will kill you.'" Taft's secretary of state, Philander C. Knox, applauded the customs receivership for curing "century-old evils" and halting corruption. The assassination of the Dominican president in November 1911 suggested that Knox spoke prematurely. And in 1912 revolutionaries operating from contiguous Haiti marauded throughout the Dominican Republic, forcing the closure of several customshouses. To restore order, Taft in September 1912 sent a commission backed by 750 marines. The commissioners redefined the Haitian-Dominican border, forced the corrupt Dominican president to resign, and avoided direct interference in a new election.

Despite his denunciation of "dollar diplomacy," President Wilson's search for stability in Latin America retraced familiar steps. When, in September 1913, revolution again threatened the Dominican government, Secretary Bryan promised "every legitimate means to assist in the restoration of order and the prevention of further insurrections." Ordering naval intervention after further Dominican disorders in May 1916, Wilson said: "If a man will not listen to you quietly in a seat, sit on his neck and make him listen." Marines brought a new treaty that gave the United States full control over Dominican finances. In November, as U.S. participation in the European war became increasingly probable, Wilson proclaimed the formal military occupation of the Dominican Republic, ostensibly to suppress revolutionaries suspected of a pro-German bias. The U.S. Navy formally governed the country until 1922. The main legacy of the occupation, in one historian's terse judgment, was "a strong anti-U.S. feeling" among the Dominican people.

The Quest for Order in Haiti and Nicaragua

The Dominican Republic shares the island of Hispaniola with Haiti, where revolution became an increasingly popular mode of changing governments. In contrast to large French and German assets, U.S. investments in Haiti were limited to ownership of a small railroad and a one-third share in the Haitian National Bank. After the outbreak of World War I, the Wilson administration worried about "the ever present danger of German control" of Haiti and its deepwater harbor of Môle Saint Nicolas. Given the precedent of the German cruiser *Panther* sinking of a Haitian gunboat in 1902, the State Department offered to buy the Môle "to take it out of the market." Wilson also pressed for an American customs receivership on the Dominican model.

The Haitians resisted successfully until July 1915, when the regime of Guillaume Sam fell in an orgy of grisly political murders. Wilson ordered the navy to "amicably take charge" of the "dusky little republic." As 2,000 troops imposed martial law, one marine recorded that "the opaque eyes in the black faces were . . . as indifferent as the lenses of cameras." Subsequent fighting between occupiers and native guerrillas killed more than 2,250 Haitians compared to 16 marine casualties. Until the marines finally departed in 1934, U.S. officials noted "the intense feeling . . . practically everywhere against the American occupation."

The United States also intervened, virtually at will, in Nicaragua. In 1907 Roosevelt proposed a peace conference to end the incessant warfare among Central American states. As Secretary Root explained, their conduct mattered because the Panama Canal put them "in the front yard of the United States." When President José Santos Zelaya solicited funds to build a second interoceanic canal, especially from Germany, Washington turned against a leader whom some Nicaraguans had compared to Roosevelt himself. For Zelaya's crime of seeking a "better economic position for Nicaragua outside the U.S. economic subsystem," the State Department labeled him "the most reprehensible ruler that ever oppressed an aspiring people."

After Zelaya "yanked Mr. Taft by the ear" by executing two Americans, Washington broke diplomatic relations in November 1909, sent a battleship for "moral effect," forced Zelaya into exile, and threatened to "knock heads together until they should maintain peace." Secretary Knox then negotiated a treaty with the victorious conservatives led by Adolfo Díaz, providing for U.S. customs control and an American loan. Instead of gratitude, "the natural sentiment of an overwhelming majority of Nicaraguans is antagonistic," the U.S. envoy reported. Rebuffed by the U.S.

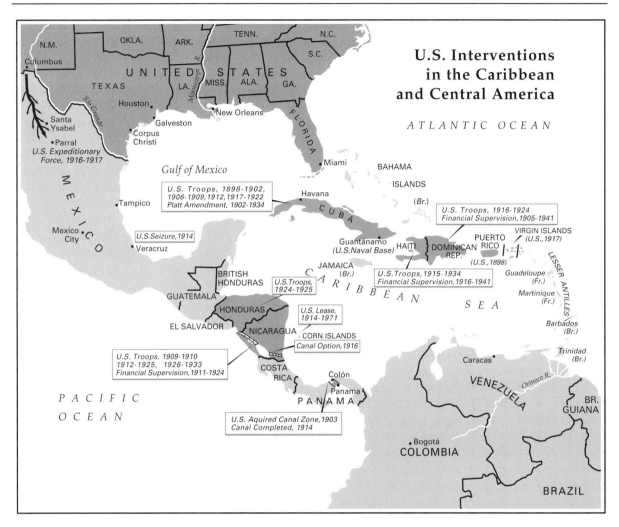

U.S. Interventions in the Caribbean and Central America

Senate, Knox and a group of bankers simply went ahead without a treaty. In September 1912, 354 U.S. marines rushed into battle on behalf of the Díaz regime, which the State Department deemed representative of "the ablest people of the country." After routing the newest revolutionary army, the leathernecks returned home, leaving one hundred behind as a legation guard in Managua.

Bryan in spring 1913 dusted off a draft treaty granting the United States a canal option in Nicaragua in exchange for $3 million. The secretary also added a clause similar to the Platt Amendment before sending the Bryan-Chamorro Treaty to the Senate. When the upper house balked, Bryan deleted the U.S. right of intervention. Ratification in February 1916 did help Nicaragua's finances. The treaty also effectively excluded European powers from naval bases in the Gulf of Fonseca, and thus U.S. warships pointedly cruised offshore during the 1916 Nicaraguan presidential campaign. Although nominally independent, Nicaragua remained a U.S. protectorate until 1933.

The Mexican Revolution Threatens U.S. Interests

Revolution in Mexico posed major problems for Washington. In 1911 Francisco I. Madero toppled Porfirio Díaz, the aged dictator who had maintained order, personal power, and a healthy environment for North American investments since the late 1870s. U.S. citizens owned more than 40 percent of Mexico's property, and Mexico had become the world's third largest oil producer, thanks to Standard Oil and other firms. When revolutionary violence endangered American lives and property, President Taft vowed to "sit tight on the lid and it will take a good deal to pry me off." In February 1913, U.S. ambassador Henry Lane Wilson encouraged one of Madero's trusted generals, Victoriano Huerta, to overthrow the revolutionary nationalist. Indeed, Huerta had Madero shot and then set about to consolidate his own power. But one of the state governors, Venustiano Carranza, organized the "Constitutionalist" revolt on February 26. With U.S. residents caught in the crossfire, the departing Taft administration refused recognition until Huerta punished the "murderers of American citizens."

Appalled by Madero's murder, President Wilson promised not to recognize a "government of butchers." He denounced Huerta as a "diverting brute! . . . seldom sober and always impossible." Seemingly unconcerned about private American properties in Mexico worth some $1.5 billion, Wilson refused to act as "the servant of those who wish to enhance the value of their Mexican investments." When Ambassador Wilson continued to urge recognition of Huerta to protect those U.S. interests, the president peremptorily recalled him in July 1913. The president thereafter treated with Mexico through special emissaries, only one of whom spoke fluent Spanish.

In August one such representative, John Lind, arrived in Mexico City. A former governor of Minnesota without diplomatic experience, Lind delivered Wilson's proposal for an armistice, "an early and free election," and Huerta's promise not to run for president. In exchange, Wilson offered recognition and aid to any elected government. "Where in the hell does he get the right to say who shall or shall not be President of Mexico," wrote one Mexican after Wilson's "counsels" were rebuffed. After this snub, Wilson announced a restrained policy of "watchful waiting." Undeterred, Huerta in October held a special election, which returned an entirely submissive congress ready to extend his presidency indefinitely. Wilson then turned to Carranza in northern Mexico, but the latter contemptuously refused Wilsonian mediation and rejected any solution short of his own triumph. Wilson then announced in November a renewed policy "to isolate General Huerta entirely . . . and so to force him out."

Most European powers, especially Germany, had recognized Huerta in defiance of Wilson. The British, however, their navy relying on Mexican oil, did not want to antagonize Wilson, with tensions mounting in Europe. London therefore notified Huerta that it would not support him against the United States, and urged him to resign—all the while viewing Wilson's policies as "most impractical and unreasonable."

With British compliance assured, Wilson lifted the U.S. arms embargo in February 1914. As Carranza's resupplied forces pushed south, the president sent U.S.

naval vessels to the oil-producing town of Tampico on the Gulf of Mexico. On April 9, at Tampico, Huerta's troops arrested several U.S. sailors loading gasoline aboard a whaleboat docked provocatively near the Mexican outpost. The Mexican colonel in charge quickly freed the bluejackets and apologized orally. Hotheaded Admiral Henry T. Mayo nonetheless demanded a formal twenty-one-gun salute because Mexico had insulted the flag. When Huerta refused, the president on April 20 asked Congress to authorize force "to obtain . . . the fullest recognition of the rights and dignity of the United States." Wilson then ordered U.S. warships to the port of Veracruz to stop a German arms shipment intended for Huerta.

On April 21, 1914, 800 American sailors and marines landed. Huerta's troops withdrew but cadets from the naval academy put up a bloody resistance. Nineteen Americans and several hundred Mexicans died. Despite Wilson's intent to undermine Huerta, the capture of Veracruz temporarily united Mexicans behind the dictator. Rejecting advice from his military advisers, who wanted to march to Mexico City, Wilson accepted mediation when proposed by Argentina, Brazil, and Chile (the ABC powers) on April 25. These mediation talks, held on the Canadian side of Niagara Falls that summer, accomplished little, but in mid-July Huerta fled to Europe, and on August 20 a triumphant Carranza paraded before enthusiastic throngs in Mexico City.

Francisco (Pancho) Villa (1878–1923). The intelligent, dedicated revolutionary nationalist bedeviled both Mexico and the United States. His daring raid on an American town was calculated to outrage President Wilson, whom he mocked as "an evangelizing professor of philosophy who is destroying the independence of a friendly people." (El Paso Public Library, Southwest Collection)

The Constitutionalist triumph did not last. One of Carranza's northern generals, Francisco (Pancho) Villa, soon broke from the ranks, marched south, and in December occupied Mexico City. Wilson saw Villa as "the only instrument of civilization in Mexico" who could "educate the turbulent masses of peons so prone to pillage." The president thus eased arms exports to him and refused to recognize Carranza. To prevent a military clash with any Mexican faction, all American troops withdrew from Veracruz on November 23, 1914. Once again, Wilson watched and waited.

Relations remained tense during early 1915. Carranza's forces gradually drove Villa north, but in the process Mexico City became a no-man's-land, with bread riots and starvation threatening its inhabitants, including 2,500 Americans and 23,000 other foreign residents. Further complications arose along the Mexico-U.S. borderland, especially in southern Texas, where the massive influx of refugees and revolutionaries exacerbated local tensions between Anglos and *Tejanos.* The ensuing raids and counterraids turned south Texas into a war zone as vigilantes and Texas rangers killed at least 150 Mexicans. Preoccupied by the *Lusitania* crisis with Germany after May 1915, Wilson reluctantly concluded that "Carranza will somehow have to be digested." With U.S. oil fields under Carranza's protection, Wilson extended de facto recognition to the Constitutionalist regime in June 1915, permitted arms exports (while banning them to opponents), and beefed up the U.S. military presence along the border.

Egged on by German agents, Villa denounced *Carranzistas* as "vassals" of the United States. In the predawn hours of March 9, 1916, Villa led a band of *Villistas* across the border into Columbus, New Mexico, leaving seventeen Americans and more than a hundred Mexicans dead. Within hours, Wilson unleashed the Punitive Expedition of 7,000 soldiers, commanded by General John J. Pershing, which soon penetrated 350 miles into Mexico in a vain search for Villa. Nonetheless, a clash with *Carranzista* troops occurred at Carrizal in June 1916. Wilson resisted demands to withdraw Pershing's troops until February 1917. Later that month, the secret Zimmermann telegram, proposing an anti-American alliance between Germany and Mexico, came into the hands of the State Department, courtesy of British intelligence. This German threat prompted the United States to extend de jure recognition of Carranza's government on August 31, 1917, in order to ensure Mexican neutrality during the fight against Germany. After four futile years, Wilson had finally given up trying to tutor the Mexicans.

Japan, China, and Dollar Diplomacy in Asia

Managing Asian affairs proved even more difficult. Secretary of State John Hay's Open Door notes did not prevent the further humiliation of China. During the Boxer Rebellion Russia stationed 175,000 troops in Manchuria and demanded exclusive rights from China, including a commercial monopoly. Roosevelt and Hay acquiesced because the Open Door had "always recognized the exceptional position of Russia" in Manchuria. Thinking it folly "to play the role of an Asian power without military power," Roosevelt retreated because the American people would not fight for nebulous principles of Chinese integrity in Manchuria.

Japan viewed the question quite differently. Russia blocked Japanese economic expansion into Manchuria, posed a potential naval menace, and endangered the Japanese position in Korea. Tokyo covered its flanks with an Anglo-Japanese Alliance in 1902 and prepared for war. On February 8, 1904, the Japanese navy destroyed Russia's Asian fleet in a surprise attack at Port Arthur. At first Roosevelt cheered privately, "for Japan is playing our game," but he worried about "the creation of either a yellow peril or a Slav peril." By spring 1905, Japanese soldiers had taken Mukden, where Russia lost 97,000 men. Revolutionary stirrings had hit St. Petersburg, and Admiral Heihachiro Togo had sunk the Russian Baltic fleet at Tsushima. On May 31, Japanese envoy Kogoro Takahira requested Roosevelt "to invite the two belligerents to come together" for direct peace negotiations.

Hoping to balance the belligerents and thus protect U.S. interests in the Pacific and Asia, Roosevelt invited Japanese and Russian diplomats to meet at Portsmouth, New Hampshire, in August 1905. Japan demanded Russia's leasehold on the Liaodong Peninsula and the railroad running from Harbin to Port Arthur, evacuation of Russian troops from Manchuria, and Japan's control of Korea. The Russians quickly conceded these points but rejected demands for an indemnity and cession of the island of Sakhalin. Roosevelt then proposed dividing Sakhalin and agreement "in principle" on an indemnity. Tsar Nicholas II agreed to partition but "not a kopeck of compensation." Japan yielded and in late August signed a peace treaty. Roosevelt had earned the Nobel Peace Prize.

The president's search for equipoise in East Asia did not end at Portsmouth. As early as March 1904, TR had conceded to Japan a relationship with Korea "just like we have with Cuba." Secretary of War Taft reaffirmed the concession with Prime Minister Taro Katsura on July 27, 1905, whereby Japan denied any designs on the Philippines, and Taft acknowledged Japanese control of Korea. A year later Tokyo

"Spread-eagleism" in China. The missionary teacher Grace Roberts teaches a Bible class in 1903 in Manchuria. Americanism and religious work, flag and missionary, became partners. The mission force was feminized—the majority of missionaries were women. (ABCFM photographs. By permission of the Houghton Library, Harvard University)

reopened southern Manchuria to foreign and American trade but discouraged foreign capital investments. Japan formally annexed Korea in 1910.

A domestic dispute in California soon soured Japanese-American cordiality. On October 11, 1906, the San Francisco School Board created a special "Oriental Public School" for all Japanese, Chinese, and Korean children. Japan immediately protested, and TR denounced the "infernal fools in California" whose educational exclusion of Japanese was "as foolish as if conceived by the mind of a Hottentot." Given existing federal-state jurisdictions, however, he could do little more than rail against the recalcitrant school board and apply political pressure to the California legislature to prevent statewide discriminatory measures. Defending segregation, the *San Francisco Examiner* editorialized:"Californians do not want their growing daughters to be intimate in daily school contact with Japanese young men. Is this remarkable?" Always the political realist, Roosevelt accepted what he personally disliked and in February 1907 reached a "Gentlemen's Agreement" with Tokyo, sharply restricting Japanese immigration on a voluntary basis.

Because "the Japanese jingoes are . . . about as bad as ours," the president shrewdly pressed for more battleships and fortification of Hawai'i and the vulnerable Philippines, now America's "heel of Achilles," so that the United States would "be ready for anything that comes." He also dramatized the importance of a strong navy to Congress and to Japan by ordering the battle fleet in 1907 to the Pacific and around the world. Just after the "Great White Fleet" visited Tokyo in October 1908, Ambassador Takahira received instructions to reach an agreement with the United States recognizing the Pacific Ocean as an open avenue of trade, pledging the integrity of Japanese and American insular possessions in the Pacific, and promising equal opportunity in China. The ensuing Root-Takahira declaration of November 30, 1908, seemed to restore Japanese-American harmony.

Conflicting Japanese-American goals toward China spoiled the new epoch. Despite the Open Door notes, American commerce with China stalled during the Roosevelt era, in part because of resurgent nationalism. When Congress barred Chinese immigration in 1904, the Chinese staged a short-lived boycott of American goods. Because Roosevelt viewed the Chinese as passive and effete, "sunk in Oriental stagnation and corruption," he placed strategic interests first and refused to antagonize Japan over China. TR's successor thought otherwise. Instead of a decrepit China in decay, Taft envisaged expanded trade with a "young China, rousing from a centuries-old slumber and rubbing the sand of its past from its eyes." During a 1905 trip to East Asia, Taft met the intensely anti-Japanese American consul general in Mukden, Willard Straight. Two years later Straight proposed the creation of a Manchurian bank, to be financed by the American railroad magnate E. H. Harriman. Under Taft, Straight and the State Department quickly inspired several New York banks to serve as the official agency of American railroad investment in China. As acting chief of the department's new Far Eastern Division, Straight demanded admission of the American bankers into a European banking consortium undertaking construction of the Huguang Railway linking Beijing and Guangzhou (Canton). Straight then resigned from the State Department to become the consortium's roving representative.

In November 1909, Washington had proposed to Britain the neutralization of Manchurian railroads through a large international loan to China for the purchase of the lines. Britain, however, joined both Japan and Russia to reject the proposal. Instead of an open door in Manchuria, Secretary of State Knox had "nailed that door closed with himself on the outside." In fall 1910, an agreement expanded the Huguang Railway consortium to include American bankers, but the Chinese Revolution broke out in May 1911 and delayed railroad construction until 1913. "Dollar diplomacy," Straight ruefully admitted, "made no friends" in the Huguang matter.

Hoping to reap tangible benefits by dissociating from the other powers, President Wilson repudiated American participation in the international consortium in March and then extended formal diplomatic recognition to the Chinese Republic in May. He had thereby renewed America's commitment to the political integrity of China, a goal pragmatically abandoned by Roosevelt, unsuccessfully resuscitated by Taft, and consistently opposed by Japan.

Events at home soon made Wilson's Asian policy resemble Taft's more than Roosevelt's. In April 1913, politicians placed before the California legislature a bill denying residents "ineligible to citizenship" the right to own land. The measure struck directly at the 50,000 Japanese living in California. Racist passions erupted, with one farmer recoiling from the prospect of racial intermarriage: "What is that baby? It isn't a Japanese. It isn't white." Basically sharing the Californians' anti-Japanese prejudices, and sensitive to states' rights, Wilson nonetheless sent Secretary Bryan to Sacramento to beg for a less harsh statute. But the California legislature passed the offensive bill on May 3, 1913. When Japan protested, Wilson and Bryan lamely argued that one state's legislation did not constitute a "national discriminatory policy."

Wilson's antipathy toward Japan reappeared in fall 1914 when Japan declared war on Germany, seized the German Pacific islands north of the equator, and swept across China's Shandong Peninsula to capture the German leasehold of Jiaozhou. "When there is a fire in a jeweller's shop," a Japanese diplomat theorized, "the neighbours cannot be expected to refrain from helping themselves." Tokyo immediately followed with the Twenty-One Demands of January 18, 1915, claiming extensive political and economic rights in Shandong, southern Manchuria, and Mongolia. Preoccupied with Mexico and the *Lusitania* crisis, the Wilson administration refused to recognize Japan's gains, which amounted to a repudiation of the Open Door policy.

Wilson's nonrecognition policy ran counter to secret treaties in which the European Allies promised to support Japan's conquests at the peace conference after World War I. Washington soon compromised. In an agreement with Viscount Kikujiro Ishii in November 1917, Secretary Lansing acknowledged that "territorial propinquity creates special relationships between countries, and consequently . . . Japan has special interests in China," while Ishii pledged his nation's dedication to the Open Door and integrity of China. The Wilson administration also revived the international banking consortium as the only way to check further unilateral Japanese economic penetration of China proper. The wheel had turned full circle for Wilson. Like Taft before him, Wilson failed to protect China's fragile sovereignty without conciliating or blocking Japan.

Anglo-American Rapprochement and Empire-Building

American policies toward Asia and Latin America often fell short of their proclaimed goals because of the pseudoscientific race thinking of the early twentieth century. Americans viewed Asians as "inscrutable and somnolent," depicted Latin Americans as black children or alluring maidens, imagined Africa as the "dark continent" of "savage beasts and beastly savages," and referred to Filipinos as "our little brown brothers," and these biased stereotypes inevitably aroused resentment from Bogotá to Beijing, from Managua to Manila. Yet such Darwinist racial attitudes also facilitated much closer relations between the United States and Great Britain. Because victory "in the international competition among the races" might go to the most populous and unscrupulous countries, England and the United States might then need "to cultivate a sense of solidarity and a capacity for cooperation." Theodore Roosevelt certainly thought so when he predicted that the "twentieth century" would "still be the century" of "men who speak English." So too did the British, as shown by their willingness to accept exclusive U.S. control of a canal in Panama. Also prompted by a search for allies against Germany, London's pursuit of "the most

John Bull in Need of Friends.
Battered by criticism over its war against the Boers in South Africa and challenged by a rising Germany, Great Britain found a new friend in the United States. (*Des Moines Leader* in *Literary Digest,* 1901)

cordial and constant cooperation" with the United States led to a celebrated "great rapprochement."

The new Anglo-American affinity, however, nearly dissolved in 1903 over the Alaska boundary controversy, which stemmed from Canadian claims to large areas of the Alaskan panhandle. As the power responsible for the Dominion's foreign relations, Britain found itself backing Ottawa's dubious contention that much of the panhandle's coastline actually belonged to Canada. Expostulating that Canada had less right "than the United States did to Cornwall or Kent," Roosevelt refused arbitration and sent 800 soldiers to Alaska to awe his opponents. London finally agreed in January 1903 to a mixed boundary commission composed of six jurists, three from each side. Taking no chances, Roosevelt appointed Senator Henry Cabot Lodge and Secretary Root, hardly disinterested judges, to the commission. He told London he would run the line himself if the commissioners failed to agree. One British commissioner sided with the Americans, and in October 1903, by a vote of 4 to 2, the commission officially decided for the United States. The British "made the inevitable choice to please a power ten times the size of Canada and with more than ten times the wealth."

Anglo-American entente also characterized the settlement of the North Atlantic fisheries dispute. Since 1782, American fishermen had insisted on retaining their pre-Revolutionary privileges off Canada's Newfoundland. Indeed, a gilded wooden cod still hung from the ceiling of the Massachusetts State House. The modus vivendi of 1888, under which they had fished for several years, collapsed in

1905 when Newfoundland placed restrictions on American fishing vessels. Senator Lodge cried for warships to protect his constituents' livelihood. Instead, Roosevelt proposed, and London accepted, arbitration at The Hague Tribunal. In 1910 the tribunal ruled that Britain could oversee fishing off Newfoundland under reasonable regulations, that a fisheries commission would hear cases, and that Americans could fish up to three miles from shore. This compromise defused the oldest dispute in American foreign relations and symbolized London's political withdrawal from the Western Hemisphere.

The naval retrenchment had occurred earlier, when the Admiralty abolished the North Atlantic station based at Jamaica. After 1902 the Royal Navy patrolled the Caribbean only with an annual visit by a token squadron of cruisers. Admiral Sir John Fisher wanted to concentrate his heavy ships in the North Sea as monitors of the growing German navy. He regarded the United States as "a kindred state with whom we shall never have a parricidal war."

Even the aggressive hemispheric diplomacy of Taft and Wilson did not undermine Anglo-American rapprochement. Foreign Secretary Sir Edward Grey tersely laid to rest all talk of a challenge: "His Majesty's Government cannot with any prospect of success embark upon an active counterpolicy to that of the United States, or constitute themselves the champions of Mexico or any of these republics against the United States." In reciprocation, Wilson protected British oil interests and made it a "point of honor" to eliminate the one potentially dangerous British grievance inherited from his predecessor. Because Taft's exemption of American intercoastal vessels from payment of Panama Canal tolls unfairly discriminated against foreign (and British) shipping, Wilson persuaded Congress to revoke the law in June 1914.

In the end, rapprochement meant mutual respect for each other's empires. Roosevelt, for example, encouraged London to frustrate native aspirations for independence in India, while the British accepted the American suppression of the Filipinos and U.S. hegemony in Latin America. U.S. leaders usually spoke favorably of independence for colonial peoples—but only after long-term tutelage to make them "civilized" enough to govern. In 1910 in Egypt, where Roosevelt applauded Britain's "great work for civilization," the ex-president even lectured Muslim nationalists about Christian respect for womanhood. In unstable Liberia, where the United States in 1912 instituted a financial receivership in the African nation like that in the Dominican Republic, the British encouraged Washington to use a strong hand in America's African "protectorate."

While building an empire, policymakers largely adhered to the tradition of aloofness from continental European affairs. Even Roosevelt overtly tampered only once with Europe's balance of power. In 1904 France acquiesced in British control of Egypt in exchange for primacy in Morocco. A year later, Germany tested the solidity of the new Anglo-French entente by challenging France's claims in Morocco. The kaiser belligerently demanded a German political role in Morocco, which France at once refused. After a brief European war scare, in which Britain stood by its ally, Germany asked Roosevelt to induce France and England to settle Morocco's future. Worried about Kaiser Wilhelm's "violent and often wholly irrational zigzags," Roosevelt accepted the personal invitation only after assuring Paris that his "sympathies . . . at bottom [were] with France." During the ensuing conference, held in early 1906 at Algeciras, Spain, Roosevelt devised a pro-French compromise and persuaded the kaiser to accept it. This political intervention isolated Germany and reinforced the Anglo-French entente, but it generated criticism at home. Roosevelt's successors made sure they did not violate the American policy of nonentanglement with Europe during the more ominous second Moroccan and Balkan crises preceding the First World War.

Nonentanglement also doomed the sweeping arbitration treaties that Secretary Hay negotiated with several world powers. When the Senate attached crippling amendments, Roosevelt withdrew the treaties because they did "not in the smallest degree facilitate settlements by arbitration." After 1905 Secretary Root persuaded Roosevelt to accept watered-down bilateral arbitration treaties, and Secretary Bryan later negotiated a series of "cooling-off" treaties that pledged nations to refrain from war during international investigations of serious disputes. None of these arrangements, however, effectively bound signatories, and like the Permanent Court of Arbitration at The Hague, they represented a backwater in international diplomacy. Ambassador Whitelaw Reid compared U.S. participation in the Hague Peace Conference of 1907 to a farmer taking his hog to market: "That hog didn't weigh as much as I expected he would, and I always knew he wouldn't."

The mainstream of American foreign policy between 1900 and 1914 flowed through the Panama Canal, a momentous political, military, and technological achievement. The United States became the unchallenged policeman of the Caribbean region, empowering Washington, in Taft's words, "to prevent revolutions" so that "we'll have no more." Despite a two-ocean navy, the United States still lacked the power to challenge Japan or Britain. As Roosevelt understood, the Open Door "completely disappears as soon as a powerful nation determines to disregard it." One military officer told Congress in 1910: "We have grown from a little frontier army to one spread all over the world—in America, Puerto Rico, Hawai'i, Alaska, the Philippines, and sometimes in Cuba—and we have not got the officers and men to do it."

American insensitivity to the nationalism of other peoples became another imperial legacy. Filipino resistance to American domination, Cuban anger against the Platt Amendment, Colombian outrage over Panama, and Mexican rejection of Wilsonian intervention bore witness to the depth of nationalistic sentiments. Like the European powers carving up Asia, Africa, and the Middle East, the United States was developing its empire and subjugating peoples and compromising their sovereignty in Latin America and the Pacific. As a Panamanian diplomat later explained, "When you hit a rock with an egg, the egg breaks. Or when you hit an egg with a rock, the egg breaks. The United States is the rock. Panama is the egg. In either case, the egg breaks." With the exception of the Virgin Islands, purchased from Denmark for $25 million in 1917 to forestall any wartime German seizure, the empire grew little from outright territorial gains. It was, instead, an informal empire administered by troops, financial advisers, and reformers who showed contempt for native peoples' culture, politics, and economies through a paternalistic discourse.

Puerto Rico thus seemed the "good" territorial possession, as political cartoons portrayed the populace as a "polite schoolchild, sometimes female, in contrast to ruffian boys" in Cuba and the Philippines. Under the Foraker Act (1900), Puerto

Rico and its naval base on Culebra became a "new constitutional animal"—an "unincorporated territory" subject to the will of the U.S. Congress and governed by the War Department (until 1934). In a series of decisions called the Insular Cases (1901–1904), the Supreme Court upheld the Foraker Act, providing Washington with a means to govern people it did not wish to organize as a state. In March 1917, Congress granted Puerto Ricans U.S. citizenship just in time for them to be drafted into the U.S. armed forces in the war against Germany. To this day, Puerto Rico remains a colony, or "commonwealth," and Puerto Ricans remain divided in their views about statehood, independence, and commonwealth status.

The adventures of American foreign relations under an imperial ideology and the male ethos in the years 1900–1914 attracted many capable, well-educated young men to diplomatic service. "It was TR's call to youth which lured me to Washington," the diplomat William Phillips recalled. Several of these young foreign-service professionals, virtually all graduates of Ivy League colleges, including Phillips, Joseph Grew, Willard Straight, former Rough Rider Henry P. Fletcher, and soldier-diplomat Frank R. McCoy, lived in an exclusive bachelors' townhouse at 1718 H Street during their Washington service. Dubbed "the Family," these youthful professionals blended camaraderie with careers and "became the elite or legendary 'inner circle' of the State Department" for the next forty years. The New York attorney Henry L. Stimson, a protégé of Elihu Root, served as secretary of war under Taft (1911–1913) and continued this tradition of recruiting some of the brightest public servants in a succession of high-level posts through the end of World War II.

Cultural foreign relations also flourished during these years. Just as Buffalo Bill Cody's Wild West Show had "hyped" American cultural myths abroad since the 1890s, Wilbur Wright's airplane tour of Europe in 1908 set records, thrilled crowds, and impressed military strategists. The cruise of the "Great White Fleet" provided as much pageantry as statecraft—"a feast, a frolic, or a fight," as one admiral put it. Colonial subjects became popular on college campuses, as anthropologists and ethnographers offered courses on "Savage Childhood" and "Peoples of the Philippines."

Hundreds of thousands of U.S. tourists ("the world's wanderers") traveled abroad clutching their Baedeker guidebooks, spending American dollars, and sometimes acquiring foreign titles through marriage, as in the case of Jennie Jerome and Lord Randolph Churchill, whose son Winston valued Anglo-American partnership. Civic leaders took pride in hosting the Olympic Games in St. Louis in 1904, hailed an American victory in the 1908 Round-the-World Automobile Race, and cheered the gold medals won by Native American Jim Thorpe at the Stockholm Olympics in 1912. Just as they seemed to take up the great game of empire from Great Britain, so too did Americans become proficient in that most diplomatic of athletic competitions, the royal and ancient Scottish sport of golf. For some Americans, true Anglo-American entente did not occur until young Francis Ouimet bested British champions Harry Vardon and Ted Ray in the U.S. Open at Brookline, Massachusetts, in 1913.

Yet beneath the glitter lurked danger. Winston Churchill later wrote of living in two different worlds: "the actual, visual world with its peaceful activities" and "a hypothetical world 'beneath the threshold' "—"a world at one moment utterly fantastic, at the next seeming to leap into reality—a world of monstrous shadows moving in convulsive combination through vistas of fathomless catastrophe." Once the world started spinning around Sarajevo, Bosnia, it became impossible for the growing American empire to escape the maelstrom of world war.

FURTHER READING FOR THE PERIOD 1900–1914

See studies listed in the last two chapters and Michael C. C. Adams, *The Great Adventure: Male Desire and the Coming of World War I* (1990); Gail Bederman, *Manliness & Civilization* (1995); Frances A. Boyle, *Foundations of World Order* (1999); Kurkpatrick Dorsey, *The Dawn of Conservation Diplomacy* (1999); Lloyd C. Gardner, *Safe for Democracy: The Anglo-American Response to Revolution, 1913–1923* (1984); Robert E. Hannigan, *The New World Empire* (2002); George R. Matthews, *America's First Olympics* (2005); Cyrus Veeser, *A World Safe for Capitalism* (2002); and Richard H. Werking, *The Master Architects* (1977) (foreign service).

Theodore Roosevelt is the subject of H. W. Brands, *T.R.* (1997); Richard H. Collin, *Theodore Roosevelt* (1985); Kathleen Dalton, *Theodore Roosevelt* (2002); Frederick W. Marks, *Velvet on Iron* (1979); Edmund Morris, *Theodore Rex* (2001); Natalie A. Naylor et al., eds., *Theodore Roosevelt* (1992); Patricia O'Toole, *When Trumpets Call* (2005); William N. Tilchin, *Theodore Roosevelt and the British Empire* (1997); and Sarah Watts, *Rough Rider in the White House* (2003).

For the Taft administration, see Paolo E. Coletta, *The Presidency of William Howard Taft* (1973); Ralph E. Minger, *William Howard Taft and American Foreign Policy* (1975); and Walter V. Scholes and Marie V. Scholes, *The Foreign Policies of the Taft Administration* (1970).

For Wilson policies, see the next chapter and Frederick S. Calhoun, *Power and Principle* (1986) and *Uses of Force and Wilsonian Foreign Policy* (1993); and Kendrick A. Clements, *The Presidency of Woodrow Wilson* (1990).

U.S. relations with Latin America are examined in Laura Briggs, *Reproducing Empire* (2002) (Puerto Rico); Bruce J. Calder, *The Impact of Intervention* (1984) (Dominican Republic); Raymond A. Carr, *Puerto Rico* (1984); Arturo M. Carrión, *Puerto Rico* (1983); Mark T. Gilderhus, *Pan American Visions* (1986) (Wilson); David Healy, *Drive to Hegemony* (1989) and *Gunboat Diplomacy in the Wilson Era* (1976) (Haiti); Lester D. Langley, *The Banana Wars* (2002); Lester D. Langley and Thomas Schoonover, *The Banana Men* (1995); Nancy Mitchell, *The Danger of Dreams* (1999); Thomas F. O'Brien, *The Revolutionary Mission* (1996); Brenda G. Plummer, *Haiti and the Great Powers, 1902–1915* (1988); Mary Renda, *Taking Haiti* (2001); Emily Rosenberg, *Financial Missionaries to the World* (1999) (dollar diplomacy); Thomas D. Schoonover, *The United States in Central America, 1860–1911* (1991); David Sheinin, *Searching for Authority* (1998) (Argentina) and *Beyond the Ideal* (2000) (Pan Americanism); and Richard P. Tucker, *Insatiable Appetite* (2000).

For the Panama Canal, see Richard H. Collin, *Theodore Roosevelt's Caribbean* (1990); Michael L. Conniff, *Panama and the United States* (2001); Richard L. Lael, *Arrogant Diplomacy* (1987); Walter LaFeber, *The Panama Canal* (1989); John Lindsay-Poland, *Emperors in the Jungle* (2003); John Major, *Prize Possession* (1993); David McCullough, *The Path Between the Seas* (1977); and Stephen J. Randall, *Colombia and the United States* (1992).

U.S. hegemony in Cuba is discussed in David Healy, *The United States in Cuba, 1898–1902* (1963); James H. Hitchman, *Leonard Wood and Cuban Independence, 1898–1902* (1971); Allan R. Millett, *The Politics of Intervention* (1968); and Louis A. Pérez, Jr., *Cuba and the United States* (2003) and *Cuba Under the Platt Amendment, 1902–1934* (1986).

Relations with Mexico are treated in Jonathan C. Brown, *Oil and Revolution in Mexico* (1993); Joseph M. Gilbert, *Revolution from Without* (1982); Mark T. Gilderhus, *Diplomacy and Revolution* (1977); John M. Hart, *Revolutionary Mexico* (1988) and *Empire and Revolution* (2002); Friedrich Katz *The Secret War in Mexico* (1981); Alan Knight, *U.S.–Mexican Relations, 1910–1940* (1987); Daniel Nugent, ed., *Rural Revolt in Mexico and U.S. Intervention* (1988); Robert L. Scheina, *Villa* (2004); and Joseph A. Stout, Jr., *Border Conflict* (1999).

For America's interactions with Asia and China, see Jongsuk Chay, *Diplomacy of Asymmetry* (1990) (Korea); Sharon Delmendo, *The Star Spangled Banner* (2004) (Philippines); Frank H. Golay, *Face of Empire* (2004) (Philippines); Jonathan Goldstein et al., eds., *America Views China* (1991); Michael H. Hunt, *The Making of a*

Special Relationship (1983); Eileen Scully, *Bargaining with the State from Afar* (2001) (Extraterritoriality); and Guanhua Wang, *In Search of Justice* (2002).

Japanese-American relations are studied in Raymond A. Esthus, *Double Eagle and Rising Sun* (1988) (Portsmouth) and *Theodore Roosevelt and Japan* (1966); Tsuyoshi Ishihara, *Mark Twain and Japan* (2005); Walter LaFeber, *The Clash* (1997); Charles E. Neu, *The Troubled Encounter* (1975); and E. P. Trani, *The Treaty of Portsmouth* (1969).

American missionaries, especially in Asia, are covered in Gael Graham, *Gender, Culture, and Christianity* (1995); Patricia R. Hill, *The World Their Household* (1985) (women); Jane Hunter, *The Gospel of Gentility* (1984) (women in China); and Xi Lian, *The Conversion of Missionaries* (1997).

U.S. relations with Europe and Great Britain, and rivalry with Germany, are discussed in Stuart Anderson, *Race and Rapprochement* (1981); Holger H. Herwig, *Politics of Frustration* (1976); Bradford Perkins, *The Great Rapprochement* (1968); Thomas and Kathleen Schaeper, *Rhodes Scholars, Oxford, and The Creation of an American Elite* (2004); and Hans-Jürgen Schröder, ed., *Confrontation and Cooperation* (1993) (Germany).

The peace movement and the role of The Hague are discussed in Calvin Davis, *The United States and the First Hague Conference* (1962) and *The United States and the Second Hague Peace Conference* (1975); Sondra R. Herman, *Eleven Against War* (1969); C. Roland Marchand, *The American Peace Movement and Social Reform, 1898–1918* (1973); and David S. Patterson, *Toward a Warless World* (1976).

See also Robert L. Beisner, ed., *Guide to American Foreign Relations Since 1600* (2003).

For comprehensive coverage of foreign-relations topics, see the articles in the four-volume *Encyclopedia of U.S. Foreign Relations* (1997), edited by Bruce W. Jentleson and Thomas G. Paterson.

CHAPTER 8

War, Peace, and Revolution in the Time of Wilson, 1914–1920

✳ The Sinking of the Lusitania, 1915

"PERFECTLY SAFE; SAFER than the trolley cars in New York City," claimed a Cunard Line official the morning of May 1, 1915. More than twice as long as an American football field, the majestic *Lusitania,* with its watertight compartments and swiftness, seemed invulnerable. The British Admiralty had stipulated that the 30,396-ton vessel could be armed if necessary, but "Lucy's" priority was pleasure, not war. Resplendent with tapestries and carpets, the luxurious floating palace dazzled. One American found the ship "more beautiful than Solomon's Temple—and big enough to hold all his wives." A crew of 702 attended the 1,257 travelers who departed from New York's Pier 54 on May 1. Deep in the *Lusitania's* storage area rested a cargo of foodstuffs and contraband. The Cunarder thus carried, said a U.S. State Department official, both "babies and bullets."

In the morning newspapers of May 1 a rather unusual announcement, placed by the German Embassy, appeared beside the Cunard Line advertisement. The German "Notice" warned passengers that the waters around the British Isles constituted a war zone wherein British vessels were subject to destruction. The State Department did not intercede to warn the 197 American passengers away from the *Lusitania.* Most Americans accepted the Cunard Line statement: "She is too fast for any submarine. No German war vessel can get her or near her."

Captained by William T. Turner, the *Lusitania* steamed into the Atlantic at half past noon on May 1. Manned by an ill-trained crew (the best now on war duty), "Lucy" enjoyed a smooth crossing in calm water. Despite lifesaving drills, complacency about the submarine danger lulled captain, crew, and passengers alike. Passengers joked about torpedoes, played cards, consumed liquor, and listened to concerts on deck. On May 6, as the *Lusitania* neared Ireland, Turner received a warning from the Naval Centre at Queenstown: "Submarines active off south coast

Mass Grave of *Lusitania* Victims. In Queenstown, Ireland, a large burial ground holds more than a hundred victims of the *Lusitania* disaster of 1915, which rudely brought Word War I to American consciousness. (U.S. War Department, National Archives)

of Ireland." The captain posted lookouts but took no other precautions, despite follow-up warnings. He had standing orders from the Admiralty to take a zigzag path at full speed to make it difficult for lurking German submarines to zero in on their targets. But Turner steamed straight ahead.

Unusually good visibility, recorded Lieutenant Walter Schwieger in his log on May 7. The young commander was piloting his *U-20* submarine along the southern Irish coast. Schwieger surfaced at 1:45 P.M. and soon spotted a four-funneled ship in the distance. He quickly submerged and set a track toward the *Lusitania*. At 700 meters the *U-20* released a torpedo. The deadly missile dashed through the water tailed by bubbles. A watchman on the starboard bow of the *Lusitania* cried out. Captain Turner did not hear the megaphone one minute before the torpedo struck. Had he heard, the ship *might* have veered sharply and avoided danger. Turner felt the explosion as it ripped into the *Lusitania*. Panic swept the passengers as they stumbled about the listing decks. Steam whistled from punctured boilers. Less than half the lifeboats lowered; some capsized or embarked only partially loaded. Within eighteen minutes the "Queen of the Atlantic" sank, killing 1,198—128 of them Americans.

President Wilson had just ended a cabinet meeting when he learned of the disaster. His special assistant, Colonel Edward House, then in London, predicted: "We shall be at war with Germany within a month." Fearing war, Secretary Bryan told the president that "ships carrying contraband should be prohibited from carrying

The *Lusitania* and *U-20*.
The majestic passenger liner was sunk by German submarine *U-20* off the coast of Ireland on May 7, 1915. "Suppose they should sink the *Lusitania* with American passengers on board," King George V had mused to Colonel Edward M. House on that fateful morning. (Peabody Museum of Salem; Bundesarchiv)

passengers. . . . It would be like putting women and children in front of an army. " Ex-president Theodore Roosevelt soon bellowed that Germany had perpetrated "piracy on a vaster scale of murder than old-time pirates ever practiced." American after American voiced horror, but few wanted war. Wilson secluded himself to ponder a response. Just months before, he had promised to hold Berlin strictly accountable for the loss of any American ships or lives because of submarine warfare. Thereafter, Wilson found himself trying to fulfill America's "double wish"—"to maintain a firm front . . . [toward] Germany and yet do nothing that might by any possibility involve us in war."

Wilson spoke in Philadelphia on May 10. His words, much misunderstood, suggested he had no backbone: "There is such a thing as a man being too proud to fight. There is such a thing as a nation being so right that it does not need to convince others by force that it is right." The next morning he told the cabinet that he would send a note to Berlin insisting that Americans had a right to travel on the high seas and demanding a German disavowal of the inhumane acts of its submarine commanders. Secretary Bryan, long upset about an apparent double standard in protesting more against German than British violations of American neutral rights, pleaded with Wilson for a simultaneous protest to London. But only one note went out on May 13—to Berlin: "The Imperial Government will not expect the United States to omit any word or any act necessary to the performance of its sacred duty of maintaining the rights of the United States and its citizens and of safeguarding their free exercise and enjoyment." In short, end submarine warfare, or else.

The German government took little pleasure in the destruction of the *Lusitania*. Chancellor Theobald von Bethmann-Hollweg had more than once chastised the navy for inviting war with the United States through submarine attacks on neutral or Allied merchant vessels. On May 28 he sent an evasive reply to Wilson's note. Claiming that the ship was armed, carried munitions, and had orders to ram submarines, Germany asked Washington to investigate. That same day, in a secret meeting with German ambassador Johann von Bernstorff, Wilson proposed that if Germany would settle the *Lusitania* crisis favorably, he would press the British to suspend their blockade and then call a conference of neutrals to mediate an end to the war.

Wilson convened the cabinet on June 1. When one member recommended a strong note demanding observance of American rights, another suggested as well a note to England to protest British interference with American commerce. Debate became heated. A majority rejected simultaneous notes. When Germany did not immediately reply to his mediation proposal, Wilson sent a second "*Lusitania* note" that vigorously demanded an end to warfare by submarine. He rejected Bryan's plea for a warning to passengers and a protest note to England. The secretary of state then quietly resigned on June 8. Wilson himself went to the golf links to free himself from the blinding headaches of the past several days.

More correspondence on the *Lusitania* followed. Washington insisted that Germany admit it had committed an illegal act; but Germany, unwilling to abandon its one effective weapon against British mastery of the ocean, refused to admit wrongdoing and asked for arbitration. "Utterly impertinent," sniffed Kaiser Wilhelm II, who preferred victory to Wilson's mediation. Eventually Berlin sought compromise. In February 1916 it expressed regret over the American deaths and offered to pay an indemnity. Wilson accepted the German concession.

The horrible deaths from the *Lusitania* remained etched in American memories. The torpedoing of the magnificent Cunarder marked a "naval victory worse than a defeat," as Britons and Americans alike depicted the "Huns" as depraved. The sinking also hardened Wilson's opinion of Germany. His secret mediation offer spurned, Wilson no longer made diplomatic life easier for the Germans by simultaneously protesting British infractions. He also refused to warn Americans away from belligerent ships. In short, if a U-boat attacked a British ship with Americans aboard,

Germany would have to take the consequences. Wilson did not spell out those consequences, but the logical implication was war—just what Bryan feared. His successor, Robert Lansing, expected "that we would ultimately become an ally of Great Britain." The sinking of the *Lusitania* pointed up, for all to see, the complexities, contradictions, and uncertainties inherent in American neutrality during the European phase of the First World War, 1914–1917.

The Travails of Neutrality

Woodrow Wilson acted virtually as his own secretary of state during those troubled years. "Wilson makes confidant of no one. No one gets his whole mind," an aide wrote. The president defined the overall character of American foreign policy—what historians call "Wilsonianism." Above all else, Wilson stood for an *open* world unencumbered by imperialism, war, or revolution. Barriers to trade and democracy had to come down, and secret diplomacy had to give way to public negotiations. The right of self-determination would force the collapse of empires. Constitutional procedures would replace revolution. A free-market, humanized capitalism would ensure democracy. Disarmament programs would restrict weapons. The Open Door of equal trade and investment would harness the economic competition that led to war. Wilson, like so many Americans, saw the United States as exceptional—"a sort of pure air blowing in world politics, destroying illusions and cleaning places of morbid miasmic gasses." His "semi-divine power to select the right" blended with realism. The president calculated the nation's economic and strategic needs and devised a foreign policy to protect them. Yet many Americans feared that his world-reforming efforts might invite war, dissipate American resources, and undermine reform at home. Wilson led a divided nation.

Few Americans, Wilson included, desired war. Most watched in shock as the European nations savagely slashed at one another in 1914. The conviction that civilization had advanced too far for such bloodletting was ruthlessly challenged. Before 1914 the new machine guns, poison gas, submarines, and dreadnoughts seemed too awesome for leaders to launch them. The outbreak of World War I smashed illusions and tested innocence. Progressive-era Americans nonetheless exuded optimism, and the crusading Wilson sought to retrieve a happier past by assuming the role of civilized instructor: America would help Europe come to its senses by teaching it the rules of humane conduct. The war's carnage justified the mission. In 1915 alone France suffered 330,000 deaths, Germany 170,000, and Britain 73,000.

Makers of American Foreign Relations, 1914–1920

President	Secretaries of State
Woodrow Wilson, 1913–1921	William Jennings Bryan, 1913–1915
	Robert Lansing, 1915–1920
	Bainbridge Colby, 1920–1921

Americans had good reason, then, to believe that Europe needed help in cleaning its own house. The outbreak of the war seemed so senseless. By June 1914, the great powers had constructed two blocs, the Triple Alliance (Germany, Austria-Hungary, and Italy) and the Triple Entente (France, Russia, and Great Britain). Some called this division of Europe a balance of power, but an assassin's bullet unbalanced it. Between Austria and Serbia lay Bosnia, a tiny province in the Austro-Hungarian Empire. Slavic nationalists sought to build a greater Serbia by annexing Bosnia, which the Austro-Hungarian Empire had absorbed in 1909. A Slavic terrorist group, the Black Hand, decided to force the issue. On June 28 the heir to the Hapsburg Crown of Austria-Hungary, Archduke Franz Ferdinand, visited Sarajevo, the capital of Bosnia. As his car moved through the streets of the city, a Black Hand assassin gunned him down.

Austria-Hungary sent impossible demands to Serbia. The Serbs rejected them. Austria-Hungary had already received encouragement from Germany, and Serbia had a pledge of support from Russia, which in turn received backing from France. A chain reaction set in. On July 28 Austria-Hungary declared war on Serbia; on August 1 Germany declared "preventive" war on Russia and two days later on France; on August 4 Germany invaded Belgium, and Great Britain declared war on Germany. In a few weeks Japan joined the Allies (Triple Entente) and Turkey the Central Powers, and Italy entered on the Allied side the next year.

Wilson issued a Proclamation of Neutrality on August 4, followed days later by an appeal to Americans to be neutral in thought, speech, and action. Laced with patriotic utterances, the decree sought to cool the passions of immigrant groups who identified with the belligerents. America must demonstrate to a troubled world that it was "fit beyond others to exhibit the fine poise of undisturbed judgment, the dignity of self-control, the efficiency of dispassionate action." A lofty call for restraint, an expression of America as the beacon of common sense in a world gone mad, a plea for unity at home—but difficult to achieve.

Few Americans proved capable of neutral thoughts. Loyalties to fatherlands and motherlands did not abate. German Americans identified with the Central Powers. Many Irish Americans wished catastrophe on Britain. But Anglo-American traditions and cultural ties, as well as slogans such as "Remember Lafayette," pulled most Americans toward a pro-Allied position. Wilson himself harbored pro-British sentiment, telling the British ambassador that "everything I love is at stake" and that a German victory "will be fatal to our form of Government and American ideals." Wilson's advisers, House and Lansing, were ardently pro-British. Ambassador Page even wanted Americans "to hang our Irish agitators and shoot our hyphenates and bring up our children with reverence for English history."

German war actions, exaggerated by British propaganda, also undermined neutrality. To Americans, the Germans, led by arrogant Kaiser Wilhelm II, became symbols of the dreaded militarism of the Old World. Germany, too, seemed an upstart nation, a noisy intruder in the Caribbean where the British had already acknowledged U.S. hegemony. Eager to grasp world power and encouraging Austria-Hungary to war, Berlin certainly had little claim on virtue. On August 4, 1914, hoping to get at France, the Germans attacked Belgium and, angered that the Belgians resisted, ruthlessly proceeded to raze villages and unleashed firing squads against

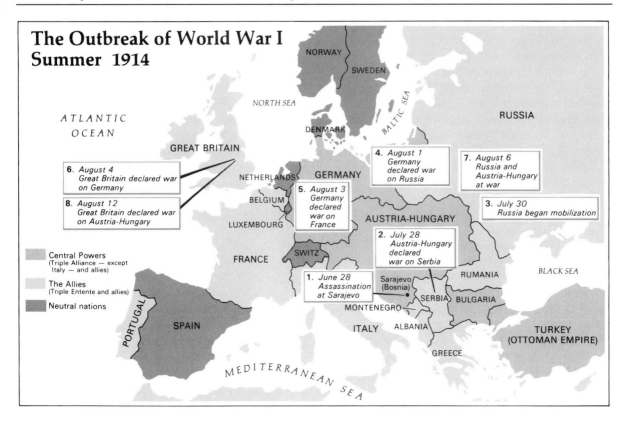

The Outbreak of World War I
Summer 1914

6. *August 4*
Great Britain declared war on Germany

8. *August 12*
Great Britain declared war on Austria-Hungary

4. *August 1*
Germany declared war on Russia

7. *August 6*
Russia and Austria-Hungary at war

5. *August 3*
Germany declared war on France

3. *July 30*
Russia began mobilization

2. *July 28*
Austria-Hungary declared war on Serbia

1. *June 28*
Assassination at Sarajevo

Central Powers
(Triple Alliance — except Italy — and allies)

The Allies
(Triple Entente and allies)

Neutral nations

townspeople. One magazine called Belgium "a martyr to civilization, sister to all who love liberty, or law; assailed, polluted, trampled in the mire, heel-marked in her breast, tattered, homeless." American hearts went out in the form of a major relief mission headed by a young, wealthy, and courageous mining engineer, Herbert Hoover.

U.S. economic links with the Allies also undercut neutrality. England had always been America's best customer, and wartime conditions simply intensified the relationship. The Allies needed both war matériel and consumer goods. Americans, inspired by huge profits and a chance to pull out of a recession, obliged. In 1914 U.S. exports to England and France equaled $754 million; in 1915 the figure shot up to $1.28 billion; and in 1916 the amount more than doubled to $2.75 billion. Comparable statistics for Germany reveal why Berlin believed the United States was taking sides. In 1914 exports to Germany totaled $345 million; in 1915 they plummeted to $29 million; and in 1916 they fell to $2 million. In 1914–1917 New York's banking house of J. P. Morgan Company served as an agent for England and France and arranged for the shipment of more than $3 billion worth of goods. By April 1917, British purchasing missions were spending $83 million a week for American copper, steel, wheat, oil, and munitions.

Britain and France sold many of their American securities to pay for these goods. This netted them several billion dollars. Next, in appeals to prominent American bankers and State Department officials, they also sought loans. In 1914 Bryan discouraged private American loans to the belligerents, because "money is the worst of all contrabands because it commands everything else." After Bryan's resignation, Robert Lansing argued that loans to the Allies would prevent "restriction of output, industrial depression, idle capital, idle labor, numerous failures, financial demoralization, and general unrest and suffering among the laboring classes." Because U.S. industries "will burst their jackets" without "free outlet to the markets of the world," Wilson thus approved $2.3 billion in loans to the Allies during 1914–1917—a sharp contrast to loans of only $27 million to Germany. Once it joined the war as a belligerent, the American economic powerhouse became even more the dispenser of munitions, food, and money to the Allies. Berlin, of course, protested such "unneutral" economic ties. Yet curbing trade with Britain, which ruled the seas, would have constituted unneutral behavior in favor of the Germans, for under international law a belligerent could buy, at its own risk, contraband and noncontraband goods from a neutral. Neutral or not, the United States had become the arsenal of the Allied war effort.

Submarines, Neutral Rights, and Mediation Efforts

To strangle Germany, the British invoked legal doctrines of retaliation and contraband without ever technically declaring a blockade. They mined the North Sea, expanded the contraband list to include foodstuffs and cotton, forced American ships into port for inspection, seized "contraband" from neutral vessels, halted American trade with Germany's neutral neighbors Denmark and Holland, armed British merchant ships, used decoy ships to lure U-boats into traps, flew neutral (often American) flags, and rammed whenever possible any U-boats that complied with international law by surfacing to warn of an imminent attack. The Wilson administration issued protests against these illegalities. The Foreign Office usually paid appropriate verbal deference to international law and went right on with its restrictive behavior. Britain sometimes compensated U.S. businesses for damages and purchased large quantities of goods at inflated prices. Americans thus came to tolerate the indignities of British economic warfare. Britain managed brilliantly to sever American economic lines to the Central Powers without rupturing Anglo-American relations.

Germans protested vehemently against American acquiescence in the British "hunger" blockade. To continue the war, Germany had to have imports and had to curb the flourishing Anglo-American trade that fueled the Allied war machine. The German surface fleet, bottled up in ports, seemed inadequate for the task, so German leaders hesitantly turned to a relatively new experimental weapon of limited maneuverability, the submarine. At the start they possessed just 21 U-boats, and only 127 at peak strength in October 1917. On February 4, 1915, Berlin retaliated by declaring a war zone around Britain. All *enemy* ships in the area would be destroyed. It warned neutral ships to *stay out* of the zone because of possible mistaken identity. Passengers from neutral countries were urged, moreover, to *stay off* enemy passenger vessels. Six days later Wilson held Germany to strict accountability for the loss of American life and property.

The British continued to arm their merchant vessels, which thereby became warships and theoretically ineligible to take on munitions in neutral ports. But Washington invoked a fine distinction between offensive and defensive armaments and permitted such "defensively" armed British craft to carry war supplies from U.S. ports. Crying foul, the Germans also argued that old international law, which Wilson invoked, did not fit the submarine. Rules adopted during the sailing-ship era held that an attacking cruiser about to sink or capture enemy merchant vessels had to give adequate warning so as to ensure the safety of passengers and crew. Yet if a submarine surfaced in its sluggish fashion, the merchant ship's crew might sink it with a deck gun. Imagine the problem for Schwieger of *U-20* when he spotted the *Lusitania.* Had he surfaced to warn the ship, the *Lusitania* probably would have attempted to ram *U-20* or send distress signals to British warships in the vicinity. Even if the *Lusitania* had stopped, it might have taken an hour for passengers to get into lifeboats before Schwieger could torpedo the Cunarder, by which time British warships might have closed in. In short, from the German point of view, to comply with an international law that failed to anticipate the submarine was not possible.

Secretary Bryan tried diplomacy in early 1915, asking Germany to give up use of unannounced submarine attacks in exchange for a British promise to disarm its merchant carriers and permit food to flow to Germany. The Germans seemed interested, but London refused. In March 1915, Wilson did send Colonel House to Europe to sound out possibilities for mediation, but to no avail. Wilson thus failed to adjust or shelve ancient international law, which had no provision for the submarine. He accepted British alterations but not German ones, for reasons of both morality and economics.

Between February and May 1915, marauding submarines sank ninety ships in the war zone. One American, on the British passenger ship *Falaba,* died in the sinking of that vessel on March 28. Then came the *Lusitania* in May. Through Wilson's many protest notes, a U.S. posture took shape: uneasy tolerance of British violations of property rights and rejection of German violations of human rights. Despite secret German orders to avoid a repetition of the *Lusitania* incident, on August 19 the *Arabic,* another British liner, was torpedoed with the loss of two American lives. A worried Ambassador Bernstorff publicly pledged that U-boats would now spare passenger ships.

In early 1916, calling the United States the "mediating nation of the world," Wilson tried to bring the warring parties to the conference table. Colonel House talked with British officials in London but left with no promises for peace. He journeyed next to Berlin, where German leaders gave no assurances. Both sides would fight on—"Hell will break loose in Europe this spring and summer as never before." House then traveled to Paris, where he rashly informed his skeptical French hosts: "If the Allies obtain a small success this spring or summer, the U.S. will intervene to promote a peaceful settlement, but if the Allies have a setback, the United States will intervene militarily and will take part in the war against Germany." House did not report his prediction to the president.

House returned to London to press Sir Edward Grey, British foreign secretary, for a peace conference. The presidential envoy recorded their apparent agreements in the House-Grey Memorandum of February 22, 1916, a document loaded with "ifs." The first paragraph read: "Colonel House told me that President Wilson was ready, on hearing from France and England that the moment was opportune, to propose that a Conference should be summoned to put an end to the war. Should the Allies accept the proposal, and should Germany refuse it, the United States would probably enter the war against Germany." House also said that the peace conference would secure terms "not unfavourable to the Allies" or else "the United States would leave the Conference as a belligerent on the side of the Allies, if Germany was unreasonable." Wilson pronounced the memorandum a diplomatic triumph, but he clouded its meaning all the more by inserting a "probably" before the word "leave" in the sentence quoted above. He took the document much more seriously than did the British or French, who shelved it, snubbed American mediation, and vowed victory over Germany.

As House moved among European capitals, Lansing offered a modus vivendi to defuse naval crises: The Allies would disarm merchant vessels, and the Germans would follow international law by warning enemy merchant ships. This suggestion revealed that Wilson understood the German argument that armed merchant vessels actually operated as offensive craft—that is, warships. The British and Colonel House protested when the Germans seemed to endorse the proposal by declaring on February 10 that submarines would henceforth attack only *armed* merchant ships without warning. Suddenly Wilson reversed policy. He abandoned the modus vivendi in order to restore his standing with the British and sustain House's mediation efforts in London.

Edward M. House (1858–1938). This Texas "colonel" served as Wilson's trusted emissary abroad. In the House-Grey Memorandum of 1916 he showed signs of the deviousness that led to his break with the president after the Versailles conference. An opponent called House "an intimate man . . . even when he was cutting your throat." (National Portrait Gallery, Smithsonian Institution/Art Resource, N.Y.)

Wilson Leads America into World War

Why let one American passenger and a trigger-happy U-boat captain start a war? Why not ban Americans from belligerent ships and require them instead to sail on American vessels? From August 1914 to mid-March 1917 only three Americans had lost their lives on an American ship torpedoed by a U-boat. In contrast, about 190 Americans, including the *Lusitania*'s 128, died on belligerent ships. After the *Falaba* was sunk, Bryan had acknowledged the right of neutrals to travel on belligerent vessels, but he wanted Wilson to forgo that right. Americans on belligerent ships seemed no different than "those who by remaining in a belligerent country assume risk of injury." Ambassador James W. Gerard in Berlin also wondered: "Why should we enter a great war because some American wants to cross on a ship where he can have a private bathroom?"

In January 1916, Representative Jeff McLemore of Texas, a Democrat, introduced a resolution to prohibit Americans from traveling on armed belligerent vessels. In February, Senator Thomas P. Gore of Oklahoma, another Democrat, submitted a similar resolution in his chamber. Wilson bristled at this challenge from Congress, flexing patronage muscle on timid legislators and insinuating that Gore-McLemore was a pro-German ploy. To forego American passage on belligerent ships, Wilson declared, would amount to national humiliation and destruction of the "whole fine fabric of international law." In short, he stuck with rigid, archaic concepts, ignoring the impact on Germany of the obvious British violations of the same law. In early March, the Gore-McLemore resolution lost 68 to 14 in the Senate and 276 to 142 in the House. The resolution asked America to give up very little. Wilson's message to Berlin rang loud and clear: Do not use your submarines.

In March 1916, another passenger ship, another U-boat, another torpedo, more American injuries: The French ship *Sussex,* moving across the English Channel, took a hit but did not sink. Aboard was a young American scholar, Samuel Flagg Bemis, later a renowned historian of foreign relations but then fresh from archival research on Jay's Treaty. Bemis glimpsed the swirling wake of a torpedo. "The entire bow was blown off," he recalled. Although four Americans sustained injuries, a wet Bemis escaped serious harm.

The *Sussex* attack violated the "*Arabic* pledge." Wilson delivered an ultimatum warning the Germans on April 18 that he would sever relations if they did not halt their submarine warfare against passenger and merchant vessels. With the stalled German offensive at Verdun costing half a million lives, Berlin did not want war with the United States. In early May Germany promised (the "*Sussex* pledge") that submarines would not attack passenger or merchant ships without prior warning. The Germans also nagged Washington to stop British infractions of international law.

The British clamped down even harder. In July, London issued a "blacklist" of more than eighty American companies that had traded with the Central Powers. Even Wilson now fumed that he was "about at the end of my patience with Great Britain and the Allies." He contemplated a ban on loans and exports to them, but he did little. Many Americans also condemned the brutal British smashing of the Irish Easter Rebellion in April 1916.

Shortly after his reelection in 1916, under the slogan "He Kept Us Out of War," the president boldly asked the belligerents to state their war aims. Neither side, still seeking military victory, welcomed Wilson's mediation. Germany coveted Poland, Lithuania, Belgium, and the Belgian Congo; Britain sought German colonies; France wanted Alsace-Lorraine. Wilson instead called for a "peace without victory" because only through a peace founded on the "equality of nations" could a lasting world order be achieved. He regarded victory as "an intoxicant that fires the national brain and leaves a craving for more." The French novelist Anatole France responded cynically: "Peace without victory is bread without yeast . . . , love without quarrels, a camel without humps, night without moon, roof without smoke, town without brothel."

In early 1917 crises mounted quickly. On January 31 Berlin announced that German submarines would attack without warning and sink all vessels, enemy and neutral, found near British waters. This declaration of unrestricted submarine warfare expressed Germany's calculated risk that it could defeat England and France before the United States could mobilize and send soldiers overseas. German naval officers persuaded the kaiser that the U-boats, now numbering about one hundred, could defeat Britain in six months. Army officers, bogged down in trench warfare, hoped to end their costly immobility through a bold stroke.

On February 3 Washington severed diplomatic relations with Berlin. Wilson had committed himself to stand firmly against unrestricted submarine warfare. Allied ships carrying war supplies soon suffered increasing losses, and the few American vessels carrying contraband stayed in port or shifted to trade outside the European war zones. Goods stacked up on wharves. The U.S. economy seemed imperiled. Next came an apparent challenge to U.S. security. In late February the British passed to Ambassador Page an intercepted telegram sent to Mexico by German foreign minister Arthur Zimmermann. The message proposed a military alliance with the U.S. neighbor. And should war with the United States break out, Germany would help Mexico "reconquer" the territory lost in 1848. Although the skeptical Mexican government never took up the German offer, Wilson now saw Germany as a "madman that should be curbed."

Wilson now asked Congress for authority to arm American merchant vessels. On March 1, to create a favorable public opinion for the request, he released the Zimmermann telegram to the press. But antiwar senators Robert La Follette and George Norris led a filibuster—a "little group of willful men," Wilson snarled—that killed the armed ship legislation. Wilson ordered the arming anyway. To no avail: during March 16–18 alone U-boats sunk the American ships *City of Memphis, Illinois,* and *Vigilancia.* Buttressed by the unanimous support of his cabinet, the president decided for war.

After several intense days writing his own speech with help from Colonel House, Wilson addressed a special joint session of Congress on the evening of April 2. He asked for a declaration of war against Germany—a war that Berlin had "thrust" on the United States. The "unmanly business" of using submarines, he asserted, constituted "warfare against mankind." Freedom of the seas, commerce, American lives, human rights—the "outlaw" U-boats challenged all. Economic self-interest, morality, and national honor compelled Americans to fight. The German government loomed as a menacing monster striking at the "very roots of human life." Wilson also hailed the Russian Revolution of March, which made Russia "a fit partner for a league of honor" in a crusade against autocracy. Then came the memorable words: "The world must be made safe for democracy." Although the oration simplified and promised too much, the moment evoked patriotic fervor. "It is [Kaiser] Bill against Woodrow, Germany against America, Hell against Heaven," proclaimed the evangelist Billy Sunday, as he demonized the enemy as "wolfish Huns, whose fangs drip with blood." By votes of 82 to 6 in the Senate on April 4 and 373 to 50 in the House on April 6, Congress endorsed Wilson's call for a war for peace.

Submarine warfare precipitated the American decision to enter the war. Had no submarine menaced American lives, property, and the U.S. definition of international law, no American soldiers would have gone to France. Critics have argued, however, that from the German perspective, the submarine became necessary because of the long list of unfriendly American acts: acquiescence in the British blockade, part of a general pro-British bias; huge munitions shipments to the Allies; large loans; an interpretation of neutral rights that insisted that American passengers could sail anywhere, even into a war zone. Take away those acts, which the Germans considered unneutral, and they might not have unleashed the U-boats. To dissenters it seemed wrong that American ideals and interests could depend so perilously on armed ships carrying contraband, heading for Britain, and steaming through a war zone. Yet Wilson and his advisers had so defined the problem.

Jeannette Rankin (1880–1973). Native of Montana, Rankin, in 1916, became the first woman to be elected to the House of Representatives. A life-long pacifist, she voted against war in 1917, only to lose her seat the following year. In the interwar period she lobbied for peace and was again elected to Congress in 1940. Once again she cast her vote against war in 1941. She later marched against the Vietnam War. (Library of Congress)

Permeating Wilson's policies was the traditional American belief that its ideals served as a beacon for the world. "We created this Nation," the president once proclaimed, "not to serve ourselves, but to serve mankind." When the Germans defied America's ideals, destroyed its property, and threatened its security through a proposed alliance with Mexico, they had to be punished. Here was an opportunity to protect both humane principles and commercial interests. When Wilson spoke passionately of the right of a neutral to freedom of the seas, he demonstrated the interconnections among American moral, economic, and strategic interests. Wilson sought the role of peacemaker and promised to remake the world in the American image—world order in which barriers to political democracy and the Open Door came down, in which revolution and aggression no longer threatened. As the philosopher John Dewey put it, war came at a "plastic juncture" in history in which Americans could fight to reshape the world according to progressive principles.

The Debate Over Preparedness

Berlin's assumption that U.S. soldiers could not reach France fast enough to reverse an expected German victory proved a gross misjudgment. American military muscle and economic power, in fact, decisively tipped the balance against Germany. In early 1917, however, the German calculation did not seem so unrealistic. In April the United States had no capacity to send a major expedition to the western front. The Regular Army counted only 130,000 officers and men, backed by 180,000 national guardsmen. Despite earlier interventions in Cuba, the Philippines, and Mexico, many soldiers lacked adequate training. Arsenals had meager supplies of such modern weapons as the machine gun. The "Air Service," then part of the army, did not have a plane of modern design with a machine gun, and some warships had never fired a gun.

An American "preparedness movement" had been under way for months, encouraged by prominent Americans such as General Leonard Wood, who argued that America's military weakness invited attack. After 1914, Wood, Theodore Roosevelt, the National Security League, the Army League, and the Navy League lobbied for bigger military appropriations with the argument that "preparedness" offered insurance against war. When the pacifist song "I Didn't Raise My Boy to Be a Soldier" became a hit in 1915, preparedness proponents countered with "I Didn't Raise My Boy to Be a Coward." One propaganda film, *The Battle Cry of Peace* (1916), depicted spike-helmeted soldiers rampaging through New York City. That same year a U.S. admiral claimed that a single hostile dreadnought could "knock down all the buildings in New York . . . , smash all the cars, break down all the bridges, and sink all the shipping." Convinced that "a great standing army" was "antidemocratic," Wilson belatedly sought moderate preparedness. His request for a half-billion-dollar naval expansion program in late 1915, including ten battleships, promised a new force that would surpass Britain as "incomparably the greatest navy in the world." He also urged that land forces be enlarged and reorganized.

Senator La Follette, Representative Claude Kitchin, and prominent reformers such as William Jennings Bryan, Lillian Wald, and Oswald Garrison Villard spurred a movement against these measures. These peace advocates, especially the Women's Peace Party, argued that war would interrupt reform at home, benefit big business, and curtail civil liberties. The American Union Against Militarism agitated against preparedness with its papier-mâché dinosaur, "Jingo," whose collar read "ALL ARMOR PLATE—NO BRAINS." Because his support of mediation, disarmament, and a postwar association of nations appealed to antiwar liberals and socialists, Wilson hoped that moderate preparedness would not alienate them. Chicago's famed social reformer Jane Addams remembered "moments of uneasiness," but she and others endorsed Wilson in the 1916 presidential campaign, for it seemed "at last that peace was assured and the future safe in the hands of an executive who had received an unequivocal mandate from the people 'to keep us out of war.' "

In January 1916, Wilson set out on a two-month speaking tour, often criticizing members of his own party for their opposition to a military buildup. U-boat sinkings aided the president's message. In May 1916, Congress passed the National Defense Act, increasing the Regular Army to some 200,000 men and 11,000 officers, and the National Guard to 440,000 men and 17,000 officers. The act also authorized summer training camps, modeled after one held in Plattsburg, New York, in 1915 for the social and economic elite. The navy bill passed in August 1916. Theodore Roosevelt thought both measures inadequate, but the anarchist Emma Goldman saw no difference between Roosevelt, "the born bully who uses a club," and Wilson, "the history professor who uses the smooth polished mask."

Once in the war, after learning that the Allies "want and need . . . men, whether trained or not," Wilson relied on the Selective Service Act of May 1917. National military service, proponents believed, would not only prepare the nation for battle but also instill respect for order, democracy, and sacrifice. Under the selective service system, 24,340,000 men eventually registered for the draft. Some 3,764,000 men received draft notices, and 2,820,000 were inducted. Over all, 4,744,000 soldiers, sailors, and marines served. The typical serviceman was a white, single, poorly educated draftee between twenty-one and twenty-three years of age. Officer training camps turned out "ninety-day wonders," thousands of commissioned officers drawn largely from people of elite background. Although excluded from combat, women became navy clerks, telephone operators in the Army Signal Corps, and nurses and physical therapists to the wounded and battle-shock cases.

With the Allies begging for soldiers, General John J. "Black Jack" Pershing, now head of the American Expeditionary Force to Europe, soon sent a "show the flag" contingent to France to boost Allied morale. Neither Wilson nor Pershing, however, would accept the European recommendation that U.S. troops be inserted in Allied units. The U.S. Army would remain separate and independent. National pride dictated this decision, but so did the realization that Allied commanders had for years wasted the lives of hundreds of thousands in trench warfare. Soldiers jumped out to charge German lines, also a maze of trenches. Machine guns mowed them down; chlorine gas, first used by Germany in 1915, poisoned them. Nor did Wilson wish to endorse exploitative Allied war aims. Thus did the United States call itself an "associated" rather than an "allied" power in the war.

Red Cross Postcard. Women served in many roles in the war. They became workers in weapons factories. They sold Liberty Bonds and publicized government mobilization programs as members of the Women's Committee of the Council of National Defense. In France, women nurses and canteen workers became envoys of the U.S. home front, representing the mothers, wives, and sisters left behind. As the historian Susan Zeiger has written, the government's sponsorship of these wartime roles for women cleverly blunted the feminist-pacifist claim that women were "inherently more peaceful than men and would oppose war out of love for their children." (Library of Congress)

The Doughboys Make the Difference in Europe

On July 4, 1917, General Pershing reviewed the first battalion to arrive in France, as nearly a million Parisians tossed flowers, hugged the "doughboys," and cheered wildly. *"Lafayette, nous sommes ici!"* ("we are here") shouted Pershing's aide.

To the dismay of American leaders, taverns and brothels quickly surrounded military camps. "Fit to Fight" became the government's slogan, as it moved to close "red-light districts," designated "sin-free zones" around camps, and banned the sale of liquor to men in uniform. Government signs declared: "A German Bullet Is Cleaner Than A Whore." The YMCA and the Jewish Welfare Board sent song leaders to camps. Movies, athletic programs, and well-stocked stores sought to keep soldiers on the base by making them feel "at home."

Success against venereal disease contrasted with a major flu epidemic, which first struck camps in spring 1918. At Camp Sherman, Ohio, one of the bases hit hardest, 1,101 people died between September 27 and October 13. Whereas about 51,000 soldiers died in battle during the war, some 62,000 soldiers died from diseases. "Doughboys" infected with the virus carried the flu with them to the European war, where it ignored national boundaries and turned into a global pandemic that killed more than 21 million people by spring 1919.

Approximately 400,000 African-American troops suffered discrimination during this war "to make the world safe for democracy." Camps were segregated and "white only" signs posted. In 1917 in Houston, Texas, whites provoked blacks into a riot that left seventeen whites and two blacks dead. In the army, three out of every four black soldiers served in labor units, where they wielded a shovel, not a gun. African Americans endured second-class citizenship and the contradiction between America's wartime rhetoric and reality. A statistic revealed the problem: 382 black Americans were lynched in the period 1914–1920.

The first official American combat death in Europe came only ten days after Congress declared war—that of Edmund Charles Clinton Genet, the great-great-grandson of French Revolutionary diplomat Citizen Genet and member of the famed American volunteer air squadron, the Lafayette Escadrille. Despite Allied impatience, General Pershing hesitated to commit his green soldiers to full-scale battle. Great numbers of troops shipped over in British vessels and had to borrow French weapons. By early 1918 the Allies had become mired in a murderous strategy of throwing ground forces directly at enemy ground forces. German troops were mauling Italian forces, and the French army was still suffering from mutinies of the year before. In March, after Germany swallowed large chunks of European Russia through the Brest-Litovsk Treaty, Wilson warned of a German "empire of force" out to "dominate the world itself" and urged Americans to "contest the mastery of the world." In April he called for "Force, Force to the utmost, Force without stint or limit." Pershing's doughboys soon trooped into battle in greater numbers.

In March the German armies, swollen by forty divisions from the Russian front, launched a great offensive. Allied forces retreated, and by late May the kaiser's soldiers surged to less than fifty miles from Paris. Saint-Mihiel, Belleau Wood, Cantigny, Château-Thierry—French sites where U.S. soldiers shed their blood—soon became household words for Americans. In June at Château-Thierry the doughboys dramatically stopped a German advance. In mid-July the Allies launched a counteroffensive; nine American divisions fought fiercely, helping to lift the German threat from Paris. In the Meuse-Argonne offensive, begun in late September, more than 1 million American soldiers joined French and British units to penetrate the crumbling German lines. "The American infantry in the Argonne [Forest] won the war," German marshal Paul von Hindenburg later commented.

On October 4, the German chancellor asked Wilson for an armistice. German troops had mutinied; revolution and riots plagued German cities; Bulgaria had left the war in September. Then Turkey dropped out in late October, and Austria-Hungary surrendered on November 3. Germany had no choice but to seek terms. The kaiser fled to Holland. On November 11, in a railroad car in the Compiègne Forest, German representatives capitulated.

The Fourteen Points
and the Peace Conference

During the combat, President Wilson had begun to explain his plans for the peace. He trumpeted his vision most dramatically in his "Fourteen Points" speech before Congress on January 8, 1918. The first five points promised an "open" world after the war, a world distinguished by "open covenants, openly arrived at," freedom of navigation on the seas, equal trade opportunity and the removal of tariffs, reduction of armaments, and an end to colonialism. Points six through thirteen called for self-determination for national minorities in Europe. Point fourteen stood paramount: a "general association of nations" to ensure "political independence and territorial integrity to great and small states alike." His Fourteen Points signaled a generous, nonpunitive postwar settlement. They served too as effective American propaganda against revenge-fed Allied aims and Russian Bolshevik appeals for European revolution.

Despite secret treaties that promised German colonies and other territorial gains, Allied leaders feared that Wilson would deny them the spoils of war. In view of the comparative wartime losses, Europeans believed that Wilson "had bought his seat at the peace table at a discount." When, in September and October 1918, Wilson exchanged notes with Germany and Austria-Hungary about an armistice, the Allied powers expressed strong reservations about the Fourteen Points. Wilson hinted at a separate peace with the Central Powers and even threatened to publicize the exploitative Allied war aims. Also facing possible reduced U.S. shipments to Europe, London, Paris, and Rome reluctantly accepted, in the armistice of November, peace negotiations on the basis of the Fourteen Points.

Wilson relished his opportunity. The United States could now claim a dominant role in deciding future international relations. The pictures of dying men dangling from barbed-wire fences and the battle-shock victims who staggered home persuaded many Americans of the need to prevent another conflagration. Wilson's call for a just peace commanded the backing of countless foreigners as well. Italians hoisted banners reading *Dio di Pace* ("God of Peace") and *Redentore dell' Humanità* ("Redeemer of Humanity") to welcome Wilson to Europe.

Yet the president weakened his position even before the peace conference. Congressional leaders wanted him to stay home to handle domestic problems. Lansing feared that Wilson would have only one vote in the day-to-day conference bickering, whereas from Washington he could symbolically marshal the votes of humankind. Wilson retorted that "England and France have not the same views with regard to peace that we have," so he had to attend personally to defend the Fourteen Points.

Domestic politics soon set Wilson back. In October 1918, Wilson "hurled a brick into a beehive" by asking Americans to return a Democratic Congress loyal to him. Partisan Republicans proceeded to capture the November election and majorities in both houses of Congress; they would sit in ultimate judgment of Wilson's peacemaking. The president also made the political mistake of appointing neither an important Republican nor a senator to the American Peace Commission. Wilson, House, and Lansing sat on it; so did Henry White, a seasoned diplomat and nominal Republican. Some concessions to his political opposition, and to senatorial pre-rogatives in foreign affairs, might have smoothed the path later for his peace treaty.

On December 4, with great fanfare, Wilson departed from New York aboard the *George Washington*. He settled into a quiet voyage, surrounded by advisers and nearly 2,000 reports on issues likely to arise at the peace conference. Confident that "we can force" the Allies "to our way of thinking" because they will be "financially in our hands," the president had made few concrete plans. After reaching France on December 15, Wilson basked in the admiration of enthusiastic Parisian crowds, and later thousands in Italy and England cheered him with near religious fervor. Wilson assumed that this generous outpouring meant that *his* peace aims were universally popular and that Americans "would be the only disinterested people" at Versailles. Such "man-in-the-street" opinion, however, did not impress David Lloyd George, prime minister of Britain, French premier Georges Clemenceau, or Italian prime minister Vittorio Orlando, Wilson's antagonists at the peace conference.

David Lloyd George (1863–1945). "America," said the British prime minister referring to the League of Nations, "had been offered the leadership of the world, but the Senate had tossed the sceptre into the sea." (Getty Images)

Excluding Germany and Bolshevik Russia, thirty-two nations sent delegations, which essentially followed the lead of the "Big Four." Most sessions worked in se-crecy, hardly befitting Wilson's first "point." Clemenceau resented Wilson's "ser-monettes" and preferred the more compliant Colonel House. "The old tiger [Clemenceau] wants the grizzly bear [Wilson] back in the Rocky Mountains before he starts tearing up the German Hog," commented Lloyd George, who sought to build a strong France and to ensure German purchases of British exports. A fervent nationalist, Orlando concerned himself primarily with enlarging Italian territory. These leaders sought a vengeful peace. Lloyd George complained of a chameleon-like Wilson—"the noble visionary, the implacable and unscrupulous partisan, the exalted idealist and the man of rather petty personal rancour." Wilson, in turn, thought the Europeans "too weatherwise to see the weather."

Much wrangling occurred over the disposition of colonies and the creation of new countries. "Tell me what's right and I'll fight for it," said Wilson as he appealed for self-determination. After hard negotiating, the conferees allocated former Ger-man and Turkish colonies to the countries that had conquered them, to be loosely supervised under League of Nations auspices. Under the mandate system—a com-promise between outright annexation and complete independence—France (with Syria and Lebanon) and Britain (with Iraq, Trans-Jordan, and Palestine) received parts of the Middle East. Japan acquired China's Shandong Province and some of Germany's Pacific islands. Regarding Shandong, the president deemed it "the best that could be accomplished out of a 'dirty past'" and planned to "let the League of Nations decide the matter later." Wilson also ignored a petition calling for self-determination in French Indochina and signed by, among others, Nguyen Ai Quoc—later famous under the name Ho Chi Minh. France gained the demilita-rization of the German Rhineland and a stake in the coal-rich Saar Basin. Italy an-nexed South Tyrol and Trieste from the collapsed Austro-Hungarian Empire. Newly independent countries also emerged from the defunct Austro-Hungarian Empire: Austria, Czechoslovakia, Hungary, Romania, and Yugoslavia. The Allies further rec-ognized a ring of hostile states already established around Bolshevik Russia: Finland, Poland, Estonia, Latvia, and Lithuania, all formerly part of the Russian empire. The mandate system smacked of imperialism, but the new states in Europe fulfilled

Wilson's self-determination pledge. To assuage fears of a revived Germany, Britain and the United States signed a security pact with France guaranteeing its border, but Wilson never submitted it for Senate approval.

Reparations proved a knotty issue. The United States wanted a limited indemnity for Germany to avoid a harsh peace that might arouse long-term German resentment or debilitate the German economy and politics. "Excessive demands," Wilson had predicted, "would most certainly sow the seeds of war." To cripple Germany, France pushed for a large bill of reparations. The conferees wrote a "war guilt clause," which held Germany responsible for all of the war's damages. Rationalizing that the League would ameliorate any excesses, Wilson gave in on both reparations and war guilt. The Reparations Commission in 1921 presented a hobbled Germany with a huge reparations bill of $33 billion, thereby helping to destabilize international economic relations for more than a decade.

The Allies played to Wilson's priorities: "Give him the League of Nations and he will give us all the rest." Drafted largely by Wilson, the League's covenant provided for an influential council of five big powers (permanent) and representatives from smaller nations (by election) and an assembly of all nations for discussion. Wilson saw the heart of the covenant as Article 10: "The Members of the League undertake to respect and preserve as against external aggression the territorial integrity and existing political independence of all Members of the League." In case of aggression or threat, "the Council shall advise upon the means by which this obligation shall be fulfilled." Wilson persuaded the conferees to merge League covenant and peace terms in a package, with the charter comprising the first 26 articles of a 440-article Treaty of Paris. Wilson deemed the League covenant the noblest part of all—"It is practical, and yet it is intended to purify, to rectify, to elevate."

The Germans signed sullenly on June 28 in the elegant Hall of Mirrors at Versailles. By stripping Germany of 13 percent of its territory, 10 percent of its population, and all of its colonies, and by demanding reparations, the treaty humiliated the Germans without crushing them. In one historian's words, the treaty contained "a witches' brew" with "too little Wilsonianism to appease, too little of Clemenceau to deter; enough of Wilson to provoke contempt, enough of Clemenceau to inspire hatred." When Wilson died on February 3, 1924, the German Embassy in Washington broke custom by not lowering its flag to half-mast.

Principle, Personality, Health, and Partisanship: The League Fight

Wilson spent almost six months in Europe. From February 24 to March 14, 1919, however, he returned to the United States for executive business. On arrival, he asserted that any U.S. failure to back the League "would break the heart of the world." In Washington, Republicans peppered Wilson with questions about the degree to which the covenant limited American sovereignty. In early March, Republican senator Henry Cabot Lodge of Massachusetts engineered a "Round Robin," a statement by thirty-nine senators (enough to deny the treaty a two-thirds vote) that questioned the League covenant and requested that the peace treaty and the covenant be acted on separately.

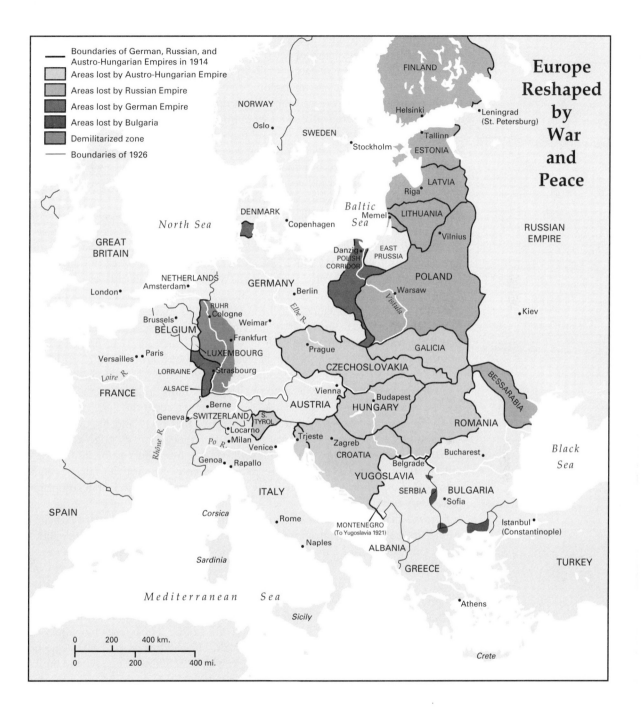

Europe
Reshaped
by
War
and
Peace

Boundaries of German, Russian, and
Austro-Hungarian Empires in 1914
Areas lost by Austro-Hungarian Empire
Areas lost by Russian Empire
Areas lost by German Empire
Areas lost by Bulgaria
Demilitarized zone
Boundaries of 1926

NORWAY
Oslo

SWEDEN
Stockholm

FINLAND
Helsinki

Leningrad
(St. Petersburg)

Tallinn
ESTONIA

RUSSIAN
EMPIRE

Riga

LATVIA

LITHUANIA
Vilnius

DENMARK
Copenhagen

Baltic
Sea

Memel

North Sea

GREAT
BRITAIN

Danzig
POLISH
CORRIDOR

EAST
PRUSSIA

POLAND
Warsaw

Kiev

NETHERLANDS
Amsterdam

GERMANY
Berlin

London

Brussels
BELGIUM

RUHR
Cologne
Weimar
Frankfurt

Elbe R.

Vistula

Versailles Paris

LUXEMBOURG
LORRAINE
Strasbourg
ALSACE

Prague

Berne

FRANCE

Geneva
SWITZERLAND
Locarno
Milan
Venice

S.
TYROL

CZECHOSLOVAKIA

Vienna

AUSTRIA

GALICIA

BESSARABIA

Budapest

HUNGARY

ROMANIA

Loire R.

Rhône R.

Po R.

Genoa
Rapallo

Trieste
Zagreb
CROATIA
Belgrade

Bucharest

Black
Sea

YUGOSLAVIA

ITALY

SERBIA

BULGARIA
Sofia

SPAIN

Corsica

Rome

MONTENEGRO
(To Yugoslavia 1921)

Istanbul
(Constantinople)

Naples

ALBANIA

TURKEY

Sardinia

GREECE

Mediterranean   Sea

Athens

Sicily

Crete

0   200   400 km.

0   200   400 mi.

A defiant Wilson sailed again for France, determined that "little Americans," full of "watchful jealousies [and] of rabid antagonisms," would not destroy his beloved League. Still, he was politician enough to seek changes in Paris. He amended the covenant so that League members could refuse mandates, League jurisdiction over purely domestic issues was precluded, and the Monroe Doctrine was safeguarded against League interference. But he would not alter Article 10. When he returned to the United States in July, Wilson submitted the long Treaty of Versailles to the Senate on July 10, with an address that resembled an evangelical sermon: "It has come about by no plan of our conceiving, but by the hand of God, who led us into this way." Asked if he would accept senatorial "reservations" to the treaty, Wilson snapped: "Anyone who opposes me in that, I'll crush."

Wilson, against strong odds, gained a good percentage of his goals as outlined in the Fourteen Points. Self-determination for nationalities advanced as never before in Europe, and the League ranked as a notable achievement. But Wilson did compromise, especially with Clemenceau. Both Italy and Japan also had threatened to walk out unless they realized some territorial goals. Still, Wilson had so built up a case for an unselfish peace that when hard bargaining and harsh terms dominated the conference, observers could only conclude that the president had betrayed his millennial rhetoric. Critics said that Wilson should have left Paris in protest, refusing to sign, or that he might have threatened the Allies with U.S. economic pressure. Believing desperately that the League, with Article 10, would rectify all, Wilson warned Congress that without it, "the United States and every other country will have to arm to the teeth."

He would not compromise at home, however. And he seldom provided systematic, technical analysis to treaty clauses. He simply expected the Senate dutifully to ratify his masterwork. Yet his earlier bypassing of that body and his own partisan speeches and self-righteousness ensured debate. Henry Cabot Lodge asked a key question: "Are you willing to put your soldiers and your sailors at the disposition of other nations?" Article 10 seemed to rattle everybody. The article did not require members to use force, but it implied they should. Senator William Borah complained that "I may be willing to help my neighbor," but he should not "decide for me when and how I shall act." Senator Hiram Johnson of California claimed that Article 10 would "freeze the world into immutability," keeping "subject peoples . . . subject until the crack of doom." The article seemed too open-ended to most opponents.

Republican Henry Cabot Lodge towered as Wilson's chief legislative obstacle. Chair of the Senate Foreign Relations Committee, nationalist-imperialist, author, like Wilson a scholar in politics, Lodge packed his committee with anti-League senators, dragged out hearings for weeks, and nurtured a personal animosity toward Wilson matched only by Wilson's detestation for Lodge. He attacked obliquely by offering "reservations" to the League covenant. They addressed the central question of American national interest—the degree to which the United States would limit its freedom of action by engaging in collective security. In fact, many of the fourteen reservations stated the obvious—that Congress would retain its constitutional role in foreign policy, for example. Another denied the League jurisdiction over American domestic legislation. The reservation on Article 10 disclaimed any obligation to preserve the territorial integrity or political independence of another country unless authorized by Congress. For Wilson this meant "nullification of the treaty."

The Senate divided into four groups. Wilson counted on about forty loyal Democrats called the Non-Reservationists. Another group, the Mild-Reservationists, led by Frank B. Kellogg, numbered about thirteen Republicans. The third faction, managed by Lodge, stood together as the Strong-Reservationists—some twenty Republicans and a few Democrats. The fourth group, consisting of sixteen Irreconcilables, ardently opposed the treaty with or without reservations. Most of them were Republicans, including La Follette, George Norris of Nebraska, and Hiram Johnson of California.

Wilson met individually with twenty-three senators over two weeks, but he suffered a minor stroke on July 19, 1919. He thereafter rigidly refused to accept any reservations. He argued that a treaty with reservations would have to be renegotiated and every nation would then rush in with its pet reservations—a hollow claim after the British announced that they would accept American reservations. In September 1919, Wilson set off on a 10,000-mile train trip across the United States. Growing more exhausted with each day, suffering severe headaches and nighttime coughing spells, Wilson pounded the podium in forty speeches. He blasted his traducers as "absolute, contemptible quitters." He confused his audiences when he stated that Article 10 meant that the United States had a moral but not legal obligation to use armed force. Failure to join the League, he prophesied in St. Louis, would result in a war "in which not a few hundred thousand fine young men from America will have to die, but as many millions as are necessary to accomplish the final freedom of the peoples of the world." On September 26, after an impassioned speech in Pueblo, Colorado, he awoke to nausea and uncontrollable facial twitching. When his doctor ordered him to cancel the rest of his trip, Wilson wept.

After Wilson returned to Washington, a massive stroke paralyzed his left side. He lay flat in bed for six weeks and saw virtually no one except his wife and Dr. Cary Grayson. For months Mrs. Wilson ran her husband's political affairs, screening messages and banishing House and Lansing, among others, from presidential favor. If the president had resigned, as Dr. Grayson advised him to do, the Senate and Vice President James Marshall almost certainly would have reached some compromise agreement on admission to the League with reservations. As it was, his concentration hampered and his stubbornness accentuated by the stroke, Wilson adamantly refused to change his all-or-nothing position.

In November 1919, the Senate balloted on the complete treaty *with* reservations and rejected it, 39 to 55 (Irreconcilables and Non-Reservationists in the negative). Then it voted on the treaty *without* reservations and also rejected it, 38 to 53 (Irreconcilables and Reservationists in the negative). The president had instructed loyal Democrats not to accept any "reserved" treaty. In March 1920, another tally saw some Democrats vote in favor of reservations. Not enough, the treaty failed, 49 to 35, short of the two-thirds majority required for approval. Still a fighter, the president claimed that the election of 1920 would be a "solemn referendum" on the treaty. Other questions actually blurred the League issue in that campaign, and Warren G. Harding, who as a senator had supported reservations, promptly condemned the League after his election as president. In July 1921, Congress officially terminated the war, and in August, by treaty with Germany, the United States claimed as valid for itself the terms of the Treaty of Versailles—exclusive of the League articles.

Woodrow Wilson After His Stroke. Recent scholarly assessments of medical evidence reveal that Wilson had a long history of cerebrovascular disease. Wilson remained in the White House after his massive stroke in October 1919, while his wife and doctor tried to keep secret the severity of his physical incapacity. (Library of Congress)

The memorable League fight had ended. The tragic denouement occurred because of political partisanship, personal animosities, senatorial resentments, the president's failing health, adherence to traditional unilateralism, and distraction and confusion in the public. Progressive internationalists, many of them harassed by wartime restrictions on civil liberties and disappointed by Wilson's compromises with the imperial powers, no longer backed a president they thought reactionary. Then, of course, there was Wilson himself—stubborn, pontificating, combative, and increasingly ill. He might have conceded that the peace had imperfections. He might have provided more careful analysis of a long, complicated document. Instead, he chose often shrill rhetoric and rigid self-righteousness. Most important, he saw the difference between himself and his critics as fundamental: whether it was in America's national interest to participate in collective security or seek safety unilaterally.

In fact, none of the great powers wished to bestow significant authority on the new League organization. Even if Washington had joined, it most likely would have acted outside the League's auspices, especially regarding its own empire in Latin America. No international association at that time could have outlawed war, dismantled empires, or scuttled navies. Wilson overshot reality in thinking that he could reform world politics through a new international body. Certainly the League represented a commendable restraint against war, but hardly a panacea for world peace.

Red Scare Abroad: Bolshevism and Intervention in Russia

"Paris cannot be understood without Moscow [Russia]," wrote Wilson's press secretary Ray Stannard Baker. Wilson himself depicted Bolshevism as "the poison of disorder, the poison of revolt, the poison of chaos." Revolutionary and anticapitalist, the Bolsheviks, or Communists, threw fright into the leaders of Europe and America. At home and abroad the peacemakers battled the radical left. In the United States the Wilson administration trampled on civil liberties during an exaggerated "Red Scare," which sent innocent people to jail or deported them. Wilson initially thought that "the only way to kill Bolshevism is . . . to open all the doors to commerce." Only belatedly, after authorizing secret aid and espionage against the "Reds," did the president openly "cast in his lot" with the other powers in a futile attempt to destroy the new revolutionary regime.

Most Americans applauded the Russian Revolution of March 1917, which toppled Tsar Nicholas II. But after the moderate Provisional government under Alexander Kerensky fell to the radical Bolsheviks in October, Americans were outraged when the new regime signed the Brest-Litovsk Treaty (March 1918) with Germany and ceded Ukraine and Finland, among other territories—one-third of Russia's best agricultural land. A necessary peace for a devastated Russia from the Bolshevik perspective, the treaty seemed a stab in the back for the Allies. Because German authorities had allowed Lenin to travel to Russia via Germany in 1917, some irate American officials even considered Bolsheviks pro-German. Others recoiled after Ambassador David Francis's testimony that Bolsheviks had "nationalized women."

Lenin actually treated the United States as a special, favored case, and he consistently sought accommodation with Washington. Soviet leaders held a series of cordial conversations from December 1917 to May 1918 with the Red Cross official Raymond Robins, a de facto U.S. representative, and reached agreements on food relief, purchase of strategic materials, and exemption of U.S. corporations from Bolshevik nationalization decrees. Prior to Brest-Litovsk, Robins urged prompt diplomatic recognition to keep Russia in the war, but President Wilson paid more heed to Francis's prediction that the Bolshevik regime would soon collapse.

Although U.S. officials in Russia engaged in espionage and cooperated with Allied and "White" agents in anti-Bolshevik activities after November 1917, Wilson knew only broad outlines of this "secret war" when he sent U.S. troops to Archangel in northern Russia in August 1918. Ordered to avoid military action in the Russian civil war, they inevitably cooperated with British and French forces in attempts to roll back Bolshevik influence. Wilson said publicly that he authorized the expedition only to prevent German seizure of military supplies, but he quickly approved $50 million in secret payments to White armies fighting the Bolsheviks. Wilson's motives were thus "simultaneously anti-German and anti-Bolshevik." Some 5,000 American troops suffered through a bitter winter of fifty-below-zero temperatures. Their morale sagged; mutiny threatened. U.S. soldiers did not leave Russia until June 1919; two hundred twenty-two of them died in what critics dubbed "Mr. Wilson's little war with Russia."

Wilson claimed to be "sweating blood over the question of what is right . . . in Russia." Pressure from the Allies and his own anti-Bolshevism inclined him to send another expedition, this time to Siberia. In July 1918 he approved the expedition, later officially explaining to the American people that he was sending 10,000 troops to rescue a group of 70,000 Czechs stranded in Russia. Organized earlier as part of the Tsarist Russian army to fight for a Czech homeland in Austria-Hungary, the Czech legion was battling Bolsheviks along the Trans-Siberian Railroad in an effort to reach Vladivostok and possible transportation to the western front. Wilson's avowed purpose of evacuating the Czech legion derived also from his "friendly feelings" for Professor Thomas Masaryk and Czechoslovakia's independence, which Wilson soon recognized in October.

Despite his disingenuous official explanation, Wilson believed that "a limited, indirect intervention to help the Russian people overcome domination by Bolsheviks and Germans would not contradict, but rather facilitate self-determination." Yet intervention in Siberia became openly anti-Bolshevik because the Czechs were fighting Lenin's forces. Once Wilson found it impossible to evacuate the Czechs in time to fight in Europe, he reluctantly bowed to Allied pressure and gave support to the anti-Bolshevik White Russian leader Admiral A. V. Kolchak in the hope that he could form a pro-Western constitutional government. Despite money and supplies from the Allies, Kolchak's armies were routed before they could reach Moscow in June 1919. U.S. troops finally withdrew from Siberia in 1920.

At the Paris peace conference, the victors tried to isolate what they considered revolutionary contagion. Accordingly, the conferees granted territory to Russia's neighbors (Poland, Romania, and Czechoslovakia) and recognized the nations of Finland, Estonia, Latvia, and Lithuania as a ring of unfriendly states around Russia.

A. Mitchell Palmer (1872–1936). When U.S. troops were intervening in Bolshevik Russia, Wilson's attorney general, A. Mitchell Palmer, was chasing suspected radicals at home. An architect of the "Red Scare," Palmer believed that the "blaze of revolution" was "eating its way into the homes of the American workmen, its sharp tongues of revolutionary heat . . . licking the altars of the churches, leaping into the belfry of the school bell, crawling into the sacred corners of American homes, burning up the foundations of society." In January 1920, the "Palmer Raids" put 4,000 people in jail. (Library of Congress)

During the conference, besides the military interventions, the Allies imposed a strict economic blockade on Russia, sent aid to the White forces, and extended relief assistance to Austria and Hungary to stem political unrest.

Even though Wilson found the anticlerical, anticapitalist Soviets distasteful, he never settled on a definitive, workable policy to co-opt or smash Bolshevism. Through "a reluctant, chaotic, and capricious process," the president allowed subordinates and circumstances to determine U.S. policy toward Russia. His growing estrangement at Versailles from Colonel House, a conduit for pro-Soviet liberals, meant that the interventionist Allies and the rabidly anti-Bolshevik Secretary Lansing exerted greater influence.

Wilson's one serious effort to end the civil war in Russia through diplomacy came in January 1919 when he invited the warring groups to meet on Prinkipo Island off the Turkish coast. The Bolsheviks cautiously accepted the invitation, but the anti-Bolsheviks refused. Next, in February, House helped arrange a trip by William C. Bullitt, a member of the U.S. delegation at Versailles, and Lincoln Steffens, the radical muckraking journalist, to Russia. Wilson envisioned only a fact-finding mission. The ambitious Bullitt nonetheless negotiated a proposal whereby the Allies would withdraw their troops, suspend military aid to White forces, and lift the economic blockade; in return the Soviets promised a cease-fire in which their opponents would hold the territories they occupied. Bullitt and Steffens returned to Paris convinced that their agreement would satisfy all parties. Lloyd George squelched it; Wilson ignored it. Bullitt resigned in protest.

The Allied counterrevolution proved costly. "It intensified the civil war and sent thousands of Russians to their deaths," the British official Bruce Lockhart later wrote. "Its direct effect was to provide the Bolsheviks with a cheap victory." Kremlin leaders also nurtured long memories. "Never have any of our soldiers been on American soil," Premier Nikita S. Khrushchev lectured Americans as late as 1959, "but your soldiers were on Russian soil." Participation by such young men as Allen and John Foster Dulles in Wilson's "secret war" against the Bolsheviks gave them expertise in "propaganda and covert action" when they later directed U.S. policies during the Cold War. Such tactics ultimately backfired, as Wilson recognized before his death. "Bolshevism is a mistake," Wilson said. "If left alone it will destroy itself. It cannot survive because it is wrong."

The Whispering Gallery of Global Disorder

More than 116,000 American soldiers died in World War I, which cost the U.S. government more than $30 billion. What President Dwight D. Eisenhower would later call the "military-industrial complex" had its origins in a high degree of government-business cooperation during the war; economic decisionmaking for the nation became centralized as never before; and the increased application of efficient methods in manufacturing contributed to U.S. economic power. The era of World War I witnessed other domestic events that impinged on foreign affairs: racial conflict, evidenced by twenty-five race riots in 1919; suppression of dissent under the Espionage and Sedition Acts; the stunting of radical commentary (Socialist leader Eugene Debs and the pacifist Alice Paul, among others, went to jail for opposing the war); and the withering of the reform impulse.

In foreign affairs, the White House assumed more authority in initiating policy and controlling execution. The State Department read diplomatic messages that Wilson had typed on his own machine. Wilson bypassed Congress on a number of occasions, failing to consult that body about the Fourteen Points, the goals at Versailles, and the intervention in Russia. The Senate finally rebelled by rejecting the League of Nations, but that negative decision did not reverse the trend of growing presidential power over foreign policy.

World War I took the lives of some 14,663,400 people—8 million soldiers and 6.6 million civilians. Russia led with 3.7 million dead; Germany followed with 2.6 million; then came France with 1.4 million, Austria-Hungary with 950,000, and Britain with 939,000. One out of every two French males between the ages of twenty and thirty-two (in 1914) died during the war. It had been a total war, involving whole societies, not merely their armies. Never before had a war left the belligerents so exhausted, so battered. New destructive weapons made their debut— "a preview of the Pandora's box of evils that the linkage of science with industry in the service of war was to mean." The war reinforced American desires to avoid foreign entanglement. Captain Harry S. Truman of Missouri claimed that most soldiers "don't give a whoop (to put it mildly) whether Russia has a Red Government or no government and if the King of the Lollipops wants to slaughter his subjects or his Prime Minister it's all the same to us." Disillusioned clergy regretted their participation in the "shrieking and hysterical patriotism." The war had ended "the artificial glow of past American idealism," wrote the novelist Ellen Glasgow.

World War I stacked the cards for an unstable future. Empires broke up—the Turkish, Austro-Hungarian, German, and Russian—creating new and weak nations, especially in central and eastern Europe. Nationalists in Asia, such as Mahatma Gandhi in British-dominated India, set goals of national liberation based in part on Wilson's ideal of self-determination. "Wilson's proposals, once set forth, could not be recalled," said Sun Zhongshan (Sun Yat-Sen) in 1924 as his China battled imperialist domination. In Latin America, prewar European economic ties withered, inviting the United States to expand its interests there, where nationalists resented the greater North American presence. The rise of Bolshevism in Russia and the hostility it aroused around the world made an already fluid international system even more so. Because of fear of a revived Germany, leaders tried to strip it of power, creating bitter resentments among the German people. Facing reconstruction problems at home, the victors tagged Germany with a huge reparations bill that would disorient the world economy. Nobody seemed happy with the postwar settlement; many would attempt to recapture lost opportunities or to redefine the terms.

World War I made the United States the world's leading economic power. As Wilson confidently put it, "The financial leadership will be ours. The industrial primacy will be ours. The commercial advantage will be ours." During the war years, to meet the need for raw materials, American companies expanded operations in developing nations. Goodyear went into the Dutch East Indies for rubber, Swift and Armour reached into South America, tin interests tapped Bolivia, copper companies mined in Chile, and oil firms sank new wells in Latin America and in the Middle East. Washington encouraged this economic expansion by building up the merchant marine, which by 1919 had grown 60 percent larger than its prewar size. By 1920, the United States produced about 40 percent of the world's coal and 50 percent of its pig iron.

Because the U.S. government and American citizens loaned heavily to the Allies during the war, the nation shifted from a debtor to a creditor, with Wall Street replacing London as the world's financial center. Whereas before the war Americans owed foreigners some $3 billion, after the conflict foreigners owed Americans and the U.S. government about $13 billion. Americans had devised plans to seize the apparent economic opportunities given them by the war—the Edge Act to permit foreign branch banks, and the Webb-Pomerene Act to allow trade associations to combine for export trading without fear of antitrust action, for example. How could Europeans pay back their debt to the United States? The answer lay somewhere in a complicated tangle of loans, reparations, tariffs, and world trade.

Economic disorder and political instability thus became the twin legacies of global war. "The world is all now one single whispering gallery," Wilson asserted in September 1919. "All the impulses . . . reach to the ends of the earth; . . . with the tongue of the wireless and the tongue of the telegraph, all the suggestions of disorder are spread." More than most Americans, Woodrow Wilson understood that global interdependence exposed America to "disorder and discontent and dissolution throughout the world." And "democracy has not yet made the world safe against irrational revolution," he admitted.

FURTHER READING FOR THE PERIOD 1914–1920

Many of the works listed in the last chapter also explore the themes, events, and personalities in the era of World War I. See also Anthony Boyle, *Foundations of World Order* (1999); Robert E. Hannigan, *The New World Power* (2002); Tony Smith, *America's Mission* (1994); David Stevenson, *The First World War and International Politics* (1988); Hew Strachan, *Over There* (2004); and Spencer C. Tucker, *The Great War* (1998).

For Woodrow Wilson and his foreign-policy views, consult Lloyd E. Ambrosius, *Wilsonianism* (2002); Louis Auchincloss, *Woodrow Wilson* (2000); H. W. Brands, *Woodrow Wilson* (2003); Thomas J. Knock, *To End All Wars* (1992); Arthur S. Link, *Woodrow Wilson* (1979); Jan Willem Schulte Nordholt, *Woodrow Wilson* (1991); and John A. Thompson, *Woodrow Wilson* (2001).

Wilson's health problems and their relationship to decisionmaking are examined in Robert H. Ferrell, *Ill-Advised* (1992), and Edwin A. Weinstein, *Woodrow Wilson* (1981). See also Bert E. Park, *Ailing, Aging, and Addicted* (1993) and *The Impact of Illness on World Leaders* (1986).

For European questions and the neutrality issue on the U.S. road to World War I, see John W. Coogan, *The End of Neutrality* (1981); Robert H. Ferrell, *Woodrow Wilson and World War I* (1985); Ross Gregory, *The Origins of American Intervention in the First World War* (1971); and Ernest R. May, *The World War and American Isolation, 1914–1917* (1959).

The German-American relationship is spotlighted in Reinhard R. Doerries, *Imperial Challenge* (1989); Manfred Jonas, *The United States and Germany* (1984); and Hans-Jürgen Schröder, ed., *Confrontation and Cooperation* (1993).

The Anglo-American relationship is featured in Kathleen Burk, *Britain, America, and the Sinews of War, 1914–1918* (1985); G. R. Conyne, *Woodrow Wilson: British Perspectives, 1912–21* (1992); and Joyce G. Williams, *Colonel House and Sir Edward Grey* (1984).

For the peace movement, see Frances H. Early, *A World Without War* (1997); Barbara S. Kraft, *The Peace Ship* (1978); Kathleen Kennedy, *Subversive Mothers and Scurrilous Citizens* (1999); Erika A. Kuhlman, *Petticoats and White Feathers* (1997); and Ernest A. McKay, *Against Wilson and War* (1996).

America's preparedness and warmaking experiences are discussed in Robert B. Bruce, *A Fraternity of Arms* (2003); Carol Byerly, *Fever of War* (2005) (influenza); John W. Chambers, *To Raise an Army* (1987); Byron Farrell, *Over There* (1999); Jennifer D. Keene, *The Doughboys, the Great War, and the Remaking of America* (2002); Thomas C. Leonard, *Above the Battle* (1978); Bullitt Lowry, *Armistice, 1918* (1997); David F. Trask, *The AEF and Coalition Warmaking* (1993) and *Captains & Cabinets* (1980); David R. Woodward, *Trial by Friendship* (1993); Susan Zeiger, *In Uncle Sam's Service* (1999) (women); and Robert H. Zieger, *America's Great War* (2001).

For the wartime home front, civil-liberties issues, and propaganda, see Allan M. Brandt, *No Magic Bullet* (1985) (venereal disease); Alfred W. Crosby, *America's Forgotten Pandemic* (1989); Leslie Midkiff DeBauche, *Reel Patriotism* (1997); Mark Ellis, *Race, War, and Surveillance* (2002); Joseph A. McCartin, *Labor's Great War* (1998); Elizabeth McKillen, *Chicago Labor and the Quest for a Democratic Diplomacy* (1995); John A. Thompson, *Reformers and War* (1986); and Stephen Vaughn, *Hold Fast the Inner Lines* (1980) (Committee on Public Information).

The Versailles peacemaking and League debate are discussed in Lloyd E. Ambrosius, *Wilsonian Statecraft* (1991) and *Woodrow Wilson and the American Diplomatic Tradition* (1987); Manfred F. Boeneke et al., eds., *The Treaty of Versailles* (1998); John M. Cooper Jr., *Breaking the Heart of the World* (2002); Inga Floto, *Colonel House in Paris* (1973); Warren F. Kuehl and Lynne K. Dunne, *Keeping the Covenant* (1997); Margaret MacMillan, *Paris 1919* (2002); Herbert F. Margulies, *The Mild Reservationists* (1989); Klaus Schwabe, *Woodrow Wilson, Revolutionary Germany, and Peacemaking* (1985); Alan Sharp, *The Versailles Settlement* (1991); Marc Trachenberg, *Reparations in World Politics* (1986); and Arthur Walworth, *America's Moment, 1918* (1977) and *Wilson and His Peacemakers* (1986).

The U.S. response to Bolshevism, intervention in Russia, and the Red Scare are investigated in Leo Bacino, *Reconstructing Russia* (1999); Donald E. Davis and Eugene P. Trani, *The First Cold War* (2000); Victor M. Fic, *The Collapse of American Policy in Russia and Siberia, 1918* (1995); David S. Foglesong, *America's Secret War Against Bolshevism* (1995); Lloyd Gardner, *Safe for Democracy* (1984); Linda Killen, *The Russian Bureau* (1983); Arno Mayer, *Politics and Diplomacy of Peacemaking* (1967); David W. McFadden, *Alternative Paths* (1993); Benjamin D. Rhodes, *The Anglo-American Winter War with Russia, 1918–1919* (1988); Neil V. Salzman, *Reform and Revolution* (1991) (Robins); Norman Saul, *War and Revolution* (2001); Ilya Somin, *Stillborn Crusade* (1996); John Thompson, *Russia, Bolshevism, and the Versailles Peace* (1966); and Betty Miller Unterberger, *America's Siberian Expedition* (1956) and *The United States, Revolutionary Russia, and the Rise of Czechoslovakia* (1989).

Also see Robert L. Beisner, ed., *Guide to American Foreign Relations Since 1600* (2003).

For comprehensive coverage of foreign-relations topics, see the articles in the four-volume *Encyclopedia of U.S. Foreign Relations* (1997), edited by Bruce W. Jentleson and Thomas G. Paterson.

Index

Italic page numbers indicate maps, photos, illustrations, or captions.